Virtual Reality and Metaverse: Impact on the Digital Transformation of Society II

Virtual Reality and Metaverse: Impact on the Digital Transformation of Society II

Guest Editor

Diego Vergara

MDPI

Basel • Beijing • Wuhan • Barcelona • Belgrade • Novi Sad • Cluj • Manchester

Guest Editor
Diego Vergara
Technology, Instruction and
Design in Engineering and
Education Research Group
(TiDEE.rg)
Catholic University of Ávila
Ávila
Spain

Editorial Office
MDPI AG
Grosspeteranlage 5
4052 Basel, Switzerland

This is a reprint of the Special Issue, published open access by the journal *Future Internet* (ISSN 1999-5903), freely accessible at: https://www.mdpi.com/journal/futureinternet/special_issues/2H0X5F10W1.

For citation purposes, cite each article independently as indicated on the article page online and as indicated below:

Lastname, A.A.; Lastname, B.B. Article Title. *Journal Name* **Year**, *Volume Number*, Page Range.

ISBN 978-3-7258-4991-8 (Hbk)
ISBN 978-3-7258-4992-5 (PDF)
https://doi.org/10.3390/books978-3-7258-4992-5

Contents

About the Editor

Diego Vergara

Diego Vergara is a distinguished academic and researcher with expertise in digital technologies applied to education and engineering, particularly within materials science and mechanical engineering. He currently holds the position of Dean of the Faculty of Sciences and Arts at Universidad Católica de Ávila (Spain) and leads the TiDEE.rg research group (Technology, Instruction, and Design in Engineering and Education). He actively engages in international conferences and contributes to high-impact publications in the fields of digital education and technological innovation. Dr. Vergara was recognized as one of the world's most influential researchers in both 2023 and 2024 by the Stanford Ranking, underscoring his significant contributions to enabling technologies and strategic materials. In 2024, he was awarded an honorary doctorate (Doctor Honoris Causa) by the Universidad Interamericana para el Desarrollo (UNID) in Peru in acknowledgment of his outstanding academic accomplishments and international collaboration.

Preface

The present Reprint focuses on the impact of immersive technologies—including virtual reality (VR), augmented reality (AR), and the metaverse—on the ongoing digital transformation of contemporary society. It garners a selection of original research articles and reviews that analyze the integration, adoption, and perception of these technologies across various professional sectors, such as health, education, industry, and tourism.

The scope of this Reprint is broad and interdisciplinary, covering technical innovations, ethical concerns, societal challenges, and the implications of emerging digital environments. It aims to provide readers with a scientifically grounded and multifaceted perspective on how immersive technologies are influencing the ways society functions, learns, communicates, and engages with both physical and digital spaces.

This Reprint seeks to contribute to ongoing discussions in academic and applied fields. It is intended for scholars, practitioners, technologists, and decision-makers interested in understanding and shaping the role of immersive digital tools in modern life.

Diego Vergara
Guest Editor

future internet

MDPI

Editorial

Editorial for the Special Issue "Virtual Reality and Metaverse: Impact on the Digital Transformation of Society—2nd Edition"

Diego Vergara

Technology, Instruction and Design in Engineering and Education Research Group (TiDEE.rg), Catholic University of Ávila, C/Canteros s/n, 05005 Ávila, Spain; diego.vergara@ucavila.es

Virtual reality (VR) is transforming society by enabling the development of diverse applications across a wide range of fields. Public perception of this technology has evolved over time, and it is now increasingly regarded as a resource with significant potential [1]. Meanwhile, the metaverse—an interconnected virtual environment that goes beyond conventional VR—has emerged as a concept poised to redefine the ways in which individuals interact, work, and participate in digital environments. Although still in its early stages of development, the metaverse is generating growing interest from both technological and societal perspectives, indicating a potentially profound impact on society as a whole. This Special Issue, entitled "Virtual Reality and Metaverse: Impact on the Digital Transformation of Society—2nd Edition" and published in the *Journal of Future Internet*, covers recent trends and advancements in the field of VR and metaverse usage for the digital transformation of society. We received 18 submissions. Following the initial screening and peer review process, nine papers were ultimately accepted for publication, eight were rejected, and one underwent an incomplete review process due to the authors' decision to withdraw. The accepted articles can be classified into two categories: (i) three reviews and (ii) six scientific papers.

Mottura's review [2] explores the rise of the "social" metaverse, emphasizing Meta's leading role in its development and noting the limited research on public opinion regarding such platforms. While the existing literature largely focuses on the technical, business, and ethical aspects of the metaverse, little attention has been paid to societal demand for a social metaverse. To address this, the author analyzes how major ICT companies engage with the metaverse and introduces a preliminary Likert scale questionnaire to assess public attitudes. Despite acknowledging its early-stage nature and limitations, the study provides a foundation for examining societal acceptance of digital social environments and encourages further investigation. Another review, by Hatami et al. [3], surveys the development of real-time metaverse technologies, which evolve beyond static virtual environments by integrating real-world data dynamically. It explores key enablers like advanced sensors, AI, edge computing, and 5G, which enable low-latency synchronization between physical and digital spaces. The study [3] highlights potential applications in areas such as entertainment, education, and urban planning, while addressing critical challenges like latency, security, and interoperability. It calls for ongoing innovation and collaboration to build a secure, scalable, and inclusive metaverse. Future research should focus on standards, 6G, multisensory integration, and ethical considerations. On the other hand, the third review, authored by Lampropoulos [4], offers an overview of the integration of artificial intelligence (AI) with extended reality (XR) technologies and the metaverse, based on an analysis of 880 articles from 2015 to 2024. This field is rapidly growing (with a 91.29% annual increase) and shows significant potential across sectors, especially education, healthcare, generative AI, virtual worlds, human–computer interactions, and industry. The results highlight the broad applicability of AI in XR, though the area is still developing. The study notes its own limitations, particularly the scope of literature reviewed, and calls for deeper, domain-specific analyses and the development of robust frameworks addressing technical, ethical, and evaluation challenges.

The scientific articles presented in this Special Issue also address topics related to the metaverse. For example, the study [5] examines global online search behavior for "metaverse" and "fashion" using Google Trends throughout 2022. It finds increasing consumer interest in these terms, though user patterns differ across Google's platforms (Search, YouTube, Images, News, Shopping). The metaverse is highlighted as a transformative force for fashion brands, offering new engagement and commerce opportunities but also introducing challenges like potential addiction and misinformation risks. Key recommendations include developing platform-specific marketing and SEO strategies tailored to each audience. The scope was limited to Google Trends and two keywords, suggesting the need for broader future research on other platforms and with more keywords. On the other hand, another paper [6] examines cybersecurity, privacy, and confidentiality challenges in Mixed Reality and metaverse environments. Key risks include data breaches, authentication issues, and threats to user anonymity due to sensitive data exchange. The authors review secure design, encryption, multi-factor authentication, and regulations to mitigate vulnerabilities; their recommendations focus on data protection, transparency, user consent, security updates, and privacy compliance. The study highlights the need for ongoing research to counter evolving threats and stresses the importance of robust security frameworks for building trust and enabling the safe adoption of MR and metaverse technologies.

This Special Issue also contains papers directly related to VR and augmented reality (AR). Regarding VR, the paper [7] compares university professors' perceptions of VR as an educational tool both in Latin American countries that are members of CABEI and those that are not, based on a questionnaire administered to 1246 educators. Professors from CABEI countries rated VR usability higher and perceived fewer disadvantages, although their improvement in digital competence significantly exceeded the increase in positive VR valuation. The gap between private and public university professors was more pronounced in CABEI countries, favoring private institutions. Nevertheless, actual VR adoption remains limited, as the increase in favorable VR perception is just over 3%. The study recommends increased investment and the development of specific protocols to enhance VR integration, particularly in public universities, while acknowledging that factors beyond CABEI membership may influence these outcomes, consistent with previous studies [8].

Another study [9] evaluates the use of VR video games to teach direct current electrical circuits at a Colombian public university, employing a mixed-methods action research approach. The results show that VR significantly enhances student comprehension, motivation, and engagement compared to traditional methods, while promoting equitable access to advanced learning tools. The VR application demonstrated safety and comfort, though moderation in usage is advised. Challenges include the need for robust technological infrastructure and curriculum adaptation. The study highlights VR's potential to transform technical education and calls for further research on long-term learning outcomes and broader applicability.

On the other hand, regarding AR, user perceptions of privacy protection in AR environments are examined in [10], focusing on three visual obfuscation techniques: blurring, masking, and pixelation. The survey results reveal that preferences vary by context and user demographics, with blurring favored for its aesthetics, masking viewed as most secure but less appealing, and pixelation ranked in the middle. Familiarity with AR influences acceptance, with more experienced users preferring blurring. These findings inform the design of privacy-preserving AR applications that balance security and usability, crucial for adoption across sectors like education and healthcare. Finally, CityBuildAR—a mobile AR app—is presented in [11]. This app allows users, especially those with limited design knowledge, to visualize and contribute to public space design. Tested at the University of Moratuwa, Sri Lanka, this study found that non-professionals favored greener spaces and found the app more useful for expressing ideas compared to professionals. CityBuildAR enhances community engagement in placemaking by bridging the gap between experts and the public. Technical issues like plane detection errors and crashes limited design detail.

Funding: This research received no external funding.

Conflicts of Interest: The author declares no conflicts of interest.

References

1. Antón-Sancho, Á.; Vergara, D.; Fernández-Arias, P. Application of virtual reality in university science education from a professors' perspective. *Multimed. Tools Appl.* **2025**. [CrossRef]
2. Mottura, S. Does Anyone Care about the Opinion of People on Participating in a "Social" Metaverse? A Review and a Draft Proposal for a Surveying Tool. *Future Internet* **2024**, *16*, 236. [CrossRef]
3. Hatami, M.; Qu, Q.; Chen, Y.; Kholidy, H.; Blasch, E.; Ardiles-Cruz, E. A Survey of the Real-Time Metaverse: Challenges and Opportunities. *Future Internet* **2024**, *16*, 379. [CrossRef]
4. Lampropoulos, G. Intelligent Virtual Reality and Augmented Reality Technologies: An Overview. *Future Internet* **2025**, *17*, 58. [CrossRef]
5. Ruiz Viñals, C.; Gil Ibáñez, M.; Del Olmo Arriaga, J.L. Metaverse and Fashion: An Analysis of Consumer Online Interest. *Future Internet* **2024**, *16*, 199. [CrossRef]
6. Pereira, C.; Marto, A.; Ribeiro, R.; Gonçalves, A.; Rodrigues, N.; Rabadão, C.; Costa, R.L.d.C.; Santos, L. Security and Privacy in Physical-Digital Environments: Trends and Opportunities. *Future Internet* **2025**, *17*, 83. [CrossRef]
7. Antón-Sancho, Á.; Fernández-Arias, P.; Ariza, E.A.; Vergara, D. The Use of Virtual Reality in the Countries of the Central American Bank for Economic Integration (CABEI). *Future Internet* **2024**, *16*, 249. [CrossRef]
8. Vergara, D.; Antón-Sancho, Á.; Dávila, L.P.; Fernández-Arias, P. Virtual reality as a didactic resource from the perspective of engineering teachers. *Comput. Appl. Eng. Educ.* **2022**, *30*, 1086–1101. [CrossRef]
9. Albarracin-Acero, D.A.; Romero-Toledo, F.A.; Saavedra-Bautista, C.E.; Ariza-Echeverri, E.A. Virtual Reality in the Classroom: Transforming the Teaching of Electrical Circuits in the Digital Age. *Future Internet* **2024**, *16*, 279. [CrossRef]
10. Cruz, A.C.; Costa, R.L.d.C.; Santos, L.; Rabadão, C.; Marto, A.; Gonçalves, A. Assessing User Perceptions and Preferences on Applying Obfuscation Techniques for Privacy Protection in Augmented Reality. *Future Internet* **2025**, *17*, 55. [CrossRef]
11. Ranasinghe, D.; Kankanamge, N.; De Silva, C.; Kangana, N.; Mahamood, R.; Yigitcanlar, T. CityBuildAR: Enhancing Community Engagement in Placemaking Through Mobile Augmented Reality. *Future Internet* **2025**, *17*, 115. [CrossRef]

future internet

MDPI

Systematic Review

Does Anyone Care about the Opinion of People on Participating in a "Social" Metaverse? A Review and a Draft Proposal for a Surveying Tool

Stefano Mottura

Institute of Intelligent Industrial Technologies and Systems for Advanced Manufacturing—National Research Council, 20133 Milano, Italy; stefano.mottura@stiima.cnr.it

Abstract: In recent years, the attention paid to the metaverse in the scientific world has increased; the hottest topics include system architecture and enabling technologies, as well as business, privacy, ethical, and security issues. On the other side, at the mainstream level, it is well known that the company Meta (formerly Facebook) is striving to realize its interpretation of a "social" metaverse. As Meta is a big leader of social media, it is reasonable to guess that, in the future, users will participate in a new social platform, such as that which the company is building by depicting unlimited and engaging opportunities. Regardless of Meta, we ask what the opinion of people is about this possible future scenario. A literature search of previous works about this topic has been done; the few results we found were not properly on topic and showed heterogeneous content. A survey on interpretations of the metaverse of major information and communication technologies (ICT) companies that impact the consumer world was undertaken; the results show that Meta is the most prominent company with the mission of building a "social" metaverse worldwide. Finally, a draft of a tool for assessing the predilection of people for a "social" metaverse, based on various facets of the future social platform, is proposed.

Keywords: metaverse; survey; questionnaire; people; opinion; society; future

1. Introduction

There is not a unique definition of a metaverse; a broad informal description could be that it is a whole of many virtual reality worlds where users can engage with a huge variety of activities, can socialize and meet people from around the world, can be represented with customizable avatars, and can benefit from the absence of limitations due do locations and traveling. The first appearance of the term "metaverse" was in 1992 in the dystopic novel *Snow Crash* [1]. At the present time, the metaverse is a system still under construction, but it has been a topic being developed in the scientific literature for many years; the first relevant works can be found in the early 2000s. The authors of [2,3] provide insights into definitions and a history of works.

Several studies have been done on the metaverse, sometimes without mentioning it explicitly, by addressing the requirements, architecture, enabling technologies, usability, user experience, acceptability, and factors related to motivation for the use of VR, privacy issues, legal and ethical issues, the future of society, and other topics. A short summary of such studies is presented below.

Studies have been done about technological aspects of the metaverse. The work presented in [4] is an early deep analysis of the transition from independent virtual worlds to a network of integrated virtual worlds (called "metaverse"). The paper, discussing the current status of technologies and requirements, presents a road map for such a transition that is composed by four key elements: realism, ubiquity, interoperability, and scalability. The research in [5] proposes a framework for supporting a visual construction of the metaverse that is composed of visualizations, graphics, and interaction techniques. A taxonomy of interaction technologies is presented, as well as two different pipelines for designing scenes in the metaverse. On the other hand, ref. [6] is a large work where a taxonomy of the metaverse has been proposed; that study notes that hardware, software, and contents are the essentials blocks for realizing the metaverse and that user interaction, implementation, and application are the three main approaches which are suitable for it. The paper also describes social influence factors and open challenges such as potential increases in inequities, legal aspects, and devices limitations. The authors of [7] first mention current developments made by some of the big tech companies, e.g., Meta aims to realize the metaverse for social purposes; Apple and Microsoft have applications for connecting users to virtual spaces, aiming to improve productivity; video-gaming and development companies such as NVIDIA and Epic Games have specific frameworks for designing and developing software for building metaverse applications. Then, scalability, accessibility, security/privacy, and legal issues are proposed and analyzed as the main requirements of the metaverse. The paper also mentions the Workrooms platform from Meta and the AltspaceVR platform from Microsoft as prototypes of the metaverse; both are virtual worlds across the internet where people can join, be present, and interact. The authors of [3] presented a systematic review analyzing and cataloguing the topics and components related to the metaverse, as well as connections with the social sciences and neurosciences. That work reported the expansion of relevant works since 2022; moreover, a set of heterogeneous definitions of the metaverse was reported, as well as enabling technologies.

Several works have been done on users and related issues, focusing in particular on questions of privacy, identity, and security. The research in [2] firstly provides a detailed report on the history, definition, and main features of the metaverse. Then, it focuses on an analysis of the metaverse in education and on its requirements and components. A framework based on enabling technologies and on a pipeline for learning is proposed, and all related components are described. The work also touches on the topics of addiction, security, and identity. In [8], a starting point is presented for discussion of the user experience and the social acceptability of immersive VR with players in public places by evoking the themes of playing among other people, safety and privacy. An experiment done on a sample of users of immersive VR who heard sounds from a simulated real social environment surrounding them showed increases in distraction, concerns about privacy, and other variables. The authors of [9] presented a detailed study on the degree of acceptance of the VR experience as a substitute for reality. The results of the experiments suggested that "active" VR experiences are less accepted as a substitution for reality compared to passive ones, in terms of the realization of sensorial, emotive, cognitive, and perceptive feelings. The authors of [10] argued that the rendering of additional senses, more than hearing and vision, is needed to fully realize an immersive VR experience; the work presented the components of an "Internet of Senses", an infrastructure made by all senses and including affective computing, quality of experience, and brain–computer interfaces. The senses are part of the elements eliciting immersion; however, virtual reality is also built on psychological components close to the narrative of virtual scenarios, role playing, and, in general, acting as affordance for immersion, as reported, for example, in [11]. A comprehensive survey addressing security issues, problems, and potential solutions, together with projects for implementing the metaverse, as well as a functional and logic architecture, is presented in [12]. The work presented in [13] is focused on the interpretation of the metaverse by Meta as a platform for a new way of living socially and on available applications. The paper mentions a tremendous increase in popularity on the world wide web of the words "meta" and "metaverse" since the presentation of Meta in October 2021. Then, the work focuses on potential applications of the metaverse to smart cities by also providing a long table of pro and cons. The analysis presented in [14] highlights three main risks of the metaverse, i.e., monitoring, manipulating and monetizing users. A road map for regulating a metaverse, focused on regulatory and non-regulatory solutions, is proposed.

Various studies about the dynamics and behavior of society and of companies can be mentioned. In [15], researchers found that most US media coverage considers the metaverse of Meta as a "space" for people with buying power; only 11% of coverage offered a critical approach to that interpretation. Research in [16] reports that several works have demonstrated that interactions in the metaverse generate an intense sense of social presence (called, for real situations, "we-mode"), because some of our neurobiological systems, typical of real communities experiences, are activated during the virtual experience. The authors of [17] provide a detailed discussion about the role of power of the big tech companies in the realization of the metaverse in relation to the dynamics of society, of addiction, and of influencing. The work analyzes the features presented by Meta and the speech [18] introducing the company; attention is also paid to the narration technique and to the depiction of the metaverse as a technology that certainly will spread in the future. The work also argues that an expansion of the metaverse could generate an increase in the power of the big tech companies and could exacerbate addiction to mass-media.

On one hand, in recent years, the topic of the metaverse has gained increased attention, both in the scientific literature (for example, ref. [3] reports a rapid increase since 2022) and in the mass media. On the other hand, Facebook in 2021 turned into brand-new company, Meta, with the mission of achieving a "social" metaverse, i.e., virtual worlds based on the internet where people can meet, share, and go "behind the boundaries". At present, the company is already delivering early apps and is spending a huge amount of energy and money on research and in development. As Meta is undoubtedly a leader in the field of social media, it is reasonable to guess that its "social" metaverse has the potential to pervade society, and that people will start acting in new virtual spaces in more immersive, vivid, engaging, and fascinating ways, and for extended periods of time. Regardless of Meta, what is the opinion of society, of people, about frequenting such a "social" metaverse scenario? Given that a radical change in habits with social media could happen in the future, we guess that a tool for assessing the opinion of people could be useful. Thus, in this paper, a draft of a tool for assessing the predilection for a "social" metaverse is proposed. To this end, the present work is structured in three main steps: (i) (Sections 2 and 3) An assessment of the interpretation of the metaverse by some of the most prominent ICT companies (Apple, IBM, Microsoft, Siemens and Meta), as they are the drivers of technology and of applications impacting at mainstream level. This helps to define whether ICT companies, other than Meta, are proposing a "social" metaverse and to collect their views of it; (ii) (Section 4) A literature review searching for previous works on the position of people regarding the "social" metaverse. This helps to outline the features of possible existing surveys on the topic; (iii) (Section 5) A draft design of a tool to survey the predilection of people to use a "social" metaverse, taking into account the outcomes of steps (i) and (ii). Section 6 outlines other considerations and presents our conclusions.

2. The Interpretation of the Metaverse by Major ICT Companies

A survey of web contents of some of the main ICT companies (Apple, IBM, Microsoft, Siemens and Meta) was undertaken in order to identify their interpretation of the metaverse and the related features exhibited to audience and to define possible ideas regarding a "social" metaverse.

Institutional web pages with contents explicitly about the "metaverse" were selected and read, and sentences and key points were collected. Institutional YouTube channels were inspected by looking for videos with a title and/or description about the metaverse; the found videos were watched and the stories told there were transcribed in our written notes.

The features which emerged from statements, verbs, key words, adjectives, and so forth, were analyzed to extract concepts describing and promoting the specific idea of the metaverse. Then, the extracted elements were summarized by means of "tags". While examining the web contents, sometimes the features were not only contained in the text but were also implicit or supported by visuals; therefore, the tags were worded taking into account this matter.

The analyzed URLs are listed in Appendix A; descriptions of the tags are shown in Tables A1–A3.

2.1. The Interpretation of the Metaverse by Apple

The survey of the Apple website [19,20] showed that there are no contents related to the metaverse. A supplementary search of the word "metaverse" in the search bar of the home page produced 10 entries. These entries were about apps for social networking, gaming, on-line dating, avatars, and not-fungible token exchange. In other words, the concept of the "metaverse" is used mainly for marketing purposes. A search for the word "metaverse" on the Apple YouTube channel [20] produced four entries, all of which were off topic.

A summary of the concepts and of the tags related to the interpretation of the metaverse by Apple was not done because not enough contents were available.

2.2. The Interpretation of the Metaverse by IBM

A survey of the website of IBM [21,22] showed that there is little content related to the metaverse. A supplementary search for the word "metaverse" in the search bar of the home page produced around 100 entries. After screening the titles and descriptions, two documents about the metaverse were found [23,24]. A search on the IBM YouTube channel [22] produced two entries, both of them off topic. A metaverse platform, called the IBM Spatial Platform [25], was found but only in IBM Japan; it is a virtual reality platform for collaborating and sharing contents in a business context.

IBM mainly considers the metaverse to be a virtual space with the purpose of doing business. The authors of [26] mentioned that the metaverse is characterized by co-presence, co-operation, and connection, and that it offers opportunities to develop products, customer experiences, and so on. The authors of [23] noted that the metaverse can serve to enhance business and marketing, perform industrial simulations, and so on. The authors of [24] described five topics that companies should explore when using the metaverse in their business.

A summary of the concepts and the tags related to the interpretation of the metaverse by IBM is not provided because not enough contents were found.

2.3. The Interpretation of the Metaverse by Microsoft

A survey of website of Microsoft [27] showed that the word "metaverse" is poorly used and that it does not appear in the home page menu items or in the sitemap. Instead, the concept of the metaverse clearly emerged in relation to Teams [28] and Mesh [29] (the software platforms for holding online meetings and online presence), as stated in [30]. A search of the word "metaverse" on the Microsoft YouTube channel [31] produced around 100 entries; after a screening the titles and the descriptions, five videos about the metaverse were inspected. A search of the word "mesh" on the associated YouTube channel and on the Microsoft Teams YouTube Channel [32] produced, respectively, about 140 and 15 entries. After screening the titles and the descriptions, 11 videos about the metaverse were inspected, for a total of 16 videos.

From an analysis of the contents of the web site and of YouTube channels, some key points about the idea of the metaverse by Microsoft were summarized:

- The metaverse takes shape in three spheres: consumer, commercial, industrial [33];
- It is a digital world where people can meet, interact, and share data (as stated, for example, in [30]);
- It allows people to communicate, meet, share data and experiences, and to improve the quality of relations. Users can enter the metaverse from everywhere and at any time;
- Its characteristics mainly focus on contexts of work, business, or entertainment (gaming). The Teams and Mesh software platforms are the main tools, while the specific word "metaverse" is poorly used.

The Tags MSTi ("MS" stands for "Microsoft"; shown in Table A1) represent the concepts presented by Microsoft while promoting the metaverse (by means of Teams and Mesh). Histograms of plain frequencies of the tags are shown in Figures 1 and 2.

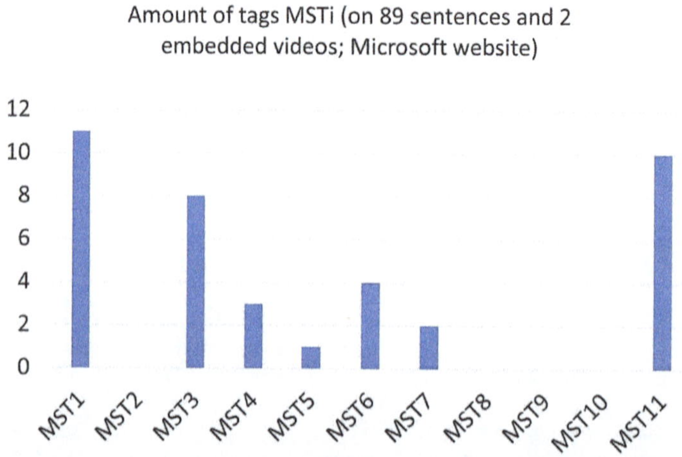

Figure 1. Histogram of the MSTi tags assigned to sentences on Microsoft web site. An inspection was performed on 89 sentences and two videos embedded in the web pages. The full tags are shown in Table A1. The (short) names of the tags are: MST1 = Sharing/working with others; MST2 = Doing activities of daily living; MST3 = Connecting from everywhere/at any time; MST4 = Representing yourself the way you want; MST5 = Representing yourself to express yourself; MST6 = Removing the barriers; MST7 = Freeing up budget; MST8 = New internet; MST9 = It can damage health; MST10 = It works on all devices; MST11 = Improving quality experiences.

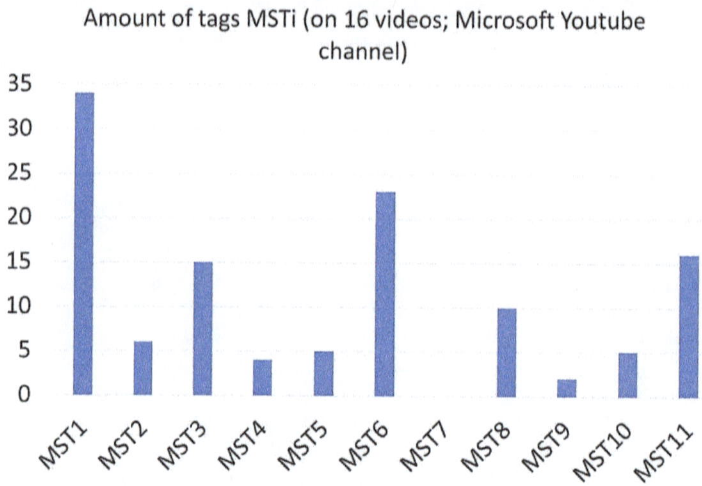

Figure 2. Histogram of MSTi tags assigned to videos watched on the Microsoft YouTube channel. An inspection was undertaken of 16 videos. The full tags are shown in Table A1. The (short) names of tags are: MST1 = Sharing/working with others; MST2 = Doing activities of daily living; MST3 = Connecting from everywhere/at any time; MST4 = Representing yourself the way you want; MST5 = Representing yourself to express yourself; MST6 = Removing the barriers; MST7 = Freeing up budget; MST8 = New internet; MST9 = It can damage health; MST10 = It works on all devices; MST11 = Improving quality experiences.

The histograms of the tags show that the most frequently encountered concepts were "Communicating, sharing, working with others" (MST1), "Connecting from everywhere/at any time" (MST3) and "Improving quality of actions/experiences" (MST11). The tag "Removing the barriers" (MST6) also had noteworthy frequency in videos (Figure 2).

2.4. The Interpretation of the Metaverse by Siemens

The survey of the Siemens website [34,35] showed that the metaverse is very important for the company. A search of word "metaverse" on the YouTube channel produced 9 entries, all of them about metaverse.

From our analysis of the contents of the web site and YouTube channel, some key points about the idea of the metaverse by Siemens may be summarized as follows:

- The metaverse takes shape in three forms: industrial, enterprise, and consumer (as stated for example in [36]);
- Siemens places itself entirely in the "industrial" metaverse;
- The industrial metaverse is a digital realm representing and simulating the manufacturing/industrial world at all levels; it proposes a new level of industrial automation and a portfolio of software platforms for it. This provides benefits for processes, production, costs, and sustainability;
- It is founded on digital twin (the most important pillar), software-defined automation, data and Artificial Intelligence (AI, especially generative AI);
- It is a real thing, it is already there, it will change the industrial domain.

The STi Tags ("S" stands for "Siemens"; shown in Table A2) represent the concepts touched on by Siemens while promoting the industrial metaverse. Histograms of the frequencies of usage of the tags are shown in Figures 3 and 4.

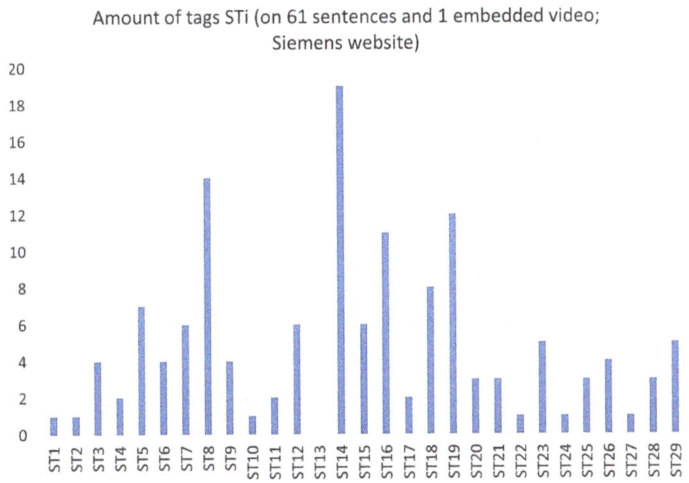

Figure 3. Histogram of the STi tags assigned to sentences on the Siemens web site. An inspection was made of 61 sentences. The full tags are shown in Table A2. The (short) names of tags are: ST1 = Three sectors; ST2 = Digital twin etc.; ST3 = The digital twin is the main pillar; ST4 = Always on; ST5 = Combination of real and digital; ST6 = Connects real to digital to simulate and solve; ST7 = Capability to solve real world problems; ST8 = Simulating/testing the whole thing; ST9 = Simulating/testing at high speed; ST10 = Making decisions; ST11 = Allowing safe environments; ST12 = Allowing sustainability; ST13 = Saving time/money; ST14 = Impacting on real world; ST15 = Realtime collaboration; ST16 = Collaborating/interoperating across systems; ST17 = Avatars for recognizing/interacting/improving; ST18 = Like a real environment; ST19 = New way of collaboration; ST20 = Changing the way organizations operate; ST21 = Getting benefit from skills of people; ST22 = Supporting/motivating people; ST23 = Breaking down distance; ST24 = Saving costs for travelling; ST25 = Need to face the possible fears of workers; ST26 = It changes our lives; ST27 = Doing activities of daily living; ST28 = It will live in the internet 3.0; ST29 = It is real.

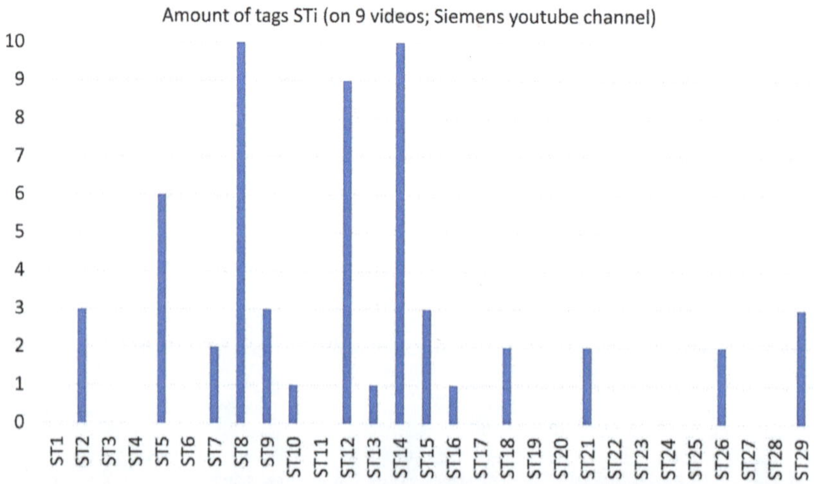

Figure 4. Histogram of the STi tags assigned to videos watched on Siemens YouTube channel. An inspection was undertaken of nine videos. The full tags are shown in Table A2. The (short) names of tags are: ST1 = Three sectors; ST2 = Digital twin etc.; ST3 = The digital twin is the main pillar; ST4 = Always on; ST5 = Combination of real and digital; ST6 = Connects real to digital to simulate and solve; ST7 = Capability to solve real world problems; ST8 = Simulating/testing the whole thing; ST9 = Simulating/testing at high speed; ST10 = Making decisions; ST11 = Allowing safe environments; ST12 = Allowing sustainability; ST13 = Saving time/money; ST14 = Impacting on real world; ST15 = Realtime collaboration; ST16 = Collaborating/interoperating across systems; ST17 = Avatars for recognizing/interacting/improving; ST18 = Like a real environment; ST19 = New way of collaboration; ST20 = Changing the way organizations operate; ST21 = Getting benefit from skills of people; ST22 = Supporting/motivating people; ST23 = Breaking down distance; ST24 = Saving costs for travelling; ST25 = Need to face the possible fears of workers; ST26 = It changes our lives; ST27 = Doing activities of daily living; ST28 = It will live in the internet 3.0; ST29 = It is real.

In this case, the inspected contents showed a great abundance of concepts; therefore, many tags were included.

Our histograms of tags show that the most frequently encountered concepts were "Simulating/testing the whole thing" (ST8) and "Improving/impacting the real world" (ST14). From the website contents (Figure 3), the concepts of "Collaborating/interoperating across systems" (ST16) and "New way of interaction/collaboration" (ST19) also emerged, while from the videos (Figure 4), "Combination of real and digital world" (ST5) and "Allowing sustainability" (ST12) also emerged.

2.5. *The Interpretation of the Metaverse by Meta*

A survey of Meta's website [37,38] showed that the promotion and development of the metaverse are the mission of the company itself. The metaverse is considered as a virtual space for social activities for people around the world. Since Meta's YouTube channel has dozens of videos, all of them about the metaverse, 13 videos were randomly selected and inspected.

From the analysis of the contents of the website and YouTube channel, some key points about the idea of the metaverse by Meta could be summarized:

- The metaverse is depicted as an awesome new virtual space for socializing, where people are free to act without the boundaries of reality (as, for example, stated in [18]);

- It is portrayed as beautiful, as the future of social interactions; it unlocks the opportunity to do what you want; the activities promoted in the metaverse represent activities of everyday life, or an "extension" of them;
- It tears down the barriers of reality and lets the user do anything and be free, better than reality;
- The goals of Meta is to make the "social" metaverse into a new internet and for social media and to gain 1 billion users by 2033 [39];
- Various features and technologies are declared to be currently in their infancy and subject to future development.

Similar topics related to the features of the idea of the metaverse of Meta were mentioned by [17], with those authors observing that they are depicted with a series of very positive and extraordinary attributes and as something with endless possibilities.

The Ti tags (shown in Table A3) represent the concepts touched on by Meta while promoting the "social" metaverse. Histograms of the frequencies of the various tags are shown in Figures 5 and 6.

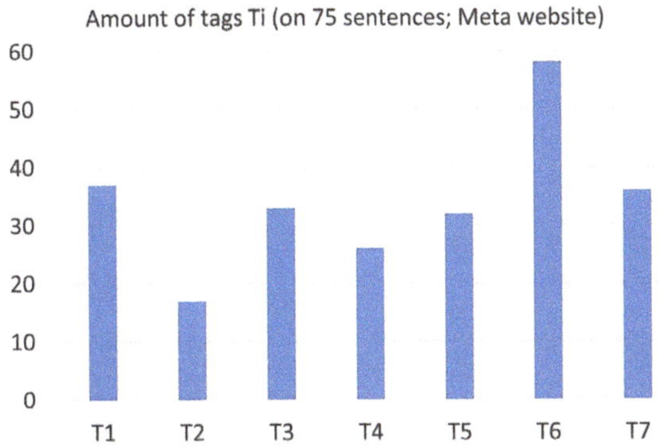

Figure 5. Histogram of the Ti tags assigned to sentences on the Meta website. An inspection was made of 75 sentences. The full tags are shown in Table A3. The (short) names of tags are: T1 = New social platform; T2 = Flooding mobile phones/devices; T3 = New internet; T4 = Doing activities of daily living; T5 = People meet/share experiences; T6 = Tearing down the boundaries; T7 = Living life in the metaverse.

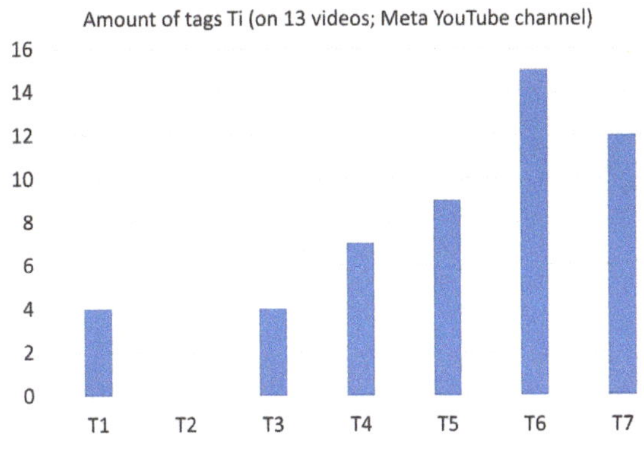

Figure 6. Histogram of the Ti tags assigned to videos watched on Meta YouTube channel. An inspection was made of 13 videos, randomly selected among dozens of available videos. The full tags are shown in Table A3. The (short) names of tags are: T1 = New social platform; T2 = Flooding mobile phones/devices; T3 = New internet; T4 = Doing activities of daily living; T5 = People meet/share experiences; T6 = Tearing down the boundaries; T7 = Living life in the metaverse.

The histograms of the tags show that the most frequently encountered concepts were "Doing activities of daily living" (T4), "People meet actively/share experiences" (T5), "Tearing down the boundaries" (T6), "Living life in the metaverse" (T7). The tags from website (Figure 5) were very frequently encountered, except "Flooding mobile phone and devices" (T2).

3. Questions about the "Social" Metaverse

Given that the purposes of the metaverse are not limited to social media and that Meta did not invent the metaverse or VR and AR, it is reasonable and realistic to consider the company as a reference player, since, currently, it is the most involved one in the development of a metaverse for social purposes, as also mentioned in [7]. This has been also confirmed by surveys (Sections 2.1–2.4) of the ideas of the metaverse developed by other companies: Microsoft is focusing on the metaverse for business/entertainment (gaming) purposes; Siemens focuses entirely on an "industrial" metaverse; while Apple and IBM only touch the topic a little.

The interpretation of the metaverse by Meta is never presented with features sounding like "useful facilities" or "solutions" or "tools" (software, apps) helping people to meet and to do things when (or if) they are in some kind of "difficulty" (for example: long travels, inability to move, pandemic, low budget, agenda full and so on). There is not just an offering of innovative and astonishing ICT applications and solutions; instead, a new level of socializing is proposed, by means of alternative virtual worlds. This emerged also from a video introducing Meta [40]. The concept of undertaking activities (associated with usual interrelationships in real life) in the virtual worlds coupled with the concepts of opportunity and feeling better than in reality, of tearing down the barriers of reality, makes us reflect. Potentially, it could be a paradigm shift in society. Therefore, we guess that it is reasonable to raise question, i.e., would people like such a "social" metaverse.

It is clear that nobody is obliged to participate or to live completely in a metaverse; on the other hand, it is well known how much the dynamics and the behavior of present-day society are mediated by the wide use of social media (for example, the authors of [41] reported that the number of internet users in October 2023 was around 5.3 billion, with 4.95 billion of them using social media). A metaverse for social purposes potentially could bring that to a higher order of magnitude. So, a literature review was done to find previous works about the question above.

4. Literature Review

A literature review was undertaken to identify previous works about aforementioned question ("Q"). The search, let's call it S1, was done on the Web of Science and Scopus databases [42,43] of document titles only, covering the period from January 2018 to December 2022 (the search strings are shown in Appendix C). The criteria for inclusion were that the titles and/or abstracts of papers had to be relevant to Q (completely or partially). A PRISMA flowchart of the process is shown in Figure 7. We found 1779 papers; after dropping duplicated documents, patents, documents not in English, datasets, clinical trials, the number of papers decreased to 111. After reading the titles and abstracts to identify the most relevant works, five papers were selected, all of them having been published in 2021–2022. Finally, two papers were retrieved. After a complete read, both [44,45] were considered to be about Q.

The work presented in [44] had two objectives. The first was "to generate new knowledge and gain a deeper understanding of the metaverse and the challenges that it faces in the future". The second was "to gain a better understanding of people's perceptions of the metaverse", which is a topic close to Q. To this end, a questionnaire was administered to 220 subjects (Appendix D).

The work in [45] is focused on the need to study the intention of participating in the metaverse (a topic close to Q) and on the involved psychological constructs, as literature is lacking in this respect. In this case, a questionnaire was administered to 450 Peruvian citizens (Appendix D; the answers are not available); the first conclusion was that "institutional support, technological literacy and participation self-efficacy have a positive and significant effect on the intention to participate in the metaverse".

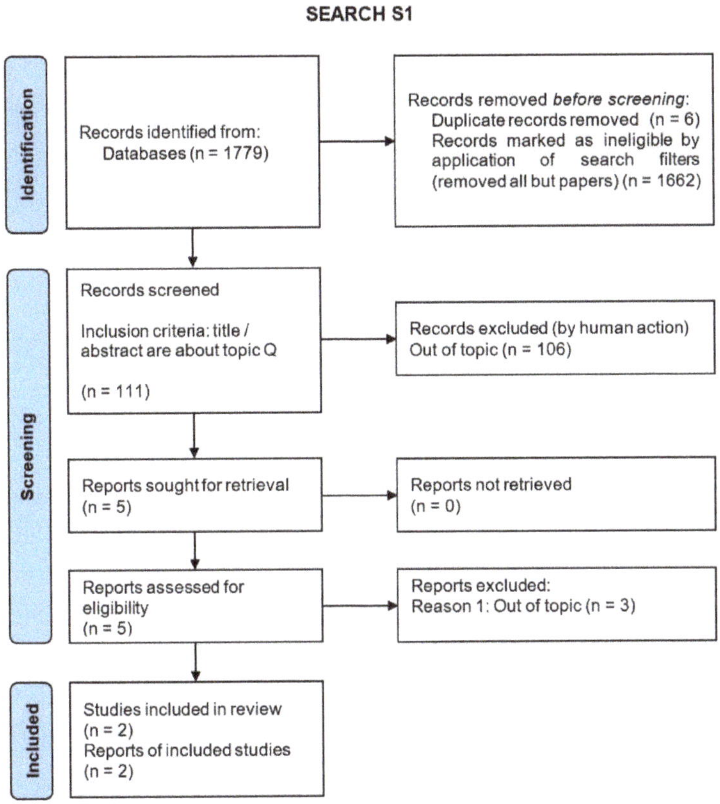

Figure 7. PRISMA flowchart of the review process of S1.

During our analysis of papers and some of the references mentioned therein, further works emerged. These works were focused on other themes connected to the metaverse, such as feasibility, enabling technologies, taxonomies, road mapping, and the current state of such technology. Such papers mentioned various topics (e.g., ethics, usage, or privacy issues) in a way that was also potentially related to Q. Therefore, a new literature review based on a search, let's call it S2, was done to identify previous works about the metaverse with questions about the future, ethics, humans, morality, which could still be relevant to Q. The search has been done on the Web of Science and Scopus databases, in document titles only and by covering the period from January 2010 to March 2023 (the search strings are shown in Appendix C). As with S1, the criteria for inclusion were that the titles and/or abstracts of papers had to be about topic Q (completely or partially). A PRISMA flowchart of the process is shown in Figure 8. We identified 730 papers. After dropping duplicated documents, patents, documents not in English, datasets, and clinical trials, the number of papers decreased to 410; after reading the titles and abstracts, 65 papers were selected, all of which were published in 2021–2023. Of these, 62 were retrieved. After a complete read, two papers [46,47] were found to be about Q.

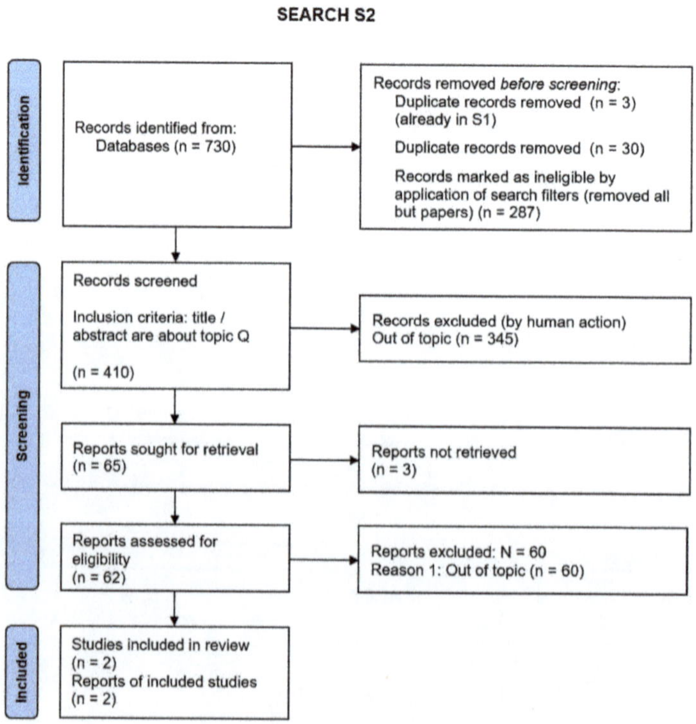

Figure 8. PRISMA flowchart of the review process for S2.

The work in [46] aimed to analyze the impact of the metaverse on humans, on one hand by consulting specific professionals such as therapists, psychologists, and neurologists, and, on the other hand, by administering a questionnaire to 250 subjects in order to understand people's view of the metaverse (see Appendix D).

The work in [47] comprised a study of the ethical implications of the metaverse in everyday life. It is remarkable that this work was probably the only one from S1 and S2 which took an explicitly critical position on the metaverse and was not directly favorable to it. It called for a "re-orienting" of the metaverse by paying more attention to human factors. The authors of [47] published the results of interviews [48] about people and the metaverse (a topic related to Q), where relevant percentages of subjects declared their concerns and fears (listed in Appendix D).

From S1 and S2, a few works emerged about Q. In these works, surveying tools, composed of many items, were administered to people, while Q was touched upon mainly in an indirect way, rather than going straight to the point. The results were fragmentary and heterogeneous; as such, a meta-analysis is out of the scope of this paper.

In order to identify a trend in terms of being "in favor" or "not in favor" of the metaverse for social purposes, from the questionnaires mentioned above (shown in Appendix D), items meeting the following criteria were selected:

- Answers were published;
- An item was relevant to Q or;
- An item was relevant to the personal and intimate sphere of the subject.

Items such as opinions about the economy, the pros and cons of a metaverse, the degree of knowledge of technology, and so on, were excluded.

Each selected item was classified as being either "in favor" or "not in favor", and has been labeled with a letter (A, B and so on). The result of this selection process is summarized in Figure 9.

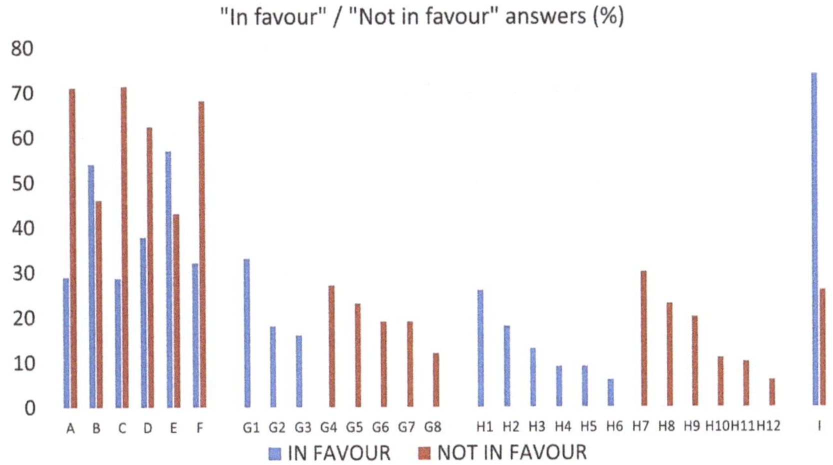

Figure 9. A plain histogram of answers "in favor"/"not in favor" (of "social" metaverse) emerged from the questionnaires found in S1 and S2. Each letter represents a selected surveying item. Items G and H were composed of different types of answers, shown respectively as G1–G8 and as H1–H12. The complete source questionnaires, scales, and all items are listed in Appendix D. The items shown in the histogram are: A = Have you been impacted by the internet? Would you say that the metaverse will affect you? B = Does the metaverse also free us from many of the limitations of the physical world? C = Can the Metaverse be a world where the digital world is more valuable than the physical world? D = Do you think you're ready for the metaverse? E = Does a Metaverse or a Virtual World excite you? F = Share of adults in the US who are interested in Meta's new virtual reality project, known as the metaverse, as of November 2021. G = Feelings toward the metaverse according to adults in the US as of January 2022 (response types: G1 = Curious; G2 = Excited; G3 = Optimistic; G4 = Uninterested; G5 = Suspicious; G6 = Concerned; G7 = Indifferent; G8 = Confused). H = Views on the metaverse according to adults in the US as of January 2022 (response types: H1 = The future of technology; H2 = A really exciting way to play/socialize; H3 = A way to intensify enjoyable experiences; H4 = A better alternative to real life; H5 = How we will do most of our shopping in the future; H6 = Will create more equality in society; H7 = Not good as real life; H8 = Tech companies trying to figure out a new way to make money; H9 = A big risk to personal privacy; H10 = A fad that will not last long; H11 = Something for young people only; H12 = A scam/predatory financial scheme). I = Share of adults in the US joining or considering joining the metaverse for various reasons as of December 2021.

A simple qualitative preliminary consideration could be that the found results approximately indicate that people giving answers favorable of the metaverse are balanced by or even fewer in number than people giving answers that were not favorable (Figure 9). Moreover, in such works, it is not clear whether people consider the metaverse as simply a new set of appealing social media functionalities, i.e., replacing Facebook, or something deeper. This simplistic assumption, that limits the understanding of the potential impact of the metaverse for social purposes, could also influence the answers (this issue was addressed in [46], where half of the subjects did not know what the metaverse is, so an idea about it was provided to them before doing the survey).

5. Draft Proposal of a Tool Assessing the Predilection to Use a "Social" Metaverse

The interpretation of the "social" metaverse reported in Section 2.5 can be considered as more interesting and profound than the usual common attributes (the metaverse is the future, you will be able to do whatever you want, and so on), because it has the potential (the intention?) to involve the most natural life habits. From S1 and S2, few documents emerged which had examined what people think about the potential future rise of the metaverse for social purposes. Therefore, a survey could reveal information about the position of people regarding participation in a "social" metaverse (that is the topic addressed in Q, defined in Section 3); it also could foster opinions or discussions about this question.

Questionnaires and scales are widely used surveying tools for measuring subjective feelings and positions. Many tools already exist for the assessment of specific technology features (as likeability, usability, acceptability, level of readiness, and so forth), for example Technology Acceptance Model (TAM) [49], Technology Acceptance Model v2 (TAM2) [50], Unified Theory of Acceptance and Use of Technology (UTAUT) [51], Technology Readiness Index (TRI) [52], Technology Readiness Level (TRL) [53,54], Human Readiness Level (HRL) [55], System Usability Scale (SUS) [56]. We found that such tools are not really suitable to investigate the topic touched on in Q, as they are aimed to be applied to technologies, i.e., to applications that are fairly specific, that are being implemented or are already working, to improve their characteristics for end users of industry and of organizations, and to enhance jobs. Instead, the features of a "social" metaverse embrace the field of human interactions and socializing. Moreover, these days, the metaverse appears to be not particularly suitable for specific surveys because it is not a specifically defined system, i.e., it is weakly diffused, and some of the required technologies (hardware and software) are still in development. An exception to this can be represented by the second version of "Unified Theory of Acceptance and Use of Technology" (UTAUT2) [57]. UTAUT2 extends the UTAUT model [51] to a consumer context by defining and including the constructs of "Hedonic Motivation", "Price Value", and "Habit" as elements influencing the "behavioral intention" of the subject to use a specific technology. The survey items of UTAUT2, according to the UTAUT model, address many specific pragmatic sides of using a given piece of technology.

Given the above considerations, the development of a new specific assessment tool may be a more focused approach. Likert scales [58,59] are widely used, self-reporting evaluation methods for measuring psychological constructs that, because of their nature, cannot be directly measured [60].

In this research, Q can be assessed by the quantification of the "predilection" to use a social metaverse, in terms of the intensity of positive feelings [61]. It is a subjective, non-observable, and not directly quantifiable variable. The Likert evaluation scale model is a tool that is suitable for such quantifications. Therefore, items for building a Likert scale assessing what Q is expressing in general terms could be designed and developed. This is made possible by focusing on the assessment of the construct, i.e., predilection for a new level of sociality in "social" metaverse (let's call it "C") and by specifically involving the design process from which those elements emerged as features of a "social" metaverse.

When a construct is a bipolar continuum, typically, its presence in the subject represents the high end of the evaluation scale, while its absence, at the low end of the scale, is associated with the opposite of that construct. On the other hand, when a construct is a unipolar continuum, the low end of the scale just represents its absence in the subject [62]. The characteristics of the metaverse for social purposes, as summarized in Section 2.5 and discussed in Section 3, reveal a shift from the real to the virtual world. So, in this context, an individual with a predilection for such social activities in the metaverse (construct C) can be deemed to be neglecting the same activities in real life; this is related to the opposite of C. Therefore, construct C can be considered a bipolar continuum ranging from "Strongly disagree" to "Strongly agree" (rather than an unipolar continuum ranging, for example, from "Not at all" to "Extremely") [61]; these types of values convey a character of bipolarity [62,63].

According to the authors of [62], the type of gradation of C to be assessed is "behavioral extremity", since it represents feelings, thoughts, behaviors; while the degrees of C reflect the level of presence of C representing the bipolar continuum. The maximum value (the high end of the scale) and the minimum value (the low end of the scale) express a complete presence (or absence) of C in the subject; the absence, as stated above, conveys the opposite of C in the subject.

The regions of the continuum with topics identifying facets of C have been mapped. This process allowed us to generate an initial large pool of items (to be reduced after the administration to a representative sample of subjects and after the analysis of the obtained answers) with which we could appropriately measure C, that is, at the beginning of the construction process of the evaluation scale [61,62,64]. Each topic in the mapping included a set of items related to it. The mapping, shown in Table 1, included the features of the metaverse for social purposes, so it took into account some of the related descriptive tags. All the Ti tags are listed in Table A3.

Table 1. In the central column, the topics for generating the pool of items for assessing construct C are shown. In the right column, the tags (Ti) involved by topic are shown (or "-" is shown if the topic does not involve tags). The tags are described in Table A3.

Topic	Involved Tags
Experiencing real life situations in a virtual space	T4, T5, T6, T7
Actual needs of real life instead of an alternative life in the virtual space	T4, T6, T7
Satisfaction/limits/barriers of real life	T4, T6, T7
Being another being	T6, T7
Time spent in virtual space	-
Value of sharing in virtual space	-
Value of actions in virtual space	-
On-site stillness of immersion	-
Pervasiveness of devices for immersion	-
Immersion in virtual space	-

As shown in Table 1, the following tags were deemed suitable for expressing facets of construct C: "Activities of daily life" (T4), "People meeting actively/sharing experiences" (T5), "Tearing down boundaries" (T6), "Living life in the metaverse" (T7). Tags T4 and T5 are related to the concept of impacting the activities of daily life, while T6 and T7 are related to the broad concept of impact on the freedom of acting. All of them are mediated by the fundamental concept of sharing experiences with other people. Additionally, other topics, not corresponding to the aforementioned tags, were identified to cover other facets of C (in Table 1; mapped to "-"). Also, in the case of topics with no involved tags, the aim was to assess the predilection of individuals for the "activity", for the "situation" represented by the topic; the specific aspects and reactions related to the consequences of experiencing virtual environments (for example: motion sickness, sense of presence, sense of reality and so on) were not considered.

On the other hand, the tags "New social platform" (T1), "Flooding mobile phones and devices" (T2), "New internet" (T3) were less suitable, because they are less related to changes in human life habits and more related to characteristics which appear to the public (especially the disenchanted ones) as normal, current, typical of existing today apps. Tag T1 was about the concept of the metaverse as a new platform for social media, which sounds like "ok, we have just a new awesome social media platform"; everyday, new ICT technologies and apps populate the online space. Tag T2 was about the concept of people accessing such new social media platforms from any device; this is an already well-known feature that is typical of existing apps. Tag T3 was about the concept of the metaverse becoming the new internet; this sounds like the "social internet has been renovated, with a new look, with new interfaces".

In a first preliminary reflection, our assessment of construct C addressed subjects aged 18–45 years; as shown in Table 2, this range was representative enough of potential and actual users. This range could be adjusted according to the characteristics of the population of a specific country or region. Moreover, people using and not using social media should be involved; the former could provide opinions as users already engaging with current social platforms (and skilled about), while the latter could provide opinions as "beginners" facing the concepts touched on in C.

Table 2. The percentages of users of Facebook and Instagram by age in January 2023. Source: [65,66]. In the left column, age range is shown. In the two center columns, percentages of Facebook users are shown. In the right column, percentages of Instagram users are shown. The values that are suitable for consideration are in bold underlined characters.

Age Range (Years)	Facebook Users %		Instagram Users %
	Male	Female	
13–17	2.7	2.1	8
18–24	**12.6**	**8.0**	**30.8**
25–34	**17.6**	**12.3**	**30.3**
35–44	**10.9**	**8.5**	**15.7**
45–54	6.1	5.5	8.4
55–64	3.5	3.8	4.3
>=65	2.6	3	2.6

6. Conclusions and Remarks

A perspective regarding the potential consolidation of actions of normal social life in a digital world emerged from a survey of the website of the Meta company, while other companies only loosely discussed the metaverse (Apple, IBM) or positioned themselves differently (Microsoft, Siemens) in relation to it. After searching the literature for works surveying opinions about question Q, few documents were found; most of the works found in the literature were focused on legal, ethical, and privacy aspects. These topics are often discussed as potential negative consequences of metaverse.

It is remarkable that most of the papers did not consider whether society in itself "wants" the metaverse (the authors of [15], mentioned in Section 1, touched on a similar topic in the field of mass media), also given that the vision of a "social" metaverse is not just related to entertainment and ICT services but also as a proposed new type of social life in the future. A curious aspect is represented by the fact that the technology push, typically used by the big tech companies, probably influences our point of view, so we tend to accept devices or paradigms coming from them, without questioning their suitability in our lives. This could be also an ethical component of the scenario. Therefore, in this paper, a preliminary analysis for the design of a Likert scale to assess the predilection of the public for a "social" metaverse has been outlined with the intent of bringing this topic to the foreground.

The presented work has limitations; the process is not complete yet, as the context could change in the future in relation to advances in the realization of "social" metaverse and in relation to behavior of other companies; the concepts and the tags summarizing views on the metaverse in this work have been outlined striving for an "objective" way, aware that it is intrinsically a subjective process (at least partially) and that some concepts could have been worded differently.

What has been designed is a draft concept underlying what should, in the future, be a questionnaire. The outcomes in the present work aim to contribute toward filling the gap in the topic of opinions about a "social" metaverse, by providing information that could be considered for further development, validation, and the application of the actual questionnaire.

Funding: This research received no external funding.

Data Availability Statement: The original contributions presented in the study are included in the article; further inquiries can be directed to the corresponding author.

Acknowledgments: Author would like to acknowledge his colleague Marta Mondellini for her effective contribution in managing the contents of the present paper.

Conflicts of Interest: The authors declare no conflicts of interest.

Appendix A

The following URLs have been surveyed for analyzing Meta web (visited in 7–21 February 2023):

https://about.meta.com/uk/what-is-the-metaverse/
https://about.meta.com/uk/company-info/
https://about.meta.com/uk/metaverse/#go-further
https://about.meta.com/uk/metaverse/#flexnaija
https://about.meta.com/uk/metaverse/are-we-there-yet/
https://about.meta.com/uk/metaverse/impact/
https://about.meta.com/uk/metaverse/#shared-experiences
https://about.meta.com/uk/metaverse/#fitness
https://about.meta.com/uk/metaverse/#work
https://about.meta.com/uk/metaverse/#education
https://about.meta.com/uk/metaverse/#virtual-reality
https://about.meta.com/uk/metaverse/#augmented-reality
https://about.meta.com/uk/metaverse/#smart-glasses
https://about.meta.com/uk/technologies/
https://www.oculus.com/horizon-worlds/
https://www.meta.com/it/quest/fitness/
https://www.meta.com/it/quest/social/
https://www.meta.com/it/quest/entertainment/
https://www.meta.com/it/quest/productivity/
https://www.meta.com/it/work/
https://www.youtube.com/watch?v=hCUyd4Y-5lo
https://www.youtube.com/watch?v=SKnc-jqLZUs
https://www.youtube.com/watch?v=L4pnQFLmHds
https://www.youtube.com/watch?v=d3ZKSmCWwJw
https://www.youtube.com/watch?v=XHmwSSxHnDw
https://www.youtube.com/watch?v=ODt3nMXu7pg
https://www.youtube.com/watch?v=VQV9%C3%973P0TDY
https://www.youtube.com/watch?v=8Ao-JG4PrGs
https://www.youtube.com/watch?v=JXP0yW80gnw
https://www.youtube.com/watch?v=pjNI9K1D_xo
https://www.youtube.com/watch?v=5FwztKGQmd8
https://www.youtube.com/watch?v=afdnbXXbBTg
https://www.youtube.com/watch?v=gQdRW44yvKw

The following URLs have been surveyed for analyzing Microsoft web (visited in 26 February 2024–4 March 2024):

https://www.microsoft.com/en-us
https://www.microsoft.com/en-us/sitemap.aspx
https://www.microsoft.com/en-us/microsoft-teams/group-chat-software
https://www.microsoft.com/en-us/microsoft-teams/group-chat-software#video
https://www.microsoft.com/en-us/microsoft-teams/enterprise
https://news.microsoft.com/source/features/innovation/microsoft-mesh/
https://www.microsoft.com/en-us/microsoft-teams/microsoft-mesh
https://www.microsoft.com/en-us/microsoft-teams/microsoft-mesh#modal-11
https://www.microsoft.com/en-us/microsoft-teams/microsoft-mesh#Customer-stories

https://www.microsoft.com/en-us/worklab/the-future-of-hybrid-events
https://www.microsoft.com/en-us/microsoft-teams/virtual-events
https://www.microsoft.com/en-us/microsoft-teams/teams-for-home
https://support.microsoft.com/en-us/office/microsoft-teams-free-08fd2b61-1c3e-47e2-821b-d312709b933d
https://support.microsoft.com/en-us/office/create-a-meeting-in-microsoft-teams-free-eb571219-517b-49bf-afe1-4fff091efa85
https://www.microsoft.com/en-us/microsoft-teams/communities
https://www.microsoft.com/en-us/microsoft-teams/education
https://www.youtube.com/watch?v=Qw6UCwCt4bE
https://www.youtube.com/watch?v=wAlcX7QaWkc
https://www.youtube.com/watch?v=tTHk0riVQ-w
https://www.youtube.com/watch?v=BJljapGLmO0
https://www.youtube.com/watch?v=lM7Yfy0OGFU
https://www.youtube.com/watch?v=Jd2GK0qDtRg
https://www.youtube.com/watch?v=IkpsJoobZmE
https://www.youtube.com/watch?v=co6sQQ64yfk
https://www.youtube.com/watch?v=LwYhAcNC0Qs&t=0s
https://www.youtube.com/watch?v=uErR_3kmRUM
https://www.youtube.com/watch?v=pdSfgRYy8Ao
https://www.youtube.com/watch?v=Pk5BVxlKL5w
https://www.youtube.com/watch?v=fOzvOM7ZX2o
https://www.youtube.com/watch?v=fSKBHOWOcSM
https://www.youtube.com/watch?v=4m6QATJW99k
https://www.youtube.com/watch?v=esBzumV_59Q

The following URLs have been surveyed for analyzing Apple web (visited in 12–13 March 2024):

https://www.apple.com/
https://www.apple.com/store
https://www.apple.com/shop/buy-mac
https://www.apple.com/shop/buy-ipad
https://www.apple.com/shop/buy-iphone
https://www.apple.com/shop/buy-watch
https://www.apple.com/mac/
https://www.apple.com/ipad/
https://www.apple.com/iphone/
https://www.apple.com/watch/
https://www.apple.com/airpods/
https://www.apple.com/tv-home/
https://www.apple.com/services/
https://www.apple.com/shop/accessories/all
https://www.apple.com/apple-vision-pro/
https://www.apple.com/shop/buy-vision
https://www.apple.com/studio-display/
https://www.apple.com/business/
https://www.apple.com/education/
https://www.apple.com/healthcare/
https://www.apple.com/augmented-reality/
https://apps.apple.com/us/app/highrise-avatar-chat-play/id924589795
https://apps.apple.com/us/app/atlas-earth/id1567636697
https://apps.apple.com/us/app/metaverse-experience-browser/id1159155137
https://apps.apple.com/us/app/imvu-3d-avatar-creator-chat/id919745844
https://apps.apple.com/us/app/zepeto-avatar-connect-play/id1350301428
https://apps.apple.com/us/app/nevermet-vr-dating-metaverse/id1601331019

https://apps.apple.com/us/app/reality-become-an-anime-avatar/id1404176564
https://apps.apple.com/us/app/meta-life-second-metaverse/id1594359997
https://apps.apple.com/us/app/habytat-metaverse/id6446708699
https://apps.apple.com/us/app/cluster-metaverse-vr/id1490075175
https://www.youtube.com/watch?v=TX9qSaGXFyg
https://www.youtube.com/watch?v=IY4x85zqoJM
https://www.youtube.com/watch?v=Vb0dG-2huJE
https://www.youtube.com/watch?v=OushE7mq0Ak

The following URLs have been surveyed for analyzing IBM web (visited in 15–19 March 2024):

https://www.ibm.com/us-en
https://www.ibm.com/consulting/customer-experience
https://www.ibm.com/thought-leadership/institute-business-value/report/enterprise-metaverse
https://www.ibm.com/downloads/cas/47X4RZJQ
https://www.ibm.com/downloads/cas/GN7B276L
https://www.ibm.com/blogs/smarter-business/business/metaverse-spatial-platform-solution-overview/
https://www.youtube.com/watch?v=rrpE8bHvf0k
https://www.youtube.com/watch?v=rrpE8bHvf0k&list=PLoELubR45xwV1My2lk7aHZmwjiAtzEPMq
https://www.ibm.com/blog/5-ways-to-get-metaverse-ready/
https://www.youtube.com/watch?v=7xfX-dmA1Rc
https://www.youtube.com/watch?v=_tl2eR7qFNU

The following URLs have been surveyed for analyzing Siemens web (visited in 20–25 March 2024):

https://www.siemens.com/global/en.html
https://www.technologyreview.com/2023/03/29/1070355/the-emergent-industrial-metaverse/
https://plm.sw.siemens.com/en-US/teamcenter/
https://xcelerator.siemens.com/global/en.html
https://www.siemens.com/global/en/company/digital-transformation/industrial-metaverse.html
https://www.youtube.com/watch?v=gRHP2IiNXKo&t=5s
https://www.siemens.com/global/en/company/digital-transformation/industrial-metaverse/what-is-the-industrial-metaverse-and-why-should-i-care.html
https://www.siemens.com/global/en/company/digital-transformation/industrial-metaverse/industrial-metaverse-glossary.html
https://www.siemens.com/global/en/company/digital-transformation/industrial-metaverse/siemens-and-nvidia-partner-to-build-the-industrial-metaverse.html
https://www.siemens.com/global/en/company/insights/siemens-and-nvidia-bringing-the-real-and-digital-worlds-together.html
https://www.siemens.com/global/en/company/insights/the-rise-of-the-industrial-metaverse-and-its-economic-impact.html
https://www.siemens.com/global/en/company/digital-transformation/industrial-metaverse/redefining-reality-3-key-building-blocks-for-the-industrial-metaverse.html
https://www.siemens.com/global/en/company/digital-transformation/industrial-metaverse/digital-twins-first-strides-into-the-industrial-metaverse.html
https://www.youtube.com/watch?v=SLVhLpVPRrU
https://www.youtube.com/watch?v=LGgccYDyGFk
https://www.youtube.com/watch?v=S9wJ7R04wac
https://www.youtube.com/watch?v=W2dQupQFv_U
https://www.youtube.com/watch?v=IsQVAXRbDs4
https://www.youtube.com/watch?v=5EtqTpQ-7mI

https://www.youtube.com/watch?v=uIT02AZs5Is
https://www.youtube.com/watch?v=9c1hlwHSel8

Appendix B

The following Table A1 contains the tags synthetized from analysis of Microsoft web.

Table A1. On the left column, the tags MSTi are shown; they classify the concepts about metaverse emerged from analysis of Microsoft web. On the right column, a description of the corresponding tag is provided; the descriptions with (*) just come from sentences explicitly positioned in a context of work, of business, of entertainment (gaming).

Tag MSTi—Represented Concept	Tag MSTi—Description
MST1—Communicating, sharing, working with others	(*) The metaverse allows people to communicate, share data/experiences, work, do things together
MST2—Doing activities of daily living	People can do in the metaverse (usual) activities of their life
MST3—Connecting from everywhere/at any time	(*) People can jump in the metaverse simply when they want and wherever they are
MST4—Representing yourself the way you want	(*) People can customize the avatar as they prefer
MST5—Representing yourself to reflect yourappearance/to express yourself	(*) People can customize their avatar to an appropriate representation of themselves
MST6—Removing the barriers	(*) People can keep in touch and act, no matter the place they are, the language they have (AI translations) and other "limitations". This allows to avoid issues of connection/presence/language, of personal life situations
MST7—Freeing up budget	Money can be saved in all those processes involving travelling/conferencing/venue costs and so on
MST8—New internet	The metaverse is a new version of internet
MST9—It can damage health	A present time, a long immersion in the metaverse (with headset) can damage health
MST10—It works on most/all devices	Metaverse can run on all the available devices
MST11—Improving quality of actions/experiences	(*) Doing things in the metaverse allows people to enhance, improve the quality of actions/experiences themselves

The following Table A2 contains the tags synthetized from analysis of Siemens web.

Table A2. On the left column, the tags STi are shown; they classify the concepts about metaverse emerged from analysis of Siemens web. On the right column, a description of the corresponding tag is provided.

Tag Sti—Represented Concept	Tag Sti—Description
ST1—Three sectors	The metaverse is present in three sectors of application: industrial, enterprise, consumer
ST2—Digital twin, software-defined automation, data and AI	The pillars of industrial metaverse are digital twin, software—defined automation, data and AI (especially generative AI)
ST3—The digital twin is the main pillar	The digital twin is the core main pillar of the whole industrial metaverse
ST4—Always on/persisting	The industrial metaverse is always running, is always on, it is a persisting system
ST5—Combination of real and digital world	In the industrial metaverse the digital and the real world are combined, joined together
ST6—Connecting real to digital to simulate and solve	In the industrial metaverse the real and digital world are connected together, by including also people, for simulating and solve problems of systems

Table A2. *Cont.*

Tag Sti—Represented Concept	Tag Sti—Description
ST7—Capability to solve real world problems	The industrial metaverse allows the capability to face and solve real-world problems that can be also very complex
ST8—Simulating/testing the whole thing	The industrial metaverse allows simulating/designing/testing/tuning the whole thing, or any side of the thing, before doing it/building it in real world or also during the real operation
ST9—Simulating/testing at high speed	The industrial metaverse allows to simulate/test/tune at unimaginable speed
ST10—Making decisions	In the industrial metaverse you can make better decisions/faster decisions
ST11—Allowing safe environments	The industrial metaverse is a virtual environment for doing experiments and actions in a safe way for people and for real environment
ST12—Allowing sustainability	The industrial metaverse allows to include matters of sustainability in simulations and optimizations
ST13—Saving time/money/resources	The digital world of simulations in industrial metaverse allows to save time, money, resources
ST14—Improving/impacting the real world	The industrial metaverse is something actually impacting the real world/making the real world better
ST15—Realtime collaboration	In the industrial metaverse the collaboration of people is in realtime
ST16—Collaborating/interoperating across systems	The industrial metaverse allows collaboration/interoperation of people/of applications across several platforms, devices, organizations, locations
ST17—Avatars for recognizing/interacting/improving	In the industrial metaverse people can use avatars for recognizing other people/for interacting with operators/for improving the job
ST18—Full immersion/like a real environment	The industrial metaverse is a fully immersive virtual environment, it is like the real environment
ST19—New way of interaction/collaboration	With the industrial metaverse new ways of interaction/of collaboration are unlocked
ST20—Changing the way organizations operate	The capabilities, the features of the industrial metaverse make organizations change the way they operate (in a better way)
ST21—Getting benefit from skills of people	In the metaverse the companies can find and get benefit from specific skills of people, by facing the shortage of skilled operators, wherever they are in the world
ST22—Supporting/motivating people	The industrial metaverse is a set of technologies allowing the engagement/the support/the motivation of people at work
ST23—Breaking down the barriers of distance	With the industrial metaverse there is no need to travel/the barriers of geographical distance among people are broken down
ST24—Saving costs for travelling	In the industrial metaverse there is no need to travel; similarly, the related costs are saved too
ST25—Need to face the possible fears of workers byexplaining opportunities/innovation	With the incoming industrial metaverse the companies can teach their workers the new opportunities offered
ST26—A new plane of existence/it changes our lives	The industrial metaverse, with all the technologies, the opportunities, the advantages it brings, can be considered as changing our lives
ST27—Doing activities of daily living	People can do in the metaverse the usual activities of their life
ST28—It will live in the internet 3.0	The industrial metaverse is a new face of internet/the internet 3.0
ST29—It is real/an emerging reality	The industrial metaverse is not an hype, it is a real thing and it is already happening

The following Table A3 contains the tags synthetized from analysis of Meta web.

Table A3. On the left column, the tags Ti are shown; they classify the concepts about metaverse emerged from analysis of Meta web. On the right column, a description of the corresponding tag is provided.

Tag Ti—Represented Concept	Tag Ti—Description
T1—New social platform	The metaverse will be the new platform for new social media
T2—Flooding mobile phones and devices	The metaverse will run on most devices as possible -smartphones, tablets, headsets, computers and other smart devices.
T3—New internet	The metaverse will be the new internet with infrastructure of contents
T4—Doing activities of daily living	People can do (or are "encouraged" to do) in the metaverse the usual activities of their life
T5—People meet actively/share experiences	People, with particular attention to relatives and friends, meet in metaverse and together they do actions and/or share experiences (depending on the context of specific sentence, this may evoke -also implicitly- no need to do it in reality)
T6—Tearing down the boundaries	The metaverse allows to do anything, by tearing down the boundaries/barriers/limits of reality (depending on the context of specific sentence, this may be also implicit)
T7—Living life in the metaverse	People can do/transfer actions typical of real life in the metaverse

Appendix C

The following search string has been used for search S1 in Web of Science (all databases, all collections):

TI = ((people OR citizen* OR user* OR "end user" OR "end users" OR society OR mainstream OR compan* OR audience) AND ("virtual reality" OR metaverse OR "meta" OR "immersive technology" OR "immersive technologies" OR "virtual world" OR "virtual worlds" OR "VR world" OR "VR worlds" OR HMD OR "head mounted display") AND ("don't want" OR "dont want" OR "do not want" OR "want it" OR want* OR deal* OR apprec* OR curio* OR expectation* OR accept* OR interest* OR enjoy* OR engage* OR involve* OR participat* OR future)) NOT TI = "meta-analysis" NOT TI = "meta-analysis" NOT TI = metaanalysis NOT TI = "meta analyses" NOT TI = "meta-analyses" NOT TI = metaanalyses NOT TI = "meta review" NOT TI = "meta-review" NOT TI = metareview

The following search string has been used for search S1 in Scopus:

TITLE ((people OR citizen* OR user* OR "end user*" OR society OR mainstream OR compan* OR audience) AND ("virtual reality" OR metaverse OR "meta" OR "immersive technolog*" OR "virtual world*" OR "VR world*" OR hmd OR "head mounted display") AND ("don't want" OR "dont want" OR "do not want" OR "want it" OR want* OR apprec* OR curio* OR expectation* OR accept* OR interest* OR enjoy* OR engage* OR involve* OR participat* OR future) AND NOT "meta analys*" AND NOT "meta-analys*" AND NOT metaanalys* AND NOT "meta review" AND NOT "meta-review" AND NOT metareview) AND PUBYEAR > 2017

The following search string has been used for search S2 in Web of Science (all databases, all collections):

TI = (metaverse AND (issue* OR problem* OR ethic* OR concern* OR substitut* OR future OR challeng* OR insight* OR alternat* OR roadmap* OR opportunit* OR possibilit* OR "3D virtual world" OR "3D virtual wolds" OR moral* OR achiev* OR dawn OR horizon* OR existence* OR realm* OR realit* OR social* OR societ* OR good OR avatar* OR behaviour* OR behavior* OR extens* OR extend* OR human* OR man OR world* OR health* OR mental* OR mind*))

The following search string has been used for search S2 in Scopus:

TITLE (metaverse AND (issue* OR problem* OR ethic* OR concern* OR substitut* OR future OR challeng* OR insight* OR alternat* OR roadmap* OR opportunit* OR possibilit* OR "3D virtual world*" OR moral* OR achiev* OR dawn OR horizon* OR existence* OR realm* OR realit* OR social* OR societ* OR good OR avatar* OR behaviour* OR behavior* OR extens* OR extend* OR human* OR man OR world* OR health* OR mental* OR mind*)) AND PUBYEAR > 2010

Appendix D

In this Appendix D are listed the questionnaires, scales items, links to interviews (with related results, when available) about metaverse; they also contain the topics that are close to Q ([44–48]), found in works selected from S1 and S2. The specific items assessed as close to Q have been selected (shown in *Underlined Italic Style*) and labeled with a letter ("A -", "B -" and so on). The selected items have been classified as "In favor" or "Not in Favor" (of metaverse) according to the percentages of answers. The results of this selection process are summarized in Figure 9.

The following is the questionnaire about metaverse in [45] (found in S1). It includes questions both in closed-form and in open-form.

The following are the questions in closed-form (Yes, No, Not Sure):

- Have you heard about the metaverse? (79.5% = Yes);
- Would you consider the metaverse to be the next evolution of the internet? (58.6% = Yes, 16.4% = No, 25% = Not Sure);
- Do you believe that the metaverse can reshape the future? (70.9% = Yes, 8.2% = No, 20.9% = Not Sure);
- Would you consider the metaverse the next frontier for online interaction? (75% = Yes);
- Would you agree that the metaverse will revolutionize online marketing in the same way that social media did? (results not shown);
- A—*Have you been impacted by the internet, Would you say that the metaverse will affect you?* (29.1% = Yes, 25.5% = No, 45.5% = Not Sure)

  In favor = 29% Not in favor = 71%;
- B—Does the metaverse also free us from many of the limitations of the physical world? (54% = Yes)

  In favor = 54% Not in favor = 46%;
- What is your opinion of the effect of metaverse on the economy? Are there opportunities for the economy to grow in the metaverse? (66.8% = Yes);
- Would you agree that the metaverse has tremendous potential to transform and improve fields (like health care, education, entertainment, and so on)? (78.6% = Yes) (this is question mentioned in the paper but, in the questionnaire, it is different);
- C—*Can Metaverse be a world where the digital world is more valuable and valuable than the physical world?* (28.6% = Yes, 37.7% = No, 33.6% = Not Sure)

  In favor = 28.6% Not in favor = 71.4%;
- Are you concerned that we may lose our connection to the real world with the metaverse? (63.2% = Yes, 20.5% = No, 16.3% = Not Sure);
- D—*Do you think you're ready for the metaverse?* (37.7% = Yes, 17.3% = No, 45.0% = Not Sure)

  In favor = 37.7% Not in favor = 62.3%;
- The metaverse is expected to fundamentally alter digital communication (75% = Yes, 8% = No, 16% = Not Sure) (question mentioned in the paper but not included in the questionnaire).

The following are the questions in opened-form:

- In your own words, how would you describe the metaverse?
- How far away do you think the metaverse is?
- In your opinion, who will benefit from using metaverse? (the majority of respondent = entertainment industry)
- Is there anything you would like to see in the metaverse?

The following are the subscales about Self-Efficacy and Intention to Participate, in [45] (found in S1). The subscales are aimed to validate the psychological constructs developed in the work. The responses are not shown in the original paper.

The following are the items of the subscale for Self-Efficacy of participating in the Facebook metaverse:

- Participating in the metaverse advertised by Facebook is a task I can perform;
- I have the necessary technological skills to participate in the metaverse advertised by Facebook;
- I have sufficient technological skills to participate in the metaverse advertised by Facebook;
- I will be able to combine my daily activities with my participation in the Facebook Metaverse.

The following are the items of the subscale for Intention to Participate in the Facebook metaverse:

- I plan to participate actively in the metaverse announced by Facebook;
- I will actively shop in the metaverse advertised by Facebook;
- I am interested in participating in job interviews in the metaverse advertised by Facebook;
- I am interested in taking training courses in the metaverse advertised by Facebook;
- I am interested in getting a new romantic partner in the metaverse advertised by Facebook;
- I will recommend my friends to participate actively in the metaverse advertised by Facebook;
- I will recommend my partner to participate actively in the metaverse advertised by Facebook;
- I will recommend my relatives to participate actively in the metaverse advertised by Facebook.

The following is the questionnaire about metaverse, in [46] (found in S2). The questions are in closed-form (Yes, No, Maybe):

- (What age group do you belong to?);
- Do you know what the metaverse is? (53% = No; "did not know what a metaverse is and had to be given an idea about a metaverse before attempting the survey.");
- E—*Do you think a Metaverse or a Virtual World excites you?* (57% = Yes, 12% = No, 31% = Maybe)

  In favor = 57% Not in favor = 43%;
- Do you think a Metaverse could create a physical communication gap between humans, and also cause hindrance in physical relationships? (47.4% = Yes, 14.3% = No, 38.2% = Maybe);
- Do you think the virtual sphere including the existing social media platforms give rise to abuse and harassment? (36.3% = Yes, 22.3% = No, 41.4% = Maybe);
- Do you think a metaverse could reduce physical activities in humans? (65.3% = Yes, 11.2% = No, 23.5% = Maybe);
- Are you concerned about your data and privacy and feel unsafe about a Metaverse? (results not shown in the paper).

The following are the reports of statistics about metaverse from interviews to samples of citizens from United States, in [47] (found in S2; sources in [48,67–70]):

- F—Share of adults in the United States who are interested in Meta's new virtual reality project known as the metaverse as of November 2021 [67]. Original question: "Based on what you know, how interested are you in using Facebook's new virtual reality project, metaverse, which would allow users to interact with each other in a computer generated environment? (values > 100% due to rounding)"

  Results: Not that/At all interested = 68%, Very = 32%
  In favor = 32% Not in favor = 68%;
- G—*Feelings toward the metaverse according to adults in the United States as of January 2022* [68]. Original question: "Which of the following best describes how you feel about Metaverse? -Select one"

  Results: Curious = 33%, Uninterested = 27%, Suspicious = 23%, Concerned = 19%, Indifferent = 19%, Excited = 18%, Optimistic = 16%, Confused = 12%, None of these = 7%
  In favor: Curious = 33%, Excited = 18%, Optimistic = 16%
  Not in favor: Uninterested = 27%, Suspicious = 23%, Concerned = 19%, Indifferent = 19%, Confused = 12%
  Note: the total amount is >100% but the access to [68] (free access) did not allow to see the results in detail
  The item "None of these" (7%) has been excluded;
- H—*Views on the metaverse according to adults in the United States as of January 2022* [69]. Original question: "[...] In the Metaverse, you could do many of the things you do now such as socialize with others, play games, watch concerts, and shop for digital and non-digital items such as clothing, home goods, and cars. Which of the following describe your views on Metaverse? -Select all that apply"

  Results: Not good as real life = 30%, The future of technology = 26%, Tech companies trying to figure out a new way to make money = 23%, A big risk to personal privacy = 20%, A really exciting way to play and socialize = 18%, A way to intensify enjoyable experiences = 13%, None of these = 11%, A fad that will not last long = 11%, Something for young people only = 10%, A better alternative to real life = 9%, How we will do most of our shopping in the future = 9%, Will create more equality in society = 6%, A scam or predatory financial scheme = 6%
  In favor: The future of technology = 26%, A really exciting way to play and socialize = 18%, A way to intensify enjoyable experiences = 13%, A better alternative to real life = 9%, How we will do most of our shopping in the future = 9%, Will create more equality in society = 6%
  Not in favor: Not good as real life = 30%, Tech companies trying to figure out a new way to make money = 23%, A big risk to personal privacy = 20%, A fad that will not last long = 11%, Something for young people only = 10%, A scam or predatory financial scheme = 6%
  The item "None of these" (11%) has been excluded;
- I—Share of adults in the United States joining or considering joining the metaverse for various reasons as of December 2021 [70]. Original question: not available

  Results: Joining or considering joining = 74%
  In Favor = 74%; Not in favor = 26%.

References

1. Stephenson, N. *Snow Crash*; Bantam Books: New York, NY, USA, 1992.
2. Zhang, X.; Chen, Y.; Hu, L.; Wang, Y. The metaverse in education: Definition, framework, features, potential applications, challenges, and future research topics. *Front. Psychol.* **2022**, *13*, 1016300. [CrossRef] [PubMed]
3. Crespo-Pereira, V.; Sánchez-Amboage, E.; Membiela-Pollán, M. Facing the challenges of metaverse: A systematic literature review from Social Sciences and Marketing and Communication. *Prof. Inf.* **2023**, *32*, e320102. [CrossRef]
4. Dionisio, J.D.N.; Burns, W.G., III; Gilbert, R. 3D Virtual Worlds and the Metaverse: Current Status and Future Possibilities. *ACM Comput. Surv.* **2013**, *45*, 34. [CrossRef]

5. Zhao, Y.; Jiang, J.; Chen, Y.; Liu, R.; Yang, Y.; Xue, X.; Chen, S. Metaverse: Perspectives from graphics, interactions and visualization. *Vis. Inform.* **2022**, *6*, 56–67. [CrossRef]
6. Park, S.-M.; Kim, Y.-G. A Metaverse: Taxonomy, Components, Applications, and Open Challenges. *IEEE Access* **2022**, *10*, 4209–4251. [CrossRef]
7. Cheng, R.; Wu, N.; Chen, S.; Han, B. Will Metaverse Be NextG Internet? Vision, Hype, and Reality. *IEEE Netw.* **2022**, *36*, 197–204. [CrossRef]
8. Vergari, M.; Kojic, T.; Vona, F.; Garzotto, F.; Moller, S.; Voigt-Antons, J.-N. Influence of Interactivity and Social Environments on User Experience and Social Acceptability in Virtual Reality. In Proceedings of the 2021 IEEE Conference on Virtual Reality and 3D User Interfaces—VR 2021, Lisboa, Portugal, 27 March–1 April 2021. [CrossRef]
9. Israel, K.; Zerres, C.; Tscheulin, D.K. Virtual Reality—Substitute for a Real Experience? The Role of User Motivation, Expectations and Experience Type. *Int. J. Innov. Technol. Manag.* **2022**, *20*, 2350018. [CrossRef]
10. Falk, T.H.; Le, L.B.; Morandotti, R. The Internet of Senses: A Position Paper on the Challenges and Opportunities of Multisensory Immersive Experiences for the Metaverse. In Proceedings of the 2022 IEEE International Conference on Metrology for Extended Reality, Artificial Intelligence and Neural Engineering (MetroXRAINE), Roma, Italy, 26–28 October 2022. [CrossRef]
11. Mystakidis, S.; Lympouridis, V. Immersive Learning Design in the Metaverse: A Theoretical Literature Review Synthesis. In *Application of the Metaverse in Education*; Liu, D., Huang, R., Metwally, A.H.S., Tlili, A., Fan Lin, E., Eds.; Smart Computing and Intelligence; Springer: Singapore, 2024. [CrossRef]
12. Choi, M.; Azzaoui, A.E.L.; Singh, S.K.; Salim, M.M.; Jeremiah, S.R.; Park, J.H. The Future of Metaverse: Security Issues, Requirements, and Solutions. *Hum.-Centric Comput. Inf. Sci.* **2022**, *12*, 60. [CrossRef]
13. Allam, Z.; Sharifi, A.; Bibri, S.E.; Jones, D.S.; Krogstie, J. The Metaverse as a Virtual Form of Smart Cities: Opportunities and Challenges for Environmental, Economic, and Social Sustainability in Urban Futures. *Smart Cities* **2022**, *5*, 771–801. [CrossRef]
14. Rosenberg, L. Regulation of the Metaverse: A Roadmap. The risks and regulatory solutions for largescale consumer platforms. In Proceedings of the ICVARS 22, 6th International Conference on Virtual and Augmented Reality Simulations, Brisbane, QLD, Australia, 25–27 March 2022. [CrossRef]
15. Maddocks, S.; Siegel, J.A.; Eaton, A.A.; Agarwal, S. Who Is Invited to the Metaverse? Analyzing Media Coverage of an Emerging Virtual World. *Cyberpsychol. Behav. Soc. Netw.* **2024**, *27*, 76–82. [CrossRef]
16. Riva, G.; Wiederhold, B.K.; Mantovani, F. Searching for the Metaverse: Neuroscience of Physical and Digital Communities. *Cyberpsychol. Behav. Soc. Netw.* **2024**, *27*, 9–18. [CrossRef] [PubMed]
17. Bojic, L. Metaverse through the prism of power and addiction: What will happen when the virtual world becomes more attractive than reality? *Eur. J. Futures Res.* **2022**, *10*, 22. [CrossRef]
18. Zuckerberg, M. The Metaverse and How We Will Build It Together. Connect 2021. Available online: https://www.youtube.com/watch?v=Uvufun6xer8 (accessed on 19 February 2023).
19. Apple Web Site. Available online: https://www.apple.com/ (accessed on 12 March 2024).
20. Apple YouTube Channel. Available online: https://www.youtube.com/@Apple (accessed on 13 March 2024).
21. IBM Web Site. Available online: https://www.ibm.com/us-en (accessed on 15 March 2024).
22. IBM YouTube Channel. Available online: https://www.youtube.com/@IBM (accessed on 15 March 2024).
23. IBM Institute for Business Value. Seven Bets. 2023. Available online: https://www.ibm.com/downloads/cas/GN7B276L (accessed on 18 March 2024).
24. IBM Consulting. 5 Ways to Get Metaverse Ready. 2024. Available online: https://www.ibm.com/blog/5-ways-to-get-metaverse-ready (accessed on 18 March 2024).
25. IBM Japan. IBM Spatial Platform. Available online: https://www.ibm.com/blogs/smarter-business/business/metaverse-spatial-platform-solution-overview/ (accessed on 19 March 2024).
26. IBM Institute for Business Value—Expert Insights. Beyond the Hype—Five Ways Retailers and Brands Can Drive Value in the Enterprise Metaverse. 2023. Available online: https://www.ibm.com/downloads/cas/47X4RZJQ (accessed on 18 March 2024).
27. Microsoft Web Site. Available online: https://www.microsoft.com/en-us (accessed on 26 February 2024).
28. Microsoft Teams Web Page. Available online: https://www.microsoft.com/en-us/microsoft-teams/ (accessed on 26 February 2024).
29. Microsoft Mesh Web Page. Available online: https://www.microsoft.com/en-us/microsoft-teams/microsoft-mesh (accessed on 27 February 2024).
30. What Is Microsoft's Metaverse? Microsoft Ignite 2021. Available online: https://www.youtube.com/watch?v=Qw6UCwCt4bE (accessed on 28 February 2024).
31. Microsoft YouTube Channel. Available online: https://www.youtube.com/@Microsoft (accessed on 28 February 2024).
32. Microsoft Teams YouTube Channel. Available online: https://www.youtube.com/@MicrosoftTeams (accessed on 27 February 2024).
33. The Industrial Metaverse. CIO Connection Series 2023. Available online: https://www.youtube.com/watch?v=wAlcX7QaWkc (accessed on 28 February 2024).
34. Siemens Web Site. Available online: https://www.siemens.com (accessed on 20 March 2024).
35. Siemens YouTube Channel. Available online: https://www.youtube.com/@siemens (accessed on 22 March 2024).

36. The Emergent Industrial Metaverse. MIT Technology Review Insights. 2023. Available online: https://www.technologyreview.com/2023/03/29/1070355/the-emergent-industrial-metaverse/ (accessed on 21 March 2024).
37. Meta Web Site. Available online: https://www.meta.com (accessed on 7 February 2023).
38. Meta YouTube Channel. Available online: https://www.youtube.com/@meta (accessed on 20 February 2023).
39. What Is the Metaverse? Meta. Available online: https://about.meta.com/uk/what-is-the-metaverse/ (accessed on 7 February 2023).
40. Zuckerberg, M. Introducing Meta. October 2021. Available online: https://www.youtube.com/watch?v=pjNI9K1D_xo (accessed on 21 February 2023).
41. Petrosyan, A. Worldwide Digital Population 2024. Statista, 31 January 2024. Available online: https://www.statista.com/statistics/617136/digital-population-worldwide/ (accessed on 30 November 2023).
42. Clarivate Web of Science. Available online: https://www.webofscience.com (accessed on 14 March 2023).
43. Elsevier Scopus. Available online: http://www.scopus.com (accessed on 15 March 2023).
44. Babu, A.; Mohan, P. Impact of the Metaverse on the Digital Future: People's Perspective. In Proceedings of the Seventh International Conference on Communication and Electronics Systems (ICCES 2022), Coimbatore, India, 22–24 June 2022. [CrossRef]
45. Alvarez-Risco, A.; Del-Aguila-Arcentales, S.; Rosen, M.A.; Yáñez, J.A. Social Cognitive Theory to Assess the Intention to Participate in the Facebook Metaverse by Citizens in Peru during the COVID-19 Pandemic. *J. Open Innov. Technol. Mark. Complex.* **2022**, *8*, 142. [CrossRef]
46. Bale, A.S.; Ghorpade, N.; Hashim, M.F.; Vaishnav, J.; Almaspoor, Z. A Comprehensive Study on Metaverse and Its Impacts on Humans. *Adv. Hum.-Comput. Interact.* 2022; 2022, 3247060. [CrossRef]
47. Bibri, S.E.; Allam, Z. The Metaverse as a virtual form of data-driven smart cities: The ethics of the hyper-connectivity, datafication, algorithmization, and platformization of urban society. *Comput. Urban Sci.* **2022**, *2*, 22. [CrossRef] [PubMed]
48. Clement, J. Metaverse—Statistics & Facts. Statista, 10 January 2024. Available online: https://www.statista.com/topics/8652/metaverse/ (accessed on 25 February 2022).
49. Davis, F.D., Jr. A Technology Acceptance Model for Empirically Testing New End-User Information Systems: Theory and Results. Ph.D. Thesis, Massachusetts Institute of Technology, Cambridge, MA, USA, 1985.
50. Venkatesh, V.; Davis, F.D. A Theoretical Extension of the Technology Acceptance Model: Four Longitudinal Field Studies. *Manag. Sci.* **2000**, *46*, 186–204. [CrossRef]
51. Venkatesh, V.; Morris, M.G.; Davis, G.B.; Davis, F.D. User Acceptance of Information Technology: Toward a Unified View. *MIS Q.* **2003**, *27*, 425–478. [CrossRef]
52. Parasuraman, A. Technology Readiness Index (TRI), A Multiple-Item Scale to Measure Readiness to Embrace New Technologies. *J. Serv. Res.* **2000**, *2*, 307–320. [CrossRef]
53. Sadin, S.R.; Povinelli, F.P.; Rosen, R. The NASA technology push towards future space mission systems. *Acta Astronaut.* **1989**, *20*, 73–77. [CrossRef]
54. Manning, C.G. Technology Readiness Levels. NASA, September 2023. Available online: https://www.nasa.gov/directorates/heo/scan/engineering/technology/technology_readiness_level (accessed on 20 January 2023).
55. *ANSI/HFES 400-2021*; Human Readiness Level Scale in the System Development Process (Draft Version). Human Factors and Ergonomics Society: Washington, DC, USA, 2021. Available online: https://hfes.org (accessed on 30 November 2022).
56. Brooke, J. *SUS—A Quick and Dirty Usability Scale*; Redhatch Consulting Ltd.: Earley, UK, 1986.
57. Venkatesh, V.; Thong, J.Y.L.; Xu, X. Consumer Acceptance and Use of Information Technology: Extending the Unified Theory of Acceptance and Use of Technology. *MIS Q.* **2012**, *36*, 157–178. [CrossRef]
58. Likert, R. A technique for the measurement of Attitudes. *Arch. Psychol.* **1932**, *22*, 55.
59. Likert, R.; Roslow, S.; Murphy, G. A simple and reliable method of scoring the Thurstone Attitude Scales. *J. Soc. Psychol.* **1934**, *5*, 228–238. [CrossRef]
60. Anjaria, K. Knowledge derivation from Likert scale using Z-numbers. *Inf. Sci.* **2022**, *590*, 234–252. [CrossRef]
61. Jebb, A.T.; Ng, V.; Tay, L. A Review of Key Likert Scale Development Advances: 1995–2019. *Front. Psychol.* **2021**, *12*, 637547. [CrossRef] [PubMed]
62. Tay, L.; Jebb, A.T. Establishing Construct Continua in Construct Validation: The Process of Continuum Specification. *Adv. Methods Pract. Psychol. Sci.* **2018**, *1*, 375–388. [CrossRef]
63. Schwarz, N. Self-reports: How the questions shape the answer. *Am. Psychol.* **1999**, *54*, 93–105. [CrossRef]
64. Clark, L.A.; Watson, D. Constructing validity: New developments in creating objective measuring instruments. *Psychol. Assess.* **2019**, *31*, 1412–1427. [CrossRef]
65. Dixon, S.J. Facebook: Distribution of Global Audiences 2024, by Age and Gender. Statista, March 2024. Available online: https://www.statista.com/statistics/376128/facebook-global-user-age-distribution/ (accessed on 23 November 2023).
66. Dixon, S.J. Instagram: Distribution of Global Audiences 2024, by Age Group. Statista, 2 May 2024. Available online: https://www.statista.com/statistics/325587/instagram-global-age-group/ (accessed on 23 November 2023).
67. Dixon, S.J. Share of Adults in the United States Who Are Interested in Meta's New Virtual Reality Project Known as the Metaverse as of November 2021. Statista, 21 February 2022. Available online: https://www.statista.com/statistics/1277855/united-states-adults-interested-meta-metaverse/ (accessed on 22 September 2023).

68. Petrosyan, A. Feelings toward the Metaverse According to Adults in the United States as of January 2022. Statista, 7 July 2022. Available online: https://www.statista.com/statistics/1290667/united-states-adults-feelings-toward-metaverse/ (accessed on 25 September 2023).
69. Petrosyan, A. Views on the Metaverse According to Adults in the United States as of January 2022. Statista, 7 July 2022. Available online: https://www.statista.com/statistics/1290435/united-states-adults-views-of-metaverse/ (accessed on 25 September 2023).
70. Dixon, S.J. Share of Adults in the United States Joining or Considering Joining the Metaverse for Various Reasons as of December 2021. Statista, 7 February 2022. Available online: https://www.statista.com/statistics/1288048/united-states-adults-reasons-for-joining-the-metaverse/ (accessed on 26 September 2023).

future internet

MDPI

Review

A Survey of the Real-Time Metaverse: Challenges and Opportunities †

Mohsen Hatami [1], Qian Qu [1], Yu Chen [1,*], Hisham Kholidy [2], Erik Blasch [3] and Erika Ardiles-Cruz [3]

1 Department of Electrical and Computer Engineering , Binghamton University, Binghamton, NY 13902, USA; mhatami1@binghamton.edu (M.H.); qqu2@binghamton.edu (Q.Q.)
2 Computer Science Department, Northern Illinois University, Dekalb, IL 60115, USA; kholidy@niu.edu
3 Air Force Research Laboratory, Rome, NY 13441, USA; erik.blasch.1@us.af.mil (E.B.); erika.ardiles-cruz@us.af.mil (E.A.-C.)
* Correspondence: ychen@binghamton.edu
† Approved for Public Release: Distribution Unlimited: Case Number AFRL-2024-5779.

Abstract: The metaverse concept has been evolving from static, pre-rendered virtual environments to a new frontier: the real-time metaverse. This survey paper explores the emerging field of real-time metaverse technologies, which enable the continuous integration of dynamic, real-world data into immersive virtual environments. We examine the key technologies driving this evolution, including advanced sensor systems (LiDAR, radar, cameras), artificial intelligence (AI) models for data interpretation, fast data fusion algorithms, and edge computing with 5G networks for low-latency data transmission. This paper reveals how these technologies are orchestrated to achieve near-instantaneous synchronization between physical and virtual worlds, a defining characteristic that distinguishes the real-time metaverse from its traditional counterparts. The survey provides a comprehensive insight into the technical challenges and discusses solutions to realize responsive dynamic virtual environments. The potential applications and impact of real-time metaverse technologies across various fields are considered, including live entertainment, remote collaboration, dynamic simulations, and urban planning with digital twins. By synthesizing current research and identifying future directions, this survey provides a foundation for understanding and advancing the rapidly evolving landscape of real-time metaverse technologies, contributing to the growing body of knowledge on immersive digital experiences and setting the stage for further innovations in the Metaverse transformative field.

Keywords: metaverse; real-time metaverse; edge computing; 5G networks; artificial intelligence (AI); virtual reality

1. Introduction

The metaverse is a complex, multi-component, hierarchical construct integrating various technologies and systems to create an immersive, three-dimensional (3D) interconnected virtual universe [1]. Figure 1 illustrates a seven-layer architecture of the metaverse. At its foundation, the *Infrastructure Layer* is the technical backbone that ensures the metaverse operates smoothly and efficiently [2]. It includes the physical hardware like servers and data centers and the cloud computing resources that provide the necessary computational power. A robust infrastructure is essential for scalability, enabling the metaverse to grow and accommodate increasing users and experiences.

The *Interface layer* determines how users interact with the metaverse [3], which includes the devices they use, such as VR headsets, AR glasses, and smartphones, as well as the software interfaces that make the metaverse accessible and user-friendly [1]. A well-designed interface is key to ensuring that the metaverse is easy to navigate and engaging, making it accessible to a wide range of users, regardless of their technical expertise.

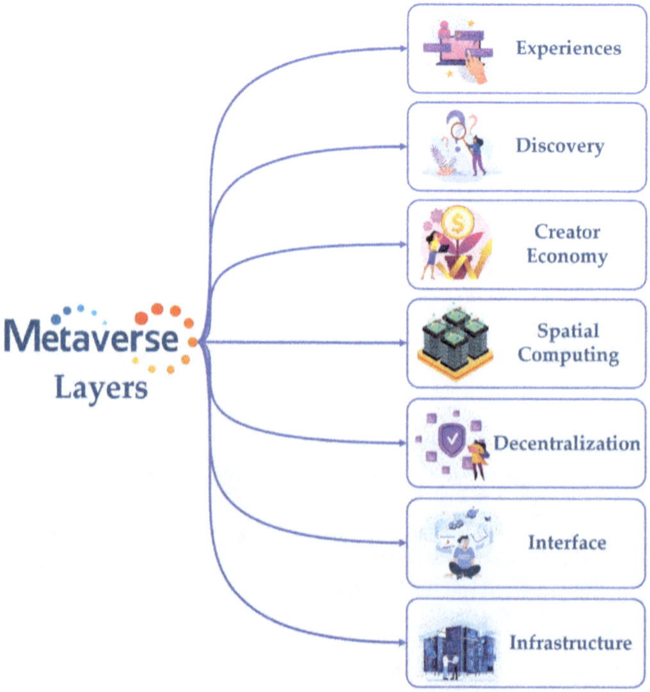

Figure 1. An illustration of the 7-layer metaverse architecture.

The core of the metaverse is the *Decentralization layer*, which ensures that the metaverse operates without being controlled by a single entity. The decentralization layer is crucial for maintaining user autonomy, privacy, and security, often achieved through blockchain technology [4]. By distributing power and data across a network of users, decentralization enables true ownership of digital assets, allowing participants to engage in transactions and interactions with confidence that their data and property are secure [5].

Spatial computing plays an essential role in a metaverse, which merges the physical and digital worlds to create immersive experiences. The computing layer utilizes technologies like virtual reality (VR) [6], augmented reality (AR) [7], mixed reality (MR) [8], and haptic feedback systems [9], allowing users to interact with digital objects as if they were part of the physical world. Spatial computing makes the metaverse more tangible and real, enabling users to experience and manipulate 3D environments in ways that go beyond the limitations of traditional computing interfaces [10].

The Creator Economy layer is the engine that drives innovation and content within the metaverse [11]. This layer supports the tools and platforms that allow users to create, distribute, and monetize digital content and experiences [12]. The creator economy fosters a vibrant, self-sustaining ecosystem where creativity is rewarded by empowering individuals to produce and profit from their creations [13]. The creator's content fuels the diversity of experiences available and encourages continual growth and expansion of the metaverse.

The Discovery layer helps users navigate the vast expanse of the metaverse [14]. It includes search engines, social networks, and recommendation systems that guide users toward content, experiences, and services that match their interests [15]. Effective discovery mechanisms are essential for helping users find and engage with what they are looking for, ensuring that the metaverse remains a dynamic and accessible space.

Finally, the *Experiences layer* is where the real value of the metaverse is realized [3]. It encompasses all the activities users can participate in, from socializing and gaming to education and commerce. The quality and variety of these experiences make the metaverse an engaging and appealing place for users to spend their time. The experience layer is constantly evolving, driven by the creativity of the community and the opportunities enabled by the other layers.

The metaverse is driven by several key technologies that collectively create an immersive, interactive, and interconnected nature [16], as conceptually shown in Figure 2. Blockchain technology underpins the decentralization and security aspects of the metaverse [17]. Blockchain ensures that digital assets, including virtual currencies, property, and identities, are securely managed and owned by users without relying on centralized authorities [18]. Blockchain technology provides transparency, immutability, and trust, enabling users to engage in secure transactions and interactions within the metaverse [19]. By leveraging blockchain, the metaverse can maintain a fair and open economy where users have full control over their digital assets and data.

Figure 2. Metaverse technologies.

Augmented reality (AR) and virtual reality (VR) are at the forefront of creating immersive experiences within the metaverse [20]. VR creates fully digital environments that users can explore and interact with using devices like headsets and gloves, effectively transporting them to another world. AR, on the other hand, overlays digital content in the real world, enhancing users' perceptions and interactions with their surroundings [21]. Together, AR and VR provide the sensory and spatial components that make the metaverse feel tangible and engaging, allowing users to interact with digital spaces in ways that mimic real-world experiences. 5G is essential for enabling the metaverse due to its ultra-high-speed connectivity and low latency [22]. This technology allows for seamless, real-time interactions within virtual environments. It supports high-bandwidth applications like augmented reality (AR), virtual reality (VR), and 3D reconstructions by providing faster data transfer, improving the user experience even in highly populated virtual spaces [23]. It also enables advanced features like haptic feedback in virtual reality, enhancing immersion by allowing users to "feel" virtual objects or textures.

Artificial intelligence (AI) technologies drive the intelligence and responsiveness of the metaverse [24]. AI powers various aspects of the metaverse, including creating realistic virtual characters to interact with users and generating dynamic and adaptive environments [25]. AI also plays a crucial role in personalization, learning from users' behaviors and preferences to tailor experiences that meet individual needs. By enabling complex decision-making and learning within the metaverse, AI ensures that the digital world is not only immersive but also intelligent and responsive. Brain–computer interfaces (BCIs) allow users to interact with virtual environments through brain signals, bypassing traditional input methods like keyboards or controllers [26]. This technology, while still in its early stages, has the potential to revolutionize the metaverse by enabling thought-based commands and avatar control. Early applications in gaming and productivity could lead to a more immersive and efficient experience. More people may use BCIs, which connect directly to the human neocortex and allow for advanced cognitive functions and interaction in virtual spaces [27].

Internet of Things (IoT) technology bridges the gap between the physical and digital worlds by connecting real-world edge devices to the metaverse [28]. IoT technology allows physical objects, from home appliances to vehicles, to communicate and interact with the digital environment. IoT integration enables real-time data exchange and interaction, making the metaverse a more seamless extension of the physical world [2,29]. For instance, IoT can allow users to control real-world devices within a virtual environment or bring physical data into the metaverse for analysis and visualization. Similarly, 3D reconstruction technology is vital in creating detailed and accurate digital representations of real-world environments [30]. This technology captures and digitizes physical spaces, objects, and people, bringing them into the metaverse with high fidelity. Three-dimensional (3D) reconstruction allows for creating virtual replicas of real-world locations, enabling users to explore and interact with these spaces as if they were physically present [31]. Three-dimensional (3D) capabilities are important for applications such as virtual tourism, real estate, and architecture within the metaverse.

All these technologies, working together, form the backbone of the metaverse, enabling users to create, explore, and interact in a fully realized digital universe [2].

While there are many survey papers about the full concept of the metaverse , this paper focuses specifically on the new frontier of the real-time metaverse paradigm. This survey is the first to examine the emerging technological ecosystem comprehensively. We present the challenges and opportunities brought by creating genuinely responsive virtual environments, from the analysis of state-of-the-art enabling technologies to their synergistic integration. It reconciles metaverse ideas and live systems and provides a starting point for researchers, developers, and industry stakeholders interested in exploring the future of immersive digital experiences. We would like to see our survey help guide this large and complex area, close the reality gap further, and lead the way toward an integral use of dynamic, interactive virtual worlds that are seamlessly integrated with our physical world.

The rest of this paper is structured as follows. Section 2 presents a general overview of the real-time metaverse concept. Section 3 introduces critical enabling technologies. The state-of-the-art real-time metaverse is discussed in Section 4, followed by sections that address multiple key issues in the real-time metaverse. Section 5 outlines the technological infrastructure that supports real-time virtual experiences. Section 6 details the engines for immersive technologies. Section 7 tackles one of the critical but long-time missed components in the metaverse ecosystem, the standard. The challenges and opportunities are illustrated in Section 8. Finally, Section 9 concludes this survey with future directions.

2. The Real-Time Metaverse

The real-time metaverse is a cutting-edge component of the ongoing digital revolution [32], serving as an advanced expansion of the broader metaverse concept. The real-time metaverse represents the next evolution in virtual worlds, transforming static digital environments into dynamic, interactive spaces continuously updated based on real-world data. The real-time metaverse goes beyond the traditional metaverse's pre-built, static worlds [33]—where users can socialize, work, play, and explore—by incorporating actual changes in the real world as they happen. This shift unlocks a new realm of possibilities, blending physical and digital realities to create more immersive and interactive experiences.

The core of the real-time metaverse instantaneously syncs real-world activities and environments with their digital counterparts. This is achieved through advanced sensor technologies and other inputs that continuously capture and send data from the physical world. These sensors gather critical information about an environment's geometry, movement, and visual details, feeding it into powerful data processing systems [34]. Data fusion techniques combine these diverse data streams into a single coherent model [35], which is then rendered in real-time within the virtual space. The result is a virtual environment that evolves in response to real-world changes, whether it is the movement of objects, changes in lighting, or adding new elements to a scene.

2.1. Dynamic Environments and Real-Time Interaction

One of the key distinguishing features of the real-time metaverse is its dynamic nature. In a traditional metaverse, environments are typically static or periodically updated [21,36], meaning that users interact with a world that may not reflect ongoing changes in the physical world. This makes the experience somewhat disconnected from reality. On the other hand, the real-time metaverse is designed to be constantly evolving [37]. As sensors capture real-world changes—such as the construction of a new building, the movement of vehicles, or even weather conditions—those changes are reflected instantly in the virtual environment [38]. This dynamic interaction opens up a wide range of applications. For example, a virtual replica of a city can be continuously updated to reflect real-time traffic patterns [39,40], construction projects [41], or even local events. Users could navigate this city virtually and interact with it as they would in the physical world. The virtual ability to mirror real-world changes in real-time has far-reaching implications for industries such as urban planning [42], architecture [43], education [44], and entertainment [45].

2.2. Enhanced Immersion and Engagement

The real-time metaverse offers a profound immersion compared to its traditional counterpart of independent systems. The user experience becomes more engaging and lifelike with the seamless integration of real-world data. Imagine attending a virtual concert that mirrors a live performance in a physical venue, with sound, lighting, and audience reactions captured in real-time [46]. This blurring of boundaries between the real and the virtual world creates a sense of presence and immediacy that is difficult to achieve in static environments. Furthermore, the real-time metaverse enhances the interactivity of virtual experiences [47]. Users are no longer just passive participants in a pre-rendered environment but can actively interact with objects and spaces that reflect real-world conditions. For example, in a real-time virtual meeting space, participants could interact with digital versions of objects [48] that are being manipulated in the physical world. The increased level of interaction could revolutionize fields like remote collaboration, virtual workspaces, and education, where the ability to manipulate and experience real-time objects and data is crucial.

2.3. The Role of Advanced Technology

The realization of the real-time metaverse hinges on several key technological advancements. One of the most important is the ability to capture, transmit, and process data in real-time. This requires a high-speed, low-latency infrastructure, such as 5G networks and edge computing, which allows sensor data to be processed locally or close to the source, reducing transmission delays [49]. Additionally, powerful AI models are necessary to analyze and interpret the incoming data, ensuring it is accurately reflected in the virtual environment. AI also plays a crucial role in managing the complexity of real-time environments [50]. Machine learning algorithms can help predict how objects will move or change over time, making the real-time metaverse more fluid and reducing the impact of any delays in data transmission. Furthermore, AI-driven data fusion techniques allow the system to combine data from multiple sensors [51] into a unified 3D model.

2.4. Applications and Potential Impact

As we approach the beginning of the digital transformation, the implications of the *real-time metaverse* extend far beyond mere entertainment. The potential applications of the real-time metaverse are vast and diverse. In terms of entertainment, live events such as sports games or concerts [52] could be experienced virtually in real-time, allowing users to engage with the event from anywhere in the world. In urban planning and architecture, creating a real-time virtual replica of a city can help planners and architects test designs and simulate the impact of changes [53] before they are made in the physical world. Education can also benefit from real-time virtual classrooms that mirror real-world laboratories or simulations [54], giving students hands-on experience in science, engineering, and medicine. The real-time metaverse also has the potential to transform social interactions [33]. Instead of static avatars meeting in a fixed environment, people could interact dynamically with each other in spaces that reflect their real-world surroundings, allowing for more meaningful and immersive connections. For example, a person in one part of the world could invite a friend to virtually experience their real-world environment in real-time, whether a stroll through a park or a live museum tour.

Figure 3 illustrates a hierarchical system for the real-time metaverse, consisting of three layers. At the physical layer, real-world actions and data are captured through sensors and devices in various domains, such as robotics, medical procedures, and fitness tracking. The data are transmitted via 5G networks to the technology layer, where cloud and high-performance computing (HPC) infrastructure processes and synchronizes it in real-time. The top metaverse layer represents digital twin environments, where the processed data are rendered into virtual replicas of physical actions, enabling immersive real-time interactions. This system ensures that real-world activities are mirrored seamlessly in the virtual world, supporting real-time metaverse experiences.

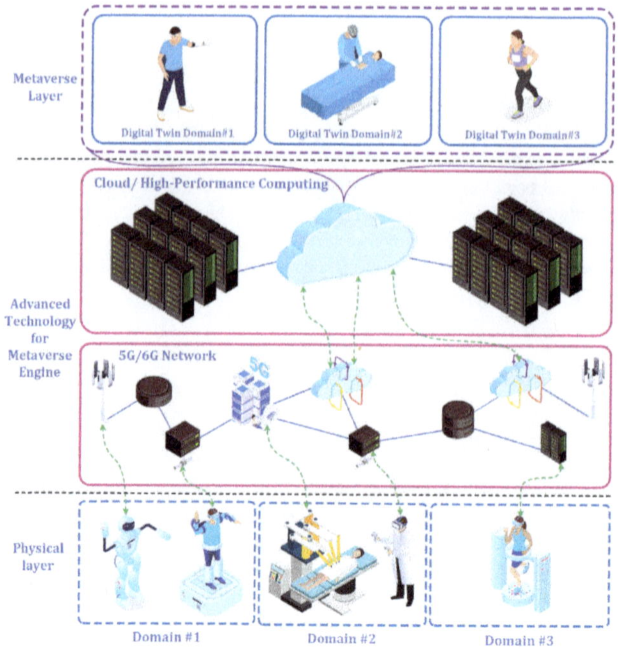

Figure 3. Real-time metaverse hierarchical system.

3. Key Enabling Technologies: An Overview

The metaverse represents a burgeoning frontier where the digital and physical worlds converge, offering immersive experiences through advancements in virtual reality (VR), augmented reality (AR), and other cutting-edge technologies. This section delves into the critical aspects of the metaverse, including blockchain integration, artificial intelligence (AI), edge computing, and the myriad challenges and implications of these innovations.

Blockchain technology is foundational for establishing a decentralized, secure, and interoperable metaverse [55]. Blockchain enhances metaverse functionalities such as data acquisition, storage, sharing, interoperability, and privacy preservation. Blockchain ensures the trustworthiness of transactions and interactions by providing a transparent and tamper-proof ledger, essential for managing digital assets and identities in a virtual world [1]. Blockchain can facilitate the creation of interoperable virtual worlds, allowing users to seamlessly transition and securely interact across different platforms, which is crucial for realizing a unified metaverse [56].

In the metaverse, *AI* is pivotal in enhancing user experiences by enabling more natural and intuitive interactions [55]. AI applications such as natural language processing, computer vision, and neural interfaces are instrumental in creating responsive and adaptive virtual environments [57]. AI-driven avatars, capable of understanding and reacting to user inputs, significantly enhance the realism and immersion of the metaverse [58]. *Edge computing* complements AI by providing computational power and low-latency communication for real-time interactions in the metaverse [59].

The deployment of the metaverse faces several technological and infrastructural challenges [21]. The role of *5G/6G technology* in overcoming these hurdles lies in its ability to provide ultra-low latency, high data rates, and enhanced reliability. The proposed layered architecture for integrating 6G with the Metaverse addresses the need for scalable and efficient network infrastructure to handle the vast amounts of data generated by Metaverse applications. Network scalability, data privacy, and security are identified as key challenges [32]. The advanced cryptographic algorithms and robust security protocols protect user data and ensure secure transactions within the metaverse are required [60]. Developing interoperability standards is also critical to facilitate seamless interactions across different virtual environments [61].

Edge computing complements VR and AI by providing the computational power and low-latency communication necessary for real-time interactions in the metaverse. Some research indicates that seamless real-time feedback ensures user safety and effectiveness. Edge computing is essential for the Metaverse, particularly in enhancing the performance and scalability of virtual environments. The role of edge-enabled technologies in managing the real-time demands of VR and AR applications is crucial. By processing data closer to the user, edge computing reduces latency and improves the overall user experience [36]. In addition, integrating advanced queue management algorithms with edge computing, as some research shows, can optimize network performance for data-intensive applications [62]. Network integration is paramount for maintaining the high levels of responsiveness and interaction fidelity required by the metaverse. By processing data closer to the user, edge computing minimizes latency. It ensures high-quality user experiences, particularly in applications that demand immediate feedback and minimal delays, such as health, education, and interactive entertainment.

VR and AR are core technologies driving the immersive experiences of the metaverse. Integrating *haptic feedback* in AR shows how tactile sensations can enhance user interactions in virtual environments [9,63]. Innovations such as the FingerTac haptic gloves provide real-time haptic feedback and improve the realism of AR applications [9]. The infrastructure supporting the metaverse must handle compute- and data-intensive tasks efficiently. Research has demonstrated that the application of VR combined with treadmill training can improve balance and mobility in individuals with traumatic brain injury (TBI) [64]. The integration of VR in rehabilitation highlights its potential in the metaverse, where real-time feedback and dynamic interaction are key. The study showed that participants engaged more with the VR-assisted training, reporting improved balance and mobility [65]. This aligns with the metaverse's vision of creating adaptive and immersive spaces customized to individual user needs, whether for entertainment, social interaction, or healthcare.

The above research underscores VR's transformative potential, especially in healthcare applications within the metaverse [66]. By offering real-time sensory feedback and stimulating neural pathways, as seen in neurorehabilitation, VR in the metaverse can provide personalized and therapeutic environments for users [67]. Therapeutic applications can have significant implications, particularly for industries such as healthcare, where virtual environments could be used for rehabilitation [68], therapy [69], and patient care [70]. Additionally, by enabling real-time interaction and multisensory engagement, VR enhances the immersive potential of the metaverse applications, making them more impactful and effective. The study on virtual taste and smell technologies further expands the sensory dimensions of VR, which is essential for a more immersive metaverse experience [71]. By integrating taste and smell, the metaverse can replicate real-world environments with a higher level of fidelity, crucial for applications in sectors such as education [72], gaming [72], and virtual tourism [73]. These technologies can enrich user experiences, offering deeper emotional and cognitive connections to the virtual world, which could be used in leisure and therapeutic contexts.

Developing multisensory technologies, such as taste and smell in VR, is essential for expanding the metaverse's immersive capabilities [74,75]. Incorporating sensory feedback beyond visual and auditory stimuli could transform user experiences across various applications, from entertainment to education and healthcare [76]. By enhancing the multisensory engagement, the metaverse can simulate real-world interactions more effectively, providing users with a richer, more connected virtual experience. Moreover, research into VR's potential in therapeutic settings showcases the broader applications of immersive virtual worlds. The metaverse could provide virtual spaces where patients receive specialized, personalized treatment plans, leveraging VR's ability to simulate realistic environments and offer real-time sensory feedback [77].

Security and *privacy* are among the top concerns in the metaverse, where vast amounts of personal data and digital assets are exchanged [78]. The immersive and persistent nature of the metaverse magnifies these concerns, as users' real-world identities, behaviors, and biometric data, such as eye movements or facial expressions, may be tracked and stored [21]. The importance of advanced cryptographic algorithms and robust security protocols to protect user data and ensure secure transactions is a fundamental requirement [79]. Also, zero-knowledge proofs and homomorphic encryption are receiving more attention as possible ways to keep private user data safe while still allowing transactions to happen without trust [80,81].

Some research explains that the decentralized nature of the metaverse offers a layer of security by eliminating the need for a central authority [17,82]. However, decentralization also presents challenges, particularly in maintaining data integrity and preventing unauthorized access. Without a centralized body to enforce security standards, the responsibility for safeguarding personal data is often distributed across numerous stakeholders. This opens up the system to vulnerabilities, where malicious actors could gain control over decentralized networks. Non-fungible tokens (NFTs) are becoming more popular and important to the metaverse economy. However, there are risks of digital asset theft, fake NFTs, and fraud, so strong identity verification systems and anti-fraud mechanisms are needed.

The findings showed that the *quality of user experience* is another critical factor in the success of the metaverse [83]. The immersive nature of VR and AR technologies can significantly enhance user engagement, but they also come with challenges. Integrating haptic feedback in AR can improve the realism of virtual interactions [9]. However, the technical difficulties in delivering consistent and intuitive haptic feedback are due to network latency and resource allocation issues [84]. AI can enhance user interaction by making virtual environments more responsive and adaptive. AI-driven avatars, capable of understanding and reacting to user inputs, can create more engaging and personalized experiences. However, ensuring these AI systems operate seamlessly across different platforms and devices remains a significant challenge.

Some research has highlighted that *scalability* is another major challenge in the development of the metaverse [85]. The current social VR platforms struggle to support large numbers of concurrent users. The bandwidth requirements for transmitting high-resolution 3D content and real-time interactions can be immense, necessitating advanced networking techniques to ensure scalability. The potential of 5G, and 6G technologies is to address these scalability issues by providing ultra-low latency, high data rates, and enhanced reliability. The proposed layered architecture for integrating 6G with the metaverse could help manage the massive data traffic and support large-scale user interactions. However, deploying such infrastructure poses significant technical and economic challenges. Recently, researchers proposed *Microverse* [16], a task-oriented, scaled-down metaverse instance, as a practical approach to current technologies [86,87].

According to some studies, *data integration* is essential for creating seamless and coherent virtual experiences in the metaverse [21,88]. The role of the edge is to compute and manage the real-time demands of data integration by processing data closer to the user. This approach reduces latency and improves the quality of experience. However, ensuring consistent and accurate data synchronization across distributed edge nodes is complex. Integrating diverse data sources, including IoT devices, digital twins, and AI systems, into the metaverse is essential. Integrating devices enables the creation of rich and dynamic virtual environments but requires robust frameworks to manage data interoperability and consistency.

In addition, *data compatibility* is another major challenge in the interoperability of different systems within the metaverse [88]. The lack of standardized data formats and protocols can hinder seamless interactions between virtual environments. Ensuring data compatibility involves developing common standards and protocols that can be adopted across various platforms and technologies. Cross-platform compatibility is essential for allowing users to access the metaverse from different devices and platforms [89]. The main challenge is achieving cross-platform compatibility, particularly in delivering consistent user experiences across devices with varying capabilities. Ensuring that applications and content are accessible and functional on different platforms requires significant effort in standardization and optimization.

Interoperability is another area of research in the metaverse, enabling seamless transitions and interactions across different virtual worlds [90]. Ensuring a cohesive experience of interoperability in the metaverse is crucial. AI and machine learning can facilitate interoperability by enabling systems to understand and adapt to different environments [91]. However, achieving true interoperability requires collaboration between developers, platform providers, and standardization bodies to establish common frameworks and protocols. To enable seamless interactions, it is required to integrate diverse technologies, such as blockchain, AI, and edge computing, and the need for standardized interfaces to enable seamless interactions [19]. Without interoperability, the metaverse risks becoming fragmented, with isolated virtual environments that cannot communicate with each other.

The metaverse holds significant potential for transforming education by creating immersive and interactive learning environments [92]. The metaverse can enable virtual classrooms where students and teachers interact in a shared virtual space, enhancing the learning experience through interactive simulations and collaborative projects. The flexibility and accessibility of the metaverse can democratize education, making high-quality learning resources available to a global audience. The concept of distance online learning in the metaverse can be expanded through evidence-based insights by leveraging immersive technologies like social virtual reality environments (SVREs) and AR. Research highlights that SVREs foster deep and meaningful learning (DML) by enabling collaborative, authentic interactions among learners [93]. These virtual environments allow students to engage in social and cognitive activities that parallel in-person experiences, thus addressing traditional distance learning challenges like isolation and disengagement [94]. AR and

VR technologies further support DML by creating simulations that encourage active, reflective, and goal-oriented learning, which enhances knowledge retention and motivation. Moreover, studies indicate that integrating SVREs into distance learning can foster a strong sense of presence and co-presence, leading to richer educational experiences that replicate the dynamics of physical classrooms [93].

Beyond technological advancements, the metaverse presents several social and ethical considerations [95]. Some issues, such as user addiction, digital harassment, and equitable representation of avatars, are highlighted. The immersive nature of the metaverse can exacerbate these issues, necessitating the development of guidelines and regulations to protect users and promote a healthy virtual environment [96]. Additionally, integrating AI and blockchain raises data privacy and security concerns, which must be addressed to ensure user trust and safety in the metaverse.

4. State-of-the-Art Real-Time Metaverse

4.1. Integration of the Physical and Virtual Worlds

Figure 4 presents a detailed view of the architecture for integrating physical, virtual, and real-time metaverse layers within a digital ecosystem. This image presents a conceptual overview of the physical–virtual world ecosystem, highlighting the synchronization of the physical and virtual environments. The *Physical layer* comprises four main components: users, IoT/sensors, virtual service providers, and physical service providers. Users engage with the virtual world using various devices, and IoT/sensors facilitate the synchronization between the physical and virtual worlds [15,97]. Virtual service providers offer digital goods and services. In contrast, physical service providers handle tangible goods and services transactions, highlighting the importance of interaction and synchronization between physical and virtual entities for a seamless user experience.

The *Virtual layer* includes avatars for virtual navigation, virtual environments for constructing the virtual world, and virtual goods/services such as virtual workspace and education [21]. The virtual layer bridges the gap between the physical and virtual worlds by providing immersive and interactive experiences. At its core, the real-time metaverse leverages data from IoT devices, sensors, and service providers to continuously update the virtual world in alignment with physical events [98]. The ability to "bring the physical world to the virtual" lies in deploying advanced sensors. These sensors capture critical information about real-world environments, such as the spatial layout, temperature, and motion of objects [99]. The data are then transmitted to cloud processing centers via high-speed communication technologies, enabling the real-time updating of virtual spaces [100]. Once the data are collected, they undergo data fusion—a process in which inputs from different sensors are combined to create a single, cohesive representation of the physical environment in the virtual world [101,102]. Fusing these diverse data types creates a rich, detailed, and accurate 3D model of the physical environment in the virtual world [103]. The data are processed in the cloud, allowing real-time synchronization between the two realms.

4.2. The Role of the Metaverse Engine

The *Metaverse engine* is crucial for maintaining the intelligence and real-time nature of the virtual environment, as shown in Figure 4. This engine incorporates a variety of advanced technologies [104], including VR/AR, haptic feedback, digital twin (DT), AI, blockchain, mixed reality [8], and advanced graphical rendering [105]. These features allow users to interact with the digital world in a way that feels natural and immersive. The metaverse engine also ensures that the virtual environment responds dynamically to user inputs and real-world changes. For example, in an industrial setting, IoT sensors embedded in machinery could transmit live data about the status and operation of physical assets to the metaverse [106]. The engine would interpret this information and update the virtual workspace to reflect real-time changes in equipment status, such as a machine overheating or requiring maintenance. AI-driven systems further enhance the realism of the environment by predicting how objects might behave in the future, ensuring the virtual world is not only reactive but also proactive [107].

AI models play a critical role in maintaining the intelligence of the real-time metaverse [108]. These models are responsible for analyzing sensor data, detecting patterns, and automating processes within the virtual environment [24]. For example, natural language processing (NLP) enables seamless human–human communication in virtual spaces, while image generation models can create realistic textures and visuals from raw data. The Metaverse engine further personalizes the user experience by suggesting virtual environments, services, or goods based on real-time preferences and interactions.

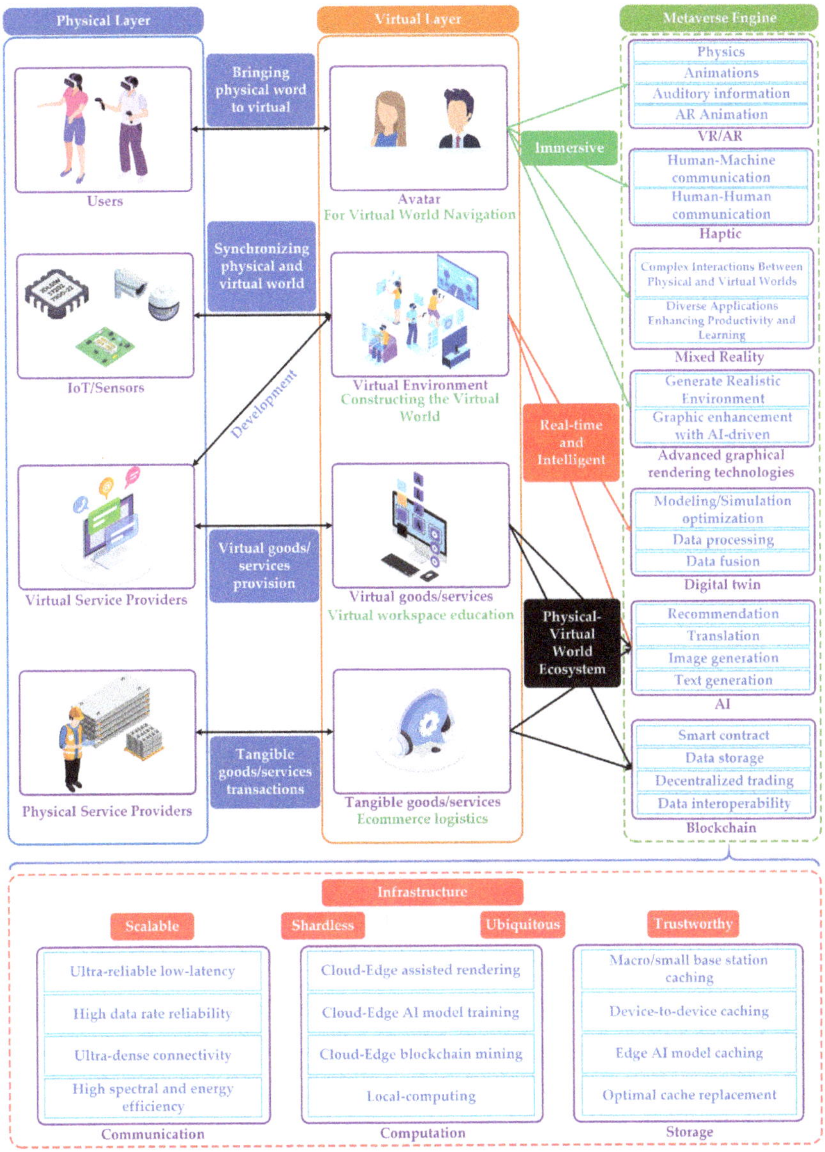

Figure 4. Metaverse architecture.

4.3. Communication and Computational Infrastructure

For the real-time metaverse to function efficiently, robust infrastructure is necessary. Figure 4 highlights key infrastructure components—communication, computation, and storage—that support the real-time data flow between the physical and virtual worlds. Scalability is essential, as the system must handle ultra-dense connectivity with high data rate reliability and low-latency communication. Technologies like 5G and edge computing are pivotal in ensuring that real-time data can be collected and transmitted without delays [109]. These communication technologies facilitate real-time data transmission and control signals between sensors, robots, and user interfaces, ensuring low latency and high reliability [110]. Real-time connectivity is essential for maintaining the interactive nature of the real-time metaverse, allowing users to experience immediate responses to their actions.

In addition to scalability, the infrastructure must be ubiquitous [37] and shardless [111]. Trustworthiness [80] is another critical factor in real-time metaverse systems, as users must trust the data and services they interact with. Localized computing, with cloud-edge-assisted rendering, cloud-edge AI model training, and blockchain mining are essential for delivering real-time experiences at scale, whether users are in urban areas with high connectivity or remote locations with limited infrastructure [90]. Technologies like blockchain provide decentralized storage, ensuring secure and verifiable transactions within the metaverse, from virtual goods to real-world e-commerce logistics.

4.4. Data Fusion and Real-Time Interaction

Figure 5 elaborates on the technical process of data fusion within the real-time metaverse. A variety of sensors, such as radar [112], LiDAR [113], RGB cameras [114], multispectral sensors [115], and hyperspectral sensors [25,116], collect data. With the high-speed connectivity of advanced communication systems, these data are transmitted to the cloud, where they are fed into the data fusion process [117,118]. For instance, LiDAR provides depth and spatial information, while RGB cameras contribute visual details like color and texture [119]. Thermal cameras capture temperature differences, and multispectral or hyperspectral sensors gather data across different wavelengths, offering unique insights into material properties [120]. This fusion of different sensor streams enables the creation of an integrated and high-fidelity virtual model that accurately reflects the physical world [121]. The fused data are then transmitted to robots and haptic control systems [122], enabling both physical and virtual objects to interact in real-time. For instance, an avatar in the metaverse could control a robot in the real world, with haptic feedback systems giving the user real-world sensations based on the robot's actions. Haptic controls play a vital role in ensuring that users can feel and interact with virtual objects as if they were physical [76]. This real-time feedback system enables greater immersion and interaction, bridging the gap between the virtual and real worlds. In combination with AI, these systems allow for complex interactions between physical and virtual entities, whether it is for remote collaboration, education, or e-commerce applications.

Cloud-edge computing, as depicted, ensures that data processing occurs as close as possible to the source, reducing the latency involved in transferring data to central servers [123]. Data and commands are processed in centralized servers or cloud-based processing centers. This setup supports complex computations and large-scale data storage, enabling the system to handle vast amounts of information and deliver real-time responses. The system benefits from scalable processing power and robust data management capabilities by leveraging cloud integration.

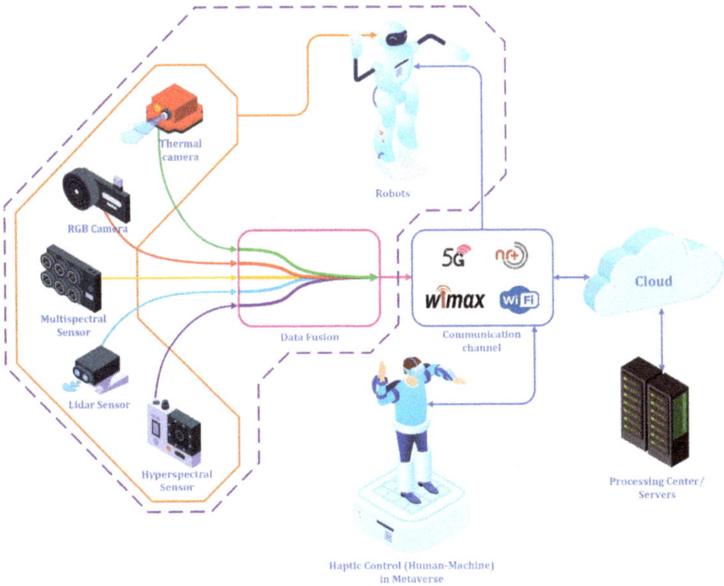

Figure 5. Real-time metaverse in a closed-loop system.

5. Technological Infrastructure

The technological infrastructure of the metaverse comprises a sophisticated and interconnected ecosystem of advanced technologies designed to support immersive, real-time virtual experiences [90]. The hardware includes high-speed and low-latency networks like 5G and fiber optics, powerful computing hardware such as graphics processing units (GPUs) and cloud computing resources, and robust data storage solutions [124]. Together, these components ensure the metaverse is a seamless, scalable, and interactive digital universe capable of supporting various applications from gaming and social interactions to professional and educational environments. Key enablers include high-performance computing, cloud and fog architectures, and edge devices as shown in Figure 6.

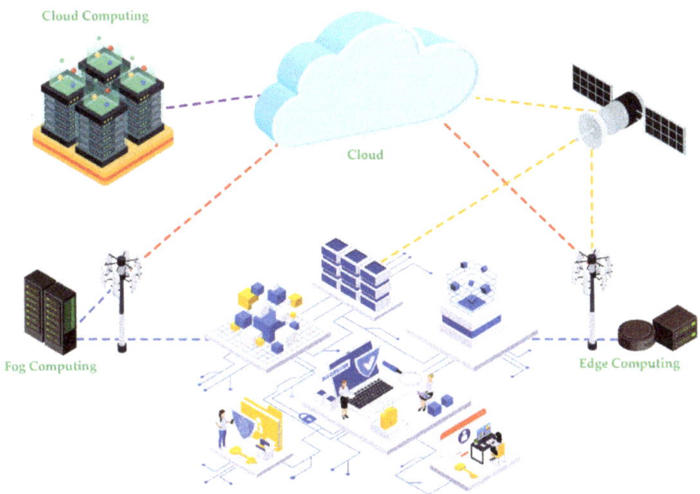

Figure 6. Structures of computing in the network.

5.1. High-Performance Computing (HPC)

High-Performance computing (HPC) leverages the combined power of supercomputers, cluster centers, and parallel processing techniques to tackle complex computational problems beyond standard desktop computers' capabilities [125]. HPC systems are essential in various domains, such as scientific research, design engineering, and data analysis, enabling large-scale simulations, systems modeling, and processing of massive datasets. Supercomputers and HPC clusters of interconnected nodes perform calculations at incredible speeds by dividing tasks into smaller sub-problems solved simultaneously. Advanced data centers equipped with high-performance servers and GPUs are essential for processing the vast amounts of data required for real-time metaverse interactions [105]. Specialized software and tools, like MPI (message passing interface), OpenMP (open multi-processing), and CUDA (compute unified device architecture), support the development and execution of HPC applications, ensuring efficient use of the vast computing resources available [126]. Applications range from climate modeling and molecular dynamics in scientific research to computational fluid dynamics and structural analysis in engineering, as well as big data analytics and machine learning in data-intensive fields.

Despite the immense capabilities of HPC for a real-time metaverse, it faces several challenges, including scalability, energy consumption, cost, and complexity [127]. Scaling applications across thousands of processors efficiently requires optimizing code to minimize communication overhead. The significant power consumption of supercomputers and large clusters necessitates the development of energy-efficient designs. The high costs of HPC infrastructure and the specialized knowledge required for developing and maintaining applications further complicate its adoption. However, the future of HPC is promising, with advancements in exascale computing, quantum computing, and AI integration. Exascale systems will enable even more complex simulations and data analyses, while quantum computing could revolutionize fields like cryptography and material science [128]. Combining HPC with AI and machine learning will drive innovations across various domains, and research into energy-efficient technologies aims to reduce the environmental impact of HPC.

5.2. Cloud Computing

Cloud computing is a transformative technology that allows individuals and organizations to access and store data, applications, and computing power over the internet rather than relying on local servers or personal devices [129]. Cloud technology offers several key advantages, including scalability, flexibility, cost-efficiency, and accessibility [130]. Cloud services are typically categorized into three main types: infrastructure as a service (IaaS) [131], which provides virtualized computing resources over the internet; platform-as-a-service (PaaS) [132], which offers hardware and software tools for application development; and software as a service (SaaS) [133], which delivers software applications over the internet on a subscription basis [134]. Major cloud service providers like Amazon Web Services (AWS), Microsoft Azure, and Google Cloud Platform (GCP) offer robust solutions that cater to a wide range of needs, from startups requiring minimal resources to enterprises needing extensive infrastructure and advanced services.

Cloud computing has revolutionized various industries by enabling more efficient and innovative business models. For instance, in the healthcare sector, cloud computing facilitates the secure storage and sharing of patient data, supports telehealth services, and enhances collaborative research through data analytics [135]. In finance, it allows for real-time transaction processing and advanced fraud detection. Additionally, cloud computing supports the growing field of remote work by providing seamless access to applications and data from any location, fostering collaboration and productivity [136]. Despite its many benefits, cloud computing also poses challenges such as data security, privacy concerns, and dependency on internet connectivity. However, ongoing advancements in cloud security protocols and hybrid cloud solutions, which combine private and public cloud resources, are addressing these issues and enhancing the reliability and security of cloud services.

5.3. Edge and Fog Computing

Edge and fog computing are paradigms that enhance data processing and analysis capabilities closer to the source of data generation, reducing latency and improving efficiency [137]. Edge computing involves processing data directly on devices or near the data source, such as sensors, IoT devices, or local servers [138]. The edge approach minimizes the need to send data to centralized cloud servers, reducing latency and bandwidth usage. Edge computing applications include real-time analytics, autonomous vehicles, and smart cities, where immediate data processing is crucial. For instance, in autonomous cars, edge computing allows for rapid decision-making based on real-time data from sensors, enhancing safety and performance.

Fog computing, on the other hand, extends the concept of edge computing by providing a distributed computing infrastructure that includes edge devices, local servers, and potentially the cloud [139]. The fog architecture acts as an intermediary layer that processes data before it reaches the cloud, providing additional storage and computational resources closer to the data source [140]. The fog–edge layered approach benefits applications requiring real-time processing and more substantial computational power or data aggregation. Fog computing is beneficial in scenarios like industrial IoT, where data from numerous devices needs to be aggregated and analyzed swiftly to optimize operations and maintenance. By distributing resources across multiple layers, fog computing improves overall system efficiency, scalability, and reliability.

Figure 6 illustrates a comprehensive architecture that integrates cloud computing, fog computing, and edge computing. At the center of the diagram is the cloud, symbolizing the centralized and extensive data processing capabilities of cloud computing. Cloud computing is depicted with multiple connections, including data centers and satellites, highlighting its broad reach and ability to handle significant computational tasks and data storage. Servers and network infrastructure placed closer to the data sources, such as IoT devices and sensors, represent fog computing. The fog layer aims to reduce latency by processing data near its origin before sending it to the cloud. Edge computing, depicted with smaller, decentralized servers and network nodes, is even closer to the end-users and devices. It emphasizes real-time data processing and immediate response actions, crucial for applications requiring low latency and high reliability. Integrating these computing paradigms ensures a balanced and efficient data handling from the core cloud to the network's edge, optimizing performance and resource utilization.

5.4. 5G Communication Technology

Fifth-generation (5G) communication technology represents a significant leap in mobile communications, offering faster data speeds, lower latency, and more excellent connectivity compared to previous generations [141].

With theoretical speeds of up to 10 Gbps and latency as low as 1 millisecond, 5G enables a wide range of applications that require real-time data transmission and high bandwidth. These include enhanced mobile broadband, ultra-reliable low-latency communications (URLLC), and massive machine-type communications (mMTC) [142]. Industries such as healthcare, automotive, and entertainment are poised to benefit immensely from 5G. For example, 5G supports telemedicine and remote surgeries in healthcare by providing reliable, high-speed connections necessary for transmitting high-definition video and large medical data files in real-time.

Beyond 5G, the focus is on developing technologies like 6G, which aims to provide even higher speeds, lower latency, and more extensive connectivity [59]. 6G is expected to integrate advanced technologies such as artificial intelligence, machine learning, and blockchain to enhance network management, security, and efficiency. Potential applications of 6G include holographic communications, advanced AR and VR, and ubiquitous IoT connectivity, enabling smart environments and autonomous systems to operate seamlessly [143]. Research and development in 6G technology are exploring new spectrum bands, such as terahertz frequencies, to achieve these ambitious goals. As society moves toward 6G, the focus will also be on sustainable and energy-efficient solutions to support the ever-growing demand for data and connectivity.

Figure 7 shows a 5G network architecture, integrating various components and technologies to create a robust communication system. The core is a massive multiple-input multiple-output (MIMO) network that connects to resources and wireless and wired links [144]. The cloud provides extensive data processing and storage capabilities, connected to the core network and servers via wired links. The internet is crucial, linking the core network and servers to broader online resources. The mobile small cell network, including 5G-enabled devices, ensures coverage and connectivity for mobile users. The edge network includes sensors, IoT devices, and connected appliances, receiving and sending data through wireless links. A residential setup is also included, demonstrating the network's ability to provide high-speed internet access to homes.

Figure 7. A general 5G cellular network architecture.

5.5. Storage Technology

Storage technology plays a critical role in the real-time metaverse by ensuring fast, secure, and efficient data handling for continuous immersive experiences [145]. As the metaverse involves interactions between physical and virtual environments, data from various sources such as sensors, edge devices, and AI systems must be cached and retrieved in real-time [146]. Technologies like macro/small base station caching [147] and device-to-device caching [148] help reduce latency by storing frequently accessed data closer to the user, ensuring faster retrieval times. This is essential in high-demand environments where real-time responsiveness directly impacts the user experience.

In addition to reducing latency, efficient storage mechanisms like edge AI model caching contribute to the real-time metaverse's ability to manage large-scale, complex interactions without overwhelming the network [149]. Edge AI model caching allows real-time AI computations to occur closer to the user by caching AI models at edge nodes, which improves performance and reduces the load on central servers [150]. This approach enhances scalability and ensures that the system can support a high number of simultaneous interactions without performance degradation, a necessity in the immersive and constantly evolving world of the real-time metaverse.

Furthermore, optimal cache replacement is crucial in ensuring that the most relevant and frequently accessed data remains readily available, while outdated or less important data are efficiently replaced [151]. As the real-time metaverse generates and processes massive amounts of data, intelligent cache management prevents storage bottlenecks and ensures the availability of real-time data [152]. This ensures seamless transitions and interactions within the real-time metaverse, allowing users to experience smooth, uninterrupted virtual environments while maintaining the overall system's trustworthiness and performance.

6. Metaverse Engine

The metaverse engine comprises seven key components: immersive technologies (including VR/AR, haptic feedback, mixed reality, and advanced graphical rendering), digital twin, AI, and blockchain. Each of these components will be detailed in the following sections.

6.1. *Immersive Technologies*

Immersive technologies for the real-time metaverse encompass a range of advanced tools and systems designed to create deeply engaging and interactive virtual experiences [105,153,154]. These technologies include VR, AR, mixed reality (MR) [155], haptic feedback [9], and advanced graphical rendering techniques [25], all of which work together to blur the lines between the physical and digital worlds. Figure 8 showcases the integration of VR/AR, haptic, and advanced graphical rendering technologies to enhance virtual and augmented reality experiences. VR/AR creates immersive environments using physics, animations, and auditory information. Haptic enhances human-machine communication and provides tactile feedback for real-life interactions. Advanced graphical rendering uses AI-driven techniques to generate realistic environments and enhance graphics, resulting in more immersive and interactive virtual experiences.

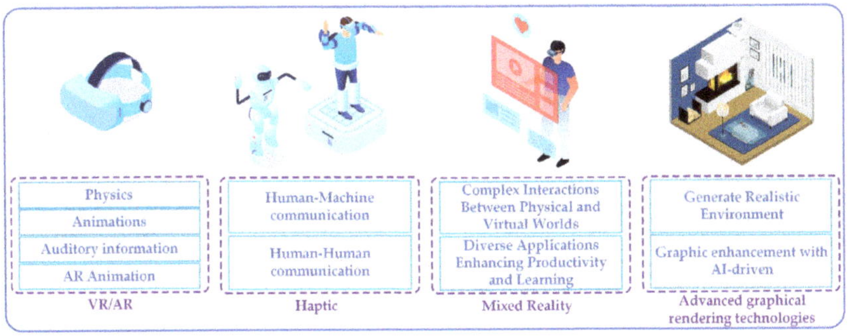

Figure 8. Immersive metaverse technologies.

6.1.1. Virtual Reality (VR)

Virtual reality (VR) is a technology that immerses users in a computer-generated environment, providing a simulated experience that can be similar to or completely different from the real-world [156]. VR typically involves headsets equipped with displays, sensors, and controllers that track the user's movements and interactions within the virtual environment [157]. VR technology is widely used in gaming and entertainment, creating immersive experiences that engage users in new and exciting ways [158]. Beyond entertainment, VR has significant applications in education, where it enables interactive learning experiences, such as virtual field trips or simulations of complex scientific concepts, allowing students to explore and understand subjects more deeply.

In addition to its impact on gaming and education, VR is transforming industries like healthcare, real estate, and training [159]. In healthcare, VR is used for surgical simulations, allowing surgeons to practice procedures in a risk-free environment and for therapeutic purposes, such as exposure therapy for patients with anxiety disorders. In real estate, VR provides virtual tours of properties, giving potential buyers a realistic sense of space without needing to visit in person [160]. In professional training, VR offers a safe and controlled environment for employees to practice skills and scenarios, such as emergency response or complex machinery operation [161]. As VR technology advances, with improvements in display resolution, motion tracking, and user interfaces, its applications are expected to expand further, offering increasingly sophisticated and practical uses across various fields.

6.1.2. Augmented Reality (AR)

Augmented reality (AR) is a technology that overlays digital information and virtual objects onto the real world, enhancing the user's perception and interaction with their environment [162]. Unlike virtual reality, which creates an entirely simulated experience, AR blends virtual elements with the physical world, often through smartphones, tablets, or AR glasses [163]. AR technology has gained widespread popularity in applications such as mobile gaming, with games like Pokémon GO allowing users to interact with virtual characters in real-world locations [164]. AR also enhances navigation and location-based services by providing real-time information and directions overlaid on the physical environment, improving user convenience and engagement [165].

Beyond entertainment and navigation, AR is making significant strides in many fields, such as retail, education [166] (distance online learning), and healthcare [167]. In retail, AR applications allow customers to visualize products in their own space before purchasing [168], such as seeing how furniture would look in their home or trying on virtual clothing [169]. AR not only enhances the shopping experience but also reduces return rates and increases customer satisfaction. In education, AR brings learning materials to life by enabling interactive and immersive experiences, such as 3D visualizations of historical events or scientific phenomena, which can deepen student understanding and engagement [54]. In healthcare, AR assists surgeons by providing real-time overlays of critical information during procedures, improving precision and outcomes [170]. As AR technology continues to evolve, its integration into everyday life and various professional fields is expected to grow, offering increasingly innovative and practical applications.

6.1.3. Mixed Reality (MR)

Mixed reality (MR) is an advanced technology that seamlessly blends the physical and digital worlds, creating environments where real and virtual elements coexist and interact in real-time [171]. Unlike VR, which immerses users in a completely virtual environment, or AR, which overlays digital information in the real world, MR allows for more complex interactions between physical and virtual objects. MR is typically achieved using advanced sensors, cameras, and displays, often incorporated into headsets like Microsoft's HoloLens or Magic Leap. These devices track the user's position and surroundings, enabling virtual objects to be anchored in the real world and interact with them naturally and intuitively [172].

The potential applications of mixed reality span numerous fields, enhancing productivity, creativity, and learning [8]. MR can be used in industry and manufacturing for remote collaboration, allowing engineers to visualize and manipulate 3D models of equipment or structures as if they were physically present [23]. This can improve design accuracy and speed up problem-solving processes. MR can provide immersive learning experiences in education, such as virtual laboratories where students can conduct experiments without the risk or expense associated with physical setups. MR can assist in medical training in the healthcare sector by simulating complex surgical procedures with real-time feedback and guidance. As MR technology continues to evolve [173], it promises to revolutionize how we interact with both the digital and physical worlds, providing a more integrated and interactive experience.

6.1.4. Haptic Feedback

Haptic feedback is a technology that simulates the sense of touch by applying forces, vibrations, or motions to the user [9,63]. Haptic sensory feedback enhances the immersive experience in virtual environments by allowing users to feel interactions with virtual objects as if they were real. In the context of the metaverse, haptic feedback is delivered through various devices such as gloves, vests, and other wearables, which can replicate sensations like texture, resistance, and impact. For instance, when a user picks up a virtual object or feels a virtual breeze, haptic devices provide physical sensations corresponding to those actions, making the virtual experience more realistic and engaging.

Integrating haptic feedback into the metaverse has significant implications for various applications, including gaming, training, and remote collaboration [174]. In gaming, haptic feedback enhances immersion by allowing players to physically feel in-game actions, such as holding equipment or surface texture. In training simulations, particularly in fields like medicine and engineering, haptic technology can provide realistic practice scenarios, helping users develop practical skills without real-world risks. For remote collaboration, haptic feedback can bridge the gap between digital and physical interactions, enabling more effective and intuitive communication. Overall, haptic feedback enriches the user experience in the metaverse by adding a critical layer of sensory interaction that deepens engagement and realism.

6.1.5. Advanced Graphical Rendering Technologies

Advanced graphical rendering (GR) technologies are crucial for creating highly realistic and visually stunning virtual environments in the metaverse [25]. One of the key advancements in GR is real-time ray tracing, a technique that simulates the way light interacts with objects in a scene to produce highly accurate reflections, refractions, and shadows [105,175]. This level of detail enhances the realism of virtual worlds, making them more immersive and visually engaging. Real-time ray tracing requires significant computational power, but recent advances in GPUs and optimization techniques have made it feasible for real-time applications, allowing users to experience lifelike visuals in interactive settings such as gaming, virtual tours, and social interactions within the metaverse.

Another significant development in advanced graphical rendering is using artificial intelligence (AI) to enhance graphics quality and performance [24,108]. AI-driven techniques, such as deep learning-based upscaling (NVIDIA's deep learning super sampling (DLSS)), can improve frame rates and image quality by predicting and generating high-resolution frames from lower-resolution inputs. High resolution not only ensures smoother performance but also allows for more detailed and complex scenes without compromising on speed. AI is also used in procedural content generation, enabling the creation of vast and diverse virtual landscapes with minimal manual effort [176]. By leveraging these advanced rendering technologies, the metaverse can offer visually rich, dynamic, and interactive environments that push the boundaries of what is possible in digital experiences, making them more compelling and lifelike for users.

6.2. Digital Twin

The integration of digital twin (DT) technology into the metaverse is transformative, serving as a crucial bridge between the physical and virtual worlds [59]. By creating a real-time digital replica of physical entities, DTs enable an immersive and interactive metaverse experience. This constant synchronization ensures that changes in the physical world are instantly reflected in the virtual environment, allowing users to engage with highly accurate and dynamic digital representations of objects, environments, and even people [177]. In this way, DTs elevate the realism and functionality of the metaverse, making it a more practical and engaging platform for users.

One of the most significant challenges in this integration is achieving real-time synchronization between the physical and digital realms [75]. Digital twins must continually update as real-world changes occur, ensuring that the metaverse remains a faithful and current representation [36]. By distributing the metaverse into smaller, localized sub-metaverses, these systems can process data closer to the source, reducing delays and enhancing the responsiveness of the digital twin environment [178]. This decentralized approach is particularly valuable in applications like autonomous vehicles [179], healthcare [180], and smart cities [181], where real-time accuracy is critical. In smart city ecosystems, the combination of DTs and the metaverse offers new dimensions for urban management and citizen interaction. Digital twins can mirror real-time city infrastructures, providing an immersive way for users to interact with urban spaces as though they are physically present. This not only improves user experience but also enhances urban planning, resource management, and disaster response through real-time simulations and predictive modeling [182]. As cities grow more complex, the ability to manage them in real-time through a metaverse-driven interface becomes increasingly valuable, offering more efficient ways to allocate resources and address challenges.

In sectors like healthcare and manufacturing, DTs integrated into the metaverse offer powerful tools for decision-making and efficiency [183]. For instance, in healthcare, digital twins can monitor patient health in real-time, allowing healthcare providers to predict potential issues and intervene before conditions worsen [180]. Similarly, in manufacturing, DTs simulate production processes, helping companies optimize performance, predict equipment failures, and reduce operational downtime [184]. By enabling these real-time simulations, the metaverse enhances decision-making capabilities and operational efficiency in critical industries. Security and trust are also essential aspects of the metaverse, where DTs play a pivotal role [185]. The decentralized nature of the metaverse, combined with blockchain technology, offers a secure and transparent framework for transactions and interactions. Blockchain ensures that all transactions are immutable, decentralized, and verifiable, making it ideal for safeguarding the integrity of digital twins and their data within the metaverse [186]. This decentralized trust mechanism is crucial as the metaverse becomes more integrated into everyday life, supporting interactions that are both secure and reliable.

6.3. *Artificial Intelligence (AI) and Machine Learning (ML)*

Artificial intelligence (AI) content generation plays a pivotal role in developing and enhancing the metaverse, a virtual universe where users can interact with each other and in digital environments in real-time [24]. Using AI to make content in a metaverse includes a lot of different technologies, such as procedural generation, natural language processing (NLP) [187], and large language models (LLMs) [188]. These technologies collectively create more immersive, interactive, and personalized user experiences. Procedural generation is a method in which content is created algorithmically rather than manually, allowing for the creation of vast and diverse virtual worlds within the metaverse. The procedural technique can generate everything from complex landscapes to intricate architecture and even entire ecosystems. Procedural generation ensures that the metaverse remains dynamic and expansive, offering users new and unique experiences each time they log in. The ability to automatically generate content also significantly reduces the time and resources needed for manual creation, enabling developers to focus on other aspects of the metaverse.

NLP is another critical component in the AI content generation for the metaverse [187]. NLP enables more natural and intuitive interactions between users and virtual entities, including non-player characters (NPCs) and digital assistants [24]. By understanding and processing human language, NLP allows these virtual entities to respond appropriately to user inputs, facilitating more engaging and meaningful conversations. The NLP capability fosters a seamless and immersive user experience [189], as it bridges the gap between human communication and digital interaction. LLMs, such as GPT-4, further enhance the capabilities of NLP in the metaverse [188].

These models are trained on vast datasets and can generate human-like text based on contextual understanding. LLMs can create complex narratives, generate dialogue for NPCs, and even assist in real-time translation between users of different languages. The integration of LLMs into the metaverse ensures that the virtual world is rich in content and can adapt to the diverse linguistic needs of its global user base. The combination of procedural generation, NLP, and LLMs in the metaverse leads to a highly dynamic and personalized user experience. For instance, users can explore unique environments tailored to their preferences, engage in meaningful conversations with virtual entities, and enjoy evolving narratives based on their interactions [190]. The advanced level of personalization not only enhances user engagement but also fosters a sense of connection and immersion within the virtual world. The AI-driven content generation ensures that the metaverse remains a vibrant and evolving space, continuously offering new experiences. In virtual environments such as the metaverse, AI-driven avatars and non-player characters (NPCs) serve distinct roles, each with unique functionalities and purposes. Although they both use artificial intelligence to power them, their approaches to user interaction, levels of autonomy, and overall goals in virtual spaces are fundamentally different.

6.3.1. AI-Driven Avatars

AI-driven avatars represent a remarkable fusion of artificial intelligence and digital animation, poised to revolutionize how we interact in virtual environments [108]. These avatars are sophisticated digital representations of individuals designed to mimic human behavior, appearance, and communication with high realism and responsiveness. At the core of these avatars is advanced AI technology, enabling them to learn, adapt, and respond to users naturally and intuitively [191]. The AI-driven avatars are integral in enhancing the user experience within the metaverse, providing a seamless and immersive interaction that bridges the gap between humans and machines. One of the most significant aspects of AI-driven avatars is their ability to understand and process natural language [192]. Using natural language processing (NLP) algorithms, these avatars can interpret spoken or written language, allowing for fluid and dynamic conversations with users. Machine learning models further enhance this capability, enabling avatars to learn from interactions and improve their responses over time. As a result, users can engage in meaningful and personalized dialogues with their avatars, making virtual interactions more engaging and lifelike.

In addition to linguistic capabilities, AI-driven avatars are equipped with advanced facial recognition and emotion detection technologies [193]. These technologies allow avatars to read and respond to human emotions, adapting their behavior and expressions accordingly. For instance, an avatar can recognize when a user is happy, sad, or frustrated and tailor its responses to provide appropriate emotional support or feedback. This emotional intelligence adds another layer of depth to virtual interactions, making AI-driven avatars not just functional tools but empathetic companions in the digital world. The applications of AI-driven avatars extend far beyond entertainment and social interactions. These avatars can serve as personalized tutors in educational settings, offering tailored instruction and feedback to students [194]. They can provide efficient and empathetic support in customer service, handling inquiries, and resolving issues with a human touch [195]. In healthcare, AI-driven avatars can act as virtual companions for patients, providing comfort and monitoring their well-being [196]. By integrating AI-driven avatars into various sectors, the metaverse can unlock new possibilities for enhancing user experiences and improving the quality of services across multiple domains.

6.3.2. Non-Player Characters (NPCs)

NPCs are fully autonomous characters embedded in the virtual environment, designed to perform roles independent of any human control. NPCs are generally pre-programmed with specific behaviors or controlled by the system's AI to serve particular functions [197]. For example, in a gaming context, NPCs often populate the environment as background characters or antagonists. However, in educational and professional settings, NPCs are increasingly being used as interactive tools to enhance user experiences. NPCs in the educational metaverse can take on roles such as virtual tutors, peers, or advisors [198]. These NPCs interact with users to foster engagement, provide feedback, or guide them through learning tasks.

NPCs are particularly useful in education because they can simulate real-world scenarios, offering dynamic, role-based interactions [199]. For instance, an NPC designed as a tutor can offer students advice on solving problems or guide them through complex design thinking processes. NPCs can also be peers or students, enabling users to practice teaching, mentoring, or collaboration skills in a controlled, simulated environment. This creates a scalable and adaptable learning space, where NPCs act as constant participants, available for interaction at any time, regardless of the availability of human peers or instructors [200]. Furthermore, NPCs often leverage advanced natural language processing (NLP) capabilities, enabling them to carry out conversations, understand user queries, and provide meaningful responses in a way that feels interactive and intuitive.

6.3.3. Differences in Purpose and Autonomy

The primary distinction between AI-driven avatars and NPCs lies in their relationship with users and their level of autonomy. AI-driven avatars are designed to represent and act on behalf of the user, making decisions based on user-defined parameters or learned behaviors [201]. They are personalized to the user's preferences and can be seen as digital extensions of the user's identity within the metaverse. These avatars help maintain a user's presence, even when they are not actively engaged in the virtual world, by taking over routine tasks or social interactions. On the other hand, NPCs exist independently of the user [202]. They are part of the virtual environment itself, managed by the system's AI to provide users with a more immersive and engaging experience. NPCs follow predefined rules or machine learning algorithms, interacting with users to fulfill specific roles—whether as educators, fellow learners, or virtual assistants. While they can simulate human-like behaviors, NPCs do not represent any specific user and are instead designed to enhance the user's experience by populating the world with interactive, responsive characters. NPCs facilitated design thinking by providing feedback, engaging in empathy-building exercises, and offering diverse perspectives that helped students reframe problems and develop solutions [203].

Another key difference between AI-driven avatars and NPCs is the degree of personalization [201]. AI-driven avatars are highly personalized to their user. They adapt and evolve based on the user's behavior, preferences, and interactions, becoming more reflective of the user over time. This level of personalization ensures that the avatar represents the user's unique identity and can act in ways that align with the user's goals and needs. For example, in a corporate setting, an AI avatar could autonomously schedule meetings, manage tasks, or even negotiate with other AI avatars based on the user's work habits and objectives. NPCs, in contrast, are designed to serve broader, more generalized purposes within the virtual environment. They are not tied to any specific user and often follow universal rules or patterns set by the system. While NPCs can adapt their behavior based on interactions with multiple users, their core function is to enhance the immersive experience for all users rather than reflecting the behavior of any individual [204]. For example, an NPC in a classroom scenario might adapt to the learning pace of different students, offering tailored guidance and feedback, but its role remains fundamentally as a system-controlled character that enriches the educational experience for everyone, not just a single user.

6.4. Blockchain

Blockchain technology is emerging as a foundational component for the realization of a secure, decentralized, and efficient real-time metaverse [205]. In a digital environment where the virtual and physical worlds merge, blockchain offers several critical benefits that ensure the smooth functioning of this complex ecosystem. By enabling decentralized control, enhancing data security, and ensuring trust, blockchain significantly contributes to the metaverse's infrastructure, making it not only more reliable but also scalable for widespread use [5]. One of the primary advantages of blockchain in the metaverse is its ability to provide a decentralized architecture [206]. Unlike traditional systems that rely on centralized servers, blockchain allows data and transactions to be distributed across a network of nodes, reducing the risk of single points of failure. In the metaverse, this decentralization ensures that no single entity has complete control over user data or interactions [207]. This is crucial for fostering a sense of trust and transparency in an environment where users engage in social, economic, and virtual activities that require accountability and fairness.

Security is another major factor that blockchain brings to the metaverse [208]. Given the vast amount of personal data, assets, and transactions occurring within this space, ensuring the integrity and security of these activities is essential. Blockchain's immutable ledger ensures that once a transaction is recorded, it cannot be altered or tampered with, providing a high level of security [209]. This is particularly important for protecting digital assets like virtual property, NFTs (non-fungible tokens), and cryptocurrencies, which are becoming integral parts of the metaverse economy. Blockchain's encryption and consensus mechanisms prevent fraud, unauthorized access, and cyberattacks, making the metaverse a safer environment for its users. In addition to decentralization and security, blockchain also plays a critical role in establishing trust and ownership within the metaverse. Smart contracts, which are self-executing contracts with the terms directly written into code, allow for transparent, automated transactions between users without the need for intermediaries [55]. This creates a system where users can buy, sell, and trade virtual goods or services with confidence, knowing that the transaction is secure and verifiable. Furthermore, blockchain's ability to record and authenticate digital ownership ensures that users can prove ownership of their virtual assets, from in-game items to virtual real estate, further solidifying the importance of blockchain in creating a functioning digital economy within the metaverse.

7. Interoperability Standards

As the real-time metaverse evolves, the need for seamless integration across various virtual worlds, platforms, and hardware has become increasingly apparent. The concept of interoperability—the ability for systems, platforms, and devices to work together harmoniously—lies at the heart of this vision. These standards ensure that different systems, devices, and applications can work together seamlessly, exchanging data and functionality without compatibility issues [55,88]. For users to experience a cohesive and immersive metaverse, regardless of the device or platform they are using, interoperability is key. Interoperability is particularly important in industries where disparate systems [210,211], such as healthcare, finance, telecommunications, and information technology, need to interconnect. By adhering to common protocols and formats, interoperability standards enable diverse systems to interoperate, reducing the need for costly custom integrations and minimizing the risk of data silos.

Figure 9 illustrates the concept of metaverse interoperability, depicting how users in the physical world can access a unified virtual world through various devices. The physical layer showcases the interoperability across these devices, allowing seamless transitions into the virtual world. Users can interact and navigate across various platforms and activities in the virtual layer once they are in the avatar-represented virtual world.

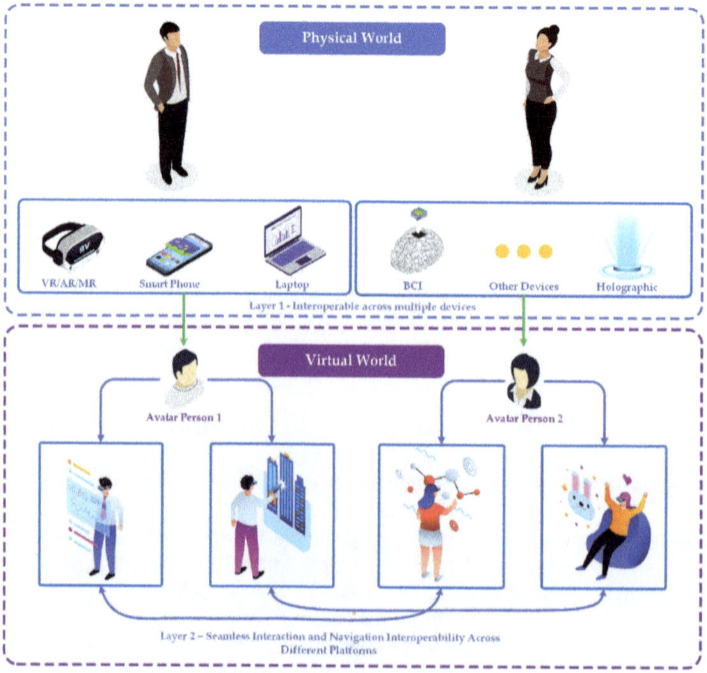

Figure 9. Interoperability of the metaverse.

7.1. Standards Development Organizations

Standards development organizations (SDOs) are key players in the advancement of the metaverse [212], ensuring that different platforms, devices, and content within this evolving virtual ecosystem are interoperable, accessible, and scalable. These organizations develop open standards to promote uniformity and collaboration across industries [88], preventing fragmentation and proprietary limitations. The W3C (World Wide Web Consortium) has been instrumental in creating WebVR and WebXR [213], standards that enable immersive VR and AR experiences through web browsers. This makes content more accessible by eliminating the need for standalone applications. Similarly, the Web3D Consortium works on the X3D standard, which enables the sharing and use of 3D graphics across web platforms, crucial for delivering 3D content in the metaverse.

The ISO/IEC MPEG group has a longstanding role in developing standards for coding, compression, and transmission of audio and video content [214]. Their MPEG-V standard ensures smooth interoperability of immersive media, such as 3D and VR/AR content, across various devices. Meanwhile, the Khronos Group, through standards like OpenXR and glTF, is focused on providing open and royalty-free interoperability standards for XR devices and 3D content, helping developers create cross-platform applications [215]. The International Telecommunication Union Telecommunication Standardization Sector (ITU-T) Correspondence Group (CG)-metaverse is dedicated to the standardization of metaverse technologies, with a focus on enabling global interoperability through telecommunication and infrastructure standards [216]. The Open Metaverse Interoperability Group complements this effort by promoting open-source interoperability in the metaverse, advocating for user-friendly transitions between virtual worlds.

IEEE's Metaverse Standards Committee, through its P2048 standards, is developing frameworks for VR/AR technologies on a global scale, ensuring technical coherence and best practices [212]. Similarly, the World Metaverse Council provides guidance on global policies and standards [217], focusing on ethical and regulatory frameworks for the metaverse. The Universal Scene Description (USD) standard improves 3D content interoperability for creation and collaboration in virtual environments [218]. Pixar, Adobe, and other companies lead the Alliance for OpenUSD [88]. Lastly, the Metaverse Standards Forum [96], which includes over 1,200 organizations, promotes open standards for the metaverse, driving industry-wide collaboration to create a more inclusive and interoperable virtual ecosystem. These SDOs collectively shape the future of the metaverse, ensuring it remains accessible, scalable, and technologically coherent across platforms, benefiting users and developers alike.

7.2. The Importance of Interoperability in the Real-Time Metaverse

In a real-time metaverse, users and assets must be able to move seamlessly across different virtual environments and platforms [219]. For instance, a user should be able to switch from a VR meeting application to an AR-enhanced virtual shopping experience, all while maintaining consistent access to their avatar, digital assets, and interactive capabilities [220]. The same applies to the integration of XR (extended reality) hardware, including virtual reality (VR) headsets, augmented reality (AR) glasses, and mixed reality (MR) systems. Suppose these devices are built on incompatible standards. In that case, users are likely to experience significant barriers to interaction, including the need for different software or restrictions on which platforms they can access [161]. Two primary open standards that seek to solve these problems are OpenXR and WebXR [221]. These standards, developed and promoted by organizations, represent an important step toward achieving greater interoperability in the metaverse. However, the road to widespread adoption and true standardization is still long and fraught with challenges.

Open standards play a crucial role in achieving interoperability. These publicly accessible specifications are the result of consensus-driven processes that frequently involve numerous stakeholders from business, academia, and government [222]. Open standards are designed to be vendor-neutral, ensuring that any organization can implement them without restrictive licensing terms. Open infrastructure promotes competition and innovation, as developers can build interoperable products without being locked into proprietary technologies. Examples of open standards include HTTP and HTML for web technologies, TCP/IP for internet communications [223], and Health Level 7 (HL7) for healthcare data exchange [224].

The adoption of open standards offers several significant advantages. First, it enhances compatibility and integration, allowing different systems to communicate and share data more easily [225]. Data compatibility is particularly beneficial in complex environments such as smart cities, where various technologies must work together to deliver seamless services. Second, open standards support long-term sustainability and flexibility [226]. Since they are not tied to a single vendor, organizations can avoid vendor lock-in and more easily adapt to changing technological landscapes. Third, open standards foster a collaborative ecosystem where communities of developers and organizations can contribute to and benefit from shared advancements and improvements [227].

7.3. OpenXR

OpenXR is an open standard for VR and AR that aims to streamline the development of applications across different hardware platforms [228]. Khronos Group, a consortium of industry-leading companies, has developed OpenXR, which provides a unified framework for VR and AR runtime interfaces. This allows developers to write code that can run on various devices without tailoring their applications to each specific platform. OpenXR provides a set of standardized APIs (application programming interfaces) that sit between XR applications and the underlying hardware, effectively decoupling software from hardware [221]. By abstracting the hardware details, OpenXR significantly reduces the complexity and cost of developing cross-platform VR and AR experiences, fostering more significant innovation and broader adoption in the immersive technology space.

The benefits of OpenXR extend beyond simplifying development. For end users, it ensures a more consistent and reliable experience across different VR and AR devices [229].

Since applications built with OpenXR can operate on multiple platforms, users are not limited to specific hardware when accessing their favorite VR and AR content. This interoperability also encourages competition among hardware manufacturers, as it levels the playing field and allows new entrants to support a rich content ecosystem without the barrier of proprietary software constraints. Ultimately, OpenXR plays a crucial role in the growth of the VR and AR industries by promoting a more open, inclusive, and efficient development environment.

By abstracting the hardware details, OpenXR significantly reduces the complexity and cost of developing cross-platform VR and AR experiences, fostering greater innovation and broader adoption in the immersive technology space [230]. This streamlined approach enables developers to spend more time focusing on the content and user experience, rather than worrying about hardware compatibility and performance optimization across different platforms. For example, OpenXR enables developers to use the same application on Meta Quest, which runs on a mobile chipset, as they would on a high-end PC VR system, with OpenXR taking care of the specific hardware adaptations. In addition to simplifying development, OpenXR offers substantial benefits for end users. It ensures a more consistent and reliable experience across different VR and AR devices [231]. This is especially important as the hardware landscape for XR continues to diversify. With the rise of new devices, from standalone headsets like Meta Quest 3 to AR glasses from companies like Magic Leap and Apple [232], users have more options than ever before. Thanks to OpenXR, users are no longer restricted to specific hardware ecosystems when accessing their favorite VR and AR content. For example, a user who purchases an app for their Oculus Quest 3 can seamlessly transition to using the same app on Valve's Index VR or Windows Mixed Reality without losing any functionality or performance, as long as both platforms support OpenXR.

This interoperability also encourages competition among hardware manufacturers [233], as it levels the playing field and allows new entrants to support a rich content ecosystem without the barrier of proprietary software constraints. Companies are incentivized to innovate in hardware design and performance rather than relying on walled gardens to retain users. For instance, smaller or newer VR/AR hardware companies that support OpenXR can leverage the existing library of OpenXR applications, thereby reducing the friction involved in building their ecosystem from scratch. Moreover, OpenXR promotes accessibility and inclusivity in the development and user communities [234]. For smaller development studios or individual creators, the costs of developing multiple versions of a VR/AR application for different platforms can be prohibitive. OpenXR mitigates this by offering a single codebase that can be deployed across devices, enabling these developers to reach more users without the financial burden of platform-specific development.

7.4. WebXR

WebXR is a robust application programming interface (API) that brings VR and AR experiences to the web, enabling developers to create immersive content accessible directly through web browsers [235]. WebXR is a standardized framework for integrating VR and AR capabilities into web applications, run by the World Wide Web Consortium (W3C). This eliminates the need for users to download specialized software or applications, allowing them to experience immersive environments simply by navigating to a webpage. As WebXR takes advantage of the widespread use of web browsers to deliver content to a large audience across a variety of devices, from desktops and laptops to smartphones and specialized VR headsets, accessibility is essential for expanding the reach of VR and AR technologies.

The W3C developed WebXR to extend the capabilities of its predecessor, WebVR, which focused exclusively on virtual reality content [213]. WebXR, by contrast, is designed to support both VR and AR, reflecting the convergence of immersive technologies under the umbrella of XR (extended reality). By building on existing web standards, such as WebGL (for rendering 3D graphics) and WebRTC (for real-time communication), WebXR enables the seamless integration of immersive experiences into the web without requiring users to install additional plugins or extensions. This shift to a more plug-and-play model significantly reduces the friction for users, making VR and AR content as easily accessible as traditional multimedia like videos or interactive maps.

In addition to accessibility, WebXR offers significant development efficiencies. By adopting WebXR, developers can create cross-platform VR and AR content without needing to maintain separate codebases for different devices or platforms [236]. WebXR provides a unified API that works across various browsers and devices, making it easier to create device-agnostic immersive experiences. This allows developers to focus on the content and interaction design rather than worrying about compatibility issues across different hardware. Google Chrome, Firefox Reality, and Microsoft Edge fully support WebXR, enabling immersive experiences across a broad range of devices, from Oculus Quest to Microsoft HoloLens, as well as traditional desktop and mobile environments.

The increasing demand for web-based XR applications across various industries has also fueled the adoption of WebXR [237]. In e-commerce, for instance, WebXR enables AR product visualizations, allowing users to view 3D models of products in their real-world environment before making a purchase. WebXR facilitates the rapid development of such applications, as it allows businesses to embed AR experiences directly into their e-commerce sites without requiring users to install a separate app. Education and training are other sectors benefiting from WebXR [221]. With the rise of remote learning and virtual classrooms, WebXR enables delivering immersive educational content through standard browsers. Schools and universities can deploy virtual lab simulations, 3D models, and interactive lessons directly on their websites, accessible from any device. This is particularly useful in low-resource environments where schools may not have access to high-end VR hardware but can still provide immersive learning experiences using WebXR on desktop or mobile devices.

Healthcare is another industry that stands to benefit significantly from WebXR's accessibility [238]. Medical professionals can use web-based VR simulations to practice procedures or conduct remote AR-assisted diagnostics. For example, WebXR-enabled telemedicine platforms could allow healthcare providers to remotely guide patients through diagnostic steps or deliver real-time AR overlays during consultations. By making such tools available via the web, WebXR expands access to critical healthcare services, particularly in remote or under-served regions where specialized hardware and software may not be readily available. In terms of future development, WebXR is expected to play a central role in the creation of the real-time metaverse. As the metaverse concept gains traction, the ability to access immersive virtual worlds via a web browser will be crucial for ensuring that the metaverse is open, accessible, and not restricted to proprietary platforms [239]. With WebXR, users could seamlessly enter and interact with the metaverse from any device, without needing specialized software or hardware. This aligns with the vision of a decentralized and open metaverse, where content and experiences are freely accessible and not locked behind walled gardens or expensive hardware ecosystems.

8. Challenges and Opportunities

8.1. Latency and Bandwidth

Latency and bandwidth are critical factors in the performance and user experience of the metaverse [240]. Latency refers to the delay between a user's action and the system's response, which is crucial for real-time interactions in virtual environments. High latency can result in lag, making movements and communications appear delayed or out of sync, thus disrupting the immersive experience [241]. Bandwidth, on the other hand, refers to the amount of data that can be transmitted over a network in a given period. Sufficient bandwidth is necessary to support the high data transfer rates required for high-resolution graphics, real-time interactions, and seamless streaming of virtual content [242]. Together, low latency and high bandwidth ensure smooth, responsive, and immersive experiences in the metaverse, allowing users to interact in real-time without interruptions or delays.

Figure 10 illustrates the critical relationship between bandwidth and latency for various applications [243], focusing on a metaverse system.

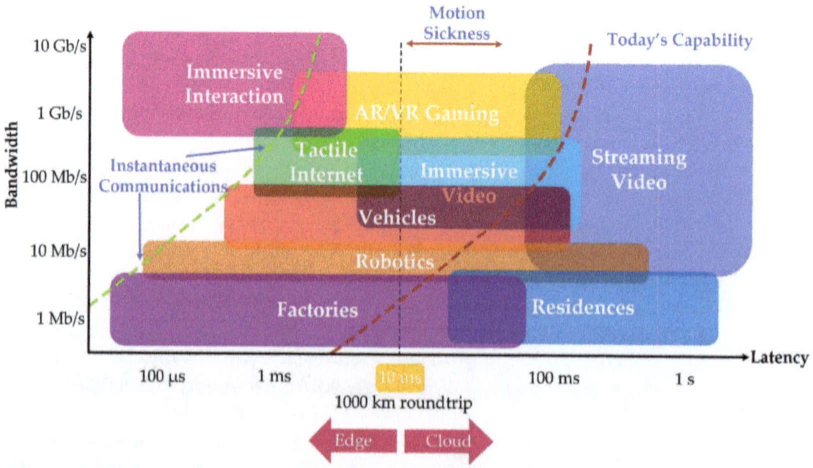

Figure 10. Metaverse applications - bandwidth versus latency.

8.1.1. Network Latency

Network latency refers to the delay between a user's action and the response from the network in a digital environment [244]. In the context of the metaverse, which relies heavily on real-time interactions and seamless connectivity, latency can significantly impact user experience. High latency can cause noticeable delays in data transmission, leading to lagging or choppy movements, delayed responses from virtual entities, and disrupted interactions between users. These delays can break the immersion and fluidity of the metaverse, making it difficult for users to enjoy a smooth and interactive experience.

The effects of network latency on the metaverse are particularly pronounced in activities that require real-time synchronization [245], such as multiplayer gaming, live events, and social interactions. When latency is high, users may experience out-of-sync movements, communication breakdowns, and inconsistencies in the virtual environment. Lack of synchronization can lead to frustration and disengagement, undermining the metaverse's overall effectiveness and appeal. Ensuring low latency is critical for maintaining the real-time responsiveness and immersive quality essential for a compelling metaverse experience. To address these challenges, advancements in network infrastructure, such as 5G technology and edge computing, are being leveraged to reduce latency and enhance the reliability of real-time interactions in the metaverse.

8.1.2. Bandwidth Limitations

Bandwidth limitation is the maximum rate at which data can be transmitted over a network. In the metaverse, bandwidth determines how much data can be exchanged between users and servers at any given time [246]. High-quality virtual experiences in the metaverse require transmitting large volumes of data, including high-resolution graphics, audio, and real-time interactive elements. When bandwidth is limited, these data transmissions can become bottlenecked, leading to slower loading times, reduced graphical fidelity, and overall degraded user experience.

The impact of bandwidth limitations on the metaverse is particularly significant during peak usage times or in areas with poor network infrastructure [247]. Users may experience lag, buffering, and disconnections, disrupting the immersive experience and hindering interactions within the virtual world [248]. Bandwidth constraints can also limit the scalability of the metaverse, as the infrastructure may struggle to support many concurrent users. To mitigate these issues, advancements in network technologies, such as fiber optics and 5G, are being deployed to increase bandwidth capacity [124]. Additionally, data compression and content delivery networks (CDNs) optimize data transmission and reduce the strain on bandwidth, ensuring a smoother and more reliable metaverse experience.

Table 1 highlights the progression of VR technologies by comparing bandwidth requirements, latency, and supported resolutions based on the latest published research. Wi-Fi 6E supports up to 8K resolution with bandwidth of up to 2.4 Gbps and approximately 20 ms latency, leveraging the 6 GHz band for enhanced performance in crowded environments [249]. Wi-Fi 7 further improves, offering bandwidth of up to 46 Gbps and latency of around 10 ms, also supporting up to 8K resolution with multi-link operations and enhanced spectrum efficiency [250]. Wi-Fi 8 is expected to make these features a lot better by using millimeter-wave technology to reach data rates up to 100 Gbps and latency levels below 1 ms. It will also support 8K and higher with features like beamforming and multiple access point (AP)-coordination [251,252]. Moreover, 5G networks provide ultra-fast speeds of 1–10 Gbps and latency between 1–10 ms, capable of smoothly streaming up to 8K VR content, especially in mobile environments [253]. The combination of NGCodec with 5G optimizes bandwidth usage through advanced video compression, reducing latency to under 5 ms while supporting up to 8K resolution [254]. Finally, FPGA-based VR streaming uses re-configurable hardware for fast video encoding and decoding, with latency below 1 ms and support for up to 8K resolution. This makes sure that users can interact and the system runs smoothly in real-time [255,256].

Table 1. Progression of VR, comparing bandwidth and latency across different technologies.

Technology	Bandwidth Requirement	Latency	Resolution
Wi-Fi 6E	Up to 2.4 Gbps	∼20 ms	HD, 2K, 4K 8K with a strong signal strength and minimal interference
Wi-Fi 7	Up to 46 Gbps	∼10 ms	Up to 8K Potential to support 16K video resolution
Wi-Fi 8	Up to 100 Gbps	<1 ms	Up to 8K Potential to support 16K video resolution
5G Network	1-10 Gbps	1–10 ms	Up to 4K 8K depends on network conditions and coverage
NGCodec + 5G	∼1–10 Gbps (optimized)	<5 ms	Up to 8K
FPGA-based VR Streaming	Depends on setup	<1 ms	Up to 8K

8.2. Blockchain in Real-Time Data Handling

Blockchain technology, while pivotal for decentralization and security in the metaverse, faces significant limitations when it comes to supporting real-time, high-frequency data exchanges [257]. Most blockchain systems, particularly those based on proof-of-work (PoW) consensus mechanisms, are designed to prioritize security and decentralization over speed. In platforms like Bitcoin and Ethereum, transaction processing times are measured in minutes, which creates unacceptable latency for real-time metaverse applications that require instant responses, such as virtual commerce, real-time collaboration, and live events. The number of transactions per second (TPS) that these networks can handle is limited—Bitcoin supports approximately 7 TPS, while Ethereum manages around 30 TPS [258]. This is inadequate when compared to traditional payment systems like Visa, which can handle over 24,000 TPS, illustrating blockchain's current scalability issues. Even newer blockchain models, such as Ethereum's transition to proof-of-stake (PoS) have improved efficiency but still face challenges in scaling to the demands of a real-time metaverse.

Additionally, the block size and transaction confirmation time exacerbate these scalability problems. Blockchains like Bitcoin limit the size of each block to 1 MB, and Ethereum's average block size is similarly constrained, meaning only a small number of transactions can be processed in each block [259]. As the transaction volume increases—especially in a bustling metaverse with a large number of users interacting simultaneously—the network becomes congested, leading to increased transaction fees and even longer confirmation times. During periods of high demand, these delays and fees can render blockchain solutions impractical for applications where low latency and high throughput are critical, such as live virtual events or fast-moving virtual economies where digital assets must be exchanged instantaneously.

Moreover, blockchain's inherent structure—where every transaction must be verified and recorded across a distributed ledger—further exacerbates latency issues in the metaverse [260]. The decentralized nature of blockchain, while crucial for security and autonomy, slows down transaction processing times due to the computational overhead required for consensus mechanisms. The synchronization of multiple nodes in a decentralized network to achieve consensus can lead to significant delays, rendering blockchain impractical for high-speed applications like real-time gaming or virtual events, where immediate feedback is necessary. For example, each transaction in Ethereum requires computationally intensive operations, such as cryptographic validation and the execution of smart contracts, which further delays the transaction finalization process [261]. In a real-time metaverse environment, where user interactions must be instantaneous to maintain immersion, these delays significantly degrade the user experience.

The energy consumption of PoW-based blockchain networks also poses a significant challenge [262]. The computational power required to solve cryptographic puzzles and validate transactions in PoW networks like Bitcoin leads to substantial energy usage, which not only limits scalability but also raises concerns about the environmental sustainability of blockchain in a highly interactive metaverse environment. Although alternative consensus mechanisms like PoS reduce energy consumption, they still face trade-offs in decentralization, as staking-based models can lead to a concentration of power among users with significant holdings, undermining the distributed, trustless nature that blockchain aims to provide.

Another limitation is the challenge of interoperability between different blockchain networks within the metaverse [263]. With a variety of blockchains supporting different applications and digital assets, ensuring seamless communication and transaction finalization across multiple blockchains becomes a major technical hurdle. Cross-chain interoperability is still in its infancy, and current solutions like bridges are often slow, susceptible to vulnerabilities, and require additional layers of trust, which defeats the purpose of decentralization. In a real-time metaverse scenario, where assets and data need to flow freely across platforms, these delays in cross-chain transactions introduce friction and reduce the fluidity of the virtual economy.

These limitations suggest that blockchain, in its current form, is not equipped to handle the high-frequency, low-latency data exchanges essential for the real-time metaverse. For blockchain to become a viable infrastructure for the metaverse, it must evolve to address these performance bottlenecks [264]. Emerging solutions, such as Layer 2 protocols—which enable off-chain processing to reduce congestion on the main chain—and sharding, which divides the blockchain into smaller, parallel chains, offer potential avenues for improvement. However, these solutions are still in the development stage and have not undergone the kind of testing that a fully developed real-time metaverse would require. Until blockchain technology can meet the demands of speed, scalability, and efficiency required by these virtual environments, alternative technologies like centralized databases or hybrid blockchain systems may need to fill the gap in supporting real-time, interactive experiences.

8.3. Interoperability and Standards

Interoperability and standards pose significant challenges in the development and functionality of the metaverse [265]. Interoperability refers to the ability of metaverse systems, platforms, and applications to work seamlessly together. The diversity of virtual environments, avatars, digital assets, and interaction mechanisms created by various developers and organizations makes achieving interoperability complex. Users might face difficulties transferring digital identities, assets, and experiences without common standards across virtual worlds. Digital fragmentation can hinder the metaverse's vision of a unified, cohesive digital universe, limiting user engagement and stifling innovation.

8.3.1. Universal Standards

Establishing universal standards for the metaverse is another formidable challenge. Standards are essential to ensure consistency, security, and compatibility across various platforms and technologies that constitute the metaverse [96]. However, reaching a consensus on these standards involves coordination among numerous stakeholders, including tech companies, developers, regulatory bodies, and users. Each group may have different priorities and interests, making it difficult to agree on a unified set of rules and protocols. Additionally, rapid technological advancements and the evolving nature of the metaverse further complicate standardization efforts. The metaverse risks becoming a collection of isolated ecosystems without robust interoperability and standardized frameworks rather than a seamless, interconnected digital reality. This major challenge is divided into two parts: fragmentation and data compatibility.

8.3.2. Fragmentation

Fragmentation refers to multiple, incompatible systems and protocols within the metaverse, leading to isolated digital environments that cannot seamlessly interact with each other [56]. Product fragmentation arises when different developers and platforms adopt unique standards for creating and managing virtual worlds, avatars, digital assets, and user interactions. Without a unified approach, users face significant challenges when navigating between different parts of the metaverse, as their digital identities, assets, and experiences may not be transferable across these isolated ecosystems.

The fragmentation issue severely impacts the user experience and the overall potential of the metaverse [266]. For instance, a user might create an avatar and acquire virtual assets in one platform, only to find that these cannot be used or recognized in another platform. The lack of interoperability discourages users from investing time and resources into the metaverse, as they may be concerned about the portability and longevity of their digital assets. Moreover, developers are also hindered by fragmentation, as they must choose which standards to support or face the burden of trying to make their platforms compatible with multiple systems. The lack of universal standards stifles innovation and growth, preventing the metaverse from becoming the interconnected and expansive digital universe it aspires to be. Addressing fragmentation requires concerted efforts to establish and adopt common standards, ensuring that all parts of the metaverse can work together harmoniously.

8.3.3. Unified Standards

Unified standards are an asset of agreed-upon protocols, formats, and guidelines that ensure compatibility and interoperability across different systems and platforms within the metaverse [96]. These standards aim to eliminate the barriers created by fragmentation, allowing for seamless integration and interaction between diverse virtual environments, digital assets, avatars, and user experiences [267]. By adopting unified standards, developers and platforms can ensure that users can move fluidly between different parts of the metaverse without losing functionality or having to recreate their digital presence.

Implementing unified standards is crucial for the metaverse to achieve its vision of a cohesive and interconnected digital universe [90,268]. These standards would cover various aspects such as data formats, communication protocols, security measures, and user interface guidelines. For example, a standardized avatar format would allow users to maintain the same digital identity across different virtual worlds. In contrast, standardized asset formats would ensure that digital goods purchased or created in one environment can be used in another. Unified standards thus foster a more inclusive and expansive metaverse, enhancing user experience, encouraging innovation, and promoting collaboration among developers and platforms.

8.3.4. Cross-Platform Compatibility

Cross-platform compatibility is the ability of different virtual environments, systems, and applications within the metaverse to work together seamlessly, regardless of the underlying platform or technology [269]. This means that users can access and interact with various parts of the metaverse using different devices (e.g., PCs, VR headsets, mobile phones, etc.) and still have a consistent and unified experience. Cross-platform compatibility ensures that digital assets, avatars, user data, and interactions can be transferred and recognized across different systems without losing functionality or user experience.

Addressing cross-platform compatibility is essential for overcoming fragmentation in the metaverse. It allows users to navigate between different virtual worlds and applications without encountering barriers or needing to adapt to different interfaces or standards [219]. For example, a user should be able to purchase a digital item in one virtual world and use it in another, regardless of which platform each world is built on. Cross-platform compatibility involves adopting common standards and protocols that enable different systems to communicate and share data effectively. Cross-platform integration enhances the user experience by providing continuity and coherence across the metaverse, fostering greater engagement and participation from a broader audience.

8.3.5. Data Compatibility

Data compatibility ensures that different systems, platforms, and applications can effectively share, interpret, and use data across various environments [270]. These issues arise when there is no common format or protocol for data representation, storage, and exchange, leading to difficulties in integrating and synchronizing data across different virtual worlds and applications.

In the metaverse, data compatibility is essential for a seamless user experience [18]. Users create and interact with various digital assets, including avatars, virtual goods, and user-generated content. When these assets are created in one environment but incompatible with others, users face significant barriers in transferring or utilizing their data across different platforms [10]. For instance, an avatar designed in one virtual world might not be recognized, or digital assets purchased in one marketplace might not be usable in another due to differences in data formats and structures.

The lack of data compatibility hampers the metaverse's potential as a unified and interconnected digital universe [271]. To address these issues, there needs to be a concerted effort to develop and adopt common data standards and protocols. These standards would define how data should be formatted, stored, and exchanged, ensuring that it can be seamlessly interpreted and used across different systems. By achieving data compatibility, the metaverse can provide a more cohesive and integrated experience, allowing users to move fluidly between different environments and fully leverage their digital assets across the entire ecosystem. Common formats and data integration are the most important factors of data compatibility [267].

Common formats in data compatibility within the metaverse are essential for ensuring seamless interoperability across various platforms, applications, and virtual environments [146,223]. These standardized formats facilitate the consistent representation, storage, and exchange of data, allowing different systems to interpret and use the same data efficiently. Common formats are critical in avatars, digital identities, digital assets, virtual goods, user data, profiles, virtual currency, transactions, communication, interaction data, environments, and world data.

Common formats like FBX (Filmbox), OBJ (wavefront object), and glTF (GL transmission format) are widely used for 3D models and animations for avatars and digital identities. These formats ensure that avatars created in one virtual world can be rendered and animated correctly in another [272]. Metadata formats such as JSON (JavaScript object notation) and XML (extensible markup language) are essential for including information about avatars, such as appearance, accessories, and customizations, ensuring consistent interpretation across platforms. Standardizing these formats helps maintain the visual and functional integrity of avatars and digital identities as they move across different virtual environments.

For digital assets and virtual goods, standardized formats for textures and materials—such as PNGs (portable network graphics), JPEG (joint photographic experts group) for textures, and PBR (physically based rendering) materials—ensure that the visual quality of digital assets is maintained across various platforms [273]. Asset bundles packaged in standard formats like Unity Asset Bundles or Unreal Engine's asset format facilitate the transfer and usage of digital assets across different virtual worlds. Additionally, blockchain standards like ERC-20 or ERC-721 for tokens ensure that virtual currencies and digital collectibles can be managed and exchanged securely and interoperably [274].

8.3.6. Data Integration

Data integration is equally important for user data and profiles, virtual currency and transactions, and communication and interaction data [275]. Standard formats for user profiles, preferences, and settings (JSON or XML) enable consistent user experiences across different platforms. Adopting blockchain protocols like ERC-20 or ERC-721 for virtual currencies and transactions ensures secure and interoperable management of digital assets [274]. In terms of communication and interaction data, standardized protocols like XMPP (extensible messaging and presence protocol) or WebRTC (web real-time communication) ensure that text, voice, and video communication services are interoperable across different platforms [276]. Using standard formats for describing virtual environments, such as XML-based X3D or JSON-based Scene Graphs, also ensures that different platforms can render and interact with these environments consistently [277].

By adopting these common formats and data integration standards, the metaverse can achieve a higher level of interoperability, enabling a more cohesive and integrated user experience. This approach not only facilitates the seamless transfer of digital assets and data across different virtual environments but also enhances user engagement and satisfaction. As the metaverse continues to evolve, the importance of standardized data formats and integration protocols will only grow, ensuring that users enjoy a unified and immersive digital universe.

8.4. Scalability

The scalability of immersive technologies, such as VR and AR, is a major concern for the metaverse. Immersive platforms are highly resource-intensive, requiring vast amounts of computational power, bandwidth, and storage to render detailed, interactive 3D environments in real-time [278,279]. As the user base grows, the system's ability to support an increasing number of concurrent users without compromising performance becomes a significant challenge. For instance, social VR platforms like VRChat or Facebook's Horizon Worlds often experience server overloads, resulting in degraded user experience due to lag, buffering, or crashes when large numbers of users are interacting simultaneously. The fact that immersive experiences necessitate the transmission of high-resolution 3D content, which necessitates significant bandwidth to maintain seamless user interaction, makes this problem worse. For example, high-resolution 3D models, complex textures, and lighting effects need to be transmitted and rendered in real-time, which places a heavy burden on both the network infrastructure and the user's hardware.

The need for real-time synchronization of users' actions and environmental changes within the metaverse further complicates the scalability issue [280]. In a fully immersive experience, every user's movement, interaction, and even facial expressions must be reflected in real-time for all other participants. This requires not only high bandwidth but also extremely low latency to avoid noticeable lag, which can severely disrupt immersion. The concept of "presence"—a core aspect of VR that makes users feel as though they are truly inside a virtual environment—depends on these real-time interactions being smooth and instantaneous. Any delay in transmitting data between users or in rendering updates to the virtual world can break the illusion, reducing the effectiveness of the immersive experience.

While current network infrastructures have seen improvements with the advent of 5G, they still face limitations in supporting the data-heavy demands of immersive systems [85]. 5G promises ultra-low latency (around 1 millisecond) and higher data rates, but even this technology may struggle under the demands of a fully populated metaverse, where thousands or even millions of users interact simultaneously. For example, the bandwidth required for real-time rendering of high-definition 3D environments and live interactions can exceed what current 5G networks can handle at scale. In large virtual events, such as live concerts or digital sports games, the number of concurrent users may push network capacity beyond its limits, resulting in a laggy or interrupted experience for many participants.

In addition to network constraints, processing power remains a critical bottleneck [281]. Rendering real-time 3D environments, especially at the quality expected in high-end VR applications, requires significant computational resources. Current GPUs (graphics processing units) are already strained in handling the complex tasks required for real-time ray tracing, realistic physics simulations, and AI-driven interactions. In a fully immersive metaverse, these requirements scale exponentially as the number of users increases. Real-time data fusion, which integrates inputs from multiple sensors (e.g., motion tracking, facial recognition, and environmental mapping), requires extensive computational power. This is especially true for systems aiming to provide haptic feedback or real-world physics, where even minor delays can degrade the overall experience.

Additionally, the diversity of devices and platforms presents another scalability challenge. Users will access the metaverse using a wide range of devices, from high-end VR headsets to mobile phones and desktop computers [267]. Each device has different processing capacities, display resolutions, and input methods, which makes it difficult to standardize the user experience. For example, a user on a low-end mobile device may experience lower-quality graphics and longer load times compared to a user on a high-end VR system, leading to disparities in the immersive experience. This inconsistency in performance can limit the scalability of the metaverse, as developers must balance the need for a high-quality experience with the technical limitations of diverse hardware. Furthermore, ensuring real-time synchronization across these varied devices without compromising the immersive experience for any user group requires sophisticated optimization techniques that are still in development.

Another significant factor is cloud infrastructure. While cloud computing can alleviate some of the processing burdens by offloading tasks to remote servers, the latency introduced by cloud-based rendering or computation can still be problematic for real-time applications [282]. Even with edge computing—where processing is done closer to the user—scalability issues remain. Edge servers must be distributed widely enough to handle the demand from local users, but deploying and maintaining this infrastructure at scale is costly and complex. Moreover, data synchronization between multiple edge servers and the central cloud can lead to consistency issues, where some users experience delays in receiving updates to the virtual world. This could be particularly problematic in environments that require precise timing, such as competitive gaming or virtual commerce platforms where milliseconds matter.

8.5. User Experience

User experience (UX) is a critical issue in the metaverse, as it directly impacts user engagement and satisfaction [283]. A seamless and intuitive UX is essential for making virtual environments enjoyable and accessible to a wide audience. However, creating an optimal UX in the metaverse is challenging due to the complexity of immersive technologies, the diversity of user needs, and the potential for adverse effects such as motion sickness [20]. Ensuring that users can navigate, interact, and communicate effectively within the metaverse requires careful design and continuous improvement based on user feedback.

8.5.1. Designing Intuitive Interfaces for Non-Expert Users

One of the greatest challenges in the real-time metaverse is ensuring that the environment is accessible to non-expert users [284]. Immersive technologies such as VR, AR, and MR (mixed reality) introduce a steep learning curve for many users who are not familiar with 3D spaces, controllers, or XR devices. For the mass adoption of the metaverse, intuitive and user-friendly interfaces are essential, allowing people to effortlessly interact with the virtual environment, regardless of their technical expertise. Simplifying the onboarding process is a critical first step. For example, using familiar UI paradigms such as gesture-based controls (e.g., swiping, pinching, or pointing) or natural language voice commands can help non-expert users engage with immersive environments more comfortably [285]. Furthermore, integrating in-world tutorials and AI-driven assistance (e.g., voice-guided navigation) can ensure that users are not overwhelmed by the complexity of virtual interactions.

Another important consideration is the use of contextual interfaces that adapt based on the user's needs and experience level. For instance, advanced users may prefer more customizable options and complex interactions, while beginners might benefit from simplified menus and guidance systems [286]. Developers should also focus on minimizing the cognitive load on users by ensuring clear visual hierarchies, intuitive navigation paths, and consistent iconography that aligns with user expectations. As XR platforms continue to evolve, standardization of these interfaces across devices and applications will be key to reducing fragmentation and ensuring a cohesive user experience across the metaverse.

8.5.2. Addressing Physical and Mental Health Risks

The immersive technologies of the metaverse, specifically VR and AR, present significant physical and mental health challenges. *Motion sickness*, also known as cybersickness in virtual environments, is a significant UX issue in the metaverse [287]. It occurs when there is a disconnect between the visual input from the virtual environment and the user's physical sensations, leading to symptoms such as nausea, dizziness, and disorientation [67]. Furthermore, users face risks of injury or accidents due to attentional distractions, especially with AR applications that blend digital content with real-world environments [288]. Psychological risks include potential aftereffects like intensified emotional responses or confusion about reality, particularly for vulnerable users like children or those with certain mental health conditions [289]. The phenomenon of "super-realism" further complicates matters, as experiences in highly realistic virtual environments may blur the lines between virtual and real experiences, potentially causing users to develop emotional or cognitive disturbances when transitioning back to the physical world [290].

To address cybersickness, developers can implement several strategies. Optimizing frame rates (ideally above 90 frames per second) is essential to ensure smooth rendering and reduce lag and visual inconsistencies, which are major contributors to motion sickness [291]. Likewise, minimizing latency in user inputs and head tracking (targeting less than 20 milliseconds) can help maintain a responsive experience, ensuring that virtual movements feel synchronized with physical actions. Designing predictable and smooth motion paths within virtual environments also helps reduce the likelihood of motion sickness. For example, rather than sudden shifts in perspective, developers can implement gradual transitions that simulate natural acceleration and deceleration, allowing users' senses to adjust to the changes in motion. Providing users with customizable comfort settings—such as adjustable field of view (FOV), camera smoothing, and snap-turning (e.g., a technique that reduces rotational motion)—can help users tailor their experience to their comfort levels, significantly reducing the risk of cybersickness [292]. Furthermore, teleportation (e.g., jumping from one location to another without continuous movement) has emerged as a popular locomotion method in VR that mitigates motion sickness by eliminating the disconnect between visual and physical motion. Offering multiple locomotion modes—such as teleportation, smooth walking, or vehicle simulation—allows users to choose their preferred method of movement based on their susceptibility to cybersickness [293].

8.5.3. Accessibility and Inclusivity in the Metaverse

Accessibility in the metaverse is another crucial aspect of UX that ensures inclusivity for users with diverse abilities and needs. Ensuring that the metaverse is accessible to all users, including those with disabilities, is a crucial aspect of UX design [294]. The immersive nature of the metaverse provides new opportunities for inclusivity, but it also introduces challenges in accommodating users with physical, sensory, and cognitive impairments. Accessibility should not be an afterthought but a core element of design, ensuring that everyone can participate fully in the metaverse. For users with mobility impairments, developers must provide multiple input methods, such as adaptive controllers, gesture-based inputs, and voice commands [295]. These options ensure that users who may not be able to use traditional controllers or keyboards can still navigate and interact with virtual environments.

Moreover, environments should be designed to support different movement speeds, seated play, and adjustable reach heights to accommodate users with limited physical mobility. For individuals with visual impairments, text-to-speech (TTS) features can enable the conversion of on-screen text into spoken words, while haptic feedback can provide tactile cues to simulate touch and interaction [296]. Audio descriptions of visual elements, such as describing the environment, actions, or characters, can further enhance the experience for users with limited sight. On the other hand, for users with hearing impairments, integrating speech-to-text (STT) features allows spoken dialogue to be transcribed in real-time, ensuring that users can engage with conversations and activities in the metaverse [297]. Additionally, ensuring compatibility with hearing aids or cochlear implants could be an important consideration for creating more inclusive soundscapes. Cognitive accessibility is another critical area. For users with cognitive disabilities, such as dyslexia, autism spectrum disorders, or attention deficits, virtual environments must be designed to minimize confusion and overload [298]. Features such as clear navigation cues, adjustable text sizes, simple language options, and color contrast settings can make the metaverse easier to understand and navigate for these users. Additionally, customizable UI layouts that allow users to control the complexity and frequency of information displayed could make virtual environments more accommodating to a wider range of cognitive abilities.

8.5.4. Social Interaction and Complexity in the Metaverse

Social interaction is one of the most promising but also challenging aspects of the metaverse [299]. It allows users to connect with others, form relationships, collaborate, and engage in shared experiences across vast virtual spaces. However, the complexity of social interactions in immersive environments brings its own set of UX challenges. In physical reality, social cues such as eye contact, body language, and tone of voice are vital for smooth communication, but replicating these nuances in a virtual environment remains difficult. Developers need to focus on creating natural communication systems that replicate these subtle social cues as much as possible [300]. For instance, spatial audio—where sound emanates from the direction of a virtual avatar—helps users better engage with conversations, creating a sense of presence and immersion. Facial tracking and emotion mapping (enabled by newer VR/AR headsets) can also enhance avatar realism, making social interactions more intuitive.

However, there are potential downsides to social interaction in the metaverse, such as the risk of harassment or exclusion [301]. Developers need to implement safety features such as personal space bubbles, mute/block functions, and reporting mechanisms to ensure that users feel safe while interacting with others in the virtual world. Moreover, AI-driven content moderation systems can help identify and mitigate toxic behaviors in real-time, ensuring a positive social experience for all users. Also, creating inclusive social spaces that accommodate users of diverse backgrounds, abilities, and cultures is key to the success of the metaverse. By facilitating customizable avatars that represent various ethnicities, body types, and disabilities, developers can promote diversity and ensure that all users feel represented and included in virtual environments.

8.6. Security and Privacy

Security and privacy issues in the metaverse are significant concerns due to the vast amount of personal and sensitive data generated and exchanged within virtual environments [302]. User interactions, transactions, and personal information, including biometric data from VR/AR devices, are vulnerable to breaches and misuse. The immersive nature of the metaverse adds complexity to security challenges, as it involves real-time data exchange and extensive user tracking to deliver personalized experiences. Ensuring the security and privacy of the data is critical to maintaining user trust and safeguarding against potential threats such as identity theft, data mining, or targeted cyberattacks. The rapid growth of metaverse technologies requires equally dynamic solutions to ensure the long-term security of these ecosystems.

Addressing *data security* in the metaverse requires robust encryption methods to protect data in transit and at rest. By utilizing cutting-edge cryptographic techniques, one can increase security and prevent malicious actors from intercepting or changing data exchanged between users and servers [303]. With the real-time nature of data exchanges in the metaverse, traditional encryption schemes may not always be efficient, especially when large volumes of 3D-rendered content, live interactions, and financial transactions occur simultaneously. Therefore, end-to-end encryption (E2EE) becomes vital to ensure that only the intended recipients can access the data, securing it against eavesdropping and tampering [304]. Employing multi-factor authentication (MFA) and secure login protocols can prevent unauthorized access to user accounts [305]. Regular security audits and vulnerability assessments are essential to identify and address potential weaknesses in the system. Developers must also establish protocols for incident response to quickly mitigate the effects of any security breaches.

Advanced cryptographic techniques, such as homomorphic encryption, are increasingly explored to enhance data security without compromising the immersive experience [81]. Homomorphic encryption allows computations to be performed on encrypted data without needing to decrypt it first, meaning that sensitive user data can be processed without exposing it to external parties, including service providers. This can be particularly useful in the metaverse for applications that involve personal data analytics or real-time decision-making. Another promising direction is the use of blockchain technology, which can enhance security through decentralization. Blockchain allows for the secure, tamper-resistant storage of transaction data, digital assets, and even user identity credentials [60]. For example, virtual assets like NFTs (non-fungible tokens) can be securely traded within the metaverse using blockchain, ensuring transparent and secure ownership. In addition to encryption and blockchain, employing multi-factor authentication (MFA) and secure login protocols helps prevent unauthorized access to user accounts. Users in the metaverse may handle sensitive data, such as virtual banking details or personal conversations [306]. By requiring multiple authentication methods—such as a password in combination with biometric verification (e.g., fingerprint, facial recognition)—MFA can significantly reduce the risks of unauthorized access. Moreover, regular security audits and vulnerability assessments should be integrated into the development lifecycle to identify and resolve weaknesses in the system.

Privacy concerns in the metaverse are equally critical, particularly as platforms may collect a wide range of personal data, from location data to behavioral patterns and biometric information (e.g., eye movement, and heart rate) [307]. The amount of data that users generate while interacting in immersive environments makes them more vulnerable to surveillance, profiling, and unauthorized data sharing. One of the central challenges in preserving user privacy is maintaining a balance between collecting data necessary for delivering personalized experiences and protecting user anonymity. To address privacy concerns, developers must implement privacy-preserving technologies such as zero-knowledge proofs (ZKPs) [308]. ZKPs allow one party to prove to another that they know a value (e.g., authentication credentials or ownership of an asset) without revealing the actual value itself. This could be crucial for ensuring that users' sensitive data, such as personal credentials or virtual asset ownership, can be verified without exposing unnecessary information. For instance, in a virtual marketplace, a ZKP-based system could allow users to verify ownership of an NFT without revealing the details of the transaction history, thereby enhancing user privacy while ensuring security.

Another approach is differential privacy, a technique that adds statistical noise to data, ensuring that individual users' actions cannot be easily distinguished when data are aggregated [309]. This technique is useful in the metaverse for collecting aggregate data (general user behavior trends) while preserving the anonymity of individual users. Homomorphic encryption, as mentioned earlier, also offers a powerful privacy solution by allowing computations on encrypted data, ensuring that service providers never have access to users' unencrypted personal data. The implementation of blockchain-based identity management systems offers another layer of privacy protection. With self-sovereign identity (SSI) models, users maintain control over their digital identities, deciding which aspects of their data to share and with whom [265]. Instead of centralized platforms owning and controlling user identity information, SSI gives users the autonomy to manage their credentials and personal data using decentralized identity solutions on blockchain networks. However, these decentralized models also carry risks. For example, if a user loses access to their private keys, they may be permanently locked out of their identity and assets, highlighting the need for secure key management solutions within the metaverse.

To further empower users, developers should adopt privacy-by-design principles, embedding privacy considerations directly into the development process from the outset [310]. This includes implementing transparent data handling practices and giving users granular control over their data, including what information is shared, how long it is stored, and with whom it is shared. For example, VR and AR applications could allow users to control which biometric data (e.g., eye movement, hand tracking) is processed and for what purposes [311]. In the regulatory space, compliance with global data protection laws such as the European Union's General Data Protection Regulation (GDPR) and the California Consumer Privacy Act (CCPA) is essential for building trust [310]. These regulations mandate that users are informed about how their data are collected, used, and stored, and give them the ability to opt out of certain types of data collection or request the deletion of their data. Adhering to such standards is particularly important in the metaverse, where sensitive data like real-time geolocation and biometric information could be exposed.

Figure 11 depicts various security challenges associated with the metaverse, focusing on the interactions between the physical and virtual worlds and the cloud infrastructure. In the physical world, users use VR headsets, smartphones, and laptops to access the virtual world. Data transmission between these devices and the cloud, which supports the metaverse, is vulnerable to packet loss and cyber-attacks. Hackers can exploit these vulnerabilities through methods like "Man in the Middle" attacks, where they intercept and potentially alter data being transmitted, and denial-of-service (DoS) attacks, which can disrupt services by overwhelming the network. These security threats can lead to compromised user experiences and data integrity in the virtual world, emphasizing the need for robust security measures to protect metaverse interactions.

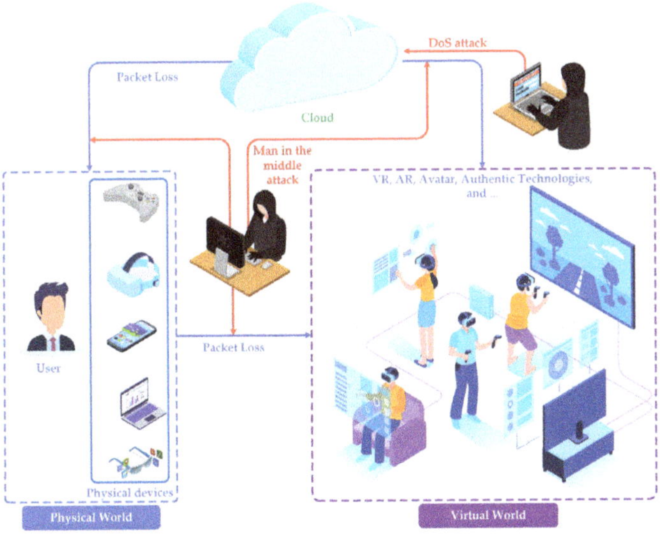

Figure 11. Security challenges associated with the metaverse.

9. Conclusions

The real-time metaverse represents a transformative evolution in how virtual environments are designed and experienced. Unlike traditional metaverse spaces, which often rely on static, pre-rendered environments, the real-time metaverse integrates real-world data to create dynamic and responsive digital landscapes. This seamless fusion of the physical and digital worlds opens up unprecedented possibilities across industries like education, healthcare, entertainment, and business. By leveraging technologies such as artificial intelligence (AI), virtual and augmented reality (VR/AR), blockchain, and advanced networking infrastructures like 5G and edge computing, the real-time metaverse can deliver immersive, interactive experiences that evolve in sync with real-world events.

Efforts to enhance the metaverse's infrastructure are crucial for its success. Incorporating edge computing is one such effort, as it brings data processing closer to the user, thereby reducing latency and improving response times. Additionally, developing robust interoperability standards is essential to ensure seamless communication and integration across different platforms and devices. These advancements will enable a more cohesive and efficient digital ecosystem, allowing users to transition smoothly between virtual environments and experiences.

However, the development of a fully functional real-time metaverse is not without its challenges. Latency and bandwidth issues remain critical hurdles, especially when attempting to deliver high-quality, real-time experiences to a large number of users. The scalability of this system depends heavily on the continuous improvement of network infrastructure, including the potential future integration of 6G technology. Additionally, there are significant security and privacy concerns, particularly regarding the handling of personal data and digital assets within these virtual spaces. Without robust privacy measures and data protection protocols, the real-time metaverse could face issues of trust and security, hindering its broader adoption.

As the metaverse evolves, industry, academia, and government collaborative efforts will be necessary to realize its transformative capabilities fully. Such collaboration will drive innovation and address existing barriers, ensuring the metaverse becomes a vibrant, user-friendly, and secure digital ecosystem. By focusing on these social, technical, and governance issues, the real-time metaverse can revolutionize how we interact, work, and learn, creating new opportunities for innovation and connectivity in the digital age.

Looking forward, future research in this area should focus on several key domains. First, the development of interoperability standards is crucial to ensure that different platforms, devices, and virtual environments can communicate and interact seamlessly. Research into 6G technology, AI-driven resource management, and edge computing is also essential for overcoming latency issues and enabling scalable, real-time applications. Another important area of study is the integration of multisensory feedback, such as haptics, smell, and taste, to further enhance the immersive quality of virtual experiences. Lastly, addressing the ethical and social challenges of the real-time metaverse, such as digital harassment and equitable representation, will be crucial for ensuring the technology's responsible and inclusive growth.

Author Contributions: Conceptualization, M.H., Q.Q. and Y.C.; methodology, M.H., Q.Q., Y.C. and H.K.; software, M.H. and Q.Q.; validation, M.H., Q.Q. and Y.C.; formal analysis, M.H. and Q.Q.; investigation, Y.C. and H.K.; resources, Y.C. and E.A.-C.; data curation, M.H. and Q.Q.; writing—original draft preparation, M.H., Q.Q. and Y.C.; writing—review and editing, Y.C., H.K., E.B. and E.A.-C.; visualization, M.H. and Q.Q.; supervision, Y.C. and E.B.; project administration, E.A.-C.; funding acquisition, Y.C. and E.A.-C. All authors have read and agreed to the published version of the manuscript.

Funding: This research was partially funded by the Air Force Research Laboratory under SFFP FA9550-20-F-0005.

Data Availability Statement: Data are available following the rules of the AFRL and Binghamton University.

Conflicts of Interest: The authors declare no conflicts of interest.

Abbreviations

The following abbreviations are used in this manuscript:

3D	three-dimensional
5G	fifth-generation
6G	sixth-generation
AI	artificial intelligence
AP	access point
API	application programming interface
AR	augmented reality
AWS	Amazon Web Services
CCPA	California Consumer Privacy Act
CDN	content delivery network
DML	deep and meaningful learning
CUDA	compute unified device architecture
DT	digital twin
DTs	digital twins
DoS	denial-of-service
DLSS	deep learning super sampling
E2EE	end-to-end encryption
FBX	Filmbox
FOV	field of view
GCP	Google Cloud Services
GDPR	General Data Protection Regulation
glTF	GL transmission format
GPU	graphics processing unit
GR	graphical rendering
HPC	high-performance computing
HL7	Health Level Seven

HTML	hypertext markup language
HTTP	hypertext transfer protocol
IaaS	infrastructure as a service
IoT	Internet of Things
JPEG	Joint Photographic Experts Group
JSON	JavaScript Object Notation
LLM	large language model
MFA	multi-factor authentication
MIMO	multiple-input multiple-output
ML	machine learning
mMTC	massive machine-type communications
MPI	message passing interface
MR	mixed reality
NFTs	non-fungible tokens
NLP	natural language processing
NPC	non-player character
OBJ	wavefront object
OpenMP	open multi-processing
PaaS	platform-as-a-service
PBR	physically based rendering
PNG	portable network graphic
PoS	proof-of-stake
PoW	proof-of-work
RBG	red, green, and blue
SaaS	software as a service
SSI	self-sovereign identity
STT	speech-to-text
SVREs	social virtual reality environments
TCP/IP	transmission control protocol/internet protocol
TPS	transactions per second
TTS	text-to-speech
URLLC	ultra-reliable low-latency communications
UX	user experience
VR	virtual reality
W3C	World Wide Web Consortium
WebGL	Web Graphics Library
WebRTC	web real-time communication
WebXR	web extended reality
XML	extensible markup language
XMPP	extensible messaging and presence protocol
ZKPs	zero-knowledge proofs

References

1. Wang, Y.; Su, Z.; Zhang, N.; Xing, R.; Liu, D.; Luan, T.H.; Shen, X. A survey on metaverse: Fundamentals, security, and privacy. *IEEE Commun. Surv. Tutor.* **2022**, *25*, 319–352. [CrossRef]
2. Li, K.; Cui, Y.; Li, W.; Lv, T.; Yuan, X.; Li, S.; Ni, W.; Simsek, M.; Dressler, F. When internet of things meets metaverse: Convergence of physical and cyber worlds. *IEEE Internet Things J.* **2022**, *10*, 4148–4173. [CrossRef]
3. Setiawan, K.D.; Anthony, A.; Meyliana; Surjandy. The essential factor of metaverse for business based on 7 layers of metaverse—Systematic literature review. In Proceedings of the 2022 International Conference on Information Management and Technology (ICIMTech), Semarang, Indonesia, 11–12 August 2022; pp. 687–692.
4. Tyagi, A.K. Decentralized everything: Practical use of blockchain technology in future applications. In *Distributed Computing to Blockchain*; Elsevier: Amsterdam, The Netherlands, 2023; pp. 19–38.
5. Truong, V.T.; Le, L.; Niyato, D. Blockchain meets metaverse and digital asset management: A comprehensive survey. *IEEE Access* **2023**, *11*, 26258–26288. [CrossRef]
6. Zhu, H.Y.; Hieu, N.Q.; Hoang, D.T.; Nguyen, D.N.; Lin, C.T. A human-centric metaverse enabled by brain-computer interface: A survey. *IEEE Commun. Surv. Tutor.* **2024**, *26*, 2120–2145. [CrossRef]
7. Park, S.M.; Kim, Y.G. A metaverse: Taxonomy, components, applications, and open challenges. *IEEE Access* **2022**, *10*, 4209–4251. [CrossRef]

8. Liu, S.; Xie, J.; Wang, X. QoE enhancement of the industrial metaverse based on Mixed Reality application optimization. *Displays* **2023**, *79*, 102463. [CrossRef]
9. Yang, Y.; Ma, M.; Van Doan, T.; Hulin, T.; Fitzek, H.F.; Nguyen, G.T. Touch the Metaverse: Demonstration of Haptic Feedback in Network-Assisted Augmented Reality. In Proceedings of the 2024 IEEE International Conference on Pervasive Computing and Communications Workshops and other Affiliated Events (PerCom Workshops), Biarritz, France, 11–15 March 2024; pp. 379–381.
10. Mystakidis, S. Metaverse. *Encyclopedia* **2022**, *2*, 486–497. [CrossRef]
11. Singla, B.; Shalender, K.; Singh, N. *Creator's Economy in Metaverse Platforms: Empowering Stakeholders Through Omnichannel Approach: Empowering Stakeholders Through Omnichannel Approach*; IGI Global: Hershey, PA, USA, 2024.
12. Park, S.; Kim, S. Identifying world types to deliver gameful experiences for sustainable learning in the metaverse. *Sustainability* **2022**, *14*, 1361. [CrossRef]
13. Mancuso, I.; Petruzzelli, A.M.; Panniello, U. Digital business model innovation in metaverse: How to approach virtual economy opportunities. *Inf. Process. Manag.* **2023**, *60*, 103457. [CrossRef]
14. Xu, M.; Ng, W.C.; Lim, W.Y.B.; Kang, J.; Xiong, Z.; Niyato, D.; Yang, Q.; Shen, X.; Miao, C. A full dive into realizing the edge-enabled metaverse: Visions, enabling technologies, and challenges. *IEEE Commun. Surv. Tutor.* **2022**, *25*, 656–700. [CrossRef]
15. Dwivedi, Y.K.; Hughes, L.; Baabdullah, A.M.; Ribeiro-Navarrete, S.; Giannakis, M.; Al-Debei, M.M.; Dennehy, D.; Metri, B.; Buhalis, D.; Cheung, C.M.; et al. Metaverse beyond the hype: Multidisciplinary perspectives on emerging challenges, opportunities, and agenda for research, practice and policy. *Int. J. Inf. Manag.* **2022**, *66*, 102542. [CrossRef]
16. Qu, Q.; Hatami, M.; Xu, R.; Nagothu, D.; Chen, Y.; Li, X.; Blasch, E.; Ardiles-Cruz, E.; Chen, G. The microverse: A task-oriented edge-scale metaverse. *Future Internet* **2024**, *16*, 60. [CrossRef]
17. Gadekallu, T.R.; Huynh-The, T.; Wang, W.; Yenduri, G.; Ranaweera, P.; Pham, Q.V.; da Costa, D.B.; Liyanage, M. Blockchain for the metaverse: A review. *arXiv* **2022**, arXiv:2203.09738.
18. Ersoy, M.; Gürfidan, R. Blockchain-based asset storage and service mechanism to metaverse universe: Metarepo. *Trans. Emerg. Telecommun. Technol.* **2023**, *34*, e4658. [CrossRef]
19. Huang, H.; Wu, J.; Zheng, Z. *From Blockchain to Web3 and Metaverse*; Springer: Berlin/Heidelberg, Germany, 2023.
20. Dincelli, E.; Yayla, A. Immersive virtual reality in the age of the Metaverse: A hybrid-narrative review based on the technology affordance perspective. *J. Strateg. Inf. Syst.* **2022**, *31*, 101717. [CrossRef]
21. Wang, H.; Ning, H.; Lin, Y.; Wang, W.; Dhelim, S.; Farha, F.; Ding, J.; Daneshmand, M. A survey on the metaverse: The state-of-the-art, technologies, applications, and challenges. *IEEE Internet Things J.* **2023**, *10*, 14671–14688. [CrossRef]
22. Kala, V.; Chudasama, S.; Bathiya, J.; Jain, D.; Barik, P.K. Optimized 5G Resource Allocation for Metaverse Applications. In Proceedings of the 2024 International Conference on Electronics, Computing, Communication and Control Technology (ICECCC), Kuala Lumpur, Malaysia, 22–24 March 2024; pp. 1–6.
23. Cardoso, L.F.d.S.; Kimura, B.Y.L.; Zorzal, E.R. Towards augmented and mixed reality on future mobile networks. *Multimed. Tools Appl.* **2024**, *83*, 9067–9102. [CrossRef]
24. Huynh-The, T.; Pham, Q.V.; Pham, X.Q.; Nguyen, T.T.; Han, Z.; Kim, D.S. Artificial intelligence for the metaverse: A survey. *Eng. Appl. Artif. Intell.* **2023**, *117*, 105581. [CrossRef]
25. Zhao, Y.; Jiang, J.; Chen, Y.; Liu, R.; Yang, Y.; Xue, X.; Chen, S. Metaverse: Perspectives from graphics, interactions and visualization. *Vis. Inform.* **2022**, *6*, 56–67. [CrossRef]
26. Hadjiaros, M.; Shimi, A.; Avraamides, M.N.; Neokleous, K.; Pattichis, C.S. Virtual Reality Brain-Computer Interfacing and the role of cognitive skills. *IEEE Access* **2024**, *12*, 129240–129261. [CrossRef]
27. Park, K.S. Brain-computer interface. In *Humans and Electricity: Understanding Body Electricity and Applications*; Springer: Berlin/Heidelberg, Germany, 2023; pp. 223–248.
28. Aloqaily, M.; Bouachir, O.; Karray, F.; Al Ridhawi, I.; El Saddik, A. Integrating digital twin and advanced intelligent technologies to realize the metaverse. *IEEE Consum. Electron. Mag.* **2022**, *12*, 47–55. [CrossRef]
29. Padmanaban, S.; Nasab, M.A.; Hatami, M.; Milani, O.H.; Dashtaki, M.A.; Nasab, M.A.; Zand, M. The Impact of the Internet of Things in the Smart City from the Point of View of Energy Consumption Optimization. In *Biomass and Solar-Powered Sustainable Digital Cities*, Wiley: Hoboken, NJ, USA; 2024; pp. 81–122.
30. Grande, R.; Albusac, J.; Vallejo, D.; Glez-Morcillo, C.; Castro-Schez, J.J. Performance Evaluation and Optimization of 3D Models from Low-Cost 3D Scanning Technologies for Virtual Reality and Metaverse E-Commerce. *Appl. Sci.* **2024**, *14*, 6037. [CrossRef]
31. Singh, A.; Mishra, S.; Jain, S.; Dogra, S.; Awasthi, A.; Roy, N.R.; Sodhi, K. 8 Exploring practical use-cases of augmented reality using photogrammetry and other 3D reconstruction tools in the Metaverse. *Augment. Virtual Real. Ind. 5.0* **2023**, *2*, 163.
32. Aslam, A.M.; Chaudhary, R.; Bhardwaj, A.; Budhiraja, I.; Kumar, N.; Zeadally, S. Metaverse for 6G and beyond: The next revolution and deployment challenges. *IEEE Internet Things Mag.* **2023**, *6*, 32–39. [CrossRef]
33. Hennig-Thurau, T.; Aliman, D.N.; Herting, A.M.; Cziehso, G.P.; Linder, M.; Kübler, R.V. Social interactions in the metaverse: Framework, initial evidence, and research roadmap. *J. Acad. Mark. Sci.* **2023**, *51*, 889–913. [CrossRef]
34. Fascista, A. Toward integrated large-scale environmental monitoring using WSN/UAV/Crowdsensing: A review of applications, signal processing, and future perspectives. *Sensors* **2022**, *22*, 1824. [CrossRef]
35. Zhao, F.; Zhang, C.; Geng, B. Deep Multimodal Data Fusion. *ACM Comput. Surv.* **2024**, *56*, 1–36. [CrossRef]
36. Yu, J.; Alhilal, A.; Hui, P.; Tsang, D.H. Bi-directional digital twin and edge computing in the metaverse. *IEEE Internet Things Mag.* **2024**, *7*, 106–112. [CrossRef]

37. Li, K.; Lau, B.P.L.; Yuan, X.; Ni, W.; Guizani, M.; Yuen, C. Towards ubiquitous semantic metaverse: Challenges, approaches, and opportunities. *IEEE Internet Things J.* **2023**, *10*, 21855–21872. [CrossRef]
38. Cao, X.; Chen, H.; Gelbal, S.Y.; Aksun-Guvenc, B.; Guvenc, L. Vehicle-in-Virtual-Environment (VVE) method for autonomous driving system development, evaluation and demonstration. *Sensors* **2023**, *23*, 5088. [CrossRef]
39. Xu, H.; Berres, A.; Yoginath, S.B.; Sorensen, H.; Nugent, P.J.; Severino, J.; Tennille, S.A.; Moore, A.; Jones, W.; Sanyal, J. Smart mobility in the cloud: Enabling real-time situational awareness and cyber-physical control through a digital twin for traffic. *IEEE Trans. Intell. Transp. Syst.* **2023**, *24*, 3145–3156. [CrossRef]
40. Kušić, K.; Schumann, R.; Ivanjko, E. A digital twin in transportation: Real-time synergy of traffic data streams and simulation for virtualizing motorway dynamics. *Adv. Eng. Inform.* **2023**, *55*, 101858. [CrossRef]
41. Tuhaise, V.V.; Tah, J.H.M.; Abanda, F.H. Technologies for digital twin applications in construction. *Autom. Constr.* **2023**, *152*, 104931. [CrossRef]
42. Gkontzis, A.F.; Kotsiantis, S.; Feretzakis, G.; Verykios, V.S. Enhancing urban resilience: Smart city data analyses, forecasts, and digital twin techniques at the neighborhood level. *Future Internet* **2024**, *16*, 47. [CrossRef]
43. Ogunsakin, R.; Mehandjiev, N.; Marin, C.A. Towards adaptive digital twins architecture. *Comput. Ind.* **2023**, *149*, 103920. [CrossRef]
44. Tian, H.; Lee, G.A.; Bai, H.; Billinghurst, M. Using virtual replicas to improve mixed reality remote collaboration. *IEEE Trans. Vis. Comput. Graph.* **2023**, *29*, 2785–2795. [CrossRef]
45. Wang, C.M.; Huang, Q.J. Design of a Technology-Based Magic Show System with Virtual User Interfacing to Enhance the Entertainment Effects. *Appl. Sci.* **2024**, *14*, 5535. [CrossRef]
46. Oh, S.; Chung, K.; Aliyu, I.; Hahn, M.; Jeong, I.K.; Yu, C.R.; Um, T.W.; Kim, J. XDN-Based Network Framework Design to Communicate Interaction in Virtual Concerts with Metaverse Platforms. *Appl. Sci.* **2023**, *13*, 9509. [CrossRef]
47. Kim, D.Y.; Lee, H.K.; Chung, K. Avatar-mediated experience in the metaverse: The impact of avatar realism on user-avatar relationship. *J. Retail. Consum. Serv.* **2023**, *73*, 103382. [CrossRef]
48. Hadi, R.; Melumad, S.; Park, E.S. The Metaverse: A new digital frontier for consumer behavior. *J. Consum. Psychol.* **2024**, *34*, 142–166. [CrossRef]
49. Liu, Y.; Deng, Y.; Nallanathan, A.; Yuan, J. Machine learning for 6G enhanced ultra-reliable and low-latency services. *IEEE Wirel. Commun.* **2023**, *30*, 48–54. [CrossRef]
50. Chen, W.; Milosevic, Z.; Rabhi, F.A.; Berry, A. Real-time analytics: Concepts, architectures and ML/AI considerations. *IEEE Access* **2023**, *11*, 71634–71657. [CrossRef]
51. Sun, T.; Feng, B.; Huo, J.; Xiao, Y.; Wang, W.; Peng, J.; Li, Z.; Du, C.; Wang, W.; Zou, G.; et al. Artificial intelligence meets flexible sensors: Emerging smart flexible sensing systems driven by machine learning and artificial synapses. *Nano-Micro Lett.* **2024**, *16*, 14. [CrossRef] [PubMed]
52. Sibley, J.; Swenson, A. Events in the metaverse. In *Virtual Events Management: Theory and Methods for Event Management and Tourism*; Goodfellow Pub Ltd.: Wolvercote, UK, 2023; p. 155.
53. Onecha, B.; Cornadó, C.; Morros, J.; Pons, O. New approach to design and assess metaverse environments for improving learning processes in higher education: The case of architectural construction and rehabilitation. *Buildings* **2023**, *13*, 1340. [CrossRef]
54. AlGerafi, M.A.; Zhou, Y.; Oubibi, M.; Wijaya, T.T. Unlocking the potential: A comprehensive evaluation of augmented reality and virtual reality in education. *Electronics* **2023**, *12*, 3953. [CrossRef]
55. Huynh-The, T.; Gadekallu, T.R.; Wang, W.; Yenduri, G.; Ranaweera, P.; Pham, Q.V.; da Costa, D.B.; Liyanage, M. Blockchain for the metaverse: A review. *Future Gener. Comput. Syst.* **2023**, *143*, 401–419. [CrossRef]
56. Lee, L.H.; Braud, T.; Zhou, P.; Wang, L.; Xu, D.; Lin, Z.; Kumar, A.; Bermejo, C.; Hui, P. All one needs to know about metaverse: A complete survey on technological singularity, virtual ecosystem, and research agenda. *arXiv* **2021**, arXiv:2110.05352.
57. Zhang, B.; Zhu, J.; Su, H. Toward the third generation artificial intelligence. *Sci. China Inf. Sci.* **2023**, *66*, 121101. [CrossRef]
58. Saxena, A.C.; Ojha, A.; Sobti, D.; Khang, A. Artificial Intelligence (AI)-Centric Model in the Metaverse Ecosystem. In *Handbook of Research on AI-Based Technologies and Applications in the Era of the Metaverse*; IGI Global: Hershey, PA, USA, 2023; pp. 1–24.
59. Duong, T.Q.; Van Huynh, D.; Khosravirad, S.R.; Sharma, V.; Dobre, O.A.; Shin, H. From digital twin to metaverse: The role of 6G ultra-reliable and low-latency communications with multi-tier computing. *IEEE Wirel. Commun.* **2023**, *30*, 140–146. [CrossRef]
60. Seo, J.; Park, S. SBAC: Substitution cipher access control based on blockchain for protecting personal data in metaverse. *Future Gener. Comput. Syst.* **2024**, *151*, 85–97. [CrossRef]
61. Hyun, W. Study on standardization for interoperable metaverse. In Proceedings of the 2023 25th International Conference on Advanced Communication Technology (ICACT), Pyeongchang, Republic of Korea, 19–22 February 2023; pp. 319–322.
62. Karunarathna, S.; Wijethilaka, S.; Ranaweera, P.; Hemachandra, K.T.; Samarasinghe, T.; Liyanage, M. The role of network slicing and edge computing in the metaverse realization. *IEEE Access* **2023**, *11*, 25502–25530. [CrossRef]
63. Sun, Z.; Zhu, M.; Shan, X.; Lee, C. Augmented tactile-perception and haptic-feedback rings as human-machine interfaces aiming for immersive interactions. *Nat. Commun.* **2022**, *13*, 5224. [CrossRef] [PubMed]
64. Hernan, G.; Ingale, N.; Somayaji, S.; Veerubhotla, A. Virtual Reality-Based Interventions to Improve Balance in Patients with Traumatic Brain Injury: A Scoping Review. *Brain Sci.* **2024**, *14*, 429. [CrossRef]
65. Tefertiller, C.; Ketchum, J.M.; Bartelt, P.; Peckham, M.; Hays, K. Feasibility of virtual reality and treadmill training in traumatic brain injury: A randomized controlled pilot trial. *Brain Inj.* **2022**, *36*, 898–908. [CrossRef]

66. Ullah, H.; Manickam, S.; Obaidat, M.; Laghari, S.U.A.; Uddin, M. Exploring the potential of metaverse technology in healthcare: Applications, challenges, and future directions. *IEEE Access* **2023**, *11*, 69686–69707. [CrossRef]
67. Sokołowska, B. Being in Virtual Reality and Its Influence on Brain Health—An Overview of Benefits, Limitations and Prospects. *Brain Sci.* **2024**, *14*, 72. [CrossRef]
68. Devane, N.; Behn, N.; Marshall, J.; Ramachandran, A.; Wilson, S.; Hilari, K. The use of virtual reality in the rehabilitation of aphasia: A systematic review. *Disabil. Rehabil.* **2023**, *45*, 3803–3822. [CrossRef] [PubMed]
69. Freeman, D.; Rosebrock, L.; Waite, F.; Loe, B.S.; Kabir, T.; Petit, A.; Dudley, R.; Chapman, K.; Morrison, A.; O'Regan, E.; et al. Virtual reality (VR) therapy for patients with psychosis: satisfaction and side effects. *Psychol. Med.* **2023**, *53*, 4373–4384. [CrossRef]
70. Suh, I.; McKinney, T.; Siu, K.C. Current perspective of metaverse application in medical education, research and patient care. *Virtual Worlds* **2023**, *2*, 115–128. [CrossRef]
71. Spence, C. Digitally enhancing tasting experiences. *Int. J. Gastron. Food Sci.* **2023**, *32*, 100695. [CrossRef]
72. Atanasio, M.; Sansone, F.; Conte, R.; Tonacci, A. Exploring Taste Sensation in the Metaverse: A Literature Review. In Proceedings of the 2024 IEEE Gaming, Entertainment, and Media Conference (GEM), Turin, Italy, 5–7 June 2024; pp. 1–6.
73. Monaco, S.; Sacchi, G. Travelling the metaverse: Potential benefits and main challenges for tourism sectors and research applications. *Sustainability* **2023**, *15*, 3348. [CrossRef]
74. Alsamhi, M.H.; Hawbani, A.; Kumar, S.; Alsamhi, S.H. Multisensory metaverse-6G: A new paradigm of commerce and education. *IEEE Access* **2024**, *12*, 75657–75677. [CrossRef]
75. Yang, B.; Yang, S.; Lv, Z.; Wang, F.; Olofsson, T. Application of digital twins and metaverse in the field of fluid machinery pumps and fans: A review. *Sensors* **2022**, *22*, 9294. [CrossRef] [PubMed]
76. Emami, M.; Bayat, A.; Tafazolli, R.; Quddus, A. A Survey on Haptics: Communication, Sensing and Feedback. Available online: https://ieeexplore.ieee.org/stamp/stamp.jsp?arnumber=10637258 (accessed on 15 October 2024).
77. Chengoden, R.; Victor, N.; Huynh-The, T.; Yenduri, G.; Jhaveri, R.H.; Alazab, M.; Bhattacharya, S.; Hegde, P.; Maddikunta, P.K.R.; Gadekallu, T.R. Metaverse for healthcare: A survey on potential applications, challenges and future directions. *IEEE Access* **2023**, *11*, 12765–12795. [CrossRef]
78. Kim, M.; Oh, J.; Son, S.; Park, Y.; Kim, J.; Park, Y. Secure and privacy-preserving authentication scheme using decentralized identifier in metaverse environment. *Electronics* **2023**, *12*, 4073. [CrossRef]
79. Yang, K.; Zhang, Z.; Youliang, T.; Ma, J. A secure authentication framework to guarantee the traceability of avatars in metaverse. *IEEE Trans. Inf. Forensics Secur.* **2023**, *18*, 3817–3832. [CrossRef]
80. Jim, J.R.; Hosain, M.T.; Mridha, M.F.; Kabir, M.M.; Shin, J. Towards trustworthy metaverse: Advancements and challenges. *IEEE Access* **2023**. [CrossRef]
81. Chen, C.; Li, Y.; Wu, Z.; Mai, C.; Liu, Y.; Hu, Y.; Kang, J.; Zheng, Z. Privacy computing meets metaverse: Necessity, taxonomy and challenges. *Ad Hoc Netw.* **2024**, *158*, 103457. [CrossRef]
82. Karaarslan, E.; Yazici Yilmaz, S. Metaverse and Decentralization. In *Metaverse: Technologies, Opportunities and Threats*; Springer: Berlin/Heidelberg, Germany, 2023; pp. 31–44.
83. Lee, H.J.; Gu, H.H. Empirical research on the metaverse user experience of digital natives. *Sustainability* **2022**, *14*, 14747. [CrossRef]
84. Mourtzis, D.; Angelopoulos, J.; Panopoulos, N. Smart manufacturing and tactile internet based on 5G in industry 4.0: Challenges, applications and new trends. *Electronics* **2021**, *10*, 3175. [CrossRef]
85. Cheng, R.; Wu, N.; Chen, S.; Han, B. Will metaverse be nextg internet? vision, hype, and reality. *IEEE Netw.* **2022**, *36*, 197–204. [CrossRef]
86. Qu, Q.; Chen, Y.; Li, X.; Blasch, E.; Chen, G.; Ardiles-Cruz, E. Low-cost collision avoidance in microverse for unmanned aerial vehicle delivery networks. In Proceedings of the Sensors and Systems for Space Applications XVII, National Harbor, MD, USA, 21–25 April 2024; Volume 13062, pp. 215–226.
87. Sun, H.; Qu, Q.; Chen, Y.; Ardiles-Cruz, E.; Blasch, E. Senior Safety Monitoring in Microverse using Fuzzy Neural Network Enhanced Action Recognition. Available online: https://www.authorea.com/users/805226/articles/1192576-senior-safety-monitoring-in-microverse-using-fuzzy-neural-network-enhanced-action-recognition (accessed on 15 October 2024).
88. Yang, L.; Ni, S.T.; Wang, Y.; Yu, A.; Lee, J.A.; Hui, P. Interoperability of the Metaverse: A Digital Ecosystem Perspective Review. *arXiv* **2024**, arXiv:2403.05205.
89. Mangrulkar, R.S.; Chavan, P.V. *Blockchain Essentials*; Springer: Berlin/Heidelberg, Germany, 2024.
90. Ritterbusch, G.D.; Teichmann, M.R. Defining the metaverse: A systematic literature review. *IEEE Access* **2023**, *11*, 12368–12377. [CrossRef]
91. Blasch, E.; Pham, T.; Chong, C.Y.; Koch, W.; Leung, H.; Braines, D.; Abdelzaher, T. Machine learning/artificial intelligence for sensor data fusion–opportunities and challenges. *IEEE Aerosp. Electron. Syst. Mag.* **2021**, *36*, 80–93. [CrossRef]
92. Lee, H.; Hwang, Y. Technology-enhanced education through VR-making and metaverse-linking to foster teacher readiness and sustainable learning. *Sustainability* **2022**, *14*, 4786. [CrossRef]
93. Mystakidis, S.; Berki, E.; Valtanen, J.P. Deep and meaningful e-learning with social virtual reality environments in higher education: A systematic literature review. *Appl. Sci.* **2021**, *11*, 2412. [CrossRef]

94. Childs, E.; Mohammad, F.; Stevens, L.; Burbelo, H.; Awoke, A.; Rewkowski, N.; Manocha, D. An overview of enhancing distance learning through emerging augmented and virtual reality technologies. *IEEE Trans. Vis. Comput. Graph.* **2023**, *30*, 4480–4496. [CrossRef]
95. Kaddoura, S.; Al Husseiny, F. The rising trend of Metaverse in education: Challenges, opportunities, and ethical considerations. *PeerJ Comput. Sci.* **2023**, *9*, e1252. [CrossRef] [PubMed]
96. Yang, L. Recommendations for metaverse governance based on technical standards. *Humanit. Soc. Sci. Commun.* **2023**, *10*, 1–10. [CrossRef]
97. Khan, M.; Hatami, M.; Zhao, W.; Chen, Y. A novel trusted hardware-based scalable security framework for IoT edge devices. *Discov. Internet Things* **2024**, *4*, 4. [CrossRef]
98. Yaqoob, I.; Salah, K.; Jayaraman, R.; Omar, M. Metaverse applications in smart cities: Enabling technologies, opportunities, challenges, and future directions. *Internet Things* **2023**, *23*, 100884. [CrossRef]
99. Wijayathunga, L.; Rassau, A.; Chai, D. Challenges and solutions for autonomous ground robot scene understanding and navigation in unstructured outdoor environments: A review. *Appl. Sci.* **2023**, *13*, 9877. [CrossRef]
100. Gill, S.S.; Wu, H.; Patros, P.; Ottaviani, C.; Arora, P.; Pujol, V.C.; Haunschild, D.; Parlikad, A.K.; Cetinkaya, O.; Lutfiyya, H.; et al. Modern computing: Vision and challenges. *Telemat. Inform. Rep.* **2024**, *13*, 100116. [CrossRef]
101. Nica, E.; Popescu, G.H.; Poliak, M.; Kliestik, T.; Sabie, O.M. Digital twin simulation tools, spatial cognition algorithms, and multi-sensor fusion technology in sustainable urban governance networks. *Mathematics* **2023**, *11*, 1981. [CrossRef]
102. Ounoughi, C.; Yahia, S.B. Data fusion for ITS: A systematic literature review. *Inf. Fusion* **2023**, *89*, 267–291. [CrossRef]
103. Wang, X.; Li, K.; Chehri, A. Multi-sensor fusion technology for 3D object detection in autonomous driving: A review. *IEEE Trans. Intell. Transp. Syst.* **2023**, *25*, 1148–1165. [CrossRef]
104. Dahan, N.A.; Al-Razgan, M.; Al-Laith, A.; Alsoufi, M.A.; Al-Asaly, M.S.; Alfakih, T. Metaverse framework: A case study on E-learning environment (ELEM). *Electronics* **2022**, *11*, 1616. [CrossRef]
105. Cheng, S. Metaverse and immersive interaction technology. In *Metaverse: Concept, Content and Context*; Springer: Berlin/Heidelberg, Germany, 2023; pp. 47–81.
106. Yao, X.; Ma, N.; Zhang, J.; Wang, K.; Yang, E.; Faccio, M. Enhancing wisdom manufacturing as industrial metaverse for industry and society 5.0. *J. Intell. Manuf.* **2024**, *35*, 235–255. [CrossRef]
107. Xu, M.; Niyato, D.; Chen, J.; Zhang, H.; Kang, J.; Xiong, Z.; Mao, S.; Han, Z. Generative AI-empowered simulation for autonomous driving in vehicular mixed reality metaverses. *IEEE J. Sel. Top. Signal Process.* **2023**, *17*, 1064–1079. [CrossRef]
108. Chamola, V.; Bansal, G.; Das, T.K.; Hassija, V.; Sai, S.; Wang, J.; Zeadally, S.; Hussain, A.; Yu, F.R.; Guizani, M.; et al. Beyond reality: The pivotal role of generative ai in the metaverse. *IEEE Internet Things Mag.* **2024**, *7*, 126–135. [CrossRef]
109. Fernández-Caramés, T.M.; Fraga-Lamas, P. Forging the Industrial Metaverse-Where Industry 5.0, Augmented and Mixed Reality, IIoT, Opportunistic Edge Computing and Digital Twins Meet. *arXiv* **2024**, arXiv:2403.11312.
110. Behnke, I.; Austad, H. Real-time performance of industrial IoT communication technologies: A review. *IEEE Internet Things J.* **2023**, *11*, 7399–7410. [CrossRef]
111. Yao, Y.; Chang, X.; Li, L.; Liu, J.; Mišić, J.; Mišić, V.B. DIDs-assisted secure cross-metaverse authentication scheme for MEC-enabled metaverse. In Proceedings of the ICC 2023-IEEE International Conference on Communications, Rome, Italy, 28 May–1 June 2023; pp. 6318–6323.
112. Zhang, L.; Du, Q.; Lu, L.; Zhang, S. Overview of the integration of communications, sensing, computing, and storage as enabling technologies for the metaverse over 6G networks. *Electronics* **2023**, *12*, 3651. [CrossRef]
113. Zhao, L.; Yang, Q.; Huang, H.; Guo, L.; Jiang, S. Intelligent wireless sensing driven metaverse: A survey. *Comput. Commun.* **2024**, *214*, 46–56. [CrossRef]
114. Gu, X.; Yuan, Y.; Yang, J.; Li, L. AI-empowered Pose Reconstruction for Real-time Synthesis of Remote Metaverse Avatars. In Proceedings of the 2024 21st International Joint Conference on Computer Science and Software Engineering (JCSSE), Phuket, Thailand, 19–22 June 2024; pp. 86–93.
115. Huang, F.; Chen, Y.; Wang, X.; Wang, S.; Wu, X. Spectral clustering super-resolution imaging based on multispectral camera array. *IEEE Trans. Image Process.* **2023**, *32*, 1257–1271. [CrossRef]
116. Tang, Y.; Song, S.; Gui, S.; Chao, W.; Cheng, C.; Qin, R. Active and low-cost hyperspectral imaging for the spectral analysis of a low-light environment. *Sensors* **2023**, *23*, 1437. [CrossRef] [PubMed]
117. Munir, A.; Aved, A.; Blasch, E. Situational awareness: Techniques, challenges, and prospects. *AI* **2022**, *3*, 55–77. [CrossRef]
118. Tang, Q.; Liang, J.; Zhu, F. A comparative review on multi-modal sensors fusion based on deep learning. *Signal Process.* **2023**, *213*, 109165. [CrossRef]
119. Zhao, L.; Zhou, H.; Zhu, X.; Song, X.; Li, H.; Tao, W. Lif-seg: Lidar and camera image fusion for 3d lidar semantic segmentation. *IEEE Trans. Multimed.* **2023**, *26*, 1158–1168. [CrossRef]
120. Smigaj, M.; Agarwal, A.; Bartholomeus, H.; Decuyper, M.; Elsherif, A.; de Jonge, A.; Kooistra, L. Thermal infrared remote sensing of stress responses in forest environments: A review of developments, Challenges, and Opportunities. *Curr. For. Rep.* **2024**, *10*, 56–76. [CrossRef]
121. Wu, G.; Chen, Z.; Dang, J. Data Fusion and Digital Modeling. In *Intelligent Bridge Maintenance and Management: Emerging Digital Technologies*; Springer: Berlin/Heidelberg, Germany, 2024; pp. 337–401.

122. Huang, M.; Feng, R.; Zou, L.; Li, R.; Xie, J. Enhancing Telecooperation Through Haptic Twin for Internet of Robotic Things: Implementation and Challenges. *IEEE Internet Things J.* **2024**, *11*, 32440–32453. [CrossRef]
123. Baidya, T.; Moh, S. Comprehensive survey on resource allocation for edge-computing-enabled metaverse. *Comput. Sci. Rev.* **2024**, *54*, 100680. [CrossRef]
124. Zawish, M.; Dharejo, F.A.; Khowaja, S.A.; Raza, S.; Davy, S.; Dev, K.; Bellavista, P. AI and 6G into the metaverse: Fundamentals, challenges and future research trends. *IEEE Open J. Commun. Soc.* **2024**, *5*, 730–778. [CrossRef]
125. Yin, F.; Shi, F. A comparative survey of big data computing and HPC: From a parallel programming model to a cluster architecture. *Int. J. Parallel Program.* **2022**, *50*, 27–64. [CrossRef]
126. Hamid, N.A.W.A.; Singh, B. High-Performance Computing Based Operating Systems, Software Dependencies and IoT Integration. In *High Performance Computing in Biomimetics: Modeling, Architecture and Applications*; Springer: Berlin/Heidelberg, Germany, 2024; pp. 175–204.
127. Navaux, P.O.A.; Lorenzon, A.F.; da Silva Serpa, M. Challenges in high-performance computing. *J. Braz. Comput. Soc.* **2023**, *29*, 51–62. [CrossRef]
128. Pyzer-Knapp, E.O.; Curioni, A. Advancing biomolecular simulation through exascale HPC, AI and quantum computing. *Curr. Opin. Struct. Biol.* **2024**, *87*, 102826. [CrossRef]
129. Thakur, S.; Jha, S.K. Cloud Computing and its Emerging Trends on Big Data Analytics. In Proceedings of the 2023 4th International Conference on Electronics and Sustainable Communication Systems (ICESC), Coimbatore, India, 6–8 July 2023; pp. 1159–1164.
130. Karunamurthy, A.; Yuvaraj, M.; Shahithya, J.; Thenmozhi, V. Cloud Database: Empowering Scalable and Flexible Data Management. *Quing Int. J. Innov. Res. Sci. Eng.* **2023**, *2*, 1–23. [CrossRef]
131. Samha, A.K. Strategies for efficient resource management in federated cloud environments supporting Infrastructure as a Service (IaaS). *J. Eng. Res.* **2024**, *12*, 101–114. [CrossRef]
132. Bharany, S.; Kaur, K.; Badotra, S.; Rani, S.; Kavita; Wozniak, M.; Shafi, J.; Ijaz, M.F. Efficient middleware for the portability of paas services consuming applications among heterogeneous clouds. *Sensors* **2022**, *22*, 5013. [CrossRef]
133. Nadeem, F. Evaluating and ranking cloud IaaS, PaaS and SaaS models based on functional and non-functional key performance indicators. *IEEE Access* **2022**, *10*, 63245–63257. [CrossRef]
134. Alhaidari, F.; Rahman, A.; Zagrouba, R. Cloud of Things: Architecture, applications and challenges. *J. Ambient Intell. Humaniz. Comput.* **2023**, *14*, 5957–5975. [CrossRef]
135. Chi, H.R.; de Fátima Domingues, M.; Zhu, H.; Li, C.; Kojima, K.; Radwan, A. Healthcare 5.0: In the perspective of consumer internet-of-things-based fog/cloud computing. *IEEE Trans. Consum. Electron.* **2023**, *69*, 745–755. [CrossRef]
136. Wang, Y.; Zhu, M.; Yuan, J.; Wang, G.; Zhou, H. The intelligent prediction and assessment of financial information risk in the cloud computing model. *arXiv* **2024**, arXiv:2404.09322. [CrossRef]
137. Hazra, A.; Rana, P.; Adhikari, M.; Amgoth, T. Fog computing for next-generation internet of things: Fundamental, state-of-the-art and research challenges. *Comput. Sci. Rev.* **2023**, *48*, 100549. [CrossRef]
138. Kong, X.; Wu, Y.; Wang, H.; Xia, F. Edge computing for internet of everything: A survey. *IEEE Internet Things J.* **2022**, *9*, 23472–23485. [CrossRef]
139. Mann, Z.A. Decentralized application placement in fog computing. *IEEE Trans. Parallel Distrib. Syst.* **2022**, *33*, 3262–3273. [CrossRef]
140. Oprea, S.V.; Bâra, A. An Edge-Fog-Cloud computing architecture for IoT and smart metering data. *Peer-Netw. Appl.* **2023**, *16*, 818–845. [CrossRef]
141. Hazarika, A.; Rahmati, M. Towards an evolved immersive experience: Exploring 5G-and beyond-enabled ultra-low-latency communications for augmented and virtual reality. *Sensors* **2023**, *23*, 3682. [CrossRef]
142. Sefati, S.S.; Halunga, S. Ultra-reliability and low-latency communications on the internet of things based on 5G network: Literature review, classification, and future research view. *Trans. Emerg. Telecommun. Technol.* **2023**, *34*, e4770. [CrossRef]
143. Qadir, Z.; Le, K.N.; Saeed, N.; Munawar, H.S. Towards 6G Internet of Things: Recent advances, use cases, and open challenges. *ICT Express* **2023**, *9*, 296–312. [CrossRef]
144. Ajmal, M.; Siddiqa, A.; Jeong, B.; Seo, J.; Kim, D. Cell-free massive multiple-input multiple-output challenges and opportunities: A survey. *ICT Express* **2023**, *10*, 194–212. [CrossRef]
145. Fang, G.; Sun, Y.; Almutiq, M.; Zhou, W.; Zhao, Y.; Ren, Y. Distributed medical data storage mechanism based on proof of retrievability and vector commitment for metaverse services. *IEEE J. Biomed. Health Inform.* **2023**, 1–9. [CrossRef] [PubMed]
146. Ooi, B.C.; Chen, G.; Shou, M.Z.; Tan, K.L.; Tung, A.; Xiao, X.; Yip, J.W.L.; Zhang, B.; Zhang, M. The metaverse data deluge: What can we do about it? In Proceedings of the 2023 IEEE 39th International Conference on Data Engineering (ICDE), Anaheim, CA, USA, 3–7 April 2023; pp. 3675–3687.
147. Chougule, S.B.; Chaudhari, B.S.; Ghorpade, S.N.; Zennaro, M. Exploring Computing Paradigms for Electric Vehicles: From Cloud to Edge Intelligence, Challenges and Future Directions. *World Electr. Veh. J.* **2024**, *15*, 39. [CrossRef]
148. Maher, S.M.; Ebrahim, G.A.; Hosny, S.; Salah, M.M. A cache-enabled device-to-device approach based on deep learning. *IEEE Access* **2023**, *11*, 76953–76963. [CrossRef]
149. Masood, A.; Tuan, D.Q.; Lakew, D.S.; Dao, N.N.; Cho, S. A Review on AI-Enabled Content Caching in Vehicular Edge Caching and Networks. In Proceedings of the 2023 International Conference on Artificial Intelligence in Information and Communication (ICAIIC), Bali, Indonesia, 20–23 February 2023; pp. 713–717.

150. Singh, R.; Gill, S.S. Edge AI: A survey. *Internet Things Cyber-Phys. Syst.* **2023**, *3*, 71–92. [CrossRef]
151. Qiu, S.; Fan, Q.; Li, X.; Zhang, X.; Min, G.; Lyu, Y. OA-cache: Oracle approximation-based cache replacement at the network edge. *IEEE Trans. Netw. Serv. Manag.* **2023**, *20*, 3177–3189. [CrossRef]
152. Sun, H.; Sun, C.; Tong, H.; Yue, Y.; Qin, X. A Machine Learning-empowered Cache Management Scheme for High-Performance SSDs. *IEEE Trans. Comput.* **2024**, *73*, 2066–2080. [CrossRef]
153. Murala, D.K.; Panda, S.K. Metaverse: A study on immersive technologies. In *Metaverse and Immersive Technologies: An Introduction to Industrial, Business and Social Applications*, Wiley: Hoboken, NJ, USA; 2023; pp. 1–41.
154. Bibri, S.E.; Jagatheesaperumal, S.K. Harnessing the potential of the metaverse and artificial intelligence for the internet of city things: Cost-effective XReality and synergistic AIoT technologies. *Smart Cities* **2023**, *6*, 2397–2429. [CrossRef]
155. Familoni, B.T.; Onyebuchi, N.C. Augmented and virtual reality in us education: A review: Analyzing the impact, effectiveness, and future prospects of ar/vr tools in enhancing learning experiences. *Int. J. Appl. Res. Soc. Sci.* **2024**, *6*, 642–663. [CrossRef]
156. Korkut, E.H.; Surer, E. Visualization in virtual reality: A systematic review. *Virtual Real.* **2023**, *27*, 1447–1480. [CrossRef]
157. Yang, Y.; Zhong, L.; Li, S.; Yu, A. Research on the Perceived Quality of Virtual Reality Headsets in Human–Computer Interaction. *Sensors* **2023**, *23*, 6824. [CrossRef] [PubMed]
158. Theodoropoulos, A.; Stavropoulou, D.; Papadopoulos, P.; Platis, N.; Lepouras, G. Developing an interactive VR CAVE for immersive shared gaming experiences. *Virtual Worlds* **2023**, *2*, 162–181. [CrossRef]
159. Raji, M.A.; Olodo, H.B.; Oke, T.T.; Addy, W.A.; Ofodile, O.C.; Oyewole, A.T. Business strategies in virtual reality: A review of market opportunities and consumer experience. *Int. J. Manag. Entrep. Res.* **2024**, *6*, 722–736. [CrossRef]
160. Miljkovic, I.; Shlyakhetko, O.; Fedushko, S. Real estate app development based on AI/VR technologies. *Electronics* **2023**, *12*, 707. [CrossRef]
161. Creed, C.; Al-Kalbani, M.; Theil, A.; Sarcar, S.; Williams, I. Inclusive AR/VR: Accessibility barriers for immersive technologies. *Univers. Access Inf. Soc.* **2024**, *23*, 59–73. [CrossRef]
162. Dargan, S.; Bansal, S.; Kumar, M.; Mittal, A.; Kumar, K. Augmented reality: A comprehensive review. *Arch. Comput. Methods Eng.* **2023**, *30*, 1057–1080. [CrossRef]
163. Mendoza-Ramírez, C.E.; Tudon-Martinez, J.C.; Félix-Herrán, L.C.; Lozoya-Santos, J.d.J.; Vargas-Martínez, A. Augmented reality: Survey. *Appl. Sci.* **2023**, *13*, 10491. [CrossRef]
164. Kim, D.; Chae, H.; Kim, Y.; Choi, J.; Kim, K.H.; Jo, D. Real-Time Motion Adaptation with Spatial Perception for an Augmented Reality Character. *Appl. Sci.* **2024**, *14*, 650. [CrossRef]
165. Sayeedunnisa, S.F.; Saberi, K.H.; Mohiuddin, M.A. Augmented GPS Navigation: Enhancing the Reliability of Location-Based Services. In Proceedings of the 2023 International Conference on Advancement in Computation & Computer Technologies (InCACCT), Gharuan, India, 5–6 May 2023; pp. 565–569.
166. Liu, D.; Huang, R.; Metwally, A.H.S.; Tlili, A.; Lin, E.F. *Application of the Metaverse in Education*; Springer: Berlin/Heidelberg, Germany, 2024.
167. Vyas, S. Extended reality and edge AI for healthcare 4.0: Systematic study. In *Extended Reality for Healthcare Systems*; Elsevier: Amsterdam, The Netherlands, 2023; pp. 229–240.
168. AL Hilal, N.S.H. The impact of the use of augmented reality on online purchasing behavior sustainability: The Saudi consumer as a model. *Sustainability* **2023**, *15*, 5448. [CrossRef]
169. Tsolis, A.; Bakogianni, S.; Angelaki, C.; Alexandridis, A.A. A review of clothing components in the development of wearable textile antennas: Design and experimental procedure. *Sensors* **2023**, *23*, 3289. [CrossRef]
170. Minopoulos, G.M.; Memos, V.A.; Stergiou, K.D.; Stergiou, C.L.; Psannis, K.E. A medical image visualization technique assisted with AI-based haptic feedback for robotic surgery and healthcare. *Appl. Sci.* **2023**, *13*, 3592. [CrossRef]
171. Buhalis, D.; Karatay, N. Mixed reality (MR) for generation Z in cultural heritage tourism towards metaverse. In *Information and Communication Technologies in Tourism 2022: Proceedings of the ENTER 2022 eTourism Conference, Tianjin, China, 11–14 January 2022*; Springer: Berlin/Heidelberg, Germany, 2022; pp. 16–27.
172. Nleya, S.M.; Velempini, M. Industrial Metaverse: A Comprehensive Review, Environmental Impact, and Challenges. *Appl. Sci.* **2024**, *14*, 5736. [CrossRef]
173. El Koshiry, A.; Eliwa, E.; Abd El-Hafeez, T.; Shams, M.Y. Unlocking the power of blockchain in education: An overview of innovations and outcomes. *Blockchain Res. Appl.* **2023**, *4*, 100165. [CrossRef]
174. Mitra, S. Metaverse: A potential virtual-physical ecosystem for innovative blended education and training. *J. Metaverse* **2023**, *3*, 66–72. [CrossRef]
175. Tan, Y.W.; Low, S.E.; Chow, J.; Teo, J.; Bhojan, A. DHR+ S: Distributed hybrid rendering with realistic real-time shadows for interactive thin client metaverse and game applications. *Vis. Comput.* **2024**, *40*, 4981–4991. [CrossRef]
176. Wang, J.; Chen, S.; Liu, Y.; Lau, R. Intelligent metaverse scene content construction. *IEEE Access* **2023**, *11*, 76222–76241. [CrossRef]
177. Xu, M.; Niyato, D.; Wright, B.; Zhang, H.; Kang, J.; Xiong, Z.; Mao, S.; Han, Z. EPViSA: Efficient Auction Design for Real-Time Physical-Virtual Synchronization in the Human-Centric Metaverse. *IEEE J. Sel. Areas Commun.* **2023**, *42*, 694–709. [CrossRef]
178. Wang, Y.; Su, Z.; Guo, S.; Dai, M.; Luan, T.H.; Liu, Y. A survey on digital twins: Architecture, enabling technologies, security and privacy, and future prospects. *IEEE Internet Things J.* **2023**, *10*, 14965–14987. [CrossRef]
179. Ali, W.A.; Fanti, M.P.; Roccotelli, M.; Ranieri, L. A review of digital twin technology for electric and autonomous vehicles. *Appl. Sci.* **2023**, *13*, 5871. [CrossRef]

180. Meijer, C.; Uh, H.W.; El Bouhaddani, S. Digital twins in healthcare: Methodological challenges and opportunities. *J. Pers. Med.* **2023**, *13*, 1522. [CrossRef]
181. Kuru, K. Metaomnicity: Toward immersive urban metaverse cyberspaces using smart city digital twins. *IEEE Access* **2023**, *11*, 43844–43868. [CrossRef]
182. Faliagka, E.; Christopoulou, E.; Ringas, D.; Politi, T.; Kostis, N.; Leonardos, D.; Tranoris, C.; Antonopoulos, C.P.; Denazis, S.; Voros, N. Trends in digital twin framework architectures for smart cities: A case study in smart mobility. *Sensors* **2024**, *24*, 1665. [CrossRef] [PubMed]
183. Turab, M.; Jamil, S. A comprehensive survey of digital twins in healthcare in the era of metaverse. *BioMedInformatics* **2023**, *3*, 563–584. [CrossRef]
184. Soori, M.; Arezoo, B.; Dastres, R. Digital twin for smart manufacturing, A review. *Sustain. Manuf. Serv. Econ.* **2023**, *2*, 100017. [CrossRef]
185. Aggarwal, S.; Kumar, N.; Singh, A.; Aujla, G.S. BlockTwins: Blockchain Empowered Supply Chain Digital Twins in Metaverse. In Proceedings of the 2024 IEEE International Conference on Communications Workshops (ICC Workshops), Denver, CO, USA, 9–13 June 2024; pp. 1456–1461.
186. Qu, Q.; Ogunbunmi, S.; Hatami, M.; Xu, R.; Chen, Y.; Chen, G.; Blasch, E. A digital twins enabled reputation system for microchain-based uav networks. In Proceedings of the 2023 IEEE 12th International Conference on Cloud Networking (CloudNet), Hoboken, NJ, USA, 1–3 November 2023; pp. 428–432.
187. Sumon, R.I.; Uddin, S.M.I.; Akter, S.; Mozumder, M.A.I.; Khan, M.O.; Kim, H.C. Natural Language Processing Influence on Digital Socialization and Linguistic Interactions in the Integration of the Metaverse in Regular Social Life. *Electronics* **2024**, *13*, 1331. [CrossRef]
188. Li, B.; Xu, T.; Li, X.; Cui, Y.; Bian, X.; Teng, S.; Ma, S.; Fan, L.; Tian, Y.; Wang, F.Y. Integrating large language models and metaverse in autonomous racing: An education-oriented perspective. *IEEE Trans. Intell. Veh.* **2024**, *9*, 59–64. [CrossRef]
189. Far, S.B.; Rad, A.I.; Bamakan, S.M.H.; Asaar, M.R. Toward Metaverse of everything: Opportunities, challenges, and future directions of the next generation of visual/virtual communications. *J. Netw. Comput. Appl.* **2023**, *217*, 103675.
190. Sun, Y.; Wang, H.; Chan, P.M.; Tabibi, M.; Zhang, Y.; Lu, H.; Chen, Y.; Lee, C.H.; Asadipour, A. Fictional Worlds, Real Connections: Developing Community Storytelling Social Chatbots through LLMs. *arXiv* **2023**, arXiv:2309.11478.
191. Partarakis, N.; Zabulis, X. A review of immersive technologies, knowledge representation, and AI for human-centered digital experiences. *Electronics* **2024**, *13*, 269. [CrossRef]
192. Hassan, S.Z.; Salehi, P.; Røed, R.K.; Halvorsen, P.; Baugerud, G.A.; Johnson, M.S.; Lison, P.; Riegler, M.; Lamb, M.E.; Griwodz, C.; et al. Towards an AI-driven talking avatar in virtual reality for investigative interviews of children. In Proceedings of the 2nd Workshop on Games Systems, Athlone Ireland, 14 June 2022; pp. 9–15.
193. Li, Y.; Hashim, A.S.; Lin, Y.; Nohuddin, P.N.; Venkatachalam, K.; Ahmadian, A. AI-based Visual Speech Recognition Towards Realistic Avatars and Lip-Reading Applications in the Metaverse. *Appl. Soft Comput.* **2024**, *164*, 111906. [CrossRef]
194. Hu, Y.H.; Yu, H.Y.; Tzeng, J.W.; Zhong, K.C. Using an avatar-based digital collaboration platform to foster ethical education for university students. *Comput. Educ.* **2023**, *196*, 104728. [CrossRef]
195. Jones, C.L.E.; Hancock, T.; Kazandjian, B.; Voorhees, C.M. Engaging the Avatar: The effects of authenticity signals during chat-based service recoveries. *J. Bus. Res.* **2022**, *144*, 703–716. [CrossRef]
196. Morrow, E.; Zidaru, T.; Ross, F.; Mason, C.; Patel, K.D.; Ream, M.; Stockley, R. Artificial intelligence technologies and compassion in healthcare: A systematic scoping review. *Front. Psychol.* **2023**, *13*, 971044. [CrossRef]
197. Campitiello, L.; Beatini, V.; Di Tore, S. Non-player Character Smart in Virtual Learning Environment: Empowering Education Through Artificial Intelligence. In *Artificial Intelligence with and for Learning Sciences. Past, Present, and Future Horizons, Proceedings of the First Workshop, WAILS 2024, Salerno, Italy, 18–19 January 2024*; Springer: Berlin/Heidelberg, Germany, 2024; pp. 131–137.
198. Chodvadiya, C.; Solanki, V.; Singh, K.G. Intelligent Virtual Worlds: A Survey of the Role of AI in the Metaverse. In Proceedings of the 2024 3rd International Conference for Innovation in Technology (INOCON), Bangalore, India, 1–3 March 2024; pp. 1–6.
199. Selznick, B.S.; Goodman, M.A.; McCready, A.M.; Duran, A. Developing Relational Leaders Through Sorority Engagement: A Quantitative Approach. *Innov. High. Educ.* **2024**, *49*, 319–347. [CrossRef]
200. Huyen, N.T. Fostering Design Thinking mindset for university students with NPCs in the metaverse. *Heliyon* **2024**, *10*, e34964. [CrossRef]
201. Qin, H.X.; Hui, P. Empowering the metaverse with generative ai: Survey and future directions. In Proceedings of the 2023 IEEE 43rd International Conference on Distributed Computing Systems Workshops (ICDCSW), Hong Kong, China, 18–21 July 2023; pp. 85–90.
202. Makowska, A.; Weiskirchen, R. Nasopharyngeal Carcinoma Cell Lines: Reliable Alternatives to Primary Nasopharyngeal Cells? *Cells* **2024**, *13*, 559. [CrossRef]
203. Pretty, E.J.; Fayek, H.M.; Zambetta, F. A case for personalized non-player character companion design. *Int. J. Hum.- Interact.* **2024**, *40*, 3051–3070. [CrossRef]
204. Uludağlı, M.Ç.; Oğuz, K. Non-player character decision-making in computer games. *Artif. Intell. Rev.* **2023**, *56*, 14159–14191. [CrossRef]
205. Mourtzis, D.; Angelopoulos, J.; Panopoulos, N. Blockchain integration in the era of industrial metaverse. *Appl. Sci.* **2023**, *13*, 1353. [CrossRef]

206. Cheng, Y.; Guo, Y.; Xu, M.; Hu, Q.; Yu, D.; Cheng, X. An adaptive and modular blockchain enabled architecture for a decentralized metaverse. *IEEE J. Sel. Areas Commun.* **2023**, *42*, 893–904. [CrossRef]
207. Ogunbunmi, S.; Hatmai, M.; Xu, R.; Chen, Y.; Blasch, E.; Ardiles-Cruz, E.; Aved, A.; Chen, G. A lightweight reputation system for uav networks. In *Security and Privacy in Cyber-Physical Systems and Smart Vehicles, Proceedings of the First EAI International Conference, SmartSP 2023, Chicago, IL, USA, 12–13 October 2023*; Springer: Berlin/Heidelberg, Germany, 2023; pp. 114–129.
208. Kumar, P.; Kumar, R.; Aloqaily, M.; Islam, A.N. Explainable AI and blockchain for metaverse: A security, and privacy perspective. *IEEE Consum. Electron. Mag.* **2023**, *13*, 90–97. [CrossRef]
209. Kottursamy, K.; Sadayapillai, B.; AlZubi, A.A.; Bashir, A.K. A novel blockchain architecture with mutable block and immutable transactions for enhanced scalability. *Sustain. Energy Technol. Assess.* **2023**, *58*, 103320. [CrossRef]
210. Torab-Miandoab, A.; Samad-Soltani, T.; Jodati, A.; Rezaei-Hachesu, P. Interoperability of heterogeneous health information systems: A systematic literature review. *BMC Med Inform. Decis. Mak.* **2023**, *23*, 18. [CrossRef]
211. Bianchi, M.; Bouvard, M.; Gomes, R.; Rhodes, A.; Shreeti, V. Mobile payments and interoperability: Insights from the academic literature. *Inf. Econ. Policy* **2023**, *65*, 101068. [CrossRef]
212. Narang, N.K. Mentor's Musings on Role of Standards, Regulations & Policies in Navigating through Metaverse and its Future Avatars. *IEEE Internet Things Mag.* **2023**, *6*, 4–11.
213. Yu, G.; Liu, C.; Fang, T.; Jia, J.; Lin, E.; He, Y.; Fu, S.; Wang, L.; Wei, L.; Huang, Q. A survey of real-time rendering on Web3D application. *Virtual Real. Intell. Hardw.* **2023**, *5*, 379–394. [CrossRef]
214. Hamidouche, W.; Bariah, L.; Debbah, M. Immersive Media and Massive Twinning: Advancing Toward the Metaverse. *IEEE Commun. Mag.* **2024**, *62*, 20–32. [CrossRef]
215. Della-Bosca, D.; Grant, G.; Patterson, D.; Roberts, S. The Multiplicitous Metaverse: Purposeful Ways of Applying and Understanding eXtended Reality in Learning and Teaching Frameworks. In *Augmented and Virtual Reality in the Metaverse*; Springer: Berlin/Heidelberg, Germany, 2024; pp. 41–63.
216. Westphal, C.; Hong, J.; Kang, S.G.; Chiariglione, L.; Jiang, T. Networking for the Metaverse: The Standardization Landscape. *arXiv* **2023**, arXiv:2312.09295. [CrossRef]
217. The World Metaverse Council. 2024. Available online: https://wmetac.com/ (accessed on 15 October 2024).
218. Tran, K.Q.; Neeli, H.; Tsekos, N.V.; Velazco-Garcia, J.D. Immersion into 3D Biomedical Data via Holographic AR Interfaces Based on the Universal Scene Description (USD) Standard. In Proceedings of the 2023 IEEE 23rd International Conference on Bioinformatics and Bioengineering (BIBE), Virtual, 4–6 December 2023; pp. 354–358.
219. Li, T.; Yang, C.; Yang, Q.; Lan, S.; Zhou, S.; Luo, X.; Huang, H.; Zheng, Z. Metaopera: A cross-metaverse interoperability protocol. *IEEE Wirel. Commun.* **2023**, *30*, 136–143. [CrossRef]
220. Yoo, K.; Welden, R.; Hewett, K.; Haenlein, M. The merchants of meta: A research agenda to understand the future of retailing in the metaverse. *J. Retail.* **2023**, *99*, 173–192. [CrossRef]
221. Liarokapis, F.; Milata, V.; Ponton, J.L.; Pelechano, N.; Zacharatos, H. XR4ED: An Extended Reality Platform for Education. *IEEE Comput. Graph. Appl.* **2024**, *44*, 79–88. [CrossRef] [PubMed]
222. Quek, H.Y.; Sielker, F.; Akroyd, J.; Bhave, A.N.; von Richthofen, A.; Herthogs, P.; van der Laag Yamu, C.; Wan, L.; Nochta, T.; Burgess, G.; et al. The conundrum in smart city governance: Interoperability and compatibility in an ever-growing ecosystem of digital twins. *Data Policy* **2023**, *5*, e6. [CrossRef]
223. Ball, M. *The Metaverse: And How It Will Revolutionize Everything*; Liveright Publishing: New York, NY, USA, 2022.
224. Song, Y.T.; Qin, J. Metaverse and personal healthcare. *Procedia Comput. Sci.* **2022**, *210*, 189–197. [CrossRef]
225. Albouq, S.S.; Abi Sen, A.A.; Almashf, N.; Yamin, M.; Alshanqiti, A.; Bahbouh, N.M. A survey of interoperability challenges and solutions for dealing with them in IoT environment. *IEEE Access* **2022**, *10*, 36416–36428. [CrossRef]
226. Perri, D.; Simonetti, M.; Tasso, S.; Gervasi, O. Open metaverse with open software. In *Computational Science and Its Applications—ICCSA 2023, Proceedings of the 23rd International Conference, Athens, Greece, 3–6 July 2023*; Springer: Berlin/Heidelberg, Germany, 2023; pp. 583–596.
227. Bühler, M.M.; Calzada, I.; Cane, I.; Jelinek, T.; Kapoor, A.; Mannan, M.; Mehta, S.; Mookerje, V.; Nübel, K.; Pentland, A.; et al. Unlocking the power of digital commons: Data cooperatives as a pathway for data sovereign, innovative and equitable digital communities. *Digital* **2023**, *3*, 146–171. [CrossRef]
228. Huzaifa, M.; Desai, R.; Grayson, S.; Jiang, X.; Jing, Y.; Lee, J.; Lu, F.; Pang, Y.; Ravichandran, J.; Sinclair, F.; et al. Illixr: An open testbed to enable extended reality systems research. *IEEE Micro* **2022**, *42*, 97–106. [CrossRef]
229. Javerliat, C.; Villenave, S.; Raimbaud, P.; Lavoué, G. Plume: Record, replay, analyze and share user behavior in 6dof xr experiences. *IEEE Trans. Vis. Comput. Graph.* **2024**, *30*, 2087–2097. [CrossRef]
230. Memmesheimer, V.; Ebert, A. A human-centered framework for scalable extended reality spaces. In *Proceedings of the International Research Training Group Conference on Physical Modeling for Virtual Manufacturing Systems and Processes*; Springer: Berlin/Heidelberg, Germany, 2023; pp. 111–128.
231. Abeywardena, I.S. OXREF: Open XR for Education Framework. *Int. Rev. Res. Open Distrib. Learn.* **2023**, *24*, 185–206. [CrossRef]
232. Sai, S.; Goyal, D.; Chamola, V.; Sikdar, B. Consumer electronics technologies for enabling an immersive metaverse experience. *IEEE Consum. Electron. Mag.* **2023**, *13*, 16–24. [CrossRef]
233. Rubinfeld, D. Data portability and interoperability: An EU-US comparison. *Eur. J. Law Econ.* **2024**, *57*, 163–179. [CrossRef]

234. De Luca, V.; Gatto, C.; Liaci, S.; Corchia, L.; Chiarello, S.; Faggiano, F.; Sumerano, G.; De Paolis, L.T. Virtual reality and spatial augmented reality for social inclusion: the "Includiamoci" project. *Information* **2023**, *14*, 38. [CrossRef]
235. Martí-Testón, A.; Muñoz, A.; Gracia, L.; Solanes, J.E. Using WebXR metaverse platforms to create touristic services and cultural promotion. *Appl. Sci.* **2023**, *13*, 8544. [CrossRef]
236. Boutsi, A.M.; Ioannidis, C.; Verykokou, S. Multi-Resolution 3D Rendering for High-Performance Web AR. *Sensors* **2023**, *23*, 6885. [CrossRef] [PubMed]
237. Sukaridhoto, S.; Hanifati, K.; Fajrianti, E.D.; Haz, A.L.; Hafidz, I.A.A.; Basuki, D.K.; Budiarti, R.P.N.; Wicaksono, H. Web-Based Extended Reality for Supporting Medical Education. In Proceedings of the SAI Intelligent Systems Conference, Amsterdam, The Netherlands, 7–8 September 2023; Springer: Berlin/Heidelberg, Germany, 2023; pp. 791–805.
238. Greenway, K.; Frisone, C.; Placidi, A.; Kumar, S.; Guest, W.; Winter, S.C.; Shah, K.; Henshall, C. Using immersive technology and architectural design to assist head and neck cancer patients' recovery from treatment: A focus group and technology acceptance study. *Eur. J. Oncol. Nurs.* **2023**, *62*, 102261. [CrossRef] [PubMed]
239. Kaarlela, T.; Pitkäaho, T.; Pieskä, S.; Padrão, P.; Bobadilla, L.; Tikanmäki, M.; Haavisto, T.; Blanco Bataller, V.; Laivuori, N.; Luimula, M. Towards metaverse: Utilizing extended reality and digital twins to control robotic systems. *Actuators* **2023**, *12*, 219. [CrossRef]
240. Cheng, R.; Wu, N.; Varvello, M.; Chen, S.; Han, B. Are we ready for metaverse? A measurement study of social virtual reality platforms. In Proceedings of the 22nd ACM Internet Measurement Conference, Nice, France, 25–27 October 2022; pp. 504–518.
241. Warburton, M.; Mon-Williams, M.; Mushtaq, F.; Morehead, J.R. Measuring motion-to-photon latency for sensorimotor experiments with virtual reality systems. *Behav. Res. Methods* **2023**, *55*, 3658–3678. [CrossRef]
242. Zhong, L.; Chen, X.; Xu, C.; Ma, Y.; Wang, M.; Zhao, Y.; Muntean, G.M. A multi-user cost-efficient crowd-assisted VR content delivery solution in 5G-and-beyond heterogeneous networks. *IEEE Trans. Mob. Comput.* **2022**, *22*, 4405–4421. [CrossRef]
243. Krauss, D. Mean-Time-to-Cloud: Enabling a Metaverse-Ready Network. 2023. Available online: https://www.ciena.com/insights/articles/2023/mean-time-to-cloud-enabling-a-metaverse-ready-network (accessed on 15 October 2024).
244. Liu, S.; Xu, X.; Claypool, M. A survey and taxonomy of latency compensation techniques for network computer games. *ACM Comput. Surv. (CSUR)* **2022**, *54*, 1–34. [CrossRef]
245. Yu, H.; Shokrnezhad, M.; Taleb, T.; Li, R.; Song, J. Toward 6g-based metaverse: Supporting highly-dynamic deterministic multi-user extended reality services. *IEEE Netw.* **2023**, *37*, 30–38. [CrossRef]
246. Chu, N.H.; Hoang, D.T.; Nguyen, D.N.; Phan, K.T.; Dutkiewicz, E.; Niyato, D.; Shu, T. Metaslicing: A novel resource allocation framework for metaverse. *IEEE Trans. Mob. Comput.* **2023**, *23*, 4145–4162. [CrossRef]
247. Zalan, T.; Barbesino, P. Making the metaverse real. *Digit. Bus.* **2023**, *3*, 100059. [CrossRef]
248. Sihare, S.; Khang, A. Effects of quantum technology on the metaverse. In *Handbook of Research on AI-Based Technologies and Applications in the Era of the Metaverse*; IGI Global: Hershey, PA, USA, 2023; pp. 174–203.
249. Mozaffariahrar, E.; Theoleyre, F.; Menth, M. A survey of Wi-Fi 6: Technologies, advances, and challenges. *Future Internet* **2022**, *14*, 293. [CrossRef]
250. Chen, C.; Chen, X.; Das, D.; Akhmetov, D.; Cordeiro, C. Overview and performance evaluation of Wi-Fi 7. *IEEE Commun. Stand. Mag.* **2022**, *6*, 12–18. [CrossRef]
251. Reshef, E.; Cordeiro, C. Future directions for Wi-Fi 8 and beyond. *IEEE Commun. Mag.* **2022**, *60*, 50–55. [CrossRef]
252. Liu, X.; Chen, T.; Dong, Y.; Mao, Z.; Gan, M.; Yang, X.; Lu, J. Wi-Fi 8: Embracing the Millimeter-Wave Era. *arXiv* **2023**, arXiv:2309.16813.
253. Domeke, A.; Cimoli, B.; Monroy, I.T. Integration of network slicing and machine learning into edge networks for low-latency services in 5G and beyond systems. *Appl. Sci.* **2022**, *12*, 6617. [CrossRef]
254. Dommeti, V.S.; Dharani, M.; Shasidhar, K.; Reddy, Y.D.R.; Moorthy, T.V. Quality Enhancement with Frame-wise DLCNN using High Efficiency Video Coding in 5G Networks. *Scalable Comput. Pract. Exp.* **2024**, *25*, 1264–1275. [CrossRef]
255. Shin, H.; Lee, J. Hardware Multi-Threaded System for High-Performance JPEG Decoding. *J. Signal Process. Syst.* **2024**, *96*, 67–79. [CrossRef]
256. Zhou, Y.; Chen, W.; Li, L.; Li, M.; Zhang, T. Initiative, Immersive Human-Computer Interactions: Software Defined Memristive Neural Networks for Non-Linear Heterogeneous Scheme in the Internet of Brains. *IEEE Internet Things J.* **2023**, *11*, 13355–13371. [CrossRef]
257. Song, R.; Xiao, B.; Song, Y.; Guo, S.; Yang, Y. A survey of blockchain-based schemes for data sharing and exchange. *IEEE Trans. Big Data* **2023**, *9*, 1477–1495. [CrossRef]
258. Zhao, C.; Zhang, S.; Wang, T.; Liew, S.C. Bodyless block propagation: Tps fully scalable blockchain with pre-validation. *Future Gener. Comput. Syst.* **2024**, *163*, 107516. [CrossRef]
259. Monem, M.; Hossain, M.T.; Alam, M.G.R.; Munir, M.S.; Rahman, M.M.; AlQahtani, S.A.; Almutlaq, S.; Hassan, M.M. A sustainable Bitcoin blockchain network through introducing dynamic block size adjustment using predictive analytics. *Future Gener. Comput. Syst.* **2024**, *153*, 12–26. [CrossRef]
260. Zafar, S.; Bhatti, K.; Shabbir, M.; Hashmat, F.; Akbar, A.H. Integration of blockchain and Internet of Things: Challenges and solutions. *Ann. Telecommun.* **2022**, *77*, 13–32. [CrossRef]
261. Kushwaha, S.S.; Joshi, S.; Singh, D.; Kaur, M.; Lee, H.N. Systematic review of security vulnerabilities in ethereum blockchain smart contract. *IEEE Access* **2022**, *10*, 6605–6621. [CrossRef]

262. Lasla, N.; Al-Sahan, L.; Abdallah, M.; Younis, M. Green-PoW: An energy-efficient blockchain Proof-of-Work consensus algorithm. *Comput. Netw.* **2022**, *214*, 109118. [CrossRef]
263. Ren, K.; Ho, N.M.; Loghin, D.; Nguyen, T.T.; Ooi, B.C.; Ta, Q.T.; Zhu, F. Interoperability in blockchain: A survey. *IEEE Trans. Knowl. Data Eng.* **2023**, *35*, 12750–12769. [CrossRef]
264. Rafique, W.; Qadir, J. Internet of everything meets the metaverse: Bridging physical and virtual worlds with blockchain. *Comput. Sci. Rev.* **2024**, *54*, 100678. [CrossRef]
265. Ghirmai, S.; Mebrahtom, D.; Aloqaily, M.; Guizani, M.; Debbah, M. Self-sovereign identity for trust and interoperability in the metaverse. In Proceedings of the 2022 IEEE Smartworld, Ubiquitous Intelligence & Computing, Scalable Computing & Communications, Digital Twin, Privacy Computing, Metaverse, Autonomous & Trusted Vehicles (SmartWorld/UIC/ScalCom/DigitalTwin/PriComp/Meta), Haikou, China, 15–18 December 2022; pp. 2468–2475.
266. Aung, N.; Dhelim, S.; Chen, L.; Ning, H.; Atzori, L.; Kechadi, T. Edge-enabled metaverse: The convergence of metaverse and mobile edge computing. *Tsinghua Sci. Technol.* **2023**, *29*, 795–805. [CrossRef]
267. Abilkaiyrkyzy, A.; Elhagry, A.; Laamarti, F.; Elsaddik, A. Metaverse key requirements and platforms survey. *IEEE Access* **2023**, *11*, 117765–117787. [CrossRef]
268. Rawat, D.B.; El Alami, H.; Hagos, D.H. Metaverse Survey & Tutorial: Exploring Key Requirements, Technologies, Standards, Applications, Challenges, and Perspectives. *arXiv* **2024**, arXiv:2405.04718.
269. Chen, B.; Song, C.; Lin, B.; Xu, X.; Tang, R.; Lin, Y.; Yao, Y.; Timoney, J.; Bi, T. A cross-platform metaverse data management system. In Proceedings of the 2022 IEEE International Conference on Metrology for Extended Reality, Artificial Intelligence and Neural Engineering (MetroXRAINE), Rome, Italy, 26–28 October 2022; pp. 145–150.
270. Jaimini, U.; Zhang, T.; Brikis, G.O.; Sheth, A. imetaversekg: Industrial metaverse knowledge graph to promote interoperability in design and engineering applications. *IEEE Internet Comput.* **2022**, *26*, 59–67. [CrossRef]
271. Zhang, Y.; Kutscher, D.; Cui, Y. Networked Metaverse Systems: Foundations, Gaps, Research Directions. *IEEE Open J. Commun. Soc.* **2024**, *5*, 5488–5539. [CrossRef]
272. Altundas, S.; Karaarslan, E. Cross-platform and personalized avatars in the metaverse: Ready player me case. In *Digital Twin Driven Intelligent Systems and Emerging Metaverse*; Springer: Berlin/Heidelberg, Germany, 2023; pp. 317–330.
273. Korbel, J.J.; Siddiq, U.H.; Zarnekow, R. Towards virtual 3D asset price prediction based on machine learning. *J. Theor. Appl. Electron. Commer. Res.* **2022**, *17*, 924–948. [CrossRef]
274. Golam, M.; Tuli, E.A.; Alief, R.N.; Kim, D.S.; Lee, J.M. Meta-Learning: A Digital Learning Management Framework using Blockchain for Metaverses. *IEEE Access* **2024**, *12*, 92774–92786. [CrossRef]
275. Lin, Y.; Liu, S. The integration strategy of information system based on artificial intelligence big data technology in metaverse environment. *Clust. Comput.* **2024**, *27*, 7049–7057. [CrossRef]
276. Deshmukh, R.; Nand, N.; Pawar, A.; Wagh, D.; Kudale, A. Video conferencing using WebRTC. In Proceedings of the 2023 International Conference on Sustainable Computing and Data Communication Systems (ICSCDS), Erode, India, 23–25 March 2023; pp. 857–864.
277. Praschl, C.; Krauss, O. Extending 3D geometric file formats for geospatial applications. *Appl. Geomat.* **2024**, *16*, 161–180. [CrossRef]
278. Al-Jundi, H.A.; Tanbour, E.Y. A framework for fidelity evaluation of immersive virtual reality systems. *Virtual Real.* **2022**, *26*, 1103–1122. [CrossRef]
279. Braud, T.; Fernández, C.B.; Hui, P. Scaling-up ar: University campus as a physical-digital metaverse. In Proceedings of the 2022 IEEE Conference on Virtual Reality and 3D User Interfaces Abstracts and Workshops (VRW), Christchurch, New Zealand, 12–16 March 2022; pp. 169–175.
280. Allam, Z.; Sharifi, A.; Bibri, S.E.; Jones, D.S.; Krogstie, J. The metaverse as a virtual form of smart cities: Opportunities and challenges for environmental, economic, and social sustainability in urban futures. *Smart Cities* **2022**, *5*, 771–801. [CrossRef]
281. Cai, Y.; Llorca, J.; Tulino, A.M.; Molisch, A.F. Compute-and data-intensive networks: The key to the metaverse. In Proceedings of the 2022 1st International Conference on 6G Networking (6GNet), Paris, France, 6–8 July 2022; pp. 1–8.
282. Paul, S.G.; Saha, A.; Arefin, M.S.; Bhuiyan, T.; Biswas, A.A.; Reza, A.W.; Alotaibi, N.M.; Alyami, S.A.; Moni, M.A. A comprehensive review of green computing: Past, present, and future research. *IEEE Access* **2023**, *11*, 87445–87494. [CrossRef]
283. Yang, S. Storytelling and user experience in the cultural metaverse. *Heliyon* **2023**, *9*, e14759. [CrossRef]
284. Omar, K.; Fakhouri, H.; Zraqou, J.; Marx Gómez, J. Usability Heuristics for Metaverse. *Computers* **2024**, *13*, 222. [CrossRef]
285. Winter, M.; Jackson, P.; Fallahkhair, S. Gesture Me: A Machine Learning Tool for Designers to Train Gesture Classifiers. In Proceedings of the International Conference on Computer-Human Interaction Research and Applications, Rome, Italy, 16–17 November 2023; pp. 336–352.
286. Chamusca, I.L.; Ferreira, C.V.; Murari, T.B.; Apolinario, A.L., Jr.; Winkler, I. Towards sustainable virtual reality: Gathering design guidelines for intuitive authoring tools. *Sustainability* **2023**, *15*, 2924. [CrossRef]
287. Ramaseri Chandra, A.N.; El Jamiy, F.; Reza, H. A systematic survey on cybersickness in virtual environments. *Computers* **2022**, *11*, 51. [CrossRef]
288. Christopoulos, A.; Mystakidis, S.; Pellas, N.; Laakso, M.J. ARLEAN: An augmented reality learning analytics ethical framework. *Computers* **2021**, *10*, 92. [CrossRef]

289. Dwivedi, Y.K.; Kshetri, N.; Hughes, L.; Rana, N.P.; Baabdullah, A.M.; Kar, A.K.; Koohang, A.; Ribeiro-Navarrete, S.; Belei, N.; Balakrishnan, J.; et al. Exploring the darkverse: A multi-perspective analysis of the negative societal impacts of the metaverse. *Inf. Syst. Front.* **2023**, *25*, 2071–2114. [CrossRef]
290. Slater, M.; Gonzalez-Liencres, C.; Haggard, P.; Vinkers, C.; Gregory-Clarke, R.; Jelley, S.; Watson, Z.; Breen, G.; Schwarz, R.; Steptoe, W.; et al. The ethics of realism in virtual and augmented reality. *Front. Virtual Real.* **2020**, *1*, 512449. [CrossRef]
291. Lu, Z.; Yu, M.; Jiang, G.; Chi, B.; Dong, Q. Prediction of motion sickness degree of stereoscopic panoramic videos based on content perception and binocular characteristics. *Digit. Signal Process.* **2023**, *132*, 103787. [CrossRef]
292. Guo, C.; Blair, G.J.; Sehgal, M.; Sangiuliano Jimka, F.N.; Bellafard, A.; Silva, A.J.; Golshani, P.; Basso, M.A.; Blair, H.T.; Aharoni, D. Miniscope-LFOV: A large-field-of-view, single-cell-resolution, miniature microscope for wired and wire-free imaging of neural dynamics in freely behaving animals. *Sci. Adv.* **2023**, *9*, eadg3918. [CrossRef]
293. Kim, A. Exploring the Relationship among Cybersickness, Locomotion Method, and Heart Rate Variability when Navigating a Virtual Environment. In Proceedings of the 2024 IEEE International Conference on Artificial Intelligence and eXtended and Virtual Reality (AIxVR), Los Angeles, CA, USA, 17–19 January 2024; pp. 215–220.
294. Radanliev, P.; De Roure, D.; Novitzky, P.; Sluganovic, I. Accessibility and inclusiveness of new information and communication technologies for disabled users and content creators in the Metaverse. *Disabil. Rehabil. Assist. Technol.* **2023**, *19*, 1849–1863. [CrossRef]
295. Henni, S.H.; Maurud, S.; Fuglerud, K.S.; Moen, A. The experiences, needs and barriers of people with impairments related to usability and accessibility of digital health solutions, levels of involvement in the design process and strategies for participatory and universal design: A scoping review. *BMC Public Health* **2022**, *22*, 35. [CrossRef]
296. Inbavalli, A.; Sakthidhasan, K.; Krishna, G. Image Generation Using AI with Effective Audio Playback System. In Proceedings of the 2024 5th International Conference for Emerging Technology (INCET), Belgaum, India, 24–26 May 2024; pp. 1–13.
297. Pari, S.N.; Ahamed, M.J.S.; Magarika, M.; Latchiyanathan, K. SLatAR-A Sign Language Translating Augmented Reality Application. In Proceedings of the 2023 12th International Conference on Advanced Computing (ICoAC), Chennai, India, 17–19 August 2023; pp. 1–8.
298. Jones, D.; Ghasemi, S.; Gračanin, D.; Azab, M. Privacy, safety, and security in extended reality: User experience challenges for neurodiverse users. In Proceedings of the International Conference on Human-Computer Interaction, Copenhagen, Denmark, 23–28 July 2023; pp. 511–528.
299. Cruz, M.; Oliveira, A. Unravelling Virtual Realities—Gamers' Perceptions of the Metaverse. *Electronics* **2024**, *13*, 2491. [CrossRef]
300. Khan, R.H.; Miah, J.; Syeed, M.M.; Uddin, M.F. Metaverse ecosystem realization for its application development. In Proceedings of the 2024 16th International Conference on Computer and Automation Engineering (ICCAE), Melbourne, Australia, 14–16 March 2024; pp. 109–113.
301. Yasuda, A. Metaverse ethics: Exploring the social implications of the metaverse. *AI Ethics* **2024**, 1–12. [CrossRef]
302. Kang, G.; Koo, J.; Kim, Y.G. Security and privacy requirements for the metaverse: A metaverse applications perspective. *IEEE Commun. Mag.* **2023**, *62*, 148–154. [CrossRef]
303. Chen, Z.; Wu, J.; Gan, W.; Qi, Z. Metaverse security and privacy: An overview. In Proceedings of the 2022 IEEE International Conference on Big Data (Big Data), Osaka, Japan, 17–20 December 2022; pp. 2950–2959.
304. Le-Khac, N.A.; Choo, K.K.R. *A Practical Hands-On Approach to Database Forensics*; Springer: Berlin/Heidelberg, Germany, 2022.
305. Mostafa, A.M.; Ezz, M.; Elbashir, M.K.; Alruily, M.; Hamouda, E.; Alsarhani, M.; Said, W. Strengthening cloud security: An innovative multi-factor multi-layer authentication framework for cloud user authentication. *Appl. Sci.* **2023**, *13*, 10871. [CrossRef]
306. Singh, M. Securing Data in the Metaverse: What We Need to Know. In *Metaverse: Technologies, Opportunities and Threats*; Springer: Berlin/Heidelberg, Germany, 2023; pp. 419–432.
307. Canbay, Y.; Utku, A.; Canbay, P. Privacy concerns and measures in metaverse: A review. In Proceedings of the 2022 15th International Conference on Information Security and Cryptography (ISCTURKEY), Ankara, Turkey, 19–20 October 2022; pp. 80–85.
308. Azam, F.; Semwal, A.; Biradar, A. A Secured Framework for Metaverse Applications. In Proceedings of the 2023 4th IEEE Global Conference for Advancement in Technology (GCAT), Bangalore, India, 6–8 October 2023; pp. 1–6.
309. Huang, Y.; Li, Y.J.; Cai, Z. Security and privacy in metaverse: A comprehensive survey. *Big Data Min. Anal.* **2023**, *6*, 234–247. [CrossRef]
310. Basyoni, L.; Tabassum, A.; Shaban, K.; Elmahjub, E.; Halabi, O.; Qadir, J. Navigating Privacy Challenges in the Metaverse: A Comprehensive Examination of Current Technologies and Platforms. *IEEE Internet Things Mag.* **2024**, *7*, 144–152. [CrossRef]
311. Parlar, T. Data privacy and security in the metaverse. In *Metaverse: Technologies, Opportunities and Threats*; Springer: Berlin/Heidelberg, Germany, 2023; pp. 123–133.

future internet

MDPI

Review

Intelligent Virtual Reality and Augmented Reality Technologies: An Overview

Georgios Lampropoulos [1,2]

[1] Department of Applied Informatics, School of Information Sciences, University of Macedonia, 54636 Thessaloniki, Greece; glampropoulos@uom.edu.gr

[2] Department of Education, School of Education, University of Nicosia, Nicosia 2417, Cyprus

Abstract: The research into artificial intelligence (AI), the metaverse, and extended reality (XR) technologies, such as augmented reality (AR), virtual reality (VR), and mixed reality (MR), has been expanding over the recent years. This study aims to provide an overview regarding the combination of AI with XR technologies and the metaverse through the examination of 880 articles using different approaches. The field has experienced a 91.29% increase in its annual growth rate, and although it is still in its infancy, the outcomes of this study highlight the potential of these technologies to be effectively combined and applied in various domains transforming and enriching them. Through content analysis and topic modeling, the main topics and areas in which this combination is mostly being researched and applied are as follows: (1) "Education/Learning/Training", (2) "Healthcare and Medicine", (3) "Generative artificial intelligence/Large language models", (4) "Virtual worlds/Virtual avatars/Virtual assistants", (5) "Human-computer interaction", (6) "Machine learning/Deep learning/Neural networks", (7) "Communication networks", (8) "Industry", (9) "Manufacturing", (10) "E-commerce", (11) "Entertainment", (12) "Smart cities", and (13) "New technologies" (e.g., digital twins, blockchain, internet of things, etc.). The study explores the documents through various dimensions and concludes by presenting the existing limitations, identifying key challenges, and providing suggestions for future research.

Keywords: artificial intelligence; AI; virtual reality; augmented reality; extended reality; mixed reality; metaverse; review; bibliometric analysis; topic modeling; scientific mapping

1. Introduction

Artificial intelligence (AI) is rapidly advancing as a field of study and due to its wide applicability and potentials, it is rapidly being integrated into different domains. AI refers to smart systems that simulate human intelligence and mimic the way they think, communicate, and act [1–3] as the development of these systems is driven by the human nervous system and humans' innate ability to learn, adapt, and reason [4–6]. Through the use of AI, intelligent systems [7–9], virtual agents and assistants [10–12], and multi-agent systems [13–15] can be created. Recent literature review studies have explored its use in various domains, such as education [16–18], industry [19–21], healthcare [22–24], business [25–27], smart cities [28–30], etc. The outcomes of these studies highlight the potential of AI to transform and enrich various sectors, which, in turn, reveals the need to further explore its capabilities to be used in combination with other novel technologies to further amplify its impact.

Immersive technologies can be greatly influenced and improved through the integration of AI. Recent studies have highlighted the benefits that this combination can potentially yield [10,11,31,32]. Specifically, emphasis is being placed on the use of AI within augmented reality (AR), virtual reality (VR), and mixed reality (MR) environments. AR focuses on embedding interactive digital information and content in users' physical environment [33,34] and is closer to the real world in the "reality-virtuality continuum" [35] while VR focuses on virtual environments that fully engulf and immerse users [36–38], thus separating them from the real environment and, as a result, it is closer to the virtual environment in the continuum. Additionally, the metaverse, which is characterized by its realistic virtual experiences and environments that constitute an extension of the real environment [39–41], is closely related to XR technologies and the creation of virtual worlds and environments with high levels of embodiment, interactivity, and persistence [42,43]. As these technologies create new ways for users to interact, communicate, and experience events, they are increasingly being used in various settings and domains including education [44–47], industry [48–50], healthcare [51–53], business [54–56], smart cities [57–59]. The studies highlighted the role of VR and AR in each domain and the benefits they can yield. The domains, although indicative, were selected to highlight the similarities in terms of application domains among AI, AR, and VR.

The outcomes of the recent studies have revealed the positive impact that they can have in different domains. Hence, studies have also started to examine their combined use. However, although these technologies constitute established fields of studies on their own, their inter-relationship has yet to be examined in detail. As a result, there has not been any study that has examined the current state of the art regarding the use of AI within VR and AR environments and the metaverse. Examining the use of AI within extended reality (XR) environments can bring about new use cases as well as new opportunities. Additionally, by integrating AI, user-tracking, monitoring, and data processing can be improved and content and activities recommendation can be enhanced. Through this approach, more adaptive and personalized experiences, unique to each individual, can be created within immersive and interactive environments. Hence, it is vital to examine the convergence of these technologies. As this field of study is advancing, it is important to have a representation and mapping of the existing literature to identify emerging thematic areas and topics, limitations and challenges, and future research areas. Therefore, to bridge this gap, the aim of this study is to provide an overview and mapping of the existing literature about the convergence of AI with VR and AR technologies as well as to reveal future research directions. The main contributions of this study are the in-depth analysis of the document characteristics, the definition of the more advanced research domains and of the emerging ones, the identification of the most widely explored topics, themes, and trends, and the provision of future research areas while considering the challenges presented in the literature. To provide a thorough, valid, and reproducible analysis, the study follows the Preferred Reporting Items for Systematic reviews and Meta-Analyses (PRISMA) [60] framework to report the document identification, processing, and selection and utilized widely accepted tools and approaches, such as Bibliometrix [61], VOSviewer [62], and topic modeling through Latent Dirichlet Allocation (LDA) [63]. The study structure is as follows: the main methods and materials used are presented in Section 2. The analysis of the document collection is presented in Section 3 and in Section 4, the findings are further discussed and summarized. In Section 5, the conclusions of this study are presented, the implications are highlighted, the limitations are detailed, and future research directions are suggested.

2. Materials and Methods

As the study strives to explore the use of AI and XR technologies from a general perspective without being limited to a specific domain, a bibliometric analysis, scientific mapping, and content analysis approach was followed to present the state of the art. This approach is deemed suitable to examine similar topics with broad reach [64]. Moreover, to ensure an accurate, valid, and reproducible analysis of the literature, the study followed the PRISMA statement [60] as well as clearly defined guidelines presented in the literature [61,65].

Furthermore, the study used different approaches and tools to analyze the related studies. Specifically, the open-source tool Bibliometrix along with the related method defined by Aria and Cuccurullo [61] were used to carry out the bibliometric and scientific mapping of the literature. To further examine the related documents and their networks, VOSviewer was also used [62]. To identify the most prominent topics discussed within the document, topic modeling through the use of LDA [63] was conducted. The tools used are being widely adopted by similar studies which highlights their suitability and effectiveness. Additionally, the use of different tools and approaches enabled a more thorough representation of the state of the art.

2.1. Systematic Literature Review Process

Taking the findings of recent studies [66,67] into account, Scopus and Web of Science were selected as the main data sources to identify studies relevant to the topic due to their being highly regarded, containing impactful documents, and being used in other literature review and bibliometric analysis studies. Another reason for the selection of these databases was the ability to use the extracted information with the aforementioned tools [61,62].

Moreover, different combinations of keywords were tested to ensure that the most relevant documents were identified. The final query defined and used was the following: ("augmented reality" OR "AR" OR "virtual reality" OR "VR" OR "mixed reality" OR "MR" OR "extended reality" OR "XR" OR "metaverse") AND ("artificial intelligence" or "AI"). It should be noted that although the abbreviations might identify some documents that are not relevant (e.g., MR can also be magnetic resonance, etc.), it was deemed appropriate for them to be used to avoid missing any potentially relevant documents. As a result, during the initial screening process, several documents were deemed to be out of scope. Additionally, as the aim of this study was to provide an overview of the topic, specialized keywords that could restrict the search to specific domains or provide explicit directions were not used. In this sense, the document collection would contain a larger number of documents but would also sufficiently provide a general representation of the current literature.

The final search for relevant documents using the aforementioned query was conducted on Scopus and Web of Science in December 2024 to identify suitable studies based on their title and abstract. In this study, only documents written in English were included. Additionally, to ensure that the most up-to-date research is being reported, the analysis involves studies that were published in the last decade, that is, 2015–2024. Following the guidelines specified within the PRISMA framework, the steps taken to search, identify, and process the related documents are presented in Figure 1.

Initially, the document collection comprised 12,281 documents with 7983 documents retrieved through Scopus and 4298 retrieved through Web of Science. The documents were then examined to identify duplicate documents using automatic and manual approaches. In total, 3533 duplicate documents were identified and removed from the document collection. As a result, the document collection consisted of 8748 documents before the initial screening which was on the existence of keywords within the title and abstract of the documents. Additionally, in order for a study to be included in the analysis, the inclusion criterion that had to be met was for it to directly focus on AI and VR and/or AR or on their combination from a theoretical or experimental perspective. Hence, studies that focused on one of these technologies or simply mentioned these terms but did not focus on their use or combination were excluded. From this process, a total of 7651 documents were removed. The remaining 1097 documents were manually examined to determine their suitability. Specifically, 65 documents were removed as they were outside the scope of this study, 41 documents were removed since they were letters, notes, and abstracts only, 38 because they were editorials, 28 because they were proceedings, 27 because they were retracted documents, 10 because they were books, 5 because they were book reviews, and finally, 3 documents were removed because they were erratum/corrections. Consequently, a total of 880 documents were included and analyzed in this study.

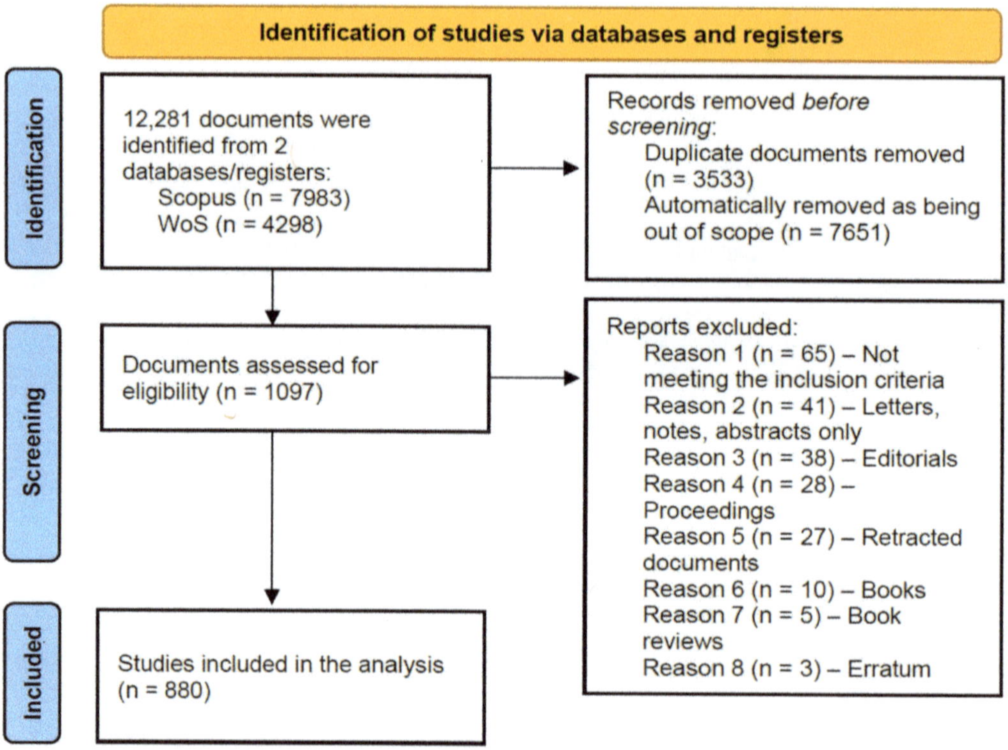

Figure 1. PRISMA flowchart.

3. Result Analysis

Various dimensions of the document collection were analyzed to map the state of the art regarding the combination of AI with AR and VR technologies in education. Initially, the details of the document collection are presented. The publication frequency and the annual citation distribution are presented. The study also looks into the authors' affiliation and countries and focuses on identifying the collaboration among the different countries. The relevant documents that have received the largest number of citations were also identified. Using keywords plus and author keywords, the trends of the topic, its thematic map, and its thematic evolution were also examined. To identify more topics, the documents were clustered using both Bibliometrix and VOSviewer to carry out a keyword-based co-occurrence analysis. To further examine the topics, LDA [63] was used to carry out a topic modeling analysis of the document collection regarding the use of AI and XR technologies in education. The related outcomes of the LDA topic modeling are presented and discussed in the discussion section.

3.1. Analysis of the Document Collection

Following the aforementioned methodology and process, a document collection comprising 880 documents was created. Table 1 presents the main information of the document collection as well as details regarding the document types, authors, the authors collaboration, and the document contents. Specifically, the documents were published in 622 different sources from 2015 to 2024 with most documents being conference/proceedings papers (n = 397, 45.1%), followed by journal articles (n = 322, 36.6%). In total, 112 documents (12.7%) were published as book chapters within edited book collections and 49 documents (5.6%) were classified as review studies. The novelty and significance of the topic is highlighted by the extremely high annual growth rate of 91.28% in scientific production. The average document age was 1.36 years and each document received 6.67 citations on average. Moreover, a total of 2938 authors from 71 countries were involved in the publication of the related documents. Out of the 880 documents, 127 were single-authored documents (14.4) written by 119 different authors and the remaining documents had 4.1 co-authors on average. The international co-authorship rate was 15.0% which showcased the global interest in this emerging field of study and the fact that collaborations among researchers and institutions on a global scale have already started being established despite the recency of the topic.

Table 1. Document collection details.

Description	Results	Description	Results
Main information about data		**Document types**	
Timespan	2015:2024	Journal article	322
Sources (Journals, Books, etc.)	622	Book chapter	112
Documents	880	Conference/Proceedings paper	397
Annual Growth Rate %	91.29	Review	49
Document Average Age	1.36	**Authors**	
Average Citations per Document	6.674	Authors	2938
References	20,100	Authors of single-authored documents	119
Document contents		**Authors collaboration**	
Keywords Plus (ID)	2868	Single-authored documents	127
Author's Keywords (DE)	2202	Co-authors per document	4.1
		International co-authorships %	15

3.2. Growth Trends in Publications and Citations

Figure 2 illustrates the sharp increase in publications from 2022 onwards, reflecting the rapid growth of interest in the field. Specifically, most documents were published in 2024 (n = 343, 39.0%), in 2023 (n = 246, 28.0%), and in 2022 (n = 119, 13.5%). Additionally, three main time periods can be observed: (1st) Initial conceptualization years: 2015–2018 in which 25 documents (2.8%) were published; (2nd) Materialization years: 2019–2021 in which 147 documents (16.7%) were published; and (3rd) Breakthrough years: 2022–2024 in which 708 documents (80.5%) were published. The outcomes are representative of the advancements in the respective fields that took place in recent years and the increasing interest in these fields. In addition to the annual number of published documents, the citable years and the mean total citations received per year were also explored. The related data is presented in Table 2.

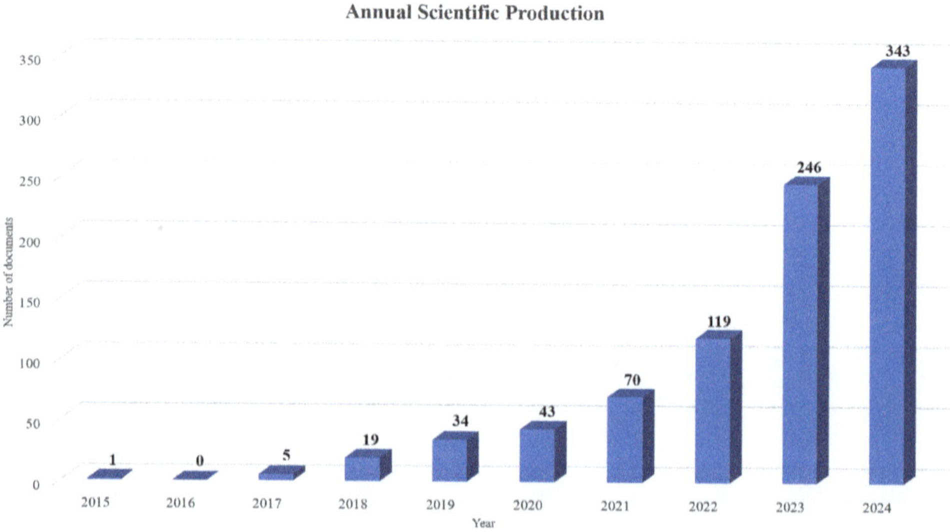

Figure 2. Annual total number of published documents.

Table 2. Annual scientific production and citations.

Year	MeanTCperDoc	Number of Published Documents	MeanTCperYear	CitableYears
2015	6	1	0.6	10
2017	2.4	5	0.3	8
2018	8.68	19	1.24	7
2019	18.65	34	3.11	6
2020	7.86	43	1.57	5
2021	16.24	70	4.06	4
2022	16.55	119	5.52	3
2023	5.28	246	2.64	2
2024	0.91	343	0.91	1

The outcomes are in line with the advancements in the respective fields in recent years. When considering the applicability of these technologies and their potential to enrich and transform the educational process, the interest in the topic is expected to continue increasing. Moreover, the citations that the documents published in each year received were also explored as can be seen in Table 2, which depicts the year, the mean total citations per document (MeanTCperDoc), the number of published documents, the mean total citations per year (MeanTCperYear), and the citable years (CitableYears). Based on the outcomes, documents from 2022 had the highest average citations per year (MeanTCperYear = 5.52), reflecting their impact despite being recent. Additionally, documents published in 2021 (MeanTCperYear = 4.06) and in 2019 (MeanTCperYear = 3.11) also presented high mean total citations per year. Nonetheless, given the increasing interest in the field, the average document age (1.36 years), and the citable years of the documents, it is expected that these outcomes will change in the future. This outcome is further validated when considering the number of documents published in 2023 and 2024, their citable years, 2 and 1 years, respectively, and their existing mean total citations per year.

3.3. Sources Analysis

To identify the most frequently used outlets and their type (e.g., journal, edited book, conference/proceedings), the total number of documents published in each outlet was considered. Most of the 880 documents were published within conferences and proceedings, followed by journals, and edited books. However, to better comprehend their relevancy, Bradford's law was applied which, in turn, resulted in the creation of three clusters with the sources in Cluster 1 being the most relevant ones. Specifically, Cluster 1 consisted of 67 sources (10.8%) in which 291 documents (33.0%) were published, Cluster 2 had 265 sources (42.6%) in which 299 documents (34.0%) were published, and Cluster 3 had 290 sources in which 290 documents (33.0%) were published.

Table 3 presents the top 10 sources of Cluster 1, based on Bradford's law ranking. The top five sources in which most documents were published were as follows: "Lecture Notes in Computer Science (including subseries Lecture Notes in Artificial Intelligence and Lecture Notes in Bioinformatics)", "Springer Series on Cultural Computing", "ACM International Conference Proceeding Series (ICPS)", "Applied Sciences", and "IEEE International Conference on Artificial Intelligence and Virtual Reality (AIVR)". It is worth noting that 3 sources had published 6 documents each, 5 sources had 5 documents each, 11 sources had 4 documents each, and 17 sources had 3 documents each. Additionally, when looking at the h-index of the sources based on the documents contained within the collection, the top four sources were as follows: "Applied Sciences", "IEEE International Conference on Artificial Intelligence and Virtual Reality (AIVR)", "Journal of Physics: Conference Series", and "Lecture Notes in Computer Science (including subseries Lecture Notes in Artificial Intelligence and Lecture Notes in Bioinformatics)" (Table 4). The mixture of journals, proceedings, and edited collections among the top sources in both cases highlights the interdisciplinarity of the field and it being actively researched.

Table 3. Top sources of cluster 1 based on Bradford's law.

Source	Rank	Freq	cumFreq	Cluster
Lecture Notes in Computer Science (including subseries Lecture Notes in Artificial Intelligence and Lecture Notes in Bioinformatics)	1	19	19	1
Springer Series on Cultural Computing	2	15	34	1
ACM International Conference Proceeding Series (ICPS)	3	13	47	1
Applied Sciences	4	13	60	1
IEEE International Conference on Artificial Intelligence and Virtual Reality (AIVR)	5	10	70	1
IEEE Access	6	9	79	1
IEEE Conference on Virtual Reality and 3D User Interfaces Abstracts and Workshops (VRW)	7	8	87	1
Analysis and Metaphysics	8	8	95	1
Applied Mathematics and Nonlinear Sciences	9	8	103	1
CEUR Workshop Proceedings	10	8	111	1

Table 4. Most impactful sources based on h-index.

Sources	h-Index	g-Index	m-Index	TC	NP	PY_Start
Applied Sciences	5	10	1.25	104	13	2021
IEEE International Conference on Artificial Intelligence and Virtual Reality (AIVR)	5	7	0.714	50	10	2018
Journal of Physics: Conference Series	4	4	0.8	23	6	2020
Lecture Notes in Computer Science (including subseries Lecture Notes in Artificial Intelligence and Lecture Notes in Bioinformatics)	4	6	0.8	49	19	2020

3.4. Authorship Patterns

Furthermore, the distribution of authors based on the number of documents to which they contributed was examined through the use of Lotka's law. The related outcomes are presented in Table 5 and are visualized in Figure 3. Specifically, 77.9% of the authors ($n = 2502$) contributed to one document while 11.5% ($n = 309$) contributed to two documents. Additionally, it can be observed that there are researchers who actively research this field of study that have contributed to five or more related documents over the period of 2015–2024.

Table 5. Distribution of authors based on the number of documents written.

Documents Written	N. of Authors	Proportion of Authors	Documents Written	N. of Authors	Proportion of Authors
1	2502	0.779	6	7	0.002
2	309	0.115	7	5	0.002
3	75	0.05	8	1	0.0
4	27	0.018	9	2	0.0
5	10	0.013			

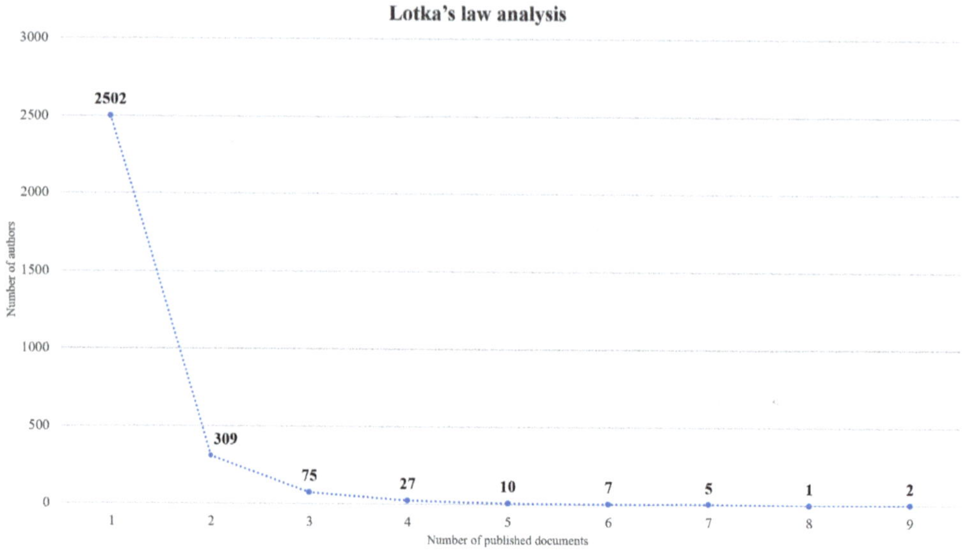

Figure 3. Lotka's law analysis.

3.5. Author's Countries and Affiliations Analysis

When considering the global interest in the topic and the international collaborations that materialized, it was deemed appropriate to examine the country whose authors most actively explore this field of study. The corresponding author's or the first author's (in case there was no corresponding author) country was considered to identify the countries whose authors have contributed to the most documents. In total, authors from 71 countries contributed to the creation and publication of the 880 documents. The related outcomes are presented in Table 6. It should be noted that SCP refers to the intra-country collaborations while MCP refers to inter-country collaborations. Based on the outcomes, China (n = 176), the United States (n = 132), India (n = 98), Italy (n = 46), and the United Kingdom (n = 34) were the top five countries based on their scientific production. China and the United States had the highest SCP among the 71 countries while the MCP value was the highest in the case of China (n = 24), followed by Singapore (n = 11). Nonetheless, the presence of countries from different continents further highlights the importance of the topic.

Table 6. Country document publication details.

Country	Documents	SCP	MCP	Freq.	MCP_Ratio
China	176	152	24	0.2	0.136
United States	132	125	7	0.15	0.053
India	98	92	6	0.111	0.061
Italy	46	41	5	0.052	0.109
United Kingdom	34	28	6	0.039	0.176
South Korea	30	24	6	0.034	0.2
Australia	26	20	6	0.03	0.231
Canada	25	19	6	0.028	0.24
Germany	24	22	2	0.027	0.083
Spain	18	15	3	0.02	0.167

Besides the number of documents published, the citations received were also explored to better understand the impact of the published work. As it can be seen in Table 7, the United States has received the most citations (n = 1335) having received on average 10.1 citations per document, followed by China with 1209 total citations and 6.9 citations on average per document. It should be noted that among the countries with the most total citations, when considering the average document citations, Vietnam (82), Singapore (34.8), and France (21.2) had the highest number. However, to better assess the outcomes the overall number of documents published from each country should also be considered. For example, Vietnam had published 2 documents, while Singapore had 16 and France 6. Hence, it can be concluded that overall, the documents published by Singapore have been the most impactful ones when considering only the average citations received per document.

Furthermore, the country collaborations were also explored. In total, six clusters arose that reveal the joint efforts toward further advancing the field. It is particularly important to note that, in many cases, collaborations between authors from different continents materialized. The related outcomes are presented in the collaboration network (Figure 4) and in the collaboration map (Figure 5). Additionally, as it can be observed, China and the United States have more actively engaged in establishing international collaborations.

Table 7. Countries that received the most citations.

Country	TC	Average Document Citations
United States	1335	10.1
China	1209	6.9
Singapore	557	34.8
South Korea	294	9.8
Italy	258	5.6
Canada	255	10.2
India	243	2.5
Vietnam	164	82
Australia	162	6.2
France	127	21.2

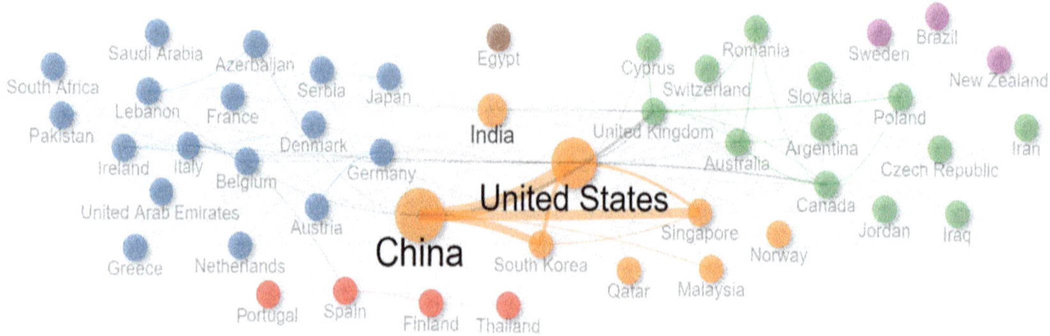

Figure 4. Country collaboration network.

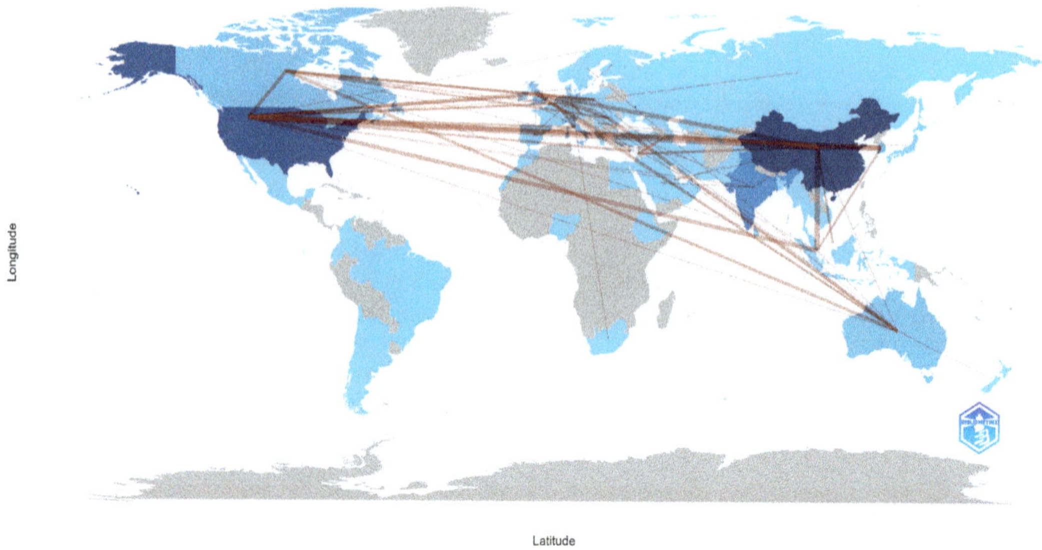

Figure 5. Country collaboration map.

Moreover, the authors' affiliation was also examined. Particularly, the information of all authors whose affiliation details were retrieved from the databases and who contributed to a document was considered. Therefore, the total number of documents published by authors from a specific country may be smaller than the sum of contributions from various affiliations within that same country. Table 8 presented the top affiliations based on the number of documents they have published. "National University of Singapore", Singapore (n = 30), "Nanyang Technological University", Singapore (n = 18), "City University of Hong Kong", Hong Kong (n = 16), "Harvard Medical School", United States (n = 15), and "Sungkyunkwan University", South Korea (n = 14) arose as the top five affiliations.

Table 8. Most relevant affiliations based on the number of documents published.

Country	Affiliation	Number of Articles	Percentage of Documents in the Collection
Singapore	National University of Singapore	30	3.4
Singapore	Nanyang Technological University	18	1.8
Hong Kong	City University of Hong Kong	16	1.7
United States	Harvard Medical School	15	1.6
South Korea	Sungkyunkwan University	14	1.5
Canada	McGill University	13	1.5
Italy	Università Politecnica delle Marche	13	1.5
Slovakia	University of Žilina	13	1.5
United States	University of Central Florida	13	1.4
United States	Carnegie Mellon University	12	1.4
Hong Kong	Chinese University of Hong Kong	12	2.0

3.6. Thematic and Topic Analysis

Focusing on the keywords, the documents were further examined. Both keywords plus (indexed keywords) and author's keywords were used since they both can effectively represent the knowledge structure of the document collection [68]. Specifically, the keywords were used to explore the co-occurrence network, the trend topics, the thematic map, and the thematic evolution of the topic. To aid in the creation of the related networks, both Bibliometrix and VOSviewer were used.

Initially, the frequency of the keywords used in the documents was examined. In addition, the frequency of the topic keywords and the most commonly used relevant keywords were also identified. Specifically, Table 9 presents the related outcomes for the keywords plus (indexed keywords) while Table 10 depicts the related data for the author's keywords. "E-learning", "machine learning", "deep learning", "immersive", "students", "human-computer interaction", "learning systems", "engineering education", "blockchain", and "education" were the most common keywords plus (indexed keywords) while "machine learning", "generative artificial intelligence", "deep learning", "education", "blockchain", "human-computer interaction", "digital twin", "internet of things", "computer vision", "explainable artificial intelligence", and "simulations" were the most frequently used author's keywords. Based on the keywords identified, it can be inferred that the role of AI within XR environments is mostly focused on the educational domain. Additionally, its close relationship with machine learning and deep learning is observed. The convergence of AI with AR and VR is also examined within the context of virtual environments, the metaverse, and digital twins. Emphasis is also placed on key technologies such as blockchain, generative AI, and explainable AI. Finally, due to their immersive and interactive nature and human-centric design, increased focus is placed on the field of human-computer interaction. It should be noted that in both cases, it is revealed that VR is more frequently examined when compared to AR, the metaverse, and MR.

Table 9. Most frequently used keywords plus (indexed keywords).

Topic Keywords		Relevant Keywords	
Words	**Occurrences**	**Words**	**Occurrences**
"virtual reality"	225	"e-learning"	53
"artificial intelligence"	182	"machine learning"	44
"augmented reality"	154	"deep learning"	37
"metaverse"	57	"immersive"	37
"mixed reality"	31	"students"	31
"extended reality"	20	"human-computer interaction"	23
		"learning systems"	23
		"engineering education"	21
		"blockchain"	19
		"education"	18

Table 10. Most frequently used author's keywords.

Topic Keywords		Relevant Keywords	
Words	**Occurrences**	**Words**	**Occurrences**
"artificial intelligence"	410	"machine learning"	65
"virtual reality"	276	"generative artificial intelligence"	46
"augmented reality"	211	"deep learning"	37
"metaverse"	144	"education"	31
"extended reality"	75	"blockchain"	27
"mixed reality"	43	"human-computer interaction"	23
		"digital twin"	22
		"internet of things"	20
		"computer vision"	18
		"explainable artificial intelligence"	16
		"simulations"	16

To better comprehend the relationships among the keywords, keyword co-occurrence networks were created using Bibliometrix and VOSviewer. The related networks are displayed in Figure 6 (Bibliometrix) and in Figure 7 (VOSviewer). It should be noted that to create the Bibliometrix-based network, keywords plus were used, as the outcomes were more representative, and to create the VOSViewer-based network, both keywords plus (indexed keywords) and author's keywords were used to provide a more thorough representation. Additionally, the total link strength of the VOSviewer keyword co-occurrence network was also examined. The 15 keywords with the highest total link strength are presented in Table 11. "Artificial intelligence" (n = 457, total link strength = 1184), "virtual reality" (n = 338, total link strength = 951), "augmented reality" (n = 251, total link strength = 677), "metaverse" (n = 152, total link strength = 431), and "machine learning" (n = 77, total link strength = 268) were the top five keywords with the highest total link strength. It should be noted that in case a keyword existed in both keyword sets, it was counted only once to avoid any bias.

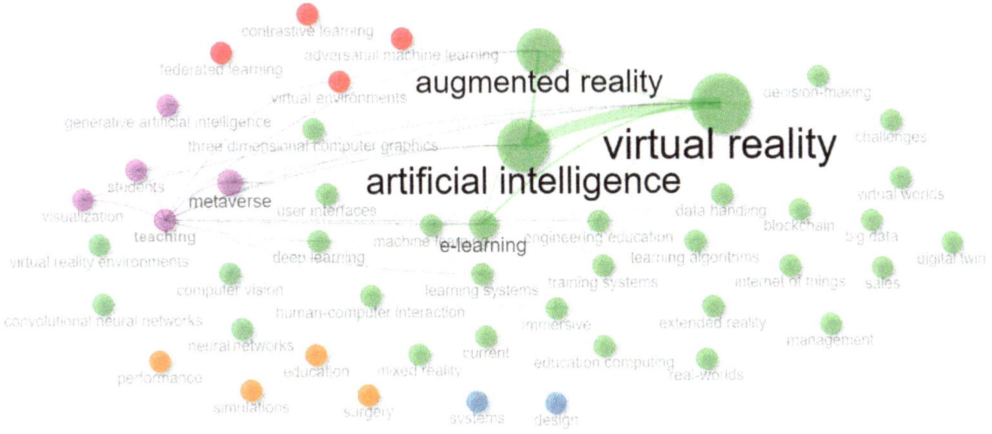

Figure 6. Keyword co-occurrence network—Bibliometrix.

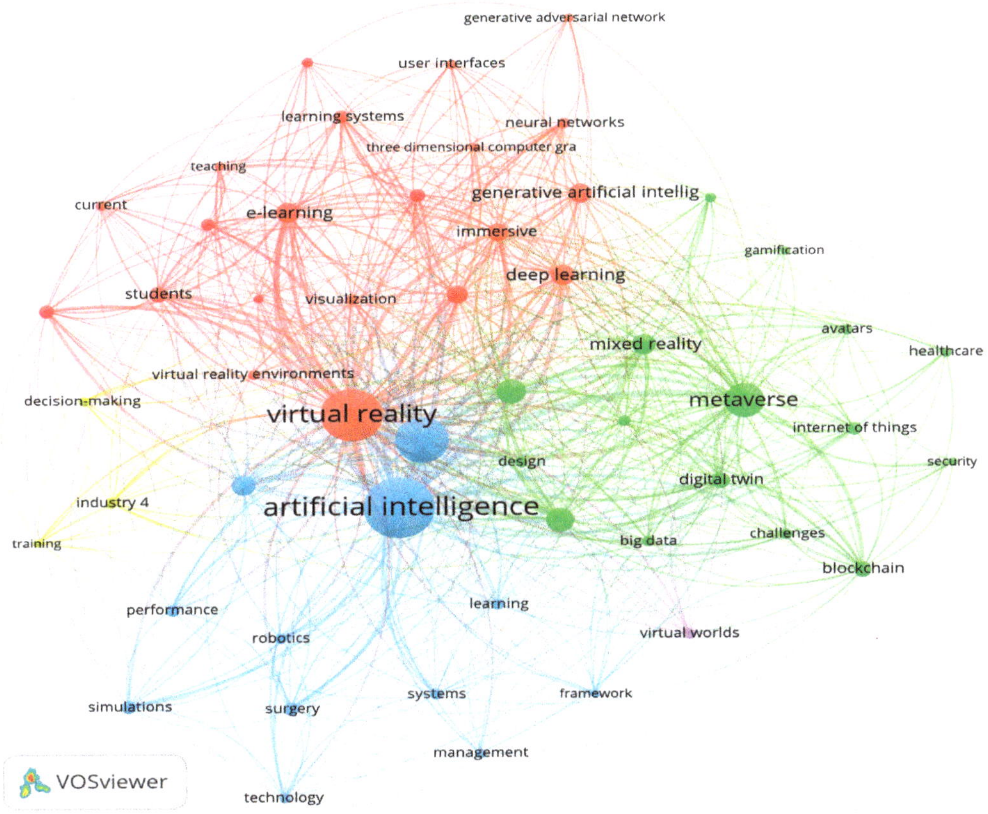

Figure 7. Keyword co-occurrence network—VOSviewer.

Table 11. Total link strength of the keyword co-occurrence network—VOSviewer.

Keywords	Occurrences	Total Link Strength	Keywords	Occurrences	Total Link Strength
"artificial intelligence"	457	1184	"deep learning"	51	188
"virtual reality"	338	951	"immersive"	43	177
"augmented reality"	251	677	"education"	51	173
"metaverse"	152	431	"digital twins"	31	142
"machine learning"	77	268	"human-computer interaction"	42	139
"extended reality"	75	243	"blockchain"	32	131
"e-learning"	52	223	"students"	32	129
"mixed reality"	51	204			

As it can be observed, a total of five clusters emerged in both networks. Table 12 summarizes the clusters and related keywords for the Bibliometrix-based network while Table 13 summarizes the clusters and related keywords for the VOSviewer-based network. The clusters that arose highlight the multidimensional role and wide applicability of combining AI with XR technologies.

Table 12. Analysis of the keyword co-occurrence network—Bibliometrix.

Cluster	Keywords
Green cluster (n = 33)	"virtual reality", "artificial intelligence", "augmented reality", "e-learning", "machine learning", "deep learning", "immersive", "mixed reality", "human-computer interaction", "learning systems", "engineering education", "extended reality", "blockchain", "challenges", "current", "user interfaces", "convolutional neural networks", "virtual reality environments", "management", "virtual worlds", "big data", "decision-making", "internet of things", "three dimensional computer graphics", "digital twin", "learning algorithms", "neural networks", "sales", "real-worlds", "training systems", "computer vision", "data handling", and "education computing"
Purple cluster (n = 5)	"metaverse", "students", "generative artificial intelligence", "visualization", and "teaching"
Orange cluster (n = 4)	"education", "performance", "surgery", and "simulations"
Read cluster (n = 4)	"virtual environments", "adversarial machine learning", "contrastive learning", and "federated learning"
Blue cluster (n = 2)	"systems" and "design"

Table 13. Analysis of the keyword co-occurrence network—VOSviewer.

Cluster	Keywords
Red cluster (n = 21)	"adversarial machine learning", "computer vision", "current", "deep learning", "e-learning", "engineering education", "generative adversarial network", "generative artificial intelligence", "human-computer interaction", "immersive", "immersive learning", "learning algorithms", "learning systems", "students", "teaching", "three dimensional computer graphics", "user interfaces", "virtual environments", "virtual reality", "virtual reality environments", and "visualization"
Green cluster (n = 16)	"avatars", "big data", "blockchain", "challenges", "design", "digital twin", "explainable artificial", "extended reality", "gamification", "healthcare", "immersive technologies", "internet of things", "machine learning", "metaverse", "mixed reality", and "security"
Blue cluster (n = 12)	"artificial intelligence", "augmented reality", "education", "framework", "learning", "management", "performance", "robotics", "simulations", "surgery", "systems", and "technology"
Yellow cluster (n = 3)	"decision-making", "industry 4", and "training"
Purple cluster (n = 1)	"virtual worlds"

Specifically, emphasis is being placed on the use of generative AI and the metaverse to aid teachers and learners as well as on the use of XR simulations to enrich medical and healthcare education. Additionally, there is a clear focus on the adoption and use of machine learning and deep learning methods. Education is revealed as one of the main domains in which their use is mostly examined due to their potential to offer immersive, personalized, and interactive learning experiences. Studies have also focused on adopting additional novel technologies and approaches including virtual agents and avatars, virtual worlds, big data, internet of things, generative AI, blockchain, etc. Particular emphasis is also placed on the design aspects of AI-enriched XR applications and on the importance of human-computer interaction is highlighted. Finally, their role in the industrial sector and security considerations are also increasingly being explored. The related outcomes are further discussed and analyzed in the discussion section.

Moreover, the keywords were used to examine the thematic evolution of the topic through the period of 2015–2024. Specifically, the following four time periods were specified: (i) 2015–2018, (ii) 2019–2020, (iii) 2021–2022, and (iv) 2023–2024. Given the limited number of documents published during 2015–2018, the specific time period was not divided any further. Based on the outcomes presented in Figure 8, the following themes arose: (i) "augmented reality" and "virtual reality" (2015–2018), (ii) "artificial intelligence", "design", "visualization", "learning systems", "robotics" (2019–2020), (iii) "virtual reality", "machine learning", "systems", "algorithm", "augmented reality", "simulation", "immersive", "impact", "internet of things", "model", "virtual worlds", "surgery", "real-world", "management", "object detection", "brain", and "avatar" (2021–2022), and (iv) "virtual reality", "surgery", "artificial intelligence", "impact", "education", "big data", "user interface", "recognition", "management", "e-commerce", "challenges", and "performance" (2023–2024). According to the thematic evolution of the topic, the gradual increase in the variety of topics explored can be observed. This fact highlights the wide applicability and potential of using AI within VR and AR environments across different domains and use cases. These outcomes become more evident when considering the trend topics that arose, which can be seen in Figure 9. Specifically, the initial emphasis on machine learning, deep learning, and neural networks has shifted toward a focus on the technologies of AR and VR. Once again, the ability of this combination to be integrated into various domains and transform them is observed with the focus being on education and training, Industry 4.0, and smart cities. However, over the last years (2022–2024), an increasing interest in exploring the field of AI and capitalizing on the use of generative AI within XR environments is observed. Finally, emphasis is also put on further exploring the adoption and use of the metaverse.

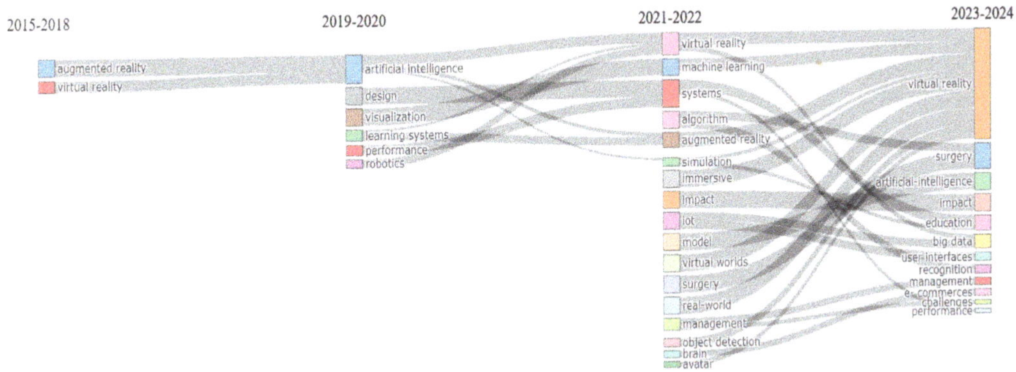

Figure 8. Thematic evolution of the topic.

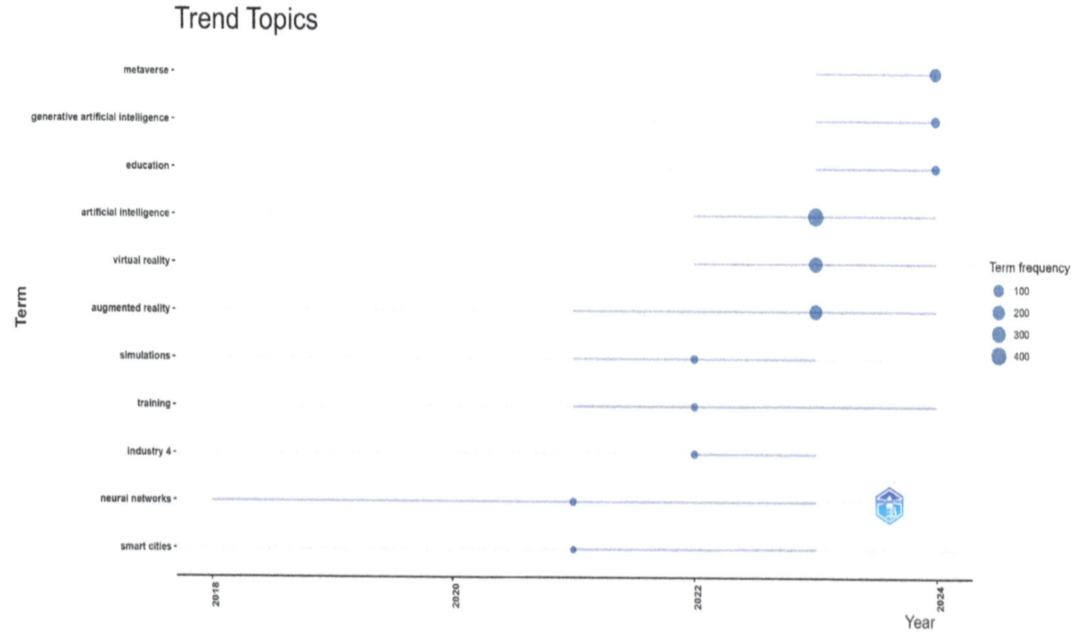

Figure 9. Trend topics based on keywords plus.

Finally, the keywords were used to examine the thematic map of the topic and cluster the documents to identify potential areas for future research. Specifically, the thematic map of the topic focuses on identifying the main themes presented within the document collection and divides the themes into Niche, Motor, Basic, and Emerging or Declining themes. Based on the data presented in Figure 10, the following five themes arose: (i) the Niche theme was related to "education" and "training", (ii) the Motor theme was related to the "metaverse", "digital twins", "blockchain", and "virtual avatars", (iii) the Basic themes were related to (a) "human-computer interaction" and (b) "artificial intelligence", "extended reality technologies" (AR, VR, and MR), "machine learning", and "deep learning", and (iv) the Emerging or Declining theme was related to "generative artificial intelligence". These outcomes are in line with the aforementioned results. When clustering the documents based on the keywords used, a total of five clusters emerged all with high impact and centrality. The first cluster was related to: "virtual environments" and "machine learning" approaches (e.g., adversarial machine learning, contrastive learning, federated learning, etc.). The second cluster was related to "augmented reality", "mixed reality", "deep learning", "machine learning", and "human-computer interaction". These outcomes further highlight the importance of machine learning and deep learning in the realization of AI within XR environments and in achieving high and effective human-computer interaction. The third cluster was associated with "augmented reality", "virtual reality", "mixed reality", "artificial intelligence", and "machine learning"; thus, highlighting their inter-relationship. The fourth cluster was related to "virtual reality", "metaverse", "artificial intelligence", "e-learning", and "students"; thus, highlighting the focus on the educational domain and the potential benefits that this combination can yield. The fifth cluster was related to the "metaverse", "machine learning", "blockchain", "non-fungible tokens", and "artificial general intelligence" which highlights the future trends in the field of virtual worlds and virtual communities.

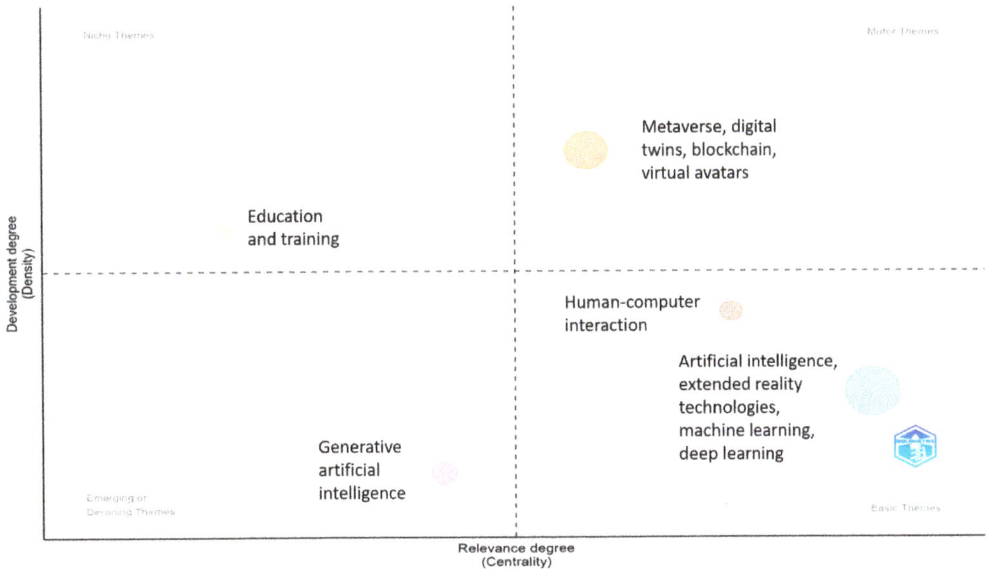

Figure 10. Thematic map of the topic.

4. Discussion

AI as well as VR and AR are increasingly being used in different sectors, yielding significant benefits and transforming them. XR technologies offer immersive, engaging, and interactive experiences [47,69,70]. However, these experiences should be carefully designed following appropriate guidelines and principles [71–76]. Studies have explored the use of AR and VR in different domains and use cases while reporting positive outcomes [77,78]. Simultaneously, AI is rapidly advancing and it is being integrated into various domains and aspects of everyday life [79,80]. Due to their nature and capabilities, these technologies can complement and enrich each other both in terms of functionality and capabilities [32].

This study focused on examining the existing literature to identify the role and integration of AI within VR and AR environments. Specifically, the study analyzed 880 documents relevant documents that were identified following the PRISMA guidelines. The related data was analyzed using content analysis, bibliometric analysis, and scientific mapping techniques. Additionally, the data is further explored through LDA as shown below. The documents had a significantly high annual growth rate (91.29%) and an average document age of 1.36 years highlighting the recency of the topic and the increased interest in further advancing this field of study. Additionally, the documents examined were written by 2938 authors and published in 622 different sources during the time period 2015–2024. Most documents were published as conference/proceedings papers, followed by journal articles. Additionally, the documents on average had 4.1 co-authors and an international co-authorship rate of 15.0%; thus, highlighting the multidisciplinary nature of the field and the need for global collaboration to further advance it.

Furthermore, most documents were published in the last three years with 2024 being the year with the most published documents, followed by 2023 and 2022. Based on the number of published documents, the 10-year time period examined was divided into three separate periods: 2015–2018: Initial conceptualization; 2019–2021: Materialization; and 2022–2024: Breakthrough. Additionally, the documents which received the highest mean total citations were published in 2019, 2022, and 2021, although this outcome is expected to change given the rapid development of the field and the increase in the number of new documents published. The sources in which the documents were published were categorized into three clusters following Bradford's law and also analyzed based on their h-index. According to the related outcomes, the most relevant sources were identified.

Moreover, using Lotka's law, the distribution of the written documents which the authors have contributed to is presented. Despite the vast majority having participated in a single document, there are authors who are actively pursuing this novel field of study and it is expected that these outcomes will also change in the near future. The authors were from 71 different countries across the globe and countries from different continents ranked among the top in terms of scientific production in the field. Similarly, the author affiliations were examined. The related outcomes highlighted the most productive and relevant countries. The development of international collaborations, which were categorized into six clusters, further highlight the diverse and complicated nature of the field and the need to examine it from multiple perspectives and incorporate the insights of authors from various backgrounds and expertise.

By examining both author's keywords and keywords plus (indexed keywords) of the documents, the thematic areas and main topics covered were examined. The results revealed the close relationship of AI, AR, and VR with the field of education and healthcare and also highlighted their inter-relation and their close relationship with other novel technologies. Particular emphasis was also put on human-computer interaction and the application of machine learning and deep learning. To better comprehend these topics, LDA, which is a probabilistic Bayesian model with a three-level hierarchical structure [63], was also used to identify topics within the document collection based on the title and abstract of the documents. Hence, using LDA, the following general topics and categories of interest emerged: "Education/Learning/Training", "Healthcare and Medicine", "Generative artificial intelligence/Large language models", "Virtual worlds/Virtual avatars/Virtual assistants", "Human-computer interaction", "Machine learning/Deep learning/Neural networks", "Communication networks", "Industry", "Manufacturing", "E-commerce", "Entertainment", "Smart cities", and "New technologies" (e.g., digital twins, blockchain, internet of things, etc.). These outcomes are in line with the results of the keywords and trends analysis and further validate the topics/areas identified.

Furthermore, focusing on the total citations received within the document collection, the top documents relevant to the topic that explore the use of AI along with VR and/or AR were identified. The related outcomes are presented in Table 14 and are analyzed to provide an overview of the most impactful studies that currently guide this field of study.

Table 14. Documents with the highest number of citations.

Document	DOI	Total Citations	Total Citations per Year	Normalized Total Citations
[81]	10.1016/j.caeai.2022.100082	400	133.33	24.17
[82]	10.1038/s41467-021-25637-w	262	65.5	16.13
[83]	10.1002/aisy.202100228	173	57.67	10.46
[84]	10.1109/OJCS.2022.3188249	166	55.33	10.03
[85]	10.1016/j.engappai.2022.105581	164	82	31.03
[86]	10.1038/s41591-019-0539-7	150	25	8.04
[87]	10.23919/ICACT53585.2022.9728808	130	43.33	7.86
[88]	10.1016/j.jsurg.2019.05.015	115	19.17	6.17
[89]	10.1080/00207543.2020.1859636	105	26.25	6.46
[90]	10.23919/jcin.2022.9815195	97	32.33	5.86
[91]	10.1007/978-3-319-93843-1_12	97	13.71	11.05

Hwan and Chien [81] explored the metaverse through the lenses of AI. Their study went over the potential research issues, role, and definition of the metaverse and the role of AI within the metaverse. The study highlighted the potentials of the AI-enriched metaverse to support and improve the educational process. Additionally, it offered future research topics and directions and commented upon the wider use of the metaverse in the near future. Wen et al. [82] focused on VR space and the use of AI to improve sign language recognition to enable bidirectional communication using haptic devices. In their study, they used a deep learning model for the recognition and translation of the sign language. Their outcomes revealed the significant benefits that can be yielded when integrating AI within VR environments to improve everyday life and communication. Zhang et al. [83] focused on the transition from AR and VR to the realization of digital twins using AI sensing technologies in the context of the internet of things. The study commented upon the role of AR, VR, and digital twins and highlighted the ability of using AI to design effective intelligent sensor systems. Finally, they pointed out the ability of AI to optimize processes and improve automation and of the metaverse and digital twins to bring about new opportunities for achieving a smarter future and commented on the existing challenges.

In another study, Yang et al. [84] examined the combination of AI and blockchain with the metaverse. The study focused on the unique characteristics and aspects of the metaverse and how they can be enhanced by using AI. The study also went over the use of blockchain and its applicability within the metaverse. Moreover, it presented key challenges and open issues related to digital economies, technological limitations, governance, regulations, as well as security and privacy. Finally, the study highlighted the important role that both AI and blockchain will play in the creation of an ever-expanding metaverse. Huynh-The et al. [85] carried out an in-depth survey regarding the use of AI within the metaverse. The study went over the categorization of the different AI types, its role in the metaverse, as well as the technical aspects in which its integration can aid with, such as natural language processing, computer vision, blockchain, digital twins, neural interfaces, and networking. Additionally, it explored various application domains, such as healthcare, manufacturing, smart cities, and gaming while also commenting on its potential use in e-commerce, real estate, and decentralized finance.

Chen et al. [86] explored the integration of AI within AR microscopes for cancer diagnosis. The study focused on presenting the proposed platform which capitalizes on AR for effective representation and interactivity and on AI for identification. Overall, the study highlights the potential that the combination of these technologies can yield in the field of healthcare. Mozumder et al. [87] provided an overview regarding the future trends of the metaverse focusing on AI, internet of things, and blockchain. Their work focused on the medical domain and commented upon the virtual environments and worlds that can be created within the metaverse. Additionally, the study highlighted the technologies which the metaverse uses and explored AI use cases within the metaverse as well as the use of the metaverse in healthcare. Winkler-Schwartz et al. [88] focused on VR simulations in the context of assessing surgical expertise. Their approach emphasized machine learning and the role of AI in medical education. Specifically, they looked into how machine learning can be used in the context of VR simulations to evaluate users' performances. The study also provides a general framework to effectively report and analyze studies that focus on machine learning and VR surgical simulations.

Sahu et al. [89] carried out a review regarding the use of AI within AR applications targeted at manufacturing. The study highlighted the benefits that AR can bring about and how AI can be used to further enrich AR applications. Specifically, the study focused on identifying the main concepts and the limitations of the existing methods and explored various AI-based approaches that could help address these challenges. The study also commented upon the benefits of AI in manufacturing and within AR-based applications. Chang et al. [90] explored 6G-enabled edge AI for the metaverse. Specifically, the study presented the main aspects of the metaverse and focused on the existing challenges that it faced. Additionally, the study looked into the limitations specified in the existing literature and provided future research directions. Holstein et al. [91] examined a mixed reality teacher awareness tool in the context of AI-enhanced classrooms. Specifically, the study focused on intelligent tutoring systems and advanced analytics which were displayed in an MR headset. Their study revealed that the use of MR-based teacher analytics can help address the learning outcome gaps observed among students of different levels of knowledge and skills. Finally, the outcomes of the study highlighted the benefits that the AI systems can bring in education and the potential that the combination of integrating human and machine intelligence can have in supporting students' learning.

The outcomes of the aforementioned studies reveal the potentials of integrating AI within AR and VR environments as well as the metaverse across different contexts. Moreover, they highlight the need to integrate and combine new technologies to meet the emerging requirements. Based on the scope of the studies, it can be inferred that emphasis is being placed on the role of AI within the metaverse as well as within XR environments in the education and healthcare domains. The sections and topics covered in the aforementioned studies are in line with the topics and areas identified within this study. Additionally, the gradual evolution and shift of focus is also in line with the thematic evolution presented in this study. Hence, the results of this study further validate those of the previous literature regarding the potentials of combining AI with XR technologies and the metaverse and highlights its ability to be effectively integrated into different domains.

However, it should be noted that there are several open challenges and barriers that need to be addressed before these technologies are more widely adopted and applied. These barriers involve privacy and security issues, ethical concerns, technical and computational limitations, algorithmic bias considerations, software and hardware limitations, sustainability and interoperability considerations, as well as development and adoption hurdles [41,92–95]. As these challenges exist for AI, the metaverse, and XR technologies, emphasis should be placed on exploring them through the lenses of each individual technology as well as of their combined use.

5. Conclusions

XR technologies are rapidly advancing and being integrated into various domains. Specifically, the adoption and use of AR and VR have brought about several benefits and new opportunities to different sectors including education, healthcare, industry, etc. Simultaneously, due to the recent advances, AI is also gaining ground and being integrated into several domains reinforcing them and enriching them. These technologies can be combined to yield even greater outcomes; hence, the research into this topic is rapidly increasing. This study aimed to provide an overview through the examination, analysis, and mapping of the existing literature regarding the use of AI within AR, VR, and the metaverse.

To provide a thorough overview, the study followed the PRISMA guidelines and used different analysis methods and tools. Specifically, the study focused on carrying out a bibliometric analysis, scientific mapping, content analysis, and topic modeling of the related literature. In total, the study examined 880 documents which were identified from Scopus and Web of Science and were published during 2015–2024. The study examined the main characteristics of the document collection and focused on identifying emerging and trend topics and areas of focus.

The results of this study highlighted the potential that the integration of AI into AR, VR, and the metaverse can yield. Additionally, it revealed its wide applicability and capabilities of being effectively integrated into various domains. The study also confirmed the significance and novelty of the topic which showcases a significantly high growth rate (91.29%). Additionally, the study revealed the main research areas and directions and highlighted the following topics as the ones being more actively researched: "Education/Learning/Training", "Healthcare and Medicine", "Generative artificial intelligence/Large language models", "Virtual worlds/Virtual avatars/Virtual assistants", "Human-computer interaction", "Machine learning/Deep learning/Neural networks", "Communication networks", "Industry", "Manufacturing", "E-commerce", "Entertainment", "Smart cities", and "New technologies" (e.g., digital twins, blockchain, internet of things, etc.).

However, the study has some limitations. Specifically, the documents identified were retrieved from two databases and only English documents were examined. Since the goal of this study was to provide a general overview of the field, a more in-depth content analysis targeted to a specific domain was not carried out. As a result, there is a clear need for future studies to further analyze the integration of AI, VR, and AR across different settings through systematic literature reviews and case studies. Additionally, effective frameworks, standards, and guidelines on how to develop relative solutions and integrate them should be created. Emphasis should also be placed on examining and addressing the challenges and barriers associated with the effective integration of AI within XR environments, such as technical, hardware, and software limitations, algorithmic bias considerations, security and privacy issues, ethical concerns, as well as development and adoption hurdles. There is also a need to create valid evaluation metrics to assess its effectiveness. Future studies should also examine security, privacy, and ethical aspects associated with the use of AI, XR technologies, and the metaverse. Finally, it is important to explore users' involvement, interactions, communications, perspectives, behaviors, and emotions while they are engaged within AI-enabled AR and VR environments as well as within the metaverse.

Funding: This research received no external funding.

Data Availability Statement: All of the data are contained within the article. The data supporting the conclusions of this article will be made available by the corresponding author upon reasonable request.

Conflicts of Interest: The author declares no conflicts of interest.

References

1. Brynjolfsson, E.; Mcafee, A. Artificial intelligence, for real. *Harv. Bus. Rev.* **2017**, *1*, 1–31.
2. Li, D.; Du, Y. *Artificial Intelligence with Uncertainty*; CRC Press: Boca Raton, FL, USA, 2017. [CrossRef]
3. Vergara, D.; Lampropoulos, G.; Antón-Sancho, Á.; Fernández-Arias, P. Impact of artificial intelligence on learning management systems: A bibliometric review. *Multimodal Technol. Interact.* **2024**, *8*, 75. [CrossRef]
4. Haenlein, M.; Kaplan, A. A brief history of artificial intelligence: On the past, present, and future of artificial intelligence. *Calif. Manag. Rev.* **2019**, *61*, 5–14. [CrossRef]
5. Duan, Y.; Edwards, J.S.; Dwivedi, Y.K. Artificial intelligence for decision making in the era of big data—Evolution, challenges and research agenda. *Int. J. Inf. Manag.* **2019**, *48*, 63–71. [CrossRef]
6. Stone, P.; Brooks, R.; Brynjolfsson, E.; Calo, R.; Etzioni, O.; Hager, G.; Hirschberg, J.; Kalyanakrishnan, S.; Kamar, E.; Kraus, S.; et al. Artificial intelligence and life in 2030: The one hundred year study on artificial intelligence. *arXiv* **2016**. [CrossRef]
7. Negnevitsky, M. *Artificial Intelligence: A Guide to Intelligent Systems*; Pearson Education: London, UK, 2005.
8. Preece, A. Asking 'why' in AI: Explainability of intelligent systems–perspectives and challenges. *Intell. Syst. Account. Financ. Manag.* **2018**, *25*, 63–72. [CrossRef]

9. Sarker, I.H. AI-Based modeling: Techniques, applications and research issues towards automation, intelligent and smart systems. *SN Comput. Sci.* **2022**, *3*, 158. [CrossRef] [PubMed]
10. Petrovic, V.M. Artificial intelligence and virtual worlds—Toward Human-Level AI agents. *IEEE Access* **2018**, *6*, 39976–39988. [CrossRef]
11. Norouzi, N.; Bruder, G.; Belna, B.; Mutter, S.; Turgut, D.; Welch, G. A systematic review of the convergence of augmented reality, intelligent virtual agents, and the internet of things. In *Transactions on Computational Science and Computational Intelligence*; Springer: Berlin/Heidelberg, Germany, 2019; pp. 1–24. [CrossRef]
12. Zhang, S.; Meng, Z.; Chen, B.; Yang, X.; Zhao, X. Motivation, social emotion, and the acceptance of artificial intelligence virtual Assistants—Trust-Based mediating effects. *Front. Psychol.* **2021**, *12*, 728495. [CrossRef] [PubMed]
13. Ferber, J.; Weiss, G. *Multi-Agent Systems: An Introduction to Distributed Artificial Intelligence*; Addison-Wesley Reading: Boston, MA, USA, 1999; Volume 1.
14. Dorri, A.; Kanhere, S.S.; Jurdak, R. Multi-Agent systems: A survey. *IEEE Access* **2018**, *6*, 28573–28593. [CrossRef]
15. Ospina-Bohórquez, A.; Rodríguez-González, S.; Vergara-Rodríguez, D. On the synergy between virtual reality and Multi-Agent systems. *Sustainability* **2021**, *13*, 4326. [CrossRef]
16. Chen, L.; Chen, P.; Lin, Z. Artificial intelligence in education: A review. *IEEE Access* **2020**, *8*, 75264–75278. [CrossRef]
17. Chiu, T.K.F.; Xia, Q.; Zhou, X.; Chai, C.S.; Cheng, M. Systematic literature review on opportunities, challenges, and future research recommendations of artificial intelligence in education. *Comput. Educ. Artif. Intell.* **2023**, *4*, 100118. [CrossRef]
18. Mustafa, M.Y.; Tlili, A.; Lampropoulos, G.; Huang, R.; Jandrić, P.; Zhao, J.; Salha, S.; Xu, L.; Panda, S.; Kinshuk; et al. A systematic review of literature reviews on artificial intelligence in education (AIED): A roadmap to a future research agenda. *Smart Learn. Environ.* **2024**, *11*, 59. [CrossRef]
19. Peres, R.S.; Jia, X.; Lee, J.; Sun, K.; Colombo, A.W.; Barata, J. Industrial artificial intelligence in industry 4.0—Systematic review, challenges and outlook. *IEEE Access* **2020**, *8*, 220121–220139. [CrossRef]
20. Javaid, M.; Haleem, A.; Singh, R.P.; Suman, R. Artificial intelligence applications for industry 4.0: A Literature-Based study. *J. Ind. Integr. Manag.* **2022**, *7*, 83–111. [CrossRef]
21. Jan, Z.; Ahamed, F.; Mayer, W.; Patel, N.; Grossmann, G.; Stumptner, M.; Kuusk, A. Artificial intelligence for industry 4.0: Systematic review of applications, challenges, and opportunities. *Expert Syst. Appl.* **2023**, *216*, 119456. [CrossRef]
22. Loh, H.W.; Ooi, C.P.; Seoni, S.; Barua, P.D.; Molinari, F.; Acharya, U.R. Application of explainable artificial intelligence for healthcare: A systematic review of the last decade (2011–2022). *Comput. Methods Programs Biomed.* **2022**, *226*, 107161. [CrossRef] [PubMed]
23. Al Kuwaiti, A.; Nazer, K.; Al-Reedy, A.; Al-Shehri, S.; Al-Muhanna, A.; Subbarayalu, A.V.; Al Muhanna, D.; Al-Muhanna, F.A. A review of the role of artificial intelligence in healthcare. *J. Pers. Med.* **2023**, *13*, 951. [CrossRef] [PubMed]
24. Secinaro, S.; Calandra, D.; Secinaro, A.; Muthurangu, V.; Biancone, P. The role of artificial intelligence in healthcare: A structured literature review. *BMC Med. Inform. Decis. Mak.* **2021**, *21*, 125. [CrossRef] [PubMed]
25. Di Vaio, A.; Palladino, R.; Hassan, R.; Escobar, O. Artificial intelligence and business models in the sustainable development goals perspective: A systematic literature review. *J. Bus. Res.* **2020**, *121*, 283–314. [CrossRef]
26. Loureiro, S.M.C.; Guerreiro, J.; Tussyadiah, I. Artificial intelligence in business: State of the art and future research agenda. *J. Bus. Res.* **2021**, *129*, 911–926. [CrossRef]
27. Enholm, I.M.; Papagiannidis, E.; Mikalef, P.; Krogstie, J. Artificial intelligence and business value: A literature review. *Inf. Syst. Front.* **2022**, *24*, 1709–1734. [CrossRef]
28. Yigitcanlar, T.; Desouza, K.; Butler, L.; Roozkhosh, F. Contributions and risks of artificial intelligence (AI) in building smarter cities: Insights from a systematic review of the literature. *Energies* **2020**, *13*, 1473. [CrossRef]
29. Ullah, Z.; Al-Turjman, F.; Mostarda, L.; Gagliardi, R. Applications of artificial intelligence and machine learning in smart cities. *Comput. Commun.* **2020**, *154*, 313–323. [CrossRef]
30. Herath, H.; Mittal, M. Adoption of artificial intelligence in smart cities: A comprehensive review. *Int. J. Inf. Manag. Data Insights* **2022**, *2*, 100076. [CrossRef]
31. Luck, M.; Aylett, R. Applying artificial intelligence to virtual reality: Intelligent virtual environments. *Appl. Artif. Intell.* **2000**, *14*, 3–32. [CrossRef]
32. Lampropoulos, G. Augmented reality and artificial intelligence in education: Toward immersive intelligent tutoring systems. In *Augmented Reality and Artificial Intelligence*; Springer: Berlin/Heidelberg, Germany, 2023; pp. 137–146. [CrossRef]
33. Azuma, R.T. A survey of augmented reality. *Presence: Teleoperators Virtual Environ.* **1997**, *6*, 355–385. [CrossRef]
34. Lee, K. Augmented reality in education and training. *TechTrends* **2012**, *56*, 13–21. [CrossRef]
35. Milgram, P.; Kishino, F. A taxonomy of mixed reality visual displays. *IEICE Trans. Inf. Syst.* **1994**, *77*, 1321–1329.
36. Burdea, G.C.; Coiffet, P. *Virtual Reality Technology*; John Wiley & Sons: Hoboken, NJ, USA, 2003.
37. Sherman, W.R.; Craig, A.B. Understanding virtual reality—Interface, application, and design. *Presence: Teleoperators Virtual Environ.* **2003**, *12*, 441–442. [CrossRef]

38. Anthes, C.; Garcia-Hernandez, R.J.; Wiedemann, M.; Kranzlmuller, D. State of the art of virtual reality technology. In Proceedings of the 2016 IEEE Aerospace Conference, Big Sky, MT, USA, 5–12 March 2016. [CrossRef]
39. Anwar, M.S.; Choi, A.; Ahmad, S.; Aurangzeb, K.; Laghari, A.A.; Gadekallu, T.R.; Hines, A. A Moving Metaverse: QoE Challenges and Standards Requirements for Immersive Media Consumption in Autonomous Vehicles. *Appl. Soft Comput.* **2024**, *159*, 111577. [CrossRef]
40. Wang, Y.; Su, Z.; Zhang, N.; Xing, R.; Liu, D.; Luan, T.H.; Shen, X. A Survey on Metaverse: Fundamentals, Security, and Privacy. *IEEE Commun. Surv. Tutor.* **2022**, *25*, 319–352. [CrossRef]
41. Wang, H.; Ning, H.; Lin, Y.; Wang, W.; Dhelim, S.; Farha, F.; Daneshmand, M. A Survey on the Metaverse: The State-of-the-Art, Technologies, Applications, and Challenges. *IEEE Internet Things J.* **2023**, *10*, 14671–14688. [CrossRef]
42. Dionisio, J.D.N.; Burns, W.G., III; Gilbert, R. 3D Virtual Worlds and the Metaverse: Current Status and Future Possibilities. *ACM Comput. Surv.* **2013**, *45*, 34. [CrossRef]
43. López-Belmonte, J.; Pozo-Sánchez, S.; Moreno-Guerrero, A.J.; Lampropoulos, G. Metaverse in Education: A Systematic Review. *Rev. Educ. Distancia (RED)* **2023**, *23*, 2. [CrossRef]
44. Kavanagh, S.; Luxton-Reilly, A.; Wuensche, B.; Plimmer, B. A systematic review of virtual reality in education. *Themes Sci. Technol. Educ.* **2017**, *10*, 85–119.
45. Avila-Garzon, C.; Bacca-Acosta, J.; Kinshuk; Duarte, J.; Betancourt, J. Augmented reality in education: An overview of Twenty-Five years of research. *Contemp. Educ. Technol.* **2021**, *13*, ep302. [CrossRef]
46. Garzón, J. An overview of Twenty-Five years of augmented reality in education. *Multimodal Technol. Interact.* **2021**, *5*, 37. [CrossRef]
47. Lampropoulos, G.; Kinshuk. Virtual reality and gamification in education: A systematic review. *Educ. Technol. Res. Dev.* **2024**, *72*, 1691–1785. [CrossRef]
48. Damiani, L.; Demartini, M.; Guizzi, G.; Revetria, R.; Tonelli, F. Augmented and virtual reality applications in industrial systems: A qualitative review towards the industry 4.0 era. *IFAC-Pap.* **2018**, *51*, 624–630. [CrossRef]
49. Guo, Z.; Zhou, D.; Zhou, Q.; Zhang, X.; Geng, J.; Zeng, S.; Lv, C.; Hao, A. Applications of virtual reality in maintenance during the industrial product lifecycle: A systematic review. *J. Manuf. Syst.* **2020**, *56*, 525–538. [CrossRef]
50. Bottani, E.; Vignali, G. Augmented reality technology in the manufacturing industry: A review of the last decade. *IISE Trans.* **2019**, *51*, 284–310. [CrossRef]
51. Eckert, M.; Volmerg, J.S.; Friedrich, C.M. Augmented reality in medicine: Systematic and bibliographic review. *JMIR Mhealth Uhealth* **2019**, *7*, e10967. [CrossRef]
52. Barteit, S.; Lanfermann, L.; Bärnighausen, T.; Neuhann, F.; Beiersmann, C. Augmented, mixed, and virtual reality-based head-mounted devices for medical education: Systematic review. *JMIR Serious Games* **2021**, *9*, e29080. [CrossRef] [PubMed]
53. Kouijzer, M.M.T.E.; Kip, H.; Bouman, Y.H.A.; Kelders, S.M. Implementation of virtual reality in healthcare: A scoping review on the implementation process of virtual reality in various healthcare settings. *Implement. Sci. Commun.* **2023**, *4*, 67. [CrossRef] [PubMed]
54. Loureiro, S.M.C.; Guerreiro, J.; Eloy, S.; Langaro, D.; Panchapakesan, P. Understanding the use of virtual reality in marketing: A text mining-based review. *J. Bus. Res.* **2019**, *100*, 514–530. [CrossRef]
55. Roxo, M.T.; Brito, P.Q. Augmented reality trends to the field of business and economics: A review of 20 years of research. *Asian J. Bus. Res.* **2018**, *8*, 94–117. [CrossRef]
56. Walentek, D.; Ziora, L. A systematic review on the use of augmented reality in management and business. *Procedia Comput. Sci.* **2023**, *225*, 861–871. [CrossRef]
57. Jamei, E.; Mortimer, M.; Seyedmahmoudian, M.; Horan, B.; Stojcevski, A. Investigating the role of virtual reality in planning for sustainable smart cities. *Sustainability* **2017**, *9*, 2006. [CrossRef]
58. Alzahrani, N.M.; Alfouzan, F.A. Augmented reality (AR) and Cyber-Security for smart Cities—A systematic literature review. *Sensors* **2022**, *22*, 2792. [CrossRef] [PubMed]
59. Kohli, V.; Tripathi, U.; Chamola, V.; Rout, B.K.; Kanhere, S.S. A review on virtual reality and augmented reality use-cases of brain computer interface based applications for smart cities. *Microprocess. Microsyst.* **2022**, *88*, 104392. [CrossRef]
60. Page, M.J.; McKenzie, J.E.; Bossuyt, P.M.; Boutron, I.; Hoffmann, T.C.; Mulrow, C.D.; Shamseer, L.; Tetzlaff, J.M.; Akl, E.A.; Brennan, S.E.; et al. The PRISMA 2020 statement: An updated guideline for reporting systematic reviews. *Int. J. Surg.* **2021**, *88*, 105906. [CrossRef] [PubMed]
61. Aria, M.; Cuccurullo, C. Bibliometrix: An r-tool for comprehensive science mapping analysis. *J. Informetr.* **2017**, *11*, 959–975. [CrossRef]
62. van Eck, N.J.; Waltman, L. Software survey: VOSviewer, a computer program for bibliometric mapping. *Scientometrics* **2010**, *84*, 523–538. [CrossRef] [PubMed]
63. Blei, D.M.; Ng, A.Y.; Jordan, M.I. Latent dirichlet allocation. *J. Mach. Learn. Res.* **2003**, *3*, 993–1022. [CrossRef]

64. Ellegaard, O.; Wallin, J.A. The bibliometric analysis of scholarly production: How great is the impact? *Scientometrics* **2015**, *105*, 1809–1831. [CrossRef] [PubMed]
65. Donthu, N.; Kumar, S.; Mukherjee, D.; Pandey, N.; Lim, W.M. How to conduct a bibliometric analysis: An overview and guidelines. *J. Bus. Res.* **2021**, *133*, 285–296. [CrossRef]
66. Mongeon, P.; Paul-Hus, A. The journal coverage of web of science and scopus: A comparative analysis. *Scientometrics* **2015**, *106*, 213–228. [CrossRef]
67. Zhu, J.; Liu, W. A tale of two databases: The use of web of science and scopus in academic papers. *Scientometrics* **2020**, *123*, 321–335. [CrossRef]
68. Zhang, J.; Yu, Q.; Zheng, F.; Long, C.; Lu, Z.; Duan, Z. Comparing keywords plus of WOS and author keywords: A case study of patient adherence research. *J. Assoc. Inf. Sci. Technol.* **2016**, *67*, 967–972. [CrossRef]
69. Allcoat, D.; Mühlenen, A. von Learning in virtual reality: Effects on performance, emotion and engagement. *Res. Learn. Technol.* **2018**, *26*, 2140. [CrossRef]
70. Zhou, F.; Duh, H.B.-L.; Billinghurst, M. Trends in augmented reality tracking, interaction and display: A review of ten years of ISMAR. In Proceedings of the 7th IEEE/ACM International Symposium on Mixed and Augmented Reality, Cambridge, UK, 15–18 September 2008; IEEE Computer Society: Washington, DC, USA, 2018; pp. 193–202. [CrossRef]
71. Vergara, D.; Extremera, J.; Rubio, M.P.; Dávila, L.P. The technological obsolescence of virtual reality learning environments. *Appl. Sci.* **2020**, *10*, 915. [CrossRef]
72. Dunleavy, M. Design principles for augmented reality learning. *TechTrends* **2013**, *58*, 28–34. [CrossRef]
73. Vergara, D.; Rubio, M.P.; Lorenzo, M.; Rodríguez, S. On the importance of the design of virtual reality learning environments. In *Advances in Intelligent Systems and Computing*; Springer: Berlin/Heidelberg, Germany, 2020; pp. 146–152. [CrossRef]
74. Lampropoulos, G.; Keramopoulos, E.; Diamantaras, K. Semantically enriched augmented reality applications: A proposed system architecture and a case study. *Int. J. Recent Contrib. Eng. Sci. IT (IJES)* **2022**, *10*, 29–46. [CrossRef]
75. Billinghurst, M.; Grasset, R.; Looser, J. Designing augmented reality interfaces. *ACM SIGGRAPH Comput. Graph.* **2005**, *39*, 17–22. [CrossRef]
76. Craig, A.B.; Sherman, W.R.; Will, J.D. *Developing Virtual Reality Applications: Foundations of Effective Design*; Morgan Kaufmann: Burlington, MA, USA, 2009.
77. Carmigniani, J.; Furht, B.; Anisetti, M.; Ceravolo, P.; Damiani, E.; Ivkovic, M. Augmented reality technologies, systems and applications. *Multimed. Tools Appl.* **2011**, *51*, 341–377. [CrossRef]
78. Wexelblat, A. *Virtual Reality: Applications and Explorations*; Academic Press: Cambridge, MA, USA, 2014.
79. Elliott, A. *The culture of AI: Everyday Life and the Digital Revolution*; Routledge: London, UK, 2019.
80. Islam, M.R.; Ahmed, M.U.; Barua, S.; Begum, S. A systematic review of explainable artificial intelligence in terms of different application domains and tasks. *Appl. Sci.* **2022**, *12*, 1353. [CrossRef]
81. Hwang, G.-J.; Chien, S.-Y. Definition, roles, and potential research issues of the metaverse in education: An artificial intelligence perspective. *Comput. Educ. Artif. Intell.* **2022**, *3*, 100082. [CrossRef]
82. Wen, F.; Zhang, Z.; He, T.; Lee, C. AI enabled sign language recognition and VR space bidirectional communication using triboelectric smart glove. *Nat. Commun.* **2021**, *12*, 5378. [CrossRef]
83. Zhang, Z.; Wen, F.; Sun, Z.; Guo, X.; He, T.; Lee, C. Artificial Intelligence-Enabled sensing technologies in the 5G/Internet of things era: From virtual Reality/Augmented reality to the digital twin. *Adv. Intell. Syst.* **2022**, *4*, 2100228. [CrossRef]
84. Yang, Q.; Zhao, Y.; Huang, H.; Xiong, Z.; Kang, J.; Zheng, Z. Fusing blockchain and AI with metaverse: A survey. *IEEE Open J. Comput. Soc.* **2022**, *3*, 122–136. [CrossRef]
85. Huynh-The, T.; Pham, Q.-V.; Pham, X.-Q.; Nguyen, T.T.; Han, Z.; Kim, D.-S. Artificial intelligence for the metaverse: A survey. *Eng. Appl. Artif. Intell.* **2023**, *117*, 105581. [CrossRef]
86. Chen, P.-H.C.; Gadepalli, K.; MacDonald, R.; Liu, Y.; Kadowaki, S.; Nagpal, K.; Kohlberger, T.; Dean, J.; Corrado, G.S.; Hipp, J.D.; et al. An augmented reality microscope with real-time artificial intelligence integration for cancer diagnosis. *Nat. Med.* **2019**, *25*, 1453–1457. [CrossRef]
87. Mozumder, M.A.I.; Sheeraz, M.M.; Athar, A.; Aich, S.; Kim, H.-C. Overview: Technology roadmap of the future trend of metaverse based on IoT, blockchain, AI technique, and medical domain metaverse activity. In Proceedings of the 2022 24th International Conference on Advanced Communication Technology (ICACT), Virtual, 13–16 February 2022; pp. 256–261. [CrossRef]
88. Winkler-Schwartz, A.; Bissonnette, V.; Mirchi, N.; Ponnudurai, N.; Yilmaz, R.; Ledwos, N.; Siyar, S.; Azarnoush, H.; Karlik, B.; Del Maestro, R.F. Artificial intelligence in medical education: Best practices using machine learning to assess surgical expertise in virtual reality simulation. *J. Surg. Educ.* **2019**, *76*, 1681–1690. [CrossRef]
89. Sahu, C.K.; Young, C.; Rai, R. Artificial intelligence (AI) in augmented reality (AR)-assisted manufacturing applications: A review. *Int. J. Prod. Res.* **2021**, *59*, 4903–4959. [CrossRef]
90. Chang, L.; Zhang, Z.; Li, P.; Xi, S.; Guo, W.; Shen, Y.; Xiong, Z.; Kang, J.; Niyato, D.; Qiao, X.; et al. 6G-Enabled edge AI for metaverse: Challenges, methods, and future research directions. *J. Commun. Inf. Netw.* **2022**, *7*, 107–121. [CrossRef]

91. Holstein, K.; McLaren, B.M.; Aleven, V. Student learning benefits of a Mixed-Reality teacher awareness tool in AI-Enhanced classrooms. In *Lecture Notes in Computer Science*; Springer: Berlin/Heidelberg, Germany, 2018; pp. 154–168. [CrossRef]
92. Park, S.M.; Kim, Y.G. A Metaverse: Taxonomy, Components, Applications, and Open Challenges. *IEEE Access* **2022**, *10*, 4209–4251. [CrossRef]
93. Kaplan, A.; Haenlein, M. Rulers of the World, Unite! The Challenges and Opportunities of Artificial Intelligence. *Bus. Horiz.* **2020**, *63*, 37–50. [CrossRef]
94. Perc, M.; Ozer, M.; Hojnik, J. Social and Juristic Challenges of Artificial Intelligence. *Palgrave Commun.* **2019**, *5*, 61. [CrossRef]
95. Bastug, E.; Bennis, M.; Médard, M.; Debbah, M. Toward Interconnected Virtual Reality: Opportunities, Challenges, and Enablers. *IEEE Commun. Mag.* **2017**, *55*, 110–117. [CrossRef]

future internet

MDPI

Article

Metaverse and Fashion: An Analysis of Consumer Online Interest

Carmen Ruiz Viñals, Marta Gil Ibáñez * and José Luis Del Olmo Arriaga

Business and Economics Department, Universitat Abat Oliba CEU, 08022 Barcelona, Spain; cruizv@uao.es (C.R.V.); jlolmo@uao.es (J.L.D.O.A.)
* Correspondence: mgili@uao.es

Abstract: Recent studies have demonstrated the value that the Internet and web applications bring to businesses. Among other tools are those that enable the analysis and monitoring of searches, such as Google Trends, which is currently used by the fashion industry to guide experiential practices in a context of augmented reality and/or virtual reality, and even to predict purchasing behaviours through the metaverse. Data from this tool provide insight into fashion consumer search patterns. Understanding and managing this digital tool is an essential factor in rethinking businesses' marketing strategies. The aim of this study is to analyse online user search behaviour by analysing and monitoring the terms "metaverse" and "fashion" on Google Trends. A quantitative descriptive cross-sectional method was employed. The results show that there is growing consumer interest in both concepts on the Internet, despite the lack of homogeneity in the behaviour of the five Google search tools.

Keywords: Google Trends; metaverse; fashion; marketing; SEO

1. Introduction

One area the fashion industry is exploring in order to drive its renewal and attract consumers is the metaverse. For the fashion industry, this new digital world offers the possibility to generate community and create brand experiences [1].

Fashion is being integrated into the metaverse in various ways: from videogames that allow players to purchase outfits for an avatar in order to customize it, through to applications with built-in augmented reality that makes it easier to visualize a product, and even non-fungible tokens or NFTs, digital assets that represent real-world objects such as art, music, game pieces, etc. They are bought and sold online, often with cryptocurrencies, and represent an interesting opportunity for the industry to increase its revenues [2].

The search for information carried out by consumers online through the new empowerment offered by the Internet and its relationship with purchasing and consumption behaviour is currently attracting significant attention. One of the topics that is currently receiving most attention from marketing specialists is the search for information online carried out by users using the terms "fashion" and "metaverse" [3], as well as its relationship with the purchasing and consumption behaviour of this product category. Here, we investigate whether search analysis and monitoring tools such as Google Trends make it possible to understand or anticipate consumer behaviour to guide digital marketing practices [4]. In this study, we aim to address three research questions: RQ1—Where are the users who most frequently use the terms "metaverse" and "fashion" in their Internet searches located? RQ2—What other words are associated with the terms "metaverse" and "fashion" in Internet searches? RQ3—Are there significant differences in search keywords between the different Google corporate communication platforms?

Google Trends is an application that provides information on Internet search trends based on keywords without specifically indicating social content. It enables the evolution of searches over a certain period (from 2004 to the present) to be graphically visualised and can, among other procedures, analyse social behaviours or possible seasonality. Other applications such as Ubersuggest, Keywordini, Google Keyword Tool, and Follow the Hashtag also provide information on Internet search trends [5].

In this study, we ask whether Google Trends could be useful for companies in the fashion sector to guide their digital marketing practices and even predict consumer behaviour using keywords such as "metaverse" and "fashion". The metaverse is a place where predominantly young fashion consumers lead lives online, with avatars that can move, talk, and be customised to be seen anywhere [6,7].

This study contributes to scientific progress by being one of the first studies to monitor the absolute values of keyword searches, thus constituting a valuable asset for the analysis of consumer search behaviour [8].

Our findings also provide a guideline for the development of efficient and effective digital marketing. Based on the results, we provide recommendations for companies in the fashion sector on how to improve the use of keywords to obtain better SEO (Search Engine Optimisation) positioning. Companies in turn can benefit from a deeper understanding of user behaviour on online search engines in exceptional periods such as that resulting from the emergence of the metaverse, which represents a fundamental change in the way consumers, brands and businesses will carry out transactions and interact in a seamlessly interconnected space of virtual realities [9].

Despite these previous studies linking Internet search activity and consumption, it is important to realize that consumer behaviour is always complex. This leads us to ask several research questions:

- Where are the users who most frequently use the terms "metaverse" and "fashion" in their Internet searches located?
- What other words are associated with the terms "metaverse" and "fashion" in Internet searches?
- Are there significant differences in search keywords between the different Google corporate communication platforms?

While the idea of the metaverse has been explored for decades in science fiction and videogames, only in recent years has it gained greater attention and popularity in the fashion industry [10]. In 2022, several fashion brands used the metaverse in their digital marketing campaigns. Therefore, we chose this period as the subject of our fieldwork. It is expected that in the coming years, the technology and infrastructure necessary for the creation of metaverses will continue to advance, and it will be of interest to analyse them in greater depth.

2. Unlocking Consumer Insights: Maximizing Google Trends for SEO Strategy Enhancement

Google is the most powerful and well-known search engine in the world. As of January 2024, Google represented 82% of the market share of leading desktop search engines worldwide, followed by Bing with a 10% share [11]. It publishes buzzword statistics on a separate website called Google Trends, which displays the popularity of specific terms, topics, or keywords by geographical location, time range, categories, and type of web search.

Google Trends searches use only a sample of Google searches due to the large volume of data handled by the platform. Through data sampling, a representative dataset of all Google searches is analysed. To achieve this, the platform normalizes the search data to facilitate comparisons between terms. Following the time and location of the queries, the search results are normalised through two processes: (1) each data point is divided by the total searches for the geographic region and the time interval it represents to compare its relative popularity (this is carried out to prevent locations with the highest search volume from appearing in the top rankings) and (2) the resulting numbers are scaled to a range of 0 to 100 based on the proportion of a topic to the total number of searches on all topics. In this respect, it should be noted that regions that register the same search interest for a term do not always have the same total search volumes.

Google Trends is a Google tool that allows the visualisation of consumer search attitudes of any word or term over time in such a way that the relative value of the volume of searches carried out can be observed. With this tool, it is possible to segment results by geographical level (by country, region, or city), by time (the last hour, the last 7 days, the last 5 years, etc.), by categories (hobbies and free time, shopping, sports, etc.), and by web search (images, news, Google Shopping, and YouTube). It also allows researchers to compare trends of up to five other words at the same time.

Users can download these data directly from the website or obtain a comparative analysis through graphs, figures and tables on specific words or terms [12]. Dergiades et al. [13] state that this "web-related data" can influence business activities and predict possible trends in the market and industry.

In the context of marketing and in relation to consumer behaviour, researchers use Google Trends data to understand consumers' interest in products, brands, and industry trends. In this regard, Silva et al. [14] state that Google Trends can be considered an indicator of consumer fashion behaviour, with specific examples of brands that could use this tool to improve decision-making, while other authors have shown that it can be used to understand the market performance of new products [15]. Along these lines, Karamitros Dimitrios and Fouskas [16] state that Google Trends can be used to recognize the impact of a company's brand and customer demand based on empirical research.

Choi and Varian [17] demonstrate through statistical methods (autoregressive models) that Google Trends can predict the present (short-term) events of economic variables such as consumer confidence. These figures are usually officially published several days after the end of each month, so Google Trends can predict them a month in advance and long before the official report comes out.

3. SEO Strategies

The Google Trends tool is very useful for boosting an SEO (Search Engine Optimisation) strategy directly linked to the search activity of consumers. For Orense Fuentes and Rojas Orduña [18], SEO as a discipline is the process by which a web page obtains and maintains notable positions in search engine results pages (SERPs), also called organic results (deriving from a large organic database) or algorithmic (depending on an algorithm for their ordering).

Mauresmo and Petrova [19] offer a guide to help entrepreneurs position their website (SEO strategies) so that they appear among the top search results. To do this, they suggest using keyword monitoring and analysis tools such as Google in order to understand what consumers are searching for on the Internet. This forms the starting point for optimizing domain names on web pages, configuring words for web pages (home page, page sections, and blogs) and also developing other marketing aspects such as blog comments or forum posts, among other things [20].

4. Exploring the Intersection of Metaverse and Fashion: Understanding the Fashion Consumer in the Metaverse

The concept of metaverse has been growing steadily for some years. Many fashion brands are now taking positions in this virtual world. But what exactly are they looking for? The metaverse (also referred to by the generic term meta) is presented as Web 3, immersive and sensory, revolutionising human interaction. It is a challenging project, but today the existing metaverse only has a few million users, 935 million in 2024 [21]. We are still far from the 5 billion or so Internet users. Futurologists propose a vision for 2030 or 2040 [22], but today, fashion brands are already taking positions in the existing metaverse.

The fashion industry is undergoing a historic metamorphosis, driven by a synergy between emerging technologies and the latest innovations of the 6G era. The emergence of blockchain and non-fungible tokens (NFTs) marks a milestone, while disruptive technologies such as artificial technology (AI) and machine learning (ML) are redefining the standards of creativity and efficiency. Virtual reality (VR) and augmented reality (AR) are intertwined with the metaverse, a space where the boundaries between the real and the virtual are blurred, giving rise to fully immersive shopping and design experiences [7].

However, the coming era of 6G connectivity promises to drive this revolution. A comprehensive study of its architecture, applications, technologies, and challenges reveals new opportunities for the fashion industry. From ultra-fast connectivity to the integration of smart sensors into garments and accessories, the 6G era offers unprecedented potential for personalisation and real-time interaction.

With the capacity to transmit data at astonishing speeds and ultra-low latency, the 6G era paves the way for truly immersive shopping experiences in which consumers can interact with products in 3D and receive personalised recommendations in real time. Moreover, the integration of extended reality (XR) technologies into the metaverse promises to take the shopping experience to new levels, allowing users to virtually explore shops and fashion shows from the comfort of their homes.

As the fashion industry adapts to these cutting-edge innovations, a new era of creativity and collaboration is emerging. Designers can take full advantage of AI- and ML-assisted design tools to create unique, sustainable collections, while consumers enjoy a more personalised and immersive shopping experience than ever before [23].

The metaverse is a three-dimensional virtual world inhabited by avatars of real people. The term was coined by Neal Stephenson in his novel Snow Crash (1992), in which avatars of real people inhabited a three-dimensional (3D) virtual world. In 2021, it became one of the most popular technology terms. Indeed, a Google Trends search shows that the word "metaverse" has been actively searched for since early 2021, beginning when Roblox went public on March 10, and subsequently when Nvidia CEO Jensen Huang stated that the company's next step was to create a metaverse [24] and when Facebook CEO Mark Zuckerberg announced his decision to change the company's name to Meta [25].

While the meanings that potential stakeholders ascribe to metaverses may differ, certain commonalities are indisputable. Metaverses universally comprise the following four commonalities: (a) a shared social space with avatars to represent users; (b) a world for avatars to inhabit and interact; (c) a space that allows users to own virtual goods as they would physical goods; and (d) a space that allows users to create their virtual property [7].

The idea of the metaverse extends an already existing concept: that of Second Life, a cross-platform online community created in 2003 in which users create avatars and essentially lead a "second life" instead of their main life in the real world [26]. Unsurprisingly, user interest in Second Life waned over time and many other metaverses currently exist or are in development. Facebook's official name change to Meta in 2021 signalled its commitment to creating a new and potentially dominant metaverse [7].

With the metaverse as a new social platform, both academics and the fashion industry are asking how these new technologies can reshape brands, reinvent the consumer experience, and alter consumer behaviour [7].

In this digital world, forward-thinking fashion brands are increasing digital product lines for this social space: a place where predominantly young consumers lead lives online with avatars that can move, talk, and customize themselves to look the way their creators want. They can own property, wear clothes, and engage in animated activities. NFTs can serve as a decentralised approach to track and establish ownership of virtual goods as they traverse metaverses owned by different corporations [27].

Recent events such as Metaverse Fashion Week (MVFW) have shown that digital fashion is real and is attracting interest from global brands and fashionistas around the world. Forever 21, for example, introduced the collection of wearables created specifically for the metaverse. For his part, Philipp Plein founded the Museum of NFT Arts, which is open to all users, and launched his first collection for the metaverse with a special catwalk fashion show in collaboration with 3D artist Antoni Tudisco.

For their part, H&M, Gucci, and Ralph Lauren are opening new virtual stores to sell their digital clothing and offer their consumers an immersive shopping experience. Other brands have partnered with gaming platforms, such as Roblox and Fortnite, to launch their digital products. Balenciaga, for example, partnered with Fortnite to give players the ability to purchase branded clothing for their avatars, helping to increase interest in Balenciaga [28].

These global companies are increasingly implementing AI in the design of interactions between their brands and consumers. Many of them are also incorporating NFTs to certify the authenticity of digital images available for purchase [7].

5. The Fashion Consumer in the Metaverse

Currently, the fashion industry is experiencing an inflection point as its core customers shift from millennials to generation Z [29]. By 2025, this generation will account for approximately half of all global sales of personal luxury goods [30]. Individuals born between 1994 and 2010 are the first digital natives, since they have been adopting any technology that facilitates and improves their daily lives from an early age [2]. This is a generation that dominates, by 60%, the metaverse, mainly through video games and applications such as Roblox, Zepeto, or Fortnite [31].

Thanks to hyper-connectivity across devices and platforms, members of this generation communicate effectively on a wide range of issues that, in turn, shape consumer preferences, based primarily on customer experience. Interaction, transparency, and social responsibility are inseparably linked to the way they consume [32].

This generation exhibits particularly unique purchasing and consumption behaviours [33]. Previous studies have shown the influence of the fashion sector's communication strategies on social networks such as Instagram on their purchasing decisions by generating positive emotions, especially among their female audiences [34].

Other studies have focused on the importance of sustainable initiatives and corporate social responsibility (CSR) strategies in the purchasing decisions of luxury fashion brands for generation Z, as a result of their growing environmental awareness [35,36]. The search for uniqueness and differentiation, on the one hand, and the bandwagon effect, on the other, seem to be the main motivations of generation Z when buying luxury fashion brands [37], which is why this generation takes into account the recommendations of their circle of friends or the influencers they follow [38].

6. Method

In order to identify the interests of consumers regarding the metaverse, this study used a quantitative descriptive cross-sectional method based on external secondary sources in which we analysed data trends to obtain a complete overview of the research.

For this, we used Google Trends to obtain the relative frequency of searches for words related to the terms "metaverse" and "fashion" on the various Google platforms: the web search engine, YouTube, Images, News and Shopping. The tool allowed us to obtain information on the number of searches that have been carried out on the Google page (https://www.google.com) on these two terms.

To analyse whether or not all the analysed platforms behave in the same way when searching for the terms "metaverse" and "fashion", a Kruskal–Wallis test was carried out. This non-parametric test is used to determine whether a dataset derives from the same population or not. The sets analysed included Google, YouTube, Google Images, Google News, and Google Shopping. The Kruskal–Wallis H test analysis confirms that Google's five communication platforms do not behave in the same way. The expected result was that the consumer behaviours do not differ according to the platform used, implying that marketers in fashion organisations should not necessarily plan different strategies for each platform. Therefore, the hypothesis is that consumer interest does not seem to vary depending on the content format (video, text, images).

The study scope covers, as work units, the period between 1 January and 31 December 2022, in a global territorial context.

While the proposed method using secondary data and Google Trends provides valuable insights into consumer behaviour related to fashion and the metaverse, it is essential to acknowledge certain limitations. Secondary data, by nature, may not capture real-time or comprehensive consumer interactions, potentially leading to gaps in understanding nuanced behaviours. Additionally, Google Trends data, while indicative of search interest, may not directly reflect actual consumer behaviour or purchasing decisions. Factors such as search volume fluctuations, algorithm changes, and user demographics can influence the data interpretation. Therefore, while the analysis offers valuable trends and patterns, it is important to interpret the findings with caution and consider the inherent limitations of using secondary data sources.

7. Results

7.1. Analysis of Results in Google Trends

As described in Section 2, Google Trends explains, "the numbers reflect search interest in relation to the maximum value of a graph in a given region and period. A value of 100 indicates the maximum popularity of a term, while 50 and 0 indicate that a term is half as popular as the maximum value or that there was not enough data for the term, respectively". Research Question 1 (RQ1) seeks to identify the geographical locations of users who extensively search for the terms "metaverse" and "fashion" on the Internet. The popularity index for these search terms on Google in 2022 peaked in March, as shown in Figure 1. Previous studies, such as Jun et al. [39], have validated the effectiveness of Google Trends as a suitable tool for analysing user interests across diverse domains.

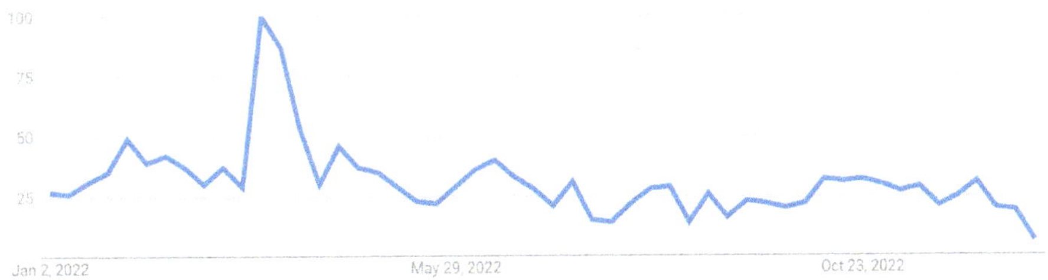

Figure 1. Interest in the concepts "metaverse" and "fashion" in the Google web search engine in 2022. Source: Google Trends (2023).

In terms of location, interest was detected in 14 different regions, with Singapore standing out above the rest. The other locations, in descending order of user interest were Hong Kong, the United Kingdom, Italy, the Netherlands, Spain, France, Australia, the United States, Canada, Germany, India, Argentina, and Brazil. Focusing on cities, London and New York stand out significantly.

To go into greater detail, regarding Research Question 2 (RQ2), which referred to what other words are associated with the terms "metaverse" and "fashion" in Internet searches, we analysed related queries in order to examine the related topics users were interested in. Thus, we observed that the leading web queries were mainly related to both concepts separately. At the company level, only Gucci and Nike appeared, albeit with little relative weight. Table 1 shows the score for each related query based on a relative scale in which 100 indicates the most frequent search query and a value of 50 indicates queries whose search frequency is half the search frequency of the most popular query, and so on.

Finally, and in relation to the previous table, it should be noted that the three searches that experienced the greatest increase in frequency compared to the previous year were "fashion in the metaverse" (+140%), "decentraland" (110%) and "nft" (70%). As has been shown before, search statistics have a certain explanatory capacity for user's interests [40]. In this way, it is possible to predict the growth of the phenomenon.

Next, our analysis proposed Research Question 3 (RQ3) to identify whether there are significant differences in search keywords between the different Google corporate communication platforms. Following the examination of the Google search engine, our attention shifted to the second Google tool, YouTube. Figure 2 shows the popularity index throughout 2022 of the search for both concepts at the same time on YouTube, reaching its maximum in March, just as for the web search engine but following a more irregular trend. Interaction with YouTube as a social space permits the detection of new interests in a self-directed mode [41].

Table 1. Queries related to the concept "metaverse and fashion" in Google in 2022.

Related Queries	Relative Scale
fashion week metaverse	100
fashion in the metaverse	44
nft fashion	34
nft	34
nft metaverse	33
digital fashion	26
decentraland	25
what is metaverse	22
metaverse fashion show	22
virtual fashion	21
metaverse fashion week decentraland	19
decentraland fashion week	19
metaverse fashion brand	17
metaverse meaning	13
gucci metaverse	10
what is the metaverse	10
roblox	9
metaverse news	8
nike metaverse	7
business of fashion	7
web3	5
facebook metaverse	5
metaverse fashion council	4
metaverse fashion summit	4
dressx	3

Source: Google Trends (2023).

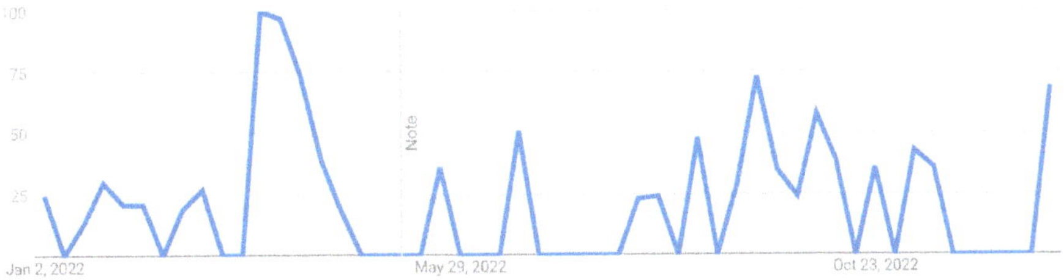

Figure 2. Interest in the concepts "metaverse" and "fashion" on YouTube in 2022. Source: Google Trends (2023).

In terms of location, interest was seen in eight different regions, with the United Kingdom standing out above the rest. The other locations, in descending order of user interest were Germany, Canada, Italy, Brazil, France, the United States. and India. Focusing on cities, New York primarily stands out.

To go into greater detail, we analysed related queries in order to examine the related topics users were interested in. Thus, the leading web queries were mainly related to the organisation of events (Table 2).

Table 2. Queries related to the concept "metaverse and fashion" on YouTube in 2022.

Related Queries	Relative Scale
metaverse fashion week	100
metaverse fashion show	50
metaverse fashion week 2022	20

Source: Google Trends (2023).

Finally, and in relation to the previous table, the search that experienced the greatest increase in frequency compared to the previous year was "metaverse fashion week" (+550%).

Next, we focused our analysis on the third Google tool mentioned in the method, Google Images. Figure 3 shows the popularity index throughout 2022 of the search for both concepts at the same time in Images, reaching its maximum in May, and following a trend more similar to YouTube than to the Google web search engine.

Figure 3. Interest in the concepts "metaverse" and "fashion" in Google Images in 2022. Source: Google Trends (2023).

At the location level, interest was detected in 10 different regions, Hong Kong standing out above the rest. The other locations, in descending order of user interest were the United Kingdom, Italy, the Netherlands, France, India, Canada, Germany, Spain and the United States. Focusing on cities, London and New York stand out, as for the web browser.

To go into greater detail, we analysed related queries in order to examine the related topics users were interested in. Thus, it can be seen, as was the case for YouTube, that the leading online queries were mainly related to the organisation of events (Table 3).

Table 3. Queries related to the concept "metaverse and fashion" in Google Images in 2022.

Related Queries	Relative Scale
Metaverse Fashion Week	100
Metaverse Fashion Show	61

Source: Google Trends (2023).

We next centred our analysis on the fourth Google tool mentioned in the method, Google News. Figure 4 shows the popularity index throughout 2022 of the search for both concepts at the same time in News, reaching its maximum in January. In this case, though, the trend was distinct from those seen in the other selected tools since no searches were carried out by users most of the time. Related to Google News, [39] point out that the search results returned by Google News offers evidence of personalisation based on browsing history. Therefore, this is a factor to consider when analysing user interests using this Google tool.

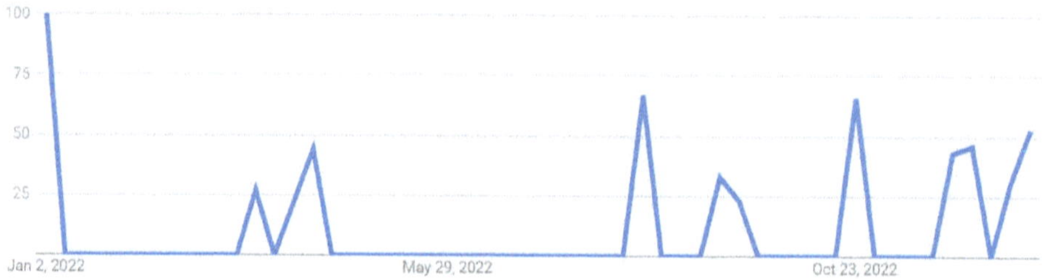

Figure 4. Interest in the concepts "metaverse" and "fashion" in Google News in 2022. Source: Google Trends (2023).

At the location level, interest was observed in three different regions, with Canada standing out above the rest. The other locations, in descending order of user interest were France and the United States. Focusing on cities, New York stands out, as it did with the previous tools. Regarding related queries, the search did not yield enough data to display results.

Finally, we analysed the fifth and last Google tool mentioned in the method, namely Google Shopping. Figure 5 shows the popularity index throughout 2022 of the search for both concepts at the same time in Shopping, reaching its maximum in November and following a similar trend to Google News, since for much of time there were no searches by users. Regarding digital markets, like Google Shopping, it is important to note that they have several characteristics, the principal two being network effects and economies of scale and scope with low marginal cost [42]. The first one means that the value of the platform increases as the number of users grows. Therefore, and applied to the case of Google Shopping and due to its growth in recent months, the information provided by the tool has become increasingly valuable.

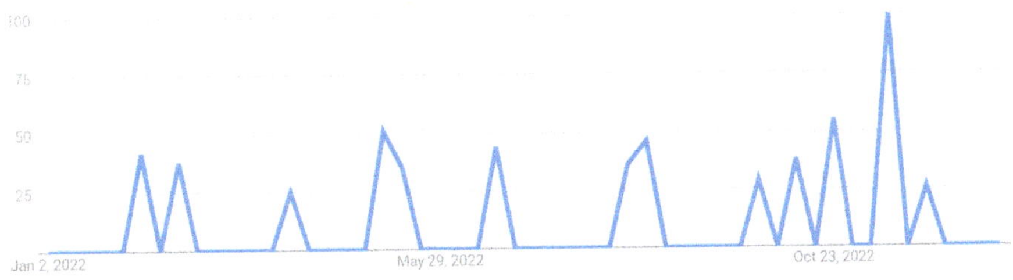

Figure 5. Interest in the concepts "metaverse" and "fashion" in Google Shopping in 2022. Source: Google Trends (2023).

For all other information, location, and related queries, the search did not yield enough data to display results.

7.2. Kruskal–Wallis Test

In order to determine whether all the analysed platforms behaved in the same way or not when searching for the terms "metaverse & fashion", a Kruskal–Wallis test was carried out. This non-parametric test is used to determine whether a set of data comes from the same population. For this reason, and as shown in Table 4, the first step was to assign the average range to each group, defined as:

- Group 1: Google Search.
- Group 2: YouTube.
- Group 3: Google Images.
- Group 4: Google News.
- Group 5: Google Shopping.

Table 4. Mean ranges, Kruskal–Wallis test.

	V1	N	Mean Range
V2	1	52	176.31
	2	52	132.49
	3	52	147.78
	4	52	97.39
	5	52	98.53
	Total	260	

Source: Authors.

As the main result and following the data in Table 5, as the p-value (asymptotic significance) is less than 0.05, the null hypothesis that the population medians are equal is rejected. Therefore, we conclude that, with a significance level of 5%, the data differ between the five corporate communication platforms. That is, the population medians are not equal.

Table 5. Test statistics, Kruskal–Wallis test *.

	V2
Kruskal–Wallis H	48.322
gl	4
Asymptotic sig.	0.000

* Grouping variable: V1. Source: Authors.

The analysis carried out is based on a Kruskal–Wallis test. This is a non-parametric statistical test used to determine whether there are significant differences between two or more independent groups on a continuous or ordinal outcome variable [43]. It is often used as an alternative to the one-way analysis of variance (ANOVA) test when the data do not meet the assumptions of normality and equal variances.

The Kruskal–Wallis test ranks the data from all groups together, calculates the sum of ranks for each group, and compares these sums to determine whether they differ significantly [44]. The test is based on the null hypothesis that the medians of all groups are equal.

To conduct the Kruskal–Wallis test, we carried out the following steps:

1. Rank the data from all groups together.
2. Calculate the sum of ranks for each group.
3. Calculate the test statistic, H, using the formula:

$$H = [(12/(n(n + 1))) \times sum(Tj\hat{}2)] - 3(n + 1)$$

where Tj is the sum of ranks in group j and n is the total number of observations.

4. Calculate the degrees of freedom (df) using the formula:

$$df = k - 1$$

where k is the number of groups.

5. Determine the *p*-value using the appropriate distribution table on the statistical software.

In our case, the *p*-value is less than the level of significance (e.g., 0.05), so we can reject the null hypothesis and conclude that there are significant differences between the analysed platforms.

As already indicated, and to conclude, the Kruskal–Wallis H test confirms that Google's five communication platforms do not behave in the same way. Google's platforms exhibit different search behaviours due to various factors. First, each platform is designed to meet different search needs. For example, Google Search is designed to provide quick answers to general questions and queries, while YouTube focuses on video results and Google Maps on geographic information [45]. Moreover, the platforms also use different ranking algorithms and metrics to rank and display search results. Each platform has its own set of ranking factors, which can include relevance, authority, freshness, and geographic location [45].

On the other hand, each platform has different usage patterns and audiences. Users may have different search intentions and expectations on each platform. For example, a user searching for information on a topic on Google Search may have a different intention than a user searching for the same thing on YouTube or Google News.

Finally, search behaviour can also be affected by personalisation. Google uses user data, including location, search history, and user activity, to personalize search results. This means that the search results may be different for different users [46].

As we have seen for the "metaverse" and "fashion" searches, Google's platforms exhibit different search behaviours due to a combination of factors, including user intent, personalisation, differences in ranking algorithms, and the usage patterns and audiences of each platform.

7.3. Words Related to the Terms "Metaverse & Fashion"

The results of the word cloud analysis related to the concepts "metaverse" and "fashion" carried out using the five Google search tools and showing the results displayed and expressing the frequency of appearance of the words extracted and derived from the word analysis in a two-dimensional space in the form of a cloud for easy recognition, are shown in Figure 6.

Figure 6. Word cloud of the terms "metaverse & fashion" based on Google Trends related queries. Source: Authors.

The results of the word cloud visualisation show the frequency of occurrence of the word according to its size and location. As shown in the results of the frequency analysis, the high frequency of "nft metaverse" is significant and locates it in the middle. It is followed, in order of relevance, by words such as "digital fashion", "nft fashion", "what is metaverse", and "decentraland".

These types of word cloud graphics make it easy for companies to recognize the most relevant search terms, which can help them when creating marketing strategies connected to the search topic. They help to understand the results of the study in a faster and more intuitive way and encourage creativity.

8. Conclusions and Discussion

Fashion brands seek to work on brand awareness and on/off-line cross-channel options (coupons, dual sales) and provide value enhancement through a virtual offer. Today, the main interest of fashion brands is to take positions in the emerging market that new technologies allow, including the metaverse. It is worth noting that the metaverse is still in its nascent stage and the extent to which fashion brands will be able to capitalize on it remains to be seen [27,40].

The metaverse has the potential to change consumer behaviour in several ways. The immersive and interactive nature of the metaverse can create new opportunities for fashion brands to engage with customers and build relationships. It can also change how consumers discover, learn about, and purchase products [24]. In the metaverse, consumers can interact with digital products in a more realistic and engaging way, allowing them to obtain a better sense of how a product will look and feel before they make a purchase. This can help to reduce the risk of buyer's remorse and increase customer satisfaction [23]. The metaverse can also create new opportunities for social commerce in which consumers can discover and purchase products through their social networks. Additionally, the metaverse can also support new forms of commerce, such as virtual item trading and digital currency.

However, the metaverse can also have a negative impact on consumer behaviour. The immersive nature of the metaverse can make it difficult for consumers to distinguish between the virtual and real world, leading to addiction and escapism [35]. Additionally, virtual environments can also facilitate the spread of misinformation and disinformation [47], and companies will have to address these issues. In RQ1, we analysed the location of users who most frequently use the terms "metaverse" and "fashion" in their Internet searches.

Overall, the metaverse has the potential to change consumer behaviour in ways that are both positive and negative. It is important for fashion brands and companies to understand how the metaverse is likely to change consumer behaviour in order to create effective strategies for engaging with customers in this new digital environment. This study aims to provide a primary tool to fashion brands by analysing Internet search behaviour for the terms "metaverse" and "fashion".

Despite the growing number of studies that have emerged on tools that allow the analysis and monitoring of searches, such as Google Trends, and that are currently used by various organisations to guide digital marketing practices and even to predict purchasing behaviour, this is, to our knowledge, one of the first studies to monitor absolute values of keyword searches. As such, it constitutes a valuable asset for the analysis of consumer search behaviour.

The literature review revealed the opportunities that new information and communication technologies offer marketing professionals to improve their strategies. Along this line, the metaverse stands out as one of the tools already currently being used, with an exponential growth trend in the short term. The present study therefore analysed interest in this concept in the fashion sector. For this, the concepts of metaverse and fashion were taken into account.

The data collected through Google Trends throughout 2022 worldwide allowed us to conclude that there is growing consumer interest in both terms on the Internet, despite the fact that the behaviour of the five Google search tools is nonhomogeneous.

Aligned with the results of other previous studies [14,39], we have shown that the purpose of using Big Data is evolving from monitoring to predicting based on the possibility of accurately forecasting using time series analysis models. In short, our findings offer guidelines for the development of efficient and effective digital marketing, both for operators in the fashion sector and those responsible for the development of new technologies in digital marketing. RQ2 examined what other words are associated with the terms "metaverse" and "fashion" in Internet searches, as the complexity of defining concepts pushes people to use different combinations of concepts to specify the meaning they want to give to their searches.

To address RQ3, in order to determine whether all the analysed platforms behaved in the same way or not when searching with the terms "metaverse & fashion", a Kruskal–Wallis H test was carried out and confirmed that Google's five communication platforms do not behave in the same way. Google's platforms exhibit different search behaviours due to different factors. Firstly, each platform is designed to meet different search needs. Secondly, each platform has different usage patterns and audiences. Finally, search behaviour can also be affected by personalisation.

The present study highlights the advantages of developing distinct strategies for each of the five Google platforms analysed in terms of SEO. By tailoring strategies to each platform, brands can potentially increase their popularity and click-through rates, establishing a framework for more successful SEO strategies. Moreover, fashion brands can elevate their digital marketing approaches by customizing content and campaigns to align with the unique user behaviour on specific platforms such as Google, YouTube, Google Images, Google News, and Google Shopping. Understanding the preferences and characteristics of users on these platforms enables brands to create targeted and compelling content that resonates with their audience. Through the analysis of platform-specific trends, engagement metrics and user demographics, fashion brands can optimize their marketing endeavours to enhance reach and impact. By integrating platform-specific strategies that cater to the behaviour of users on each channel, brands can boost brand visibility, engagement levels, and conversion rates in the digital landscape.

This research has a number of limitations that offer possibilities for future research. Firstly, only the analysis and monitoring tool Google Trends was used. Therefore, to generalize and confirm the results obtained in this study, it could be replicated with other applications such as Keywordini, Google Keyword Tool, or Follow the Hashtag [5]. Moreover, to broaden the research, other keywords could be included in the analysis. Finally, it would be useful to study and compare user reaction to those keywords, including industry-specific brands.

Author Contributions: Methodology, C.R.V.; Investigation, M.G.I. and J.L.D.O.A.; Resources, J.L.D.O.A.; Writing—original draft, M.G.I. and J.L.D.O.A.; Writing—review & editing, C.R.V. All authors have read and agreed to the published version of the manuscript.

Funding: This article is part of the project "Social Media and Entrepreneurship" (B02.0402-P2) financed by the Chair of Entrepreneurship and Family Business UAO CEU (2021-2024).

Data Availability Statement: The data presented in this study are available in this article.

Conflicts of Interest: The authors declare no conflict of interest.

References

1. Weiss, C. Fashion retailing in the metaverse. *Fash. Style Popul. Cult.* **2022**, *9*, 523–538. [CrossRef]
2. González, P. *Digital Fashion in the Metaverse*; Politécnico de Milán: Milan, Italy, 2022. Available online: https://bit.ly/gonzalez-gucci (accessed on 28 May 2024).
3. Shin, J.Y.; Suk, J.; Chung, J.E. Consumer Responses to Fashion in the Metaverse: A Text-Mining Analysis on Online News Comments. In *Advances in Information and Communication: Proceedings of the 2023 Future of Information and Communication Conference (FICC)*; Springer Nature Switzerland: Cham, Switzerland, 2023; Volume 1, pp. 12–24.
4. Estrada, F.A.P.; von Wobeser, L.H. Google Trends y Ubersuggest como herramientas de análisis del com-portamiento del consumidor. Estudio de caso de la microempresa Yaxkin, Cancún-México. *RECAI Rev. Estud. Contaduría Adm. Inf.* **2017**, *6*, 25–46.
5. Gutiérrez, J.J.P. Herramientas para el análisis y monitoreo en Redes Sociales. *Int. Rev. Inf. Ethics* **2011**, *16*, 33–40. [CrossRef]
6. Garcia, C.C. Contemporary changes and challenges in the practice of trend forecasting. *Int. J. Fash. Stud.* **2023**, *10*, 75–98. [CrossRef]
7. Joy, A.; Zhu, Y.; Peña, C.; Brouard, M. Digital future of luxury brands: Metaverse, digital fashion, and non-fungible tokens. *Strateg. Chang.* **2022**, *31*, 337–343. [CrossRef]
8. Keywords Everywhere. Keyword Research on the Go. 2023. Available online: https://keywordseverywhere.com/ (accessed on 28 May 2024).
9. Barrera, K.G.; Shah, D. Marketing in the metaverse: Conceptual understanding, framework, and research agenda. *J. Bus. Res.* **2023**, *155*, 113420. [CrossRef]
10. Grillo, M. Moda e metaverso: Uno studio esporativo sulla prima metaverso fashion week. *Int. Vis. Cult. Rev.* **2022**, *9*, 1–10. [CrossRef]
11. Statista. *Market Share of Leading Desktop Search Engines Worldwide from January 2015 to January 2024*; Statista: Hamburg, Germany, 2024.
12. Rativa, A.S.; van Limpt, Z.; Kraaijeveld, S. Branding and Google Trends: Software companies' names, the metaverse and virtual reality. In Proceedings of the Finnish Academy of Marketing Annual Conference: FAMAC 2022, Helsinki, Finland, 2–3 May 2022.
13. Dergiades, T.; Mavragani, E.; Pan, B. Google Trends and Tourists' Arrivals: Emerging Biases and Proposed Corrections. *Tour. Manag.* **2018**, *66*, 108–120. [CrossRef]
14. Silva, E.; Madsen, D.Ø. Google Trends. In *Encyclopedia of Tourism Management and Marketing*; Buhalis, D., Ed.; Edward Elgar: Northampton, MA, USA, 2022.
15. Chumnumpan, P.; Shi, X. Understanding new products' market performance using Google Trends. *Australas. Mark. J. (AMJ)* **2019**, *27*, 91–103. [CrossRef]
16. Karamitros Dimitrios, T.O.; Fouskas, K. A study of digital customer journey through google trends. In Proceedings of the Xiv Balkan Conference on Operational Research—Virtual Balcor 2020, Thessaloniki, Greece, 30 September–3 October 2020.
17. Choi, H.; Varian, H. Predicting the Present with Google Trends. *Econ. Rec.* **2012**, *88*, 2–9. [CrossRef]
18. Orense Fuentes, M.; Rojas Orduña, O.I. *SEO Como Triunfar en Buscadores*; ESIC: New Delhi, India, 2010.
19. Mauresmo, K.; Petrova, A. *SEO for WordPress, How I Hit Page*; Read2Learn: Beverly Hills, CA, USA, 2016; Volume 1.
20. Brydges, T.; Hracs, B.J.; Lavanga, M. Evolution versus entrenchment: Debating the impact of digitization, de-mocratization and diffusion in the global fashion industry. *Int. J. Fash. Stud.* **2018**, *5*, 365–372. [CrossRef] [PubMed]
21. Statista. *Número de Usuarios del Metaverso a Nivel Mundial Entre 2022 y 2030*; Statista: Hamburg, Germany, 2024.
22. Anderson, J.; Rainie, L. *The Metaverse in 2040*; Pew Research Center: Washington, DC, USA, 2022. Available online: https://www.pewresearch.org/internet/2022/06/30/the-metaverse-in-2040/ (accessed on 28 May 2024).
23. Zarantonello, L.; Schmitt, B.H. Experiential AR/VR: A consumer and service framework and research agenda. *J. Serv. Manag.* **2022**, *34*, 34–55. [CrossRef]

24. Shapiro, E.; Artificial Intelligence Will Change World, Says Nvidia CEO. Time. 2021. Available online: https://time.com/5955412/artificial-intelligence-nvidia-jensen-huang/ (accessed on 28 May 2024).
25. Bosworth, A.; Clegg, N. *Building the Metaverse Responsibly*; Meta: Menlo Park, CA, USA, 2021.
26. Tidy, J. Zuckerberg's Metaverse: Lessons from Second Life. *BBC News*, 13 November 2021; 5.
27. Orland, K. So What Is the "Metaverse" Exactly? 2021. Available online: https://arstechnica.com/gaming/2021/11/everyone-pitching-the-metaverse-has-a-different-idea-of-what-it-is/ (accessed on 28 May 2024).
28. McDowell, M.; Meta's New Digital Fashion Marketplace Will Sell PRADA, Balenciaga and Thom Browne. Vogue Business. 2022. Available online: https://cutt.ly/PLCSIlQ (accessed on 28 May 2024).
29. Wang, W. How Has the Fashion Industry Reacted to Gen z's Completely Different Consumption Concepts and Shopping Habits? *Acad. J. Humanit. Soc. Sci.* **2021**, *4*, 72–80. [CrossRef]
30. Salpini, C.; Millennials, Gen Z to Account for 45% of Luxury Market. Retail Drive. 2017. Available online: https://bit.ly/salpini-gucci (accessed on 28 May 2024).
31. Colomo, A. *Gen Z and the Metaverse: Key Insights*; Inlea: Barcelona, Spain, 2022. Available online: https://bit.ly/colomo-gucci (accessed on 28 May 2024).
32. Kocai, E.; Smaliukiene, R.; Tamuleviciute, A. Generation Z and Consumption: How communication environment shapes youth choices. *Media Stud.* **2020**, *11*, 24–45.
33. Jain, V.; Takayanagi, M.; Malthouse, E.C. Effects of show windows on female consumers' shopping behaviour. *J. Consum. Mark.* **2014**, *31*, 380–390. [CrossRef]
34. Djafarova, E.; Bowes, T. Instagram made Me buy it: Generation Z impulse purchases in fashion industry. *J. Retail. Consum. Serv.* **2021**, *59*, 102345. [CrossRef]
35. McCormick, H.; Ram, P. Take a Stand: The Importance of Social Sustainability and Its Effect on Generation Z Consumption of Luxury Fashion Brands. In *Sustainable Luxury*; Palgrave Advances in Luxury; Henninger, C.E., Athwal, N.K., Eds.; Palgrave Macmillan Cham: Cham, Switzerland, 2022.
36. Youn, S.-Y.; Cho, E. CSR ads matter to luxury fashion brands: A construal level approach to understand Gen Z consumers' eWOM on social media. *J. Fash. Mark. Manag. Int. J.* **2021**, *26*, 516–533. [CrossRef]
37. Cho, E.; Kim-Vick, J.; Yu, U.-J. Unveiling motivation for luxury fashion purchase among Gen Z consumers: Need for uniqueness versus bandwagon effect. *Int. J. Fash. Des. Technol. Educ.* **2022**, *15*, 24–34. [CrossRef]
38. The Center for Generational Kinetics. Generation Z Research State of Gen Z. *Consumers*. 2020. Available online: https://bit.ly/tcgk-gucci (accessed on 28 May 2024).
39. Jun, S.; Hyoung, S.; San, C. Ten years of research change using Google Trends: From the perspective of big data utilizations and applications. *Technol. Forecast. Soc. Change* **2018**, *130*, 69–87. [CrossRef]
40. Gomes, M.A.; Marques, S.; Dias, A. The impact of digital influencers' characteristics on purchase intention of fashion products. *J. Glob. Fash. Mark.* **2022**, *13*, 187–204. [CrossRef]
41. Dubovi, I.; Tabak, I. An empirical analysis of knowledge co-construction in YouTube comments. *Comput. Educ.* **2020**, *156*, 103939. [CrossRef]
42. Alves, M.P. *An Overview of Google Shopping Case in Brazil and Europe Union*; UNIGOU Remote, Czech-Brazilian Academic Program; INCBAC: Prague, Czech Republic, 2022.
43. Carrasco, J.; García, S.; Rueda, M.; Das, S.; Herrera, F. Recent trends in the use of statistical tests for comparing swarm and evolutionary computing algorithms: Practical guidelines and a critical review. *Swarm Evol. Comput.* **2020**, *54*, 100665. [CrossRef]
44. Edelman, B.; Lai, Z. Design of Search Engine Services: Channel Interdependence in Search Engine Results. *J. Mark. Res.* **2016**, *53*, 881–900. [CrossRef]
45. Erdmann, A.; Arilla, R.; Ponzoa, J.M. Search engine optimization: The long-term strategy of keyword choice. *J. Bus. Res.* **2022**, *144*, 650–662. [CrossRef]
46. Rangaswamy, A.; Giles, C.L.; Seres, S. A Strategic Perspective on Search Engines: Thought Candies for Practitioners and Researchers. *J. Interact. Mark.* **2009**, *23*, 49–60. [CrossRef]
47. Chen-Yu, J.H.; Kincade, D.H.; Rhee, Y. Effects of consumer characteristics and product presentations on online apparel impulse buying. *J. Glob. Fash. Mark.* **2022**, *13*, 205–220. [CrossRef]

future internet

Article

Security and Privacy in Physical–Digital Environments: Trends and Opportunities

Carolina Pereira , Anabela Marto , Roberto Ribeiro , Alexandrino Gonçalves , Nuno Rodrigues , Carlos Rabadão , Rogério Luís de Carvalho Costa *and Leonel Santos

Computer Science and Communication Research Center (CIIC), Escola Superior de Tecnologia e Gestão (ESTG), Polytechnic University of Leiria, 2411-901 Leiria, Portugal; 2232644@my.ipleiria.pt (C.P.); anabela.marto@ipleiria.pt (A.M.); roberto.ribeiro@ipleiria.pt (R.R.); alex@ipleiria.pt (A.G.); nunorod@ipleiria.pt (N.R.); carlos.rabadao@ipleiria.pt (C.R.); leonel.santos@ipleiria.pt (L.S.)

* Correspondence: rogerio.l.costa@ipleiria.pt

Abstract: Over recent decades, internet-based communication has grown exponentially, accompanied by a surge in cyber threats from malicious actors targeting users and organizations, heightening the demand for robust security and privacy measures. With the emergence of physical–digital environments based on Mixed Reality (MR) and the Metaverse, new cybersecurity, privacy, and confidentiality challenges have surfaced, requiring innovative approaches. This work examines the current landscape of cybersecurity concerns in MR and Metaverse environments, focusing on their unique vulnerabilities and the risks posed to users and their data. Key challenges include authentication issues, data breaches, and risks to user anonymity. The work also explores advancements in secure design frameworks, encryption techniques, and regulatory approaches to safeguard these technologies. Additionally, it identifies opportunities for further research and innovation to strengthen data protection and ensure a safe, trustworthy experience in these environments.

Keywords: confidentiality; metaverse; mixed reality; privacy; cybersecurity

1. Introduction

The growing integration of technology into everyday life has fueled the rapid evolution of the Internet and digital communications, reshaping human–computer interaction (HCI). Over time, the Internet has transitioned from a mere communication tool to a ubiquitous presence, embedding itself deeply in daily activities. Information exchange now transcends human interactions, extending to machine-to-machine communications on an unprecedented scale.

Paul Milgram and Fumio Kishino's 1994 groundbreaking paper [1] marked the introduction of the term Mixed Reality(MR). This pioneering concept combines the physical and virtual worlds within the virtuality continuum [2] in the same visual display environment, encompassing Augmented Reality (AR), Augmented Virtuality (AV), Virtual Reality (VR), and any technology that allows interactions between digital material and real-world objects.

The technological advancements of these systems within the spectrum have enabled the creation of immersive technologies, which has led to the emergence of the *Metaverse*. In 1992, Neal Stephenson introduced the Metaverse in his novel "Snow Crash" [3]. According to Stephenson, the Metaverse is a virtual environment that runs parallel to the physical world and allows users to interact with each other through digital avatars. It is a virtual reality space where users can engage in several activities, including gaming, socializing, and commerce. It is a shared, persistent environment that allows users to create and customize their digital representations or avatars, through which users can interact with each other in real time.

While these innovations present unprecedented opportunities, they also introduce complex security, privacy, and confidentiality challenges. As physical–digital environments like MR and the Metaverse evolve, they become targets for novel threats and vulnerabilities. By addressing the intersection of security, privacy, and immersive technologies, this paper sheds light on the opportunities and risks in physical–digital environments, offering a roadmap for future advancements and challenges.

Therefore, the following research questions are posed:

- RQ1—What are the leading security risks stemming from the development and expansion of Metaverse and Mixed Reality technologies?
- RQ2—How can a user's privacy be maintained in the context of involving and participatory experiences in the Metaverse and Mixed Reality environments?
- RQ3—What are the ethical issues related to the collection, utilization, and distribution of data in Metaverse and Mixed Reality technologies, and how can these issues be mitigated?

A comprehensive search was conducted to support answering these questions. Keywords like "Metaverse", "Mixed Reality", "Augmented Reality", "Augmented Virtuality", "Virtual Reality", "security", "privacy", "confidentiality", "threats", "vulnerabilities", and "countermeasures" were among the many terms utilized to run the search in the multiple available databases, including Scopus, Web of Science, Google Scholar, MDPI, and IEEEXplore. Following this, data extraction was conducted using a standardized extraction form to capture key information, including author(s), publication year, research methodology, findings, and conclusions. Then, we conducted a thematic analysis to identify and organize significant themes and patterns within the selected literature.

The remainder of this paper is organized as follows. The next section introduces concepts related to MR and the Metaverse, describes their architecture, and presents application areas. Section 3 identifies potential attack vectors and discusses threats and countermeasures. Section 4 delves into challenges and possible solutions. Section 5 discusses research findings and outlines future research directions in securing and protecting these environments. Finally, Section 6 concludes the paper.

2. The Metaverse and Mixed Reality

MR is a technological paradigm that merges physical and digital worlds to create a unified and interactive environment where real-world and virtual elements coexist and interact in real-time. Positioned along the virtuality continuum [2], MR spans the spectrum between totally physical environments and fully immersive virtual realities, encompassing technologies such as AR, AV, and VR. Unlike purely virtual experiences, MR enables users to interact with real and virtual objects simultaneously, offering immersive and contextually enriched experiences. By leveraging advanced sensors, display systems, and processing power, MR enables seamless integration between digital content and the physical world, facilitating different applications in many areas, like education, healthcare, entertainment, and industrial training.

Milgram and Kishino's one-dimensional reality virtuality continuum provides an intelligible way to visualize the different concepts, as represented in Figure 1. The spectrum is a straight line with two ends. The physical and the virtual environments are placed on the line's left and right ends, respectively. AR lies towards the left end of the spectrum, while VR is at the right end. Although both these environments are MR systems, they are positioned differently on the "Mixed Reality Spectrum".

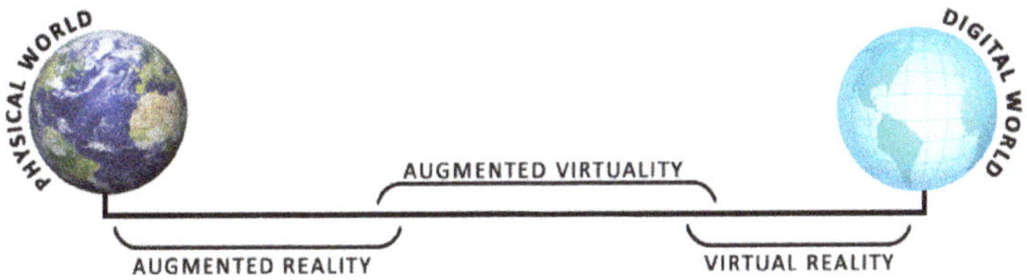

Figure 1. Simplified representation of the reality–virtuality continuum.

The term "Metaverse" originates from the Greek prefix "meta-", meaning "beyond" or "after", combined with "verse", derived from "universe". This fusion represents a reality transcending the physical universe, encompassing immersive virtual environments or digital worlds. The Metaverse refers to a digital realm that operates in parallel with the physical world. Within this virtual space, users can interact and communicate with one another through personalized avatars, utilizing VR and AR technologies to immerse themselves in the experience. This concept is gradually becoming tangible, allowing individuals to feel present through the whole experience, even if they are physically elsewhere.

The input devices, such as orientation trackers, magnetic trackers, and eye-tracking devices, coupled with the recent advancements in processing power, have made it possible to capture data about the physical environment and build a connection between humans, computers, and the environment by utilizing computer perceptions of the environment. The development of such systems has opened new doors for integrating virtual and physical worlds, creating a bridge between reality and virtuality, as shown in Figure 2.

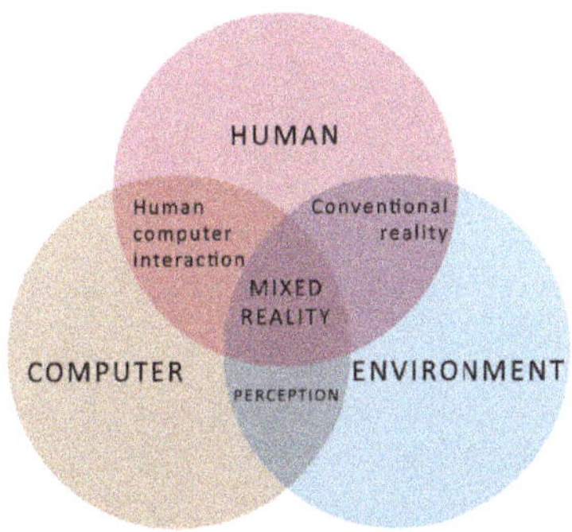

Figure 2. The interactions between humans, computers, and environments. Image adapted from [4].

2.1. Architectures

Understanding the architecture of the MR and the Metaverse is of considerable importance to gain insight into their infrastructure and operations and to address issues concerning scalability and performance. It is crucial to ensure the privacy and security of the users, protect their sensitive information, and thwart any risk of data breaches.

2.1.1. Mixed Reality

MR systems handle real-time data, complex interactions between physical and digital objects, and an increasing number of users, making scrutinizing their architecture vital to ensure efficient performance, privacy, and security. Protecting user data and preventing information breaches are critical concerns, especially as ME technologies keep advancing in applications ranging from healthcare to entertainment.

Figure 3 presents the typical architecture of MR systems, which consists of five layers that work together to enable immersive experiences by merging the real and virtual worlds. These layers form the foundation of MR systems, facilitating key operations such as data integration, interaction, and visualization. The first group comprises layers 1 to 4 and focuses on the technical infrastructure—system components, integration, application, and user interface layers—while layer 5 handles the user interaction that allows for real-time, intuitive engagement with the MR environment.

LAYER	LAYER NAME	LAYER DESCRIPTION
1	System Components	5G, WI-FI 6, HMDs, Cameras, Sensors, GPUs, MEMS (microelectromechanical systems)
2	Integration Architecture	Object Tracking, Spatial Mapping, AI Agents, Calibration Systems
3	Application	3D Engines, VR/AR/XR, Multitasking UI for immersive environments, Geospatial Mapping
4	User Interface	Smartglasses, Wearables, Haptic Gloves, Voice Commands, Gaze Control
5	User Interaction	Immersive Apps, Games, Real-time Collaboration, Mixed Reality Simulations

Figure 3. Layer architecture of Mixed Reality adapted from [5].

This architecture ensures that MR environments are robust, responsive, and capable of handling the diverse scenarios of real-world applications [5,6]. In the following, we describe each layer in further detail to provide a comprehensive understanding of how MR systems operate.

Layer 1: System Components

This layer consists of the hardware, such as head-mounted displays (HMDs), sensors, and cameras. Devices are chosen and calibrated based on the MR application goals.

Layer 2: Integration Architecture

In this layer, real-world objects are modeled and tracked, allowing interactions between real and virtual objects. Algorithms for calibration, object recognition, and tracking fall under this category, enabling MR systems to interpret physical and virtual environments.

Layer 3: Application

This handles the software logic that controls how virtual and real elements behave and interact. For instance, this layer governs how virtual objects would respond when a user interacts with them in the real world.

Layer 4: User Interface

This layer deals with user interaction. It allows users to control and interact with virtual objects through gestures, voice, or gaze without needing physical controllers.

Layer 5: User Interaction

This layer manages how users perceive and manipulate the MR space, ensuring immersion and real-time feedback.

2.1.2. Metaverse

The Metaverse comprises seven tiers that form the value chain of its marketplace, which can be broadly classified into two groups, as shown in Figure 4. The first group, comprising layers 1 to 6, concentrates on its foundational infrastructure, while the second group, consisting solely of layer 7, is dedicated to social activities within the Metaverse. Each layer will be expounded upon in greater detail in the following.

LAYER	LAYER FOCUS	LAYER NAME	LAYER DESCRIPTION
1	BASIC INFRASTRUCTURES	Infrastructure	5G, WIFI 8, 6G, CLOUD, 7NM TI 1.4 NM, MEMS, GPUs, Materials
2		Human Interface	Mobile, Smartglasses, Wearables, Haptic, Gestures, Voice, Neural
3		Decentralization	Edge Computing, AI Agents, Microservices, Blockchain
4		Spatial Computing	3D Engines, VR/AR,/XR, Multitasking UI Geospatial Mapping
5		Creator Economy	Design Tools, Asset Markets, Workflow, Commerse
6		Discovery	Ad Network, Social Curation, Ratings,Stores, Agents
7	SOCIAL ACTIVITIES	Experience	Games, Social, Esports, Theater, Shopping

Figure 4. Layer architecture of the Metaverse adapted from [7].

Layer 1: Infrastructure

This particular layer comprises the requisite technological infrastructure that enables the seamless operation of 5G, WiFi, Cloud, and other layers.

Layer 2: Human Interface

The second layer focuses on the hardware utilized to facilitate spatial computing, encompassing a range of devices such as mobile phones, smartwatches, smart glasses, and wearables. This integration of technology provides swift and accurate data collection concerning our environment.

Layer 3: Decentralization

The decentralization of the Metaverse is facilitated through the implementation of edge computing, AI agents, microservices, and blockchain, which allow user participation without the need for permission. This approach allows for a more democratic and inclusive environment that empowers users to engage with the Metaverse on their terms. With this technology, individuals have greater control over their experiences and can contribute to the development of the Metaverse in a more meaningful way. These decentralized technologies represent a significant step towards creating a more equitable and accessible virtual world.

Layer 4: Spatial Computing

Spatial computing combines digital and augmented realities, allowing us to digitize objects, enable sensors to detect moving objects, and map the physical world in 3D engines, VR, AR, and multitasking UI.

Layer 5: Creator Economy

This particular layer of the Metaverse is dedicated to the financial sector, where designers and creators utilize design tools and asset markets to establish the economy of Web 3.0. This sector is currently experiencing exponential growth and is poised to play a significant role in shaping the future of online commerce.

Layer 6: Discovery

Within the Metaverse ecosystem, two distinct discovery systems exist: inbound and outbound. Inbound discovery is characterized by individuals intentionally seeking out information, while outbound discovery involves proactively pushing messages to individuals, regardless of their request.

Layer 7: Experience

This layer defines user experience in the Metaverse, which includes video games, social interaction, shopping, sports, and many others.

2.2. Areas of Application

The Metaverse and MR were designed as versatile technologies that support several applications. With their ability to seamlessly bridge the physical and virtual worlds, they have the potential to revolutionize various fields, including education, smart cities, culture, medicine, business, and manufacturing. By leveraging the power of the Metaverse and MR, one can develop innovative solutions that address complex challenges and create new opportunities for growth and progress. Figure 5 displays examples of several domains and subdomains on which these technologies have been applied.

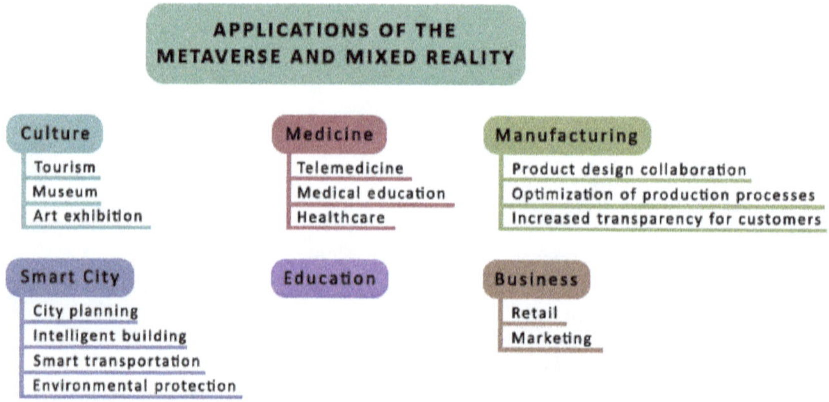

Figure 5. Some of the areas of application of the Metaverse and MR adapted from [8].

2.2.1. Culture

The Metaverse presents a significant opportunity to enhance cultural experiences by merging virtual and physical environments to create highly engaging and authentic interactions. This innovative technology has the potential to overcome traditional tourism's physical barriers and limitations, enabling visitors to engage with historic sites and monuments remotely. Through this, it facilitates new immersive experiences that not only captivate visitors but also transform their traveling and consumption habits.

MR enables the creation of virtual models of ancient buildings and monuments, enabling visitors to have an enhanced experience when interacting with them. Additionally, this technology may revolutionize the tourism industry by creating digital reconstructions of ancient cultural monuments that would otherwise be impossible to physically reconstruct without damaging the original piece.

2.2.2. Smart Cities

On another note, incorporating the Metaverse into smart cities can also provide significant advantages, particularly in traffic management, monitoring, planning, design, and transportation services. This integration may enhance the overall quality of life for residents.

Traditionally, the physical presence of architects is necessary at construction sites to perform urban construction planning. However, digital twins can create a virtual replica of the space, allowing architects and administrators to access it through the Metaverse without needing a physical presence. This technological innovation has the potential to revolutionize current construction planning methods by simulating construction possibilities and providing real-time status updates to construction workers.

Incorporating MR into smart cities can offer significant benefits across various sectors, particularly urban planning, construction, and infrastructure management. MR allows city planners, architects, and engineers to overlay virtual models onto real-world environments, facilitating real-time visualization and interaction with future city layouts, transportation systems, and public spaces. For instance, MR can enhance traffic management by enabling virtual simulations of traffic flow and pedestrian behavior, helping authorities design better roads, manage congestion, and improve overall transportation efficiency.

In construction, MR can complement digital twins by allowing architects and construction workers to interact with holographic models of buildings at the actual site. This technology enables real-time design adjustments, immediate feedback on construction progress, and more accurate visualizations of how new developments will integrate into the urban landscape. By combining virtual and physical perspectives, MR enhances decision-making and collaboration, reducing the need for physical presence while increasing the precision and efficiency of urban development projects. This innovation holds great potential for transforming urban infrastructure planning and management [5,6].

2.2.3. Medicine

As for healthcare, the Metaverse is transforming the industry by enabling medical professionals to communicate with patients more effectively through virtual interactions. This technology also provides a platform for creating calming virtual environments that can help alleviate patients' stress during treatment. Additionally, creating virtual representations of patients enables simulations of different treatments to determine the most appropriate course of action. The high level of realism of these virtual representations also allows for simulated and safe training of medical students without any risk of harm to patients. As a result, Metaverse technology is improving patient outcomes and revolutionizing healthcare education.

In healthcare, MR plays a transformative role by enhancing how medical professionals interact with patients and medical data. MR allows real-time collaboration between healthcare providers, enabling remote consultations and more interactive patient care. By overlaying virtual data on real-world medical environments, MR facilitates the visualization of patient information, such as MRI scans or 3D models, directly during physical examinations or surgeries. This augmented view helps clinicians make better-informed decisions. Additionally, MR is revolutionizing medical training by enabling simulations that combine physical practice with virtual guidance, allowing medical students to practice surgeries or procedures without having any real-life consequences while receiving immediate feedback. A notable component of this innovation is the creation of virtual patient scenarios, a concept that has been around for nearly 40 years [9]. The American Association of Medical Colleges (AAMC) defines these scenarios as "a specific type of computer-based program that simulates real-life clinical scenarios; learners emulate the roles of healthcare providers to obtain a patient history, conduct physical exams, and make diagnostic and therapeutic decisions" [10]. This approach facilitates the simulation of a variety of medical conditions, which can be derived from case studies available on websites or CD-ROMs, virtual reality simulations, or even robotic human-scale mannequins equipped with sensors [9], and can incorporate individual patient parameters such as age, medical history, and associated diseases. This realistic training environment helps to reduce errors and improve skill proficiency, all without risking patient safety. MR also aids in rehabilitation, where immersive experiences can support recovery by simulating real-world scenarios for therapeutic purposes. As a result, MR enhances both the quality of care and educational experiences in healthcare.

2.2.4. Education

In general, the Metaverse presents a promising opportunity for students to access a wide range of tools and engage in experiments that may be deemed unsafe in the physical world, which is particularly relevant when considering experiments involving hazardous chemical reactions. Furthermore, the Metaverse has the potential to provide a solution for the education of disabled children. Specifically, using avatars to simulate sign language human gestures can facilitate the learning process for children with hearing impairments. By leveraging the Metaverse, we can potentially improve the accessibility and safety of educational environments for a diverse range of students.

In contrast to the Metaverse, MR offers a unique opportunity to enhance education by blending the physical and virtual worlds, providing students with interactive experiences that bridge both realms. Through MR, students can engage with digital simulations of complex experiments, such as molecular chemistry or engineering processes, while maintaining a connection to their physical environment and ensuring safety without sacrificing the hands-on aspect of learning. For instance, students can manipulate virtual hazardous materials in real-time without any risk, making MR a valuable tool for conducting experiments that would be dangerous or impractical in a traditional classroom.

Moreover, MR holds significant potential for inclusive education, particularly for students with disabilities. It provides immersive tools like holographic projections and gesture-based interactions that facilitate learning. For example, MR allows hearing-impaired students to engage in sign language lessons through holograms or avatars that accurately replicate human gestures in their real-world environment. This approach not only supports the needs of students with disabilities but also fosters a more dynamic and engaging learning experience for all. By harnessing the power of MR, we can create safer, more accessible, and highly interactive educational environments that accommodate diverse learning needs.

2.2.5. Manufacturing

The application of MR in the manufacturing domain offers an even more immersive and interactive opportunity to enhance productivity, cut costs, and optimize factory processes. By overlaying digital information onto real-world environments, MR allows designers and engineers to visualize and interact with 3D models of products in real-time. This enables more efficient collaboration across teams, as design modifications can be immediately seen and tested in virtual spaces without needing physical prototypes. Through the development of digital twins, manufacturers can simulate production processes and solve problems in real-time, emphasizing user interaction with digital information. They can create physical models of equipment using tools like Simulink, while MATLAB is used to manage data, configure simulations, and enable real-time adjustments. Additionally, data can be integrated from Data Acquisition (DAQ) devices to monitor parameters such as temperature, power consumption, and pressure. Using AR interfaces, manufacturers can intuitively visualize these parameters, simulate faults, and facilitate more effective troubleshooting and decision-making. By analyzing system behavior under malfunction conditions, manufacturers can optimize workflows and identify inefficiencies before they occur in the real world. MR also aids in training employees by providing immersive, hands-on experiences in virtual factory setups, thereby reducing downtime and errors, ultimately leading to more streamlined and cost-effective operations.

Using the Metaverse technology in the manufacturing domain offers a significant opportunity to increase productivity, reduce costs, and enhance the understanding of factory performance. By enabling designers to collaborate on product design, the technology saves resources for both the creation and presentation of the product while also facilitating changes based on feedback from manufacturers. As a result, manufacturers can simulate blueprints, identify potential problems, and prevent them before they occur. This technology thus empowers manufacturers to streamline their workflows and improve efficiency, leading to a more productive and cost-effective operation.

2.2.6. Business

The Metaverse technology has the potential to significantly enhance businesses's productivity by enabling users to peruse online stores, search for desired products, and engage with them via their digital avatars. It represents a paradigm shift in conducting e-commerce, as users can now experience products in an immersive manner rather than merely adding them to their shopping carts. Additionally, by integrating AR with the Metaverse, businesses can develop innovative advertising strategies that allow users to try the product instead of merely viewing it being displayed.

The integration of the Metaverse into various sectors of our society is a critical undertaking. One of the key considerations in this process is ensuring the protection of user privacy, security, and confidentiality. Given the novelty and complexity of this emerging technology, there is a pressing need to establish precautions and standards that safeguard the interests of all stakeholders involved. Therefore, developing a regulatory framework that addresses potential risks and threats while promoting innovation and growth is essential. By doing so, one can harness the full potential of the Metaverse while upholding the ethical and legal standards that underpin our society.

MR also holds tremendous potential to revolutionize business operations and enhance productivity by blending real-world environments with digital interactions. In e-commerce, MR allows users to interact with virtual representations of products in real time, examining them from different angles and manipulating them within the physical space, creating a more engaging and informed shopping experience. This immersive approach can increase consumer confidence and reduce the gap between online shopping and in-store experiences. Additionally, by integrating MR into advertising strategies, businesses can offer customers the ability to "try before they buy", allowing them to interact with products virtually within their environment—something far more interactive than static online displays.

As MR technology becomes more integrated into various industries, safeguarding user privacy, security, and data confidentiality is crucial. Like the Metaverse, MR faces unique challenges regarding user data protection and the ethical use of immersive technologies. Establishing standards and regulatory frameworks is essential to mitigate risks such as unauthorized data access or the misuse of personal information. This framework should promote innovation while ensuring that users' rights are maintained, creating an environment where effectively adopting MR does not compromise ethical or legal standards.

2.3. *Ethical Issues*

Due to the reliance of these technologies on visual and auditory information, there are concerns about how their interactive nature manages the collection and use of user data. While these technologies are in use, they gather information about users and their actions. This data collection serves various purposes, including advising, informing, tracking, manipulating, and entertaining the end user [11]. Studies have shown that large-scale collection of user data can contribute to privacy risks, particularly when users are unaware of the extent to which their data are being stored or analyzed [12].

An ethical issue related to these technologies is their persuasive nature, especially regarding novelty, the exploitation of positive reputation, persistence, and control [11,13]. Because these technologies are relatively new in our daily lives, their novelty can easily obscure the designers' persuasive intentions from users, leading to potential misinformation and overreliance on these systems. Additionally, the widespread enthusiasm for new and innovative technological products enhances their reputation, fostering an unquestioning level of trust from users [14]. This trust can be exploited by designers and developers, leading to ethical concerns regarding user manipulation and autonomy. Another concerning issue is the targeting of vulnerable groups, including children, aged people, individuals with low socio-economic status, those with intellectual challenges, and those with mental illnesses [15]. If persuasive actions seem designed to exploit these groups, it raises significant ethical concerns that warrant further investigation and regulation [16].

The information collected may include personal details and data, such as how long users stay on certain websites, how frequently they visit them, and their locations through GPS tracking, and also data about bystanders. Then, it raises questions about how this information is managed: whether and where it is stored, who may access it, and how it is used [12]. In many cases, users are unaware of the extent of data retention policies or their implications for privacy [17].

Moreover, technologies such as facial recognition can collect and store users' biometric data, often without their full awareness of the associated risks [15,18]. Many users do not recognize the risks associated with storing facial recognition data, as they tend to focus on its future applications rather than its present dangers. Consequently, they may underestimate potential threats, such as the risk of being identified by matching those data with publicly available online photos [15]. This tendency can lead to increased complacency regarding data privacy and security.

3. Security, Privacy, and Confidentiality

Adopting new technologies in various fields has expanded the virtual world's reach, making it more susceptible to security vulnerabilities. Therefore, it is relevant to understand the potential security risks that can arise from using Metaverse and MR applications.

The Open Systems Interconnection model (OSI model) facilitates the comprehension of how information is managed for user consumption within the Metaverse and the MR. This model comprises seven layers, as illustrated in Figure 6, where the physical, data link, and network layers form the foundation of the Metaverse and MR. These layers enable the connection between networks and the creation and interaction of individual realities. In contrast, the transport, session, presentation, and application layers allow access to manipulate data, leading to the Metaverse and MR, resulting in virtual, augmented, and mixed realities. It is important to note that the OSI model is an essential tool for comprehending the information flow, and its utilization allows for creating more efficient and effective systems.

LAYER	OSI	EXTENDED REALITY
1	APPLICATION	How XR is interacted with and manipulated by users
2	PRESENTATION	How XR is seen by users
3	SESSION	The XR ecosystem
4	TRANSPORT	Blockchain/Decentralized routing protocols
5	NETWORK	Blockchain/Decentralized networks
6	DATA LINK	Optical/Cable lines
7	PHYSICAL	Server space

Figure 6. OSI layers from the extended reality, adapted from [19].

This model is vulnerable to distinct topics of security and privacy risks, which include blockchain security, interactive technology security, cloud service and Internet of Things security, artificial intelligence security, and digital twins security [20], just as shown in Figure 7.

SECURITY RISK	DESCRIPTION	IMPACT ON MIXED REALITY
BLOCKCHAIN SECURITY	Vulnerabilities in consensus mechanisms	Risk of double-spending, fraudulent transactions
INTERACTIVE TECHNOLOGY SECURITY	Biometric authentication weaknesses	Identity theft, impersonation
CLOUD AND IOT SECURITY	Decentralized data exposure risks	Breaches of private spaces, sensitive data leaks
AI SECURITY	Exploitrable AI weakneses	Adversarial attacks, data manipulation
DIGITAL TWINS SECURITY	Unauthorized acess to virtual models	Real-world asset compromise, privacy breaches

Figure 7. Comparison of key security risks in the Metaverse and MR.

3.1. Blockchain Security

Blockchain technology provides a secure and dependable means of storing user data by employing a combination of consensus mechanisms, smart contracts, and encryption algorithms. Nevertheless, such designs are vulnerable to malicious attacks due to their inherent inadequacies. Therefore, it is imperative for blockchain developers to adopt robust security measures in the design and implementation of blockchain systems to ensure they meet the highest standards of security and reliability.

The consensus algorithm plays a pivotal role in upholding the safety and efficiency of blockchain technology. It is responsible for ensuring that all nodes in a decentralized network are in agreement with respect to the state of the ledger. Practical Byzantine Fault Tolerance (PBFT), Proof of Work (PoW), Proof of Stake (PoS), and Delegated Proof of Stake (DPoS) [21] are a few examples of consensus mechanisms that help achieve the consistency and accuracy of data across different nodes. However, these algorithms are susceptible to security risks. For instance, the PoW mechanism is vulnerable to the double spend attack, which involves the fraudulent use of a cryptocurrency more than once.

In MR, blockchain security is crucial for managing and verifying the authenticity of interactions and assets that bridge the digital and physical worlds. Blockchain systems can be used to protect MR assets by creating immutable records of virtual items and experiences, which can be "anchored" in real-world locations. However, similar to the Metaverse, MR experiences face risks associated with consensus mechanisms, where double-spending or unauthorized duplication of digital assets could compromise user trust. Furthermore, decentralized ledgers need to efficiently handle real-time data from MR environments without sacrificing security [22].

3.2. Interactive Technology Security

The proper functioning of the Metaverse relies heavily on interactive technologies such as Augmented Reality (AR) and Virtual Reality (VR). These technologies play a fundamental role in shaping the Metaverse's functionalities. Despite their importance, AR and VR are susceptible to security and privacy challenges. The extent of information shared within them and the difficulties associated with identity authentication in the virtual world are among the most pressing.

For example, traditional methods of user authentication, such as password entry, are considered unsuitable. As such, alternative authentication solutions have become imperative. Although voice recognition technology has been considered a viable option, it is susceptible to various risks, such as voice synthesis techniques. Consequently, biometric authentication mechanisms have been developed to use the unique biological traits of users for secure authentication. Of these options, facial recognition technology has emerged as an effective mechanism for verifying the user's identity. However, the reliability of facial recognition technology has been challenged by unscrupulous actors who can easily download a user's image and create a virtual reality representation of their face. Such manipulations can then be used to bypass the security system, thereby exposing vulnerabilities that must be addressed in order to enhance the overall security posture of an organization.

The security challenges of interactive technologies in MR extend beyond those in AR and VR due to the unique blend of physical and digital interaction that MR entails. MR environments rely heavily on precise spatial mapping and real-time user tracking, often using biometric data and continuous environmental scanning. Facial recognition, gesture tracking, and other biometrics are essential for providing responsive interactions, yet they introduce significant privacy concerns if hacked or misused [23].

3.3. *Cloud Service and Internet of Things (IoT) Security*

Both cloud services and the IoT have the ability to process large amounts of information. However, their decentralized deployment can create management challenges and make them susceptible to security attacks.

Cloud computing enables users to store and share their data in a centralized location, which can be accessed with the appropriate permissions. To ensure the confidentiality of sensitive data, encryption is used as a protective measure. In doing so, even if malicious actors gain access to the data, they will be unable to comprehend it [24].

Similarly, IoT devices are designed to collect and transmit enormous amounts of data, often without human intervention. However, the security of these devices is critical, as they are susceptible to several types of attacks, such as denial-of-service attacks, botnets, and data breaches.

In MR environments, cloud services and IoT play a significant role in providing real-time processing power and managing massive data flows. MR devices and applications often rely on edge computing and IoT sensors to synchronize digital objects within the physical environment, creating unique security challenges. Malicious attacks on IoT devices or cloud services could disrupt the seamless integration of physical and digital components, leading to potential breaches of private spaces and sensitive user data [25].

3.4. *Artificial Intelligence Security*

The rapid advancement of technology has made artificial intelligence (AI) increasingly capable of identifying and classifying potential cyber threats. These threats can then be communicated to relevant personnel for prompt action. Nevertheless, due to the black box (i.e., a system to which the user interacts through its external parameters without any or limited knowledge of what happens inside it) characteristics of AI and the identification of certain cyber attacks can present significant challenges.

Despite the efficacy and accuracy of AI in identifying threats, the lack of transparency in the decision-making process can make it difficult to comprehend the basis for certain classifications. The Generative Adversarial Networks (GANs) attack is one of the most commonly used attack models that targets black box systems [26]. The GAN model comprises a pair of networks, where one generates data and the other determines whether the output is authentic or counterfeit. The two networks continuously interact in this manner until the first network reliably produces content that can deceive the other [27].

Artificial intelligence (AI) in MR is crucial for enhancing user interactions by dynamically adjusting digital elements based on real-world inputs. However, MR's dependency on AI-driven contextual recognition, object identification, and behavioral prediction exposes it to additional security risks. AI models in MR must process vast amounts of personal data in real time, making them vulnerable to attacks that exploit model weaknesses, such as adversarial attacks [25].

3.5. Digital Twins Security

The advent of the Metaverse has brought a proliferation of digital services that collect, transmit, process, govern, and store user data. However, this process also poses significant risks to user privacy, particularly with the inclusion of digital twins. The latter may compromise sensitive user information such as location, habits, and living styles throughout the lifecycle of these digital services.

To facilitate immersive interactions with digital twins in the Metaverse, it is imperative to conduct comprehensive data collection procedures. These procedures encompass acquiring personal information, behavioral data, and user preferences. It is of utmost importance to ensure the privacy of these data to prevent unauthorized access or misuse by third parties.

Also, the effective creation and rendering of avatars and virtual environments in Metaverse services necessitate the aggregation and processing of voluminous data collected from the human body and its surrounding environment. However, this undertaking carries the potential for sensitive information to be exposed. Specifically, centralizing the private data of different users for training personalized avatar appearance models challenges user privacy and contravenes extant regulations such as the General Data Protection Regulation (GDPR). Besides that, due to the ability of avatars to reflect the behavior patterns, preferences, habits, and activities of their real-life counterparts, attackers can exploit this similarity to collect the digital footprints of avatars and create accurate user profiles that enable them to carry out illicit activities, posing a significant threat to the security and privacy of users. As such, it is imperative to safeguard users' data privacy and security in the Metaverse [28].

Digital twins in MR represent real-world objects or systems within the digital space, enabling interactions that blend the physical and virtual realms. In MR applications, digital twins are often used to visualize complex data or provide interactive simulations, such as in manufacturing or medical training. Security concerns arise as these digital twins can access and mirror sensitive data from physical assets. Unauthorized access to digital twins in MR environments could lead to serious data breaches or manipulations, compromising physical assets. To address this, MR security models must ensure that data exchanged between digital twins and their real-world counterparts are securely encrypted [29].

3.6. Threats and Countermeasures

Digital environments can also be a breeding ground for privacy violations and other security threats. As the Metaverse and MR technologies evolve, so do concerns about privacy threats and the need for countermeasures.

3.6.1. Threats

The Metaverse is built upon a foundation of data, which necessitates that user data are gathered and stored as they engage with the virtual world. This information may include sensitive data such as personal identification particulars, physical addresses, and even financial data. However, these data are not limited to virtual interactions alone. Wearable devices such as HMDs may acquire extensive data, subsequently transferred via wired and wireless communications. Even if the information is encrypted, nefarious actors can still access the unprocessed data by infiltrating a specific channel or tracking the user's location [28].

To enable the creation of virtual environments and avatars, it is necessary to accumulate and process massive amounts of data collected from users and their surroundings, which may lead to the unintended exposure of private information [30].

As the field of technology continues to advance, the utilization of wearable sensors is becoming increasingly prevalent. These sensors capture the movements and surroundings of individuals and their surrounding environment. By doing so, avatars can emulate natural eye contact and capture hand gestures and facial expressions in real-time. Nonetheless, a major concern arises concerning the ability of these wearable sensors to create an entirely authentic representation of an individual, including their manner of speech, behavior, and self-expression [28]. It is important to note that compromised end devices can become a source of risk, as hackers may gain access to an individual's avatar in the Metaverse, thereby enabling them to collect data on the individual's eye tracking and hand gestures, which may be used to replicate the individual's actions and potentially obtain sensitive passwords for personal accounts.

In MR, devices capture real-world data to create seamless interactions between users and virtual elements, extending privacy concerns, as devices like AR glasses or MR headsets gather and process spatial mapping information, potentially exposing users to physical surveillance and environmental tracking risks. For example, AR applications that scan a user's environment may inadvertently reveal sensitive or private details of their physical space.

Additionally, cross-device data synchronization is common in MR systems, which means that data collected on one device might be accessible through others, increasing the risk of data breaches across multiple devices [31].

3.6.2. Countermeasures

To mitigate the risks associated with digital threats, users can take several measures, such as the ones in Figure 8, to protect their online presence.

COUNTERMEASURE	DESCRIPTION	EFFECTIVENESS
Edge Computing	Processes data locally to reduce exposure	High
Context-Aware Privacy Controls	Adjusts data sharing dynamically	Medium
Field-of-View Restrictions	Limits unnecesary data capture	High
Data Sanitization (SafeAR)	Applies obfuscation to sensitive data	Medium

Figure 8. Comparison of countermeasures for MR privacy risks.

One of the most pivotal measures is carefully managing their digital footprint. Managing one's digital footprint involves being conscious of the information collected, stored, and shared online, including personal data such as name, address, date of birth, and credit card details. Users should be mindful of the websites and platforms they interact with and take steps to limit the amount of personal information they share. Users should also use strong passwords and two-factor authentication to safeguard their online presence, helping prevent unauthorized access to accounts and sensitive information. Two-factor authentication provides an additional layer of security by requiring users to enter a unique code sent to their mobile device or email.

In addition to these measures, it is also essential to renew consent permissions periodically, ensuring users' awareness of the data collected and their usage. By regularly reviewing and updating consent permissions, users can better control their digital footprint and mitigate the risks associated with cyber threats.

To mitigate MR threats, MR systems require strong security protocols. One fruitful approach is edge computing, which allows data to be processed locally on the device rather than transmitted to remote servers, reducing data exposure and latency [32]. By keeping sensitive data on the local device, edge computing minimizes the risks of interception and unauthorized access. This approach is particularly useful for processing biometric data, such as eye tracking and facial recognition, directly on MR headsets without sending it to external cloud servers, thereby enhancing privacy and security.

Furthermore, context-aware privacy controls enable users to adjust the level of data sharing based on their environment or activity [33]. These controls allow MR devices to dynamically modify privacy settings depending on the user's location, interaction context, or personal preferences. For instance, users in private spaces might set their MR devices to a high-privacy mode, limiting data collection to only essential functions, while in public settings, data-sharing permissions could be more flexible. Another example is the adaptive permission model, where MR applications request access to specific data only when necessary, rather than maintaining continuous access to personal or spatial information.

Another countermeasure is the implementation of field-of-view restrictions, where the device blurs or limits data capture outside of specific focal points. This technique helps prevent the collection of unnecessary spatial information [34]. In MR, data sanitization before rendering may also reduce privacy risks. For instance, SafeAR [35,36] automatically identifies instances of sensitive data and applies obfuscation techniques to image streams before rendering. In [37], the authors evaluate qualitative and quantitative methodologies for applying different obfuscation strategies to protect private data in MR applications. The authors collected opinions from tens of users through a specific questionnaire. They conclude that factors like age and occupation influence the users' concerns about privacy-maintenance methods and preferences regarding obfuscation. Overall, the participants identified blurring as the obfuscation method that provides the best aesthetic appeal.

By integrating edge computing and context-aware privacy controls with existing security measures, MR environments can offer improved user privacy protections while maintaining seamless interactions and performance. Future work in this area should explore adaptive privacy mechanisms that provide greater user control while ensuring data security in dynamic MR settings.

4. Challenges and Solutions

As individuals spend more time in virtual environments, it becomes increasingly paramount to ensure that their personal information remains secure and confidential. Furthermore, concerns arise regarding the susceptibility of virtual communities to cybercriminals and hackers, thereby increasing the likelihood of virtual crimes spilling over into the physical realm. Additionally, challenges emerge with respect to empowering users with control over their shared information while maintaining their privacy.

To effectively organize the issues and challenges, they can be broadly categorized into four categories: socialization, immersive interaction, real-world building, and expandability [38].

4.1. Socialization

The Metaverse represents a virtual world where individuals can interact without being bound by traditional geographic limitations. The underlying infrastructure relies on internet servers to facilitate connectivity, exposing it to network-related security and privacy concerns analogous to those in social networks. As such, the Metaverse's potential to enable seamless communication across vast distances is under constant threat from vulnerabilities inherent to modern networked systems.

The Metaverse, being an interactive virtual space, is operated through user inputs. However, it presents an opportunity for hackers to engage in unauthorized access to sensitive data through injection attacks (untrusted inputs or unauthorized code sent from attackers and interpreted as valid commands or queries) [39].

The majority of cyber-attacks are the result of security vulnerabilities, often stemming from a lack of input validation. To mitigate the risks associated with these attacks, employing the SQL defense model [40] is a recommended best practice. The SQL defense model involves a three-step process to validate input information. Firstly, the server side verifies the legitimacy of the IP address, followed by testing input values for format, length, type, and range. Lastly, the server verifies the user's privileges, and in the event that the user's access permissions exceed the allowable limit, the user is immediately blocked and the system administrator is notified.

One prevalent type of cyber attack is the man-in-the-middle attack [41], in which a malicious actor eavesdrops on or interferes with the communication between a user and a server, with the ultimate goal of intercepting confidential data. To mitigate the risk of such attacks, it is recommended to invest in authentication algorithms that can be applied to safeguard data integrity. The effectiveness of these algorithms stems from their ability to verify the identity of both parties involved in a communication session, thereby ensuring that the data exchanged between them are authentic and secure.

In the Metaverse, where MR technologies are increasingly used, socialization relies on real-time data exchanges that enable users to interact within virtual spaces. In MR environments, socialization can include shared virtual experiences overlaid on physical spaces, creating additional security risks. Because MR devices often capture audio, video, and environmental data, they introduce vulnerabilities to eavesdropping attacks and man-in-the-middle attacks. Attackers can intercept or manipulate MR data streams, potentially altering the shared experience or extracting sensitive data.

MR platforms should, therefore, enforce end-to-end encryption and adopt secure session management techniques to protect data as they flow between users. Additionally, regular security updates and vulnerability assessments for MR applications can help protect against emerging threats [25].

4.2. Immersive Interaction

In order to achieve a more immersive level of interaction, it is necessary to employ wearable devices, headsets, and controllers that exchange a significant amount of data. To ensure seamless communication, these data are serialized and deserialized. However, the use of these devices also poses a significant security risk. Malicious actors can exploit Insecure Deserialization (untrusted data are used to bypass authentication or otherwise abuse the logic behind an application) vulnerabilities by injecting hostile serialized data into the communication stream, thereby gaining an initial entry point to a more complex system. There are several defensive measures available to prevent insecure deserialization attacks. Data serialization can be encrypted and monitored, or data source authentication can be established. However, selecting the most suitable method requires a preliminary analysis of the attack report.

To ensure the prevention of insecure deserialization attacks, it is critical to consider all possible methods. Encryption of data serialization can provide an additional layer of protection against unauthorized access. Additionally, monitoring data serialization can detect any suspicious activities and allow immediate remedial action. Creating authentication for data sources can also prevent unauthorized access, ensuring that only verified and authenticated data sources are used.

It is essential to analyze the attack report before selecting a method for prevention. This analysis enables a better understanding of the attack and its vulnerability points, allowing for a more targeted and effective response. It is only through effective analysis that the most suitable prevention method can be selected.

It is imperative to consider that biometric-based authentication methods, such as voice, fingerprint, and facial recognition, offer convenience but also entail the risk of compromising users' biometric data. To mitigate this risk, it is crucial to adhere to the best practice of storing biometric data exclusively on the local device and abstaining from transmitting it outside. This approach ensures that the data are encrypted and remain in a local space instead of being exposed to a remote server. During the authentication process, only the user's input is compared with the stored data, and the output is a simple boolean value. This methodology safeguards the biometric data against any potential breaches, as even in the event of an attack on the device or remote service, the data remain secure. It is also necessary to take into consideration that biometric-based authentication, such as voice, fingerprint, and face, which can be very popular due to its convenience, also causes the risk of leaking users' biometrics. To prevent them from being accessed or collected by malicious entities, it is necessary to follow the best practice of keeping all biometrics in the local device and never sending them out. This allows the data to be stored and encrypted in a local space instead of a remote server, meaning that in the authentication process, it is only necessary to compare the user input with the stored data, and the only output is a boolean. This way, even if the device or remote service is attacked, the data are still safe.

4.3. Real-World Building

In light of the recent development of a digital replica of the physical world, users are afforded the opportunity to create a virtual representation of themselves, incorporating personal information such as interests, friendships, and hobbies. However, this poses a significant risk to user privacy, as extensive profiling could potentially result in the unauthorized disclosure of sensitive information. The creation of such digital profiles opens the door to exploitation by malicious actors, as such profiles can be used to target users with tailored advertising, phishing attacks, and other forms of cybercrime. Furthermore, the sheer volume of data generated by such profiles means that the potential for data breaches and leaks is substantial.

The "Graph-based privacy-preserving data publication" essay [42] proposes a framework for securely sharing data while protecting individual privacy. This approach utilizes graph theory, where individuals, devices, or locations are represented as nodes (vertices) in a network, and their relationships (e.g., friendships, connections, interactions) are represented as edges. By leveraging this graph structure, the framework can effectively anonymize sensitive information, such as personal identities or locations, while still allowing for valuable data analysis. This is achieved through techniques such as node degree modification, edge perturbation, or differential privacy. In the context of edge computing, where data processing occurs closer to the data source, this graph-based approach can be particularly advantageous for enabling privacy-preserving data sharing in decentralized and resource-constrained environments.

4.4. Expandability

The Metaverse is a revolutionary concept that transcends the physical boundaries of the real world by offering advanced functionalities that are unattainable in reality. It provides a virtual environment that enables individuals to interact with each other, participate in virtual meetings, and engage in shopping experiences in virtual malls, among other activities.

The Metaverse system consists of a diverse range of applications designed to facilitate several features. These applications are interconnected through communication channels, creating a unified and multifunctional Metaverse, similar to mobile devices' interconnectivity. However, this level of interconnectedness presents a potential vulnerability for third-party tracking, as these communication channels allow an application to access system components' status and other applications' outgoing information.

It is essential to consider the implications of this interconnectedness and potential vulnerability when engaging in activities within the Metaverse. As such, it is recommended to take the necessary precautions to safeguard against any such threat. The first step towards ensuring the system's integrity is to restrict certain channels in the system, thereby blocking any unnecessary third-party tracking.

By taking these necessary precautions, the Metaverse system can be utilized to its full potential while minimizing the risk of third-party tracking and preserving user privacy.

5. Discussion and Future Directions

This section starts with an analysis of the research questions previously defined, providing a detailed explanation of the findings derived from the literature review. This analysis highlights the key insights and implications of the reviewed studies, offering a clearer understanding of the studied topics. Then, Section 5.2 discusses open issues and possible future research directions.

5.1. Discussion

In the following, the main findings related to the research questions are highlighted.

RQ1: What are the leading security risks stemming from the development and expansion of Metaverse and Mixed Reality technologies?

The development and expansion of Metaverse and MR technologies pose multifaceted security risks. As shown in Figure 9, these risks include vulnerabilities in underlying technologies such as blockchain, which lead to issues such as double spending and unauthorized asset duplication, especially those that rely on biometric data for authentication, face challenges related to privacy maintenance, and the potential for forgery. Cloud services and IoT devices critical to MR operations are vulnerable to attacks such as denial of service and data breaches. Furthermore, integrating artificial intelligence into MR systems raises concerns about the "black box" nature of AI models and the possibility of adversary attacks. Finally, using the information about users (including their personal data and experiences) and their physical assets might potentially violate privacy, and using digital twins in MR raises concerns about how stakeholders use such data.

RQ2: How can a user's privacy be maintained in the context of involving and participatory experiences in the Metaverse and Mixed Reality environments?

Preserving user privacy in an immersive and interactive experience across the Metaverse and MR requires a multi-pronged approach. Key strategies, as shown in Figure 9, include limiting data collection to only what is necessary, using privacy-preserving techniques such as differential privacy and integrated learning, and granular control over their data through context-aware privacy settings. Techniques like field-of-view restrictions can limit the collection of unnecessary spatial information, while data sanitization can help protect sensitive data before they are rendered. In addition, robust certification authorization processes with approvals, authorizations, and regular reviews are required to ensure user control over their data. Edge computing and secure data storage practices are essential to minimize data exposure. Ultimately, transparency and user control are paramount, empowering individuals to make informed decisions about their privacy in these evolving digital environments.

RQ3: What are the ethical issues related to the collection, utilization, and distribution of data in Metaverse and Mixed Reality Technologies, and how can these issues be mitigated?

Concerns about ethics in the Metaverse and MR environments, as shown in Figure 9, revolve around issues like privacy violations stemming from extensive data collection, the potential for algorithmic bias in AI systems, and the insufficient transparency and user control regarding how data are used. The ongoing collection of data also raises worries about surveillance and manipulation. Additionally, the digital divide may worsen existing inequalities by restricting access to and engagement with these technologies. Addressing these ethical challenges calls for a comprehensive strategy that includes minimizing data collection, adopting privacy-preserving technologies, ensuring transparency and user control, promoting fairness in algorithms, and creating clear ethical guidelines and regulations. By emphasizing ethical considerations and encouraging responsible development, we can work towards ensuring that Metaverse and MR technologies serve society positively while honoring individual rights and freedoms.

CATEGORY	IDENTIFIED RISKS	MITIGATION STRATEGIES
Security Risks	- Blockchain vulnerabilities (e.g., double spending, asset forgery) - AI adversarial attacks and opacity - IoT and cloud vulnerabilities (e.g., data breaches, DDoS attacks)	- Strong cryptographic protocols - AI explainability & adversarial training - Secure cloud storage & edge computing
Privacy Concerns	- Excessive data collection - Biometric data misuse - Location and spatial tracing risks	- Differential privacy & federated learning - Field-of-view restrictions - User-controlled data settings
Ethical Issues	- Lack of transparency in AI & data usage - Algorithmic bias - Digital divide & exclusion risks	- Fair AI governance & audits - User data transparency policies - Ethical AI guidelines & regulatory frameworks

Figure 9. Security risks, privacy measures, and ethical mitigation strategies in Metaverse and MR.

5.2. Future Directions

In light of the constantly evolving concept of MR and Metaverse, it is of utmost importance to address the issues of privacy and security within this virtual world. MR and Metaverse constitute a vast interconnected network of virtual spaces, games, and social platforms, which inevitably renders data security and privacy concerns more complex than in the physical world.

Subsequently, the following subtopics will provide a comprehensive overview of the future direction of the MR and Metaverse with respect to security, privacy, and confidentiality. The aim of this discourse is to critically analyze the potential threats and challenges that arise within the MR and Metaverse and to elucidate practical measures that can be undertaken to mitigate the risks.

5.2.1. Endogenous Security Empowered

With the increasing use of technology, the security and privacy risks associated with the physical–digital environments have become a major concern. Endogenous security theory [43] provides a promising solution for addressing these issues by incorporating built-in security mechanisms with self-protection, self-evolution, and autoimmunity capabilities.

This approach takes into account security and privacy factors during the system design phase, which results in more secure and resilient physical–digital environments. The self-protection mechanisms ensure that the physical–digital environments can defend themselves against known and unknown security threats, while the self-evolution capabilities enable the system to adapt to changing security threats. The autoimmunity capabilities allow the physical–digital environments to identify and eliminate malicious software and prevent unauthorized access to sensitive data.

Endogenous security theory is a proactive approach to security that can significantly minimize the risk of security breaches and privacy violations in the physical–digital environments. By integrating secure-by-design mechanisms into the system, the future physical–digital environments can provide a safe and secure environment for people to interact and conduct business in the digital world.

5.2.2. Cloud-Edge-End Orchestrated Secure

In the physical–digital environments, the gathering of vast amounts of multi-sensory and multimodal information from the real world is a challenge that can be addressed through the orchestration of cloud-edge-end computing. This approach leverages the collaborative and dynamic sharing of computation, communication, and storage resources among various entities to enhance the quality of experience (QoE) for users/avatars and the quality of service (QoS) for MR and Metaverse services.

Cloud-edge-end computing [44] involves a distributed architecture that spans across cloud data centers, edge devices, and end devices. By leveraging this architecture, it is possible to process data closer to the source, improving the speed and efficiency of data processing. This approach can also help with edge intelligence and user privacy protection by aggregating and processing user private data on edge devices.

Furthermore, cloud-edge-end computing can help address the challenges of data transmission in the physical–digital environments. With collaborative use of computational resources, it is possible to reduce the amount of data that need to be transmitted, thereby reducing network congestion and latency.

5.2.3. Cross-Chain Interoperable and Regulatory

Blockchain technology is a revolutionary concept that eliminates the need for trusted third parties. It is a decentralized system that allows digital assets to be exchanged without the involvement of intermediaries, such as banks or financial institutions. In the Metaverse, a trust-free economic ecosystem is essential to ensure the security and privacy of digital assets. This is where efficient cross-chain authentication and governance mechanisms come into play.

To ensure the security of digital assets, we must investigate the effectiveness, efficiency, and security of identity authentication across different domains and blockchains. The cross-chain authentication process ensures that users can access and manage their digital assets securely and efficiently across multiple blockchains. It also eliminates the need for users to create multiple accounts on different blockchains [28].

Moreover, to ensure that digital asset transactions are fair and trustworthy, we need decentralized, hierarchical, and comprehensive cross-chain governance mechanisms. Decentralization of governance ensures that no single entity has control over the decision-making process. Hierarchical governance ensures that decisions are made at different levels of the system, allowing for greater transparency and accountability. Comprehensive governance ensures that all aspects of the system are governed, including the codebase, smart contracts, and protocols.

Participants should be able to express their preferences, make decisions, and resolve conflicts without relying on centralized authorities. This is where the decentralized governance mechanisms come into play. They allow participants to propose and vote on changes to the system, resolve disputes, and make decisions that affect the entire ecosystem. This ensures that the system remains fair and trustworthy and that the interests of all participants are protected.

6. Conclusions

Physical–digital environments have emerged as an exciting new frontier that offers countless possibilities for individuals, businesses, and governments alike. However, this new digital realm also brings a host of security, privacy, and confidentiality challenges that must be addressed for it to reach its full potential.

One of the most significant concerns is data security. The physical–digital environments provide a vast platform for data sharing. Therefore, sensitive information such as bank details, passwords, and personal information can be easily compromised. Implementing a robust data encryption protocol that can prevent unauthorized access to data is essential.

Another critical aspect is user authentication. It is vital to ensure that users are who they claim to be. This can be achieved by implementing two-factor authentication, which requires users to provide additional information beyond a password to log in, thus making it harder for hackers to gain access to user accounts.

In addition to security measures, privacy and confidentiality must be respected and protected, including implementing guidelines and regulations to prevent the misuse or exploitation of personal information. For instance, users should be informed about how their data are being collected, used, and shared and have the option to opt out if they wish to do so.

As physical–digital environments continue to evolve, it is essential to prioritize security, privacy, and confidentiality to create a secure and trustworthy virtual world for everyone, which involves implementing regular security updates, complying with privacy regulations, and being vigilant against emerging threats. By taking a proactive approach to security and privacy, we can ensure that physical–digital environments remain safe and inclusive spaces for all.

Author Contributions: Conceptualization, C.P., A.M., R.R., A.G., N.R., C.R., R.L.d.C.C. and L.S.; Funding acquisition, C.R. and R.L.d.C.C.; Investigation, C.P., A.M., R.R., A.G., N.R., C.R., R.L.d.C.C. and L.S.; Project administration, C.R. and R.L.d.C.C.; Supervision, A.M., R.R., A.G. and N.R.; Visualization, C.P.; Writing—original draft, C.P., R.L.d.C.C. and L.S.; Writing—review & editing, C.P., R.L.d.C.C. and L.S. All authors have read and agreed to the published version of the manuscript.

Funding: This work is partially funded by national funds through FCT—Fundação para a Ciência e a Tecnologia, I.P., in the context of the projects SafeAR—2022.09235.PTDC, UIDB/04524/2020, and under the Scientific Employment Stimulus—CEECINS/00051/2018.

Data Availability Statement: No new data were created in this study. Data sharing is not applicable to this article.

Conflicts of Interest: The authors declare no conflicts of interest.

References

1. Milgram, P.; Kishino, F. A Taxonomy of Mixed Reality Visual Displays. *IEICE Trans. Inf. Syst.* **1994**, *E77-D*, 1321–1329.
2. Milgram, P.; Takemura, H.; Utsumi, A.; Kishino, F. Augmented reality: A class of displays on the reality-virtuality continuum. In Proceedings of the Telemanipulator and Telepresence Technologies, Boston, MA, USA, 31 October–4 November 1995; SPIE: Bellingham, WA, USA, 1995; Volume 2351, pp. 282–292.
3. Stephenson, N. *Snow Crash: A Novel*; Bantam Books (US): New York, NY, USA, 2003.
4. qianw211. What Is Mixed Reality?—Mixed Reality—learn.microsoft.com. Available online: https://learn.microsoft.com/en-us/windows/mixed-reality/discover/mixed-reality (accessed on 6 February 2025).

5. Rokhsaritalemi, S.; Sadeghi-Niaraki, A.; Choi, S.M. A review on mixed reality: Current trends, challenges and prospects. *Appl. Sci.* **2020**, *10*, 636. [CrossRef]
6. Ikeuchi, K.; Matsushita, Y.; Sagawa, R.; Kawasaki, H.; Mukaigawa, Y.; Furukawa, R.; Miyazaki, D.; Ikeuchi, K.; Matsushita, Y.; Sagawa, R.; et al. Visualization/AR/VR/MR Systems. In *Active Lighting and Its Application for Computer Vision: 40 Years of History of Active Lighting Techniques*; Springer: Cham, Swizerland, 2020; pp. 213–239. [CrossRef]
7. Setiawan, K.D.; Anthony, A.; Meyliana; Surjandy. The Essential Factor of Metaverse for Business Based on 7 Layers of Metaverse – Systematic Literature Review. In Proceedings of the 2022 International Conference on Information Management and Technology (ICIMTech), Semarang, Indonesia, 11–12 August 2022; pp. 687–692. [CrossRef]
8. Sun, J.; Gan, W.; Chao, H.C.; Yu, P.S. Metaverse: Survey, applications, security, and opportunities. *arXiv* **2022**, arXiv:2210.07990. [CrossRef]
9. Cendan, J.; Lok, B. The use of virtual patients in medical school curricula. *Adv. Physiol. Educ.* **2012**, *36*, 48–53. [CrossRef] [PubMed]
10. Association of American Medical Colleges. *Effective Use of Educational Technology in Medical Education: Summary Report of the 2006 AAMC Colloquium on Educational Technology*; Association of American Medical Colleges: Washington, DC, USA, 2007.
11. Pase, S. Ethical Considerations in Augmented Reality Applications. Available online: https://worldcomp-proceedings.com/proc/p2012/EEE6059.pdf (accessed on 6 February 2025).
12. Zuboff, S. *The Age of Surveillance Capitalism: The Fight for a Human Future at the New Frontier of Power*; PublicAffairs: New York, NY, USA, 2019.
13. Fogg, B.J. Persuasive technology: Using computers to change what we think and do. *Ubiquity* **2002**, *2002*, 2. [CrossRef]
14. Ruckenstein, M.; Pantzar, M. Beyond the quantified self: Thematic exploration of a dataistic paradigm. *New Media Soc.* **2017**, *19*, 401–418. [CrossRef]
15. Smith, M.; Miller, S. The ethical application of biometric facial recognition technology. *Ai Soc.* **2022**, *37*, 167–175. [CrossRef]
16. Helberger, N. Profiling and Targeting Consumers in the Internet of Things—A New Challenge for Consumer Law. Available online: https://dare.uva.nl/search?identifier=81275d9e-284a-4975-8555-77c74f54cc75 (accessed on 6 February 2025).
17. Nissenbaum, H. Privacy in context: Technology, policy, and the integrity of social life. *J. Inf. Policy* **2011**, *1*, 149–151.
18. Whittaker, M.; Crawford, K.; Dobbe, R.; Fried, G.; Kaziunas, E.; Mathur, V.; West, S.M.; Richardson, R.; Schultz, J.; Schwartz, O.; et al. *AI Now Report 2018*; AI Now Institute at New York University: New York, NY, USA, 2018.
19. Journal, J. Why You Need a Metaverse Strategy | The Jabian Journal — journal.jabian.com. Available online: https://journal.jabian.com/why-you-need-a-metaverse-strategy/ (accessed on 6 February 2025).
20. Chen, Z.; Wu, J.; Gan, W.; Qi, Z. Metaverse security and privacy: An overview. In Proceedings of the 2022 IEEE International Conference on Big Data (Big Data), Osaka, Japan, 17–20 December 2022; IEEE: Piscataway, NJ, USA, 2022; pp. 2950–2959. [CrossRef]
21. Mingxiao, D.; Xiaofeng, M.; Zhe, Z.; Xiangwei, W.; Qijun, C. A review on consensus algorithm of blockchain. In Proceedings of the 2017 IEEE International Conference on Systems, Man, and Cybernetics (SMC), Banff, AB, Canada, 5–8 October 2017; IEEE: Piscataway, NJ, USA, 2017; pp. 2567–2572. [CrossRef]
22. Islam, A.; Masuduzzaman, M.; Akter, A.; Shin, S.Y. Mr-block: A blockchain-assisted secure content sharing scheme for multi-user mixed-reality applications in internet of military things. In Proceedings of the 2020 International Conference on Information and Communication Technology Convergence (ICTC), Jeju, Republic of Korea, 21–23 October 2020; IEEE: Piscataway, NJ, USA, 2020; pp. 407–411. [CrossRef]
23. Wu, M.; Dai, S.L.; Yang, C. Mixed reality enhanced user interactive path planning for omnidirectional mobile robot. *Appl. Sci.* **2020**, *10*, 1135. [CrossRef]
24. Vurukonda, N.; Rao, B.T. A study on data storage security issues in cloud computing. *Procedia Comput. Sci.* **2016**, *92*, 128–135. [CrossRef]
25. De Guzman, J.A.; Thilakarathna, K.; Seneviratne, A. Security and privacy approaches in mixed reality: A literature survey. *ACM Comput. Surv. (CSUR)* **2019**, *52*, 1–37. [CrossRef]
26. Yan, X.; Cui, B.; Xu, Y.; Shi, P.; Wang, Z. A method of information protection for collaborative deep learning under GAN model attack. *IEEE/ACM Trans. Comput. Biol. Bioinform.* **2019**, *18*, 871–881. [CrossRef] [PubMed]
27. Zhao, S.; Li, J.; Wang, J.; Zhang, Z.; Zhu, L.; Zhang, Y. attackGAN: Adversarial Attack against Black-box IDS using Generative Adversarial Networks. *Procedia Comput. Sci.* **2021**, *187*, 128–133; . [CrossRef]
28. Wang, Y.; Su, Z.; Zhang, N.; Xing, R.; Liu, D.; Luan, T.H.; Shen, X. A survey on metaverse: Fundamentals, security, and privacy. *IEEE Commun. Surv. Tutorials* **2022**, *25*, 319–352. [CrossRef]
29. Asad, U.; Khan, M.; Khalid, A.; Lughmani, W.A. Human-centric digital twins in industry: A comprehensive review of enabling technologies and implementation strategies. *Sensors* **2023**, *23*, 3938. [CrossRef]
30. Li, X.; He, J.; Vijayakumar, P.; Zhang, X.; Chang, V. A verifiable privacy-preserving machine learning prediction scheme for edge-enhanced HCPSs. *IEEE Trans. Ind. Inform.* **2021**, *18*, 5494–5503. [CrossRef]

31. Roesner, F.; Denning, T.; Newell, B.C.; Kohno, T.; Calo, R. Augmented reality: Hard problems of law and policy. In Proceedings of the 2014 ACM International Joint Conference on Pervasive and Ubiquitous Computing: Adjunct Publication, Seattle, WA, USA, 13–17 September 2014; pp. 1283–1288. [CrossRef]
32. Satyanarayanan, M. The emergence of edge computing. *Computer* **2017**, *50*, 30–39. [CrossRef]
33. Schilit, B.; Adams, N.; Want, R. Context-aware computing applications. In Proceedings of the 1994 First Workshop on Mobile Computing Systems and Applications, Santa Cruz, CA, USA, 8–9 December 1994; IEEE: Piscataway, NJ, USA, 1994; pp. 85–90.
34. Chen, S.; Li, Z.; Dangelo, F.; Gao, C.; Fu, X. A case study of security and privacy threats from augmented reality (ar). In Proceedings of the 2018 International Conference on Computing, Networking and Communications (ICNC), Maui, HI, USA, 5–8 March 2018; IEEE: Piscataway, NJ, USA, 2018; pp. 442–446. [CrossRef]
35. Alves, M.; Ribeiro, T.; Santos, L.; Marto, A.; Gonçalves, A.; Rabadão, C.; Costa, R.L.d.C. Evaluating Service-based Privacy-Protection for Augmented Reality Applications. In Proceedings of the 16th International Conference on Management of Digital Ecosystems (MEDES 2024), Naples, Italy, 18–20 November 2024.
36. Ribeiro, T.; Marto, A.; Gonçalves, A.; Santos, L.; Rabadão, C.; Costa, R.L.d.C. SafeARUnity: Real-Time Image Processing to Enhance Privacy Protection in LBARGs. In Proceedings of the 14th International Conference on Videogame Sciences and Arts (VideoJogos 2024), Leiria, Portugal, 5–6 December 2024; pp. 186–200. [CrossRef]
37. Cruz, A.C.; Costa, R.L.d.C.; Santos, L.; Rabadão, C.; Marto, A.; Gonçalves, A. Assessing User Perceptions and Preferences on Applying Obfuscation Techniques for Privacy Protection in Augmented Reality. *Future Internet* **2025**, *17*, 55. [CrossRef]
38. Huang, Y.; Li, Y.J.; Cai, Z. Security and Privacy in Metaverse: A Comprehensive Survey. *Big Data Min. Anal.* **2023**, *6*, 234–247. [CrossRef]
39. Sharma, R.C.; Zamfiroiu, A. Cybersecurity Threats and Vulnerabilities in the Metaverse. In Proceedings of the 2023 International Conference on Intelligent Metaverse Technologies & Applications (iMETA), Tartu, Estonia, 18–20 September 2023; IEEE: Piscataway, NJ, USA, 2023; pp. 1–7. [CrossRef]
40. Qian, L.; Zhu, Z.; Hu, J.; Liu, S. Research of SQL injection attack and prevention technology. In Proceedings of the 2015 International Conference on Estimation, Detection and Information Fusion (ICEDIF), Harbin, China, 10–11 January 2015; IEEE: Piscataway, NJ, USA, 2015; pp. 303–306. [CrossRef]
41. Sharma, S.; Singh, J.; Gupta, A.; Ali, F.; Khan, F.; Kwak, D. User Safety and Security in the Metaverse: A Critical Review. *IEEE Open J. Commun. Soc.* **2024**, *5*, 5467–5487. [CrossRef]
42. Li, X.Y.; Zhang, C.; Jung, T.; Qian, J.; Chen, L. Graph-based privacy-preserving data publication. In Proceedings of the IEEE INFOCOM 2016-The 35th Annual IEEE International Conference on Computer Communications, San Francisco, CA, USA, 10–14 April 2016; IEEE: Piscataway, NJ, USA, 2016; pp. 1–9. [CrossRef]
43. Zhou, Z.; Kuang, X.; Sun, L.; Zhong, L.; Xu, C. Endogenous security defense against deductive attack: When artificial intelligence meets active defense for online service. *IEEE Commun. Mag.* **2020**, *58*, 58–64. [CrossRef]
44. Kai, C.; Zhou, H.; Yi, Y.; Huang, W. Collaborative cloud-edge-end task offloading in mobile-edge computing networks with limited communication capability. *IEEE Trans. Cogn. Commun. Netw.* **2020**, *7*, 624–634. [CrossRef]

future internet

MDPI

Article

The Use of Virtual Reality in the Countries of the Central American Bank for Economic Integration (CABEI)

Álvaro Antón-Sancho [1], Pablo Fernández-Arias [1], Edwan Anderson Ariza [2] and Diego Vergara [1,*]

1 Technology, Instruction and Design in Engineering and Education Research Group (TiDEE.rg), Catholic University of Avila, C/Canteros s/n, 05005 Ávila, Spain; alvaro.anton@ucavila.es (Á.A.-S.); pablo.fernandezarias@ucavila.es (P.F.-A.)

2 Grupo de Nuevos Materiales, Facultad de Ingeniería, Universidad del Magdalena, Santa Marta 470004, Colombia; earizaec@unimagdalena.edu.co

* Correspondence: diego.vergara@ucavila.es

Abstract: In recent years, virtual reality (VR) technologies have become one of the teaching tools with the greatest training potential in higher education. Thus, the study of factors that influence the adoption and valuation of VR by the educational agents involved is a fruitful line of research, because it can provide keys to promote its incorporation. This article compares the assessments of VR as a teaching technology in higher education given by professors from countries that are members of the Central American Bank for Economic Integration (CABEI) with those of professors from countries in the Latin American region that are not members of CABEI. For this purpose, a validated questionnaire on the perception of VR use was administered to a sample of 1246 professors from the entire Latin American region, and their responses were statistically analyzed. As a result, it was found that professors from CABEI countries give better ratings to the usability dimensions of VR and report a lower number of disadvantages in its use than professors from countries outside CABEI. However, the increase in the digital competence of professors in CABEI countries is more than twice as high as the increase in the valuation of VR. It follows that there is still much room for the integration of VR in higher education in CABEI countries. Furthermore, in CABEI countries there is a more pronounced gap between professors from private and public universities with respect to the above-mentioned ratings than in non-CABEI countries. As a consequence, some implications and suggestions derived from the results are reported.

Keywords: virtual reality; virtual learning environments; information and communication technologies; university tenure; developing countries

1. Introduction

The term Virtual Reality (VR) refers to computer technologies that create environments, objects, and scenes with the appearance of reality and with which the user can have an interactive experience [1]. Thus, certain technical characteristics are inherent to VR, such as the three-dimensional design of virtual environments [2], which should give as realistic a feeling as possible [3], and interactivity [4], since the user experience should be able to allow interaction with that environment. In addition, a certain degree of immersiveness is required from VR, i.e., the user is sensorially immersed in the environment, inhibiting users from experiencing their real environment. This degree of immersion can be greater or lesser depending on the VR technological application in question; it is a continuum that allows distinguishing, in extreme situations, between immersive VR and non-immersive VR [5]. All these technical characteristics allow VR technologies (together with augmented or mixed reality technologies) to have a multitude of applications in the most diverse fields of technology [6–10].

Within the educational world, VR is one Information and Communication Technology (ICT) that has shown great potential to develop the knowledge of students at all educational stages [11]. This potential arises from the ability of VR technologies to recreate diverse and dynamic learning situations such that users have all their senses focused on the environment and are able to interact with it in a realistic way. In this way, the virtual environment does not lose the practicality of the real environment but gains in amenities over other non-immersive technological resources. Therefore, in general terms, VR brings unquestionably numerous advantages for use in the classroom, including the following: (i) it allows the recreation of environments in a realistic way that could likely not be recreated with that same realism through other technological resources, which is of special interest in fields such as medicine [12], architecture [13], engineering [14], or art [15]; (ii) the three-dimensional, immersive, and realistic nature facilitates the achievement of learning objectives, which often leads to an increase in academic performance [16]; and (iii) the interactive nature of the environments and the strong underlying technological foundation is motivating for most students, who generally increase their involvement in learning activities [17].

It is also necessary to point out that the implementation of VR technologies in education has some limitations. These include the costs involved in implementation [18] and the digital and techno-pedagogical skills that educators must develop to effectively incorporate these technologies into their teaching activities [19]. Certainly, the initial expense involved in implementing VR technologies is high. Nonetheless, research indicates that over time, their adoption leads to considerable cost savings across various domains, including expenditure on consumables or laboratory equipment [20]. Consequently, the incorporation of VR technologies by educational institutions represents a sustainable initiative [21]. Conversely, the accessibility of VR is hindered by limitations in teacher training, particularly in regions experiencing technological advancement, where the integration of ICT into educational practices is less robust [22].

Digital transformation in Central America faces significant obstacles, which impact regional development and competitiveness. A considerable digital divide and limitations in technological infrastructure, coupled with a lack of advanced digital skills and cybersecurity challenges, hinder the transition to a more digital and connected economy. In response to these challenges, the Central American Bank for Economic Integration (CABEI) has played a crucial role in financing projects that seek to overcome these barriers. For example, CABEI financed in 2023 the construction and improvement of educational infrastructure in Guatemala, benefiting more than 107,000 students [23], provided a USD 80 million loan in 2019 to the Republic of Honduras for the "Program for the Integral Improvement of Educational Infrastructure and Training in Honduras" [24] to promote progress in improving the infrastructure of public education centers, and also supported, in 2022, the creation of an immersive virtual room in the National Art Museum of Guatemala to enrich the cultural experience of visitors through advanced technology [25]. These initiatives not only improve access to education and culture, but also lay the groundwork for integrating emerging technologies such as virtual reality into the educational environment.

In addition, the increase in infrastructure and digital capabilities thanks to CABEI's efforts has provided a special context for examining the reception of virtual reality (VR) in the region's universities. Another outstanding example of CABEI's promotion of advanced technologies in the Latin American and Caribbean region was the financing of the Agriculture and Technology (AgTec) 2022 event, organized by Zamorano University, with the sponsorship of CABEI's DYNAMIC II initiative [26]. This event brought together nearly 900 participants, including students, graduates, industry, and development institutions, to share innovations in processes, products, and services aimed at improving the resilience and equity of agri-food systems. This event discussed how the inclusion of technologies such as the Internet of Things and Artificial Intelligence offers a relevant framework for considering the expansion and acceptance of virtual reality in educational contexts, given its low adoption in the region, which does not exceed 2% among small-scale farmers [26]. Along the same lines, in 2020 CABEI held the forum "Science, Technology and Innovation for Development: the necessary normality" [27], in which the possibility of regional integration was proposed based on science and technology systems linked between countries and their productive systems. This forum also discussed possible solutions to the most urgent problems based on investment in research and development in Latin America, as the COVID-19 pandemic revealed the low scientific and technological capacity as well as the relative backwardness in the use of information technologies. Likewise, CABEI's initiative to support the development of the Artificial Intelligence Strategy in coordination with the Executive Directorate of the Innovation Cabinet of the Dominican Republic exemplifies the entity's commitment to the promotion and adoption of advanced technologies [28]. These supports, initiatives, and efforts provide a solid framework to drive research and development, which is crucial to understand the potential for integration of technologies such as virtual reality in higher education in the region.

Despite CABEI's firm commitment to the digitalization of its member countries, especially in higher education, there are no studies in the specialized literature that analyze the impact of CABEI's actions in this digital integration process. For this reason, the main purpose of this paper is to contribute to closing this gap. The general objective of this research is to analyze the reception of VR technologies by Latin American university professors, distinguishing between CABEI countries and non-CABEI countries. Specifically, it aims to achieve the following objectives: (i) to analyze the perceptions that Latin American professors have about the didactic use of VR and their self-concept of digital competence for its use; (ii) to identify gaps in the above perceptions between CABEI and non-CABEI countries; and (iii) to analyze whether the behavior of the differences in the perception of VR between private and public universities in CABEI countries is similar or different from those in non-CBEI countries. Therefore, we seek to answer the following research questions:

- RQ1: Are there significant differences in perceptions of the didactic use of VR between teachers in CABEI and non-CBEI countries within the Latin American region?
- RQ2: Are differences by university tenure in perceptions of VR in CABEI countries similar to or different from those of teachers in non-CABEI countries?

2. Related Works

The digital competence expressed by university professors in the Latin American region is low, both in general terms [29] and in relation to the use of VR [22]. In this sense, the area of specialty of the professors conditions their digital competence [30] which, in general, is higher among professors in scientific and technical areas [31]. As far as we have been able to explore, there are no studies that analyze differences in digital skills between private and public university teachers in general. However, there are contextualized studies on professors of Engineering [32] and Health Sciences [33] that claim that professors from private universities report having better digital competence than those from public universities. This disparity is attributed to several factors. Predominantly, private universities tend to have a larger contingent of distance learning students, necessitating substantial investments in digital infrastructure and resources [32]. Moreover, private institutions might also prioritize comprehensive training programs in digital skills for their faculty, which not only enhance technical abilities but also improve pedagogical and professional capacities to integrate these technologies effectively into their teaching practices. These strategies are integral to fostering an environment that supports digital competence, tailored to the evolving educational needs and modalities of the modern academic landscape.

However, the digital competence of faculty in the Latin American region also changes depending on the particular country studied. Specifically, it has been shown that the level of digitization of the country correlates positively with the level of digital competence expressed by university teachers [22]. In addition, it has also been shown that in certain Latin American countries there are gaps in the digital competence of university professors that do not exist in countries in more strongly digitized regions. For example, in Mexico, engineering professors express the best digital competence [34], while in Spain, no gaps in digital competence by knowledge area have been identified [35].

University professors give very good ratings to VR technologies as a teaching resource in higher education [36]. In this sense, the aspect most highlighted by the literature is the very high acceptance generated by these technologies among students [37], which leads to a significant increase in students' motivation and engagement with learning activities [38]. However, these high ratings are accompanied by the identification of a high number of limitations or disadvantages, mainly linked to the cost of implementation and the needs VR poses in terms of faculty training [39].

The specialized literature identifies numerous factors that condition the reception of digital technologies in general and VR in particular, in higher education. The factors most frequently present in the literature are sociological factors such as the gender and age of teachers. In the case of gender, the literature presents diverse results. There are works that report a better reception of digital technologies by men compared to women [29], works that report that women are the ones who show a better reception [40], and works that report no significant differences by gender [35]. As far as we have been able to explore, it has not been possible to describe the extraneous variables that explain these divergences. A similar phenomenon occurs with age. In fact, it has been found that the digital generation (digital natives or digital immigrants) affects professors' evaluations of digital technologies [41]. However, it has also been found that the field of expertise of a professor significantly influences how age affects their evaluation of virtual reality (VR). Specifically, the area of knowledge acts as a critical variable that could explain the variance in VR ratings across different age groups [42]. This suggests not only that age impacts technological adoption but that this effect is moderated by the specific disciplinary contexts in which the technology is used. Thus, the interaction between the age of a professor and their field of knowledge provides a detailed understanding of their perception and valuation of VR technology, highlighting the importance of considering both individual and contextual factors in studies of technology adoption in educational settings.

It has also been found that the teacher's area of knowledge conditions the way in which age influences his or her evaluations of VR [42]. Thus, knowledge area appears as a possible explanatory extraneous variable for age gaps in VR ratings.

University tenure has been shown to be an explanatory variable for faculty perceptions of VR within specific subject areas, such as Health Sciences [31] and Engineering [32]. In both knowledge areas, faculty from private universities value VR more than those from public universities [31,32]. However, the gap between the two is wider in Health Sciences [31]. This shows that university tenure is not only an explanatory variable for VR ratings but also an extraneous variable that explains, secondarily, the influence of other factors on the above-mentioned ratings.

3. Materials and Methods

3.1. Participants

The target population for this research was university professors in the Latin American and Caribbean region. Specifically, the authors designed and taught a master class on the didactic use of VR in higher education focused on Latin American university professors, which was accessed through free registration in the course, and which was repeated every two weeks between January and June 2023. This session had the following objectives: (i) to present VR technologies as didactic tools and elucidate their technical characteristics of realism, three-dimensionality, interactivity, and immersion; (ii) to discuss the logistical, equipment, and training needs necessary for the implementation of VR technologies in university classrooms; and (iii) to present different examples of practical applications of the use of VR technologies in the various areas of knowledge in higher education. The criteria for inclusion were the following: (i) being a professor at a Latin American university and (ii) being a registered attendee at a training session on the use of VR in higher education given by the authors. Attendance at the above-mentioned training session allows assuming that the participants had, at the time of their participation in the study, similar and homogeneous knowledge about the didactic use of VR, even though they were professors with no previous experience in the use of VR. After each training session, the attendees were asked to respond telematically to the questionnaire used as a research instrument, which was sent to them by means of a GoogleForms® (v1, Mountain View, CA, USA) questionnaire. Participation was informed and consented to in writing, as well as free and anonymous. At no point in the process were participant data recorded that could lead to identification. A total of 1559 professors attended the training session, of whom 1246 responded to the questionnaire. All the responses received were considered valid by the authors, in the sense that they were complete.

3.2. Research Variables and Instrument

In this study, the main explanatory variable considered is whether or not the country of origin of the participating professors belongs to CABEI. This is a dichotomous nominal variable. The secondary explanatory variable is the tenure, private or public, of the university where the professors teach. This is also a dichotomous variable.

The following explained variables are also considered: (i) self-concept of the participants' digital competence in the use of VR technologies; (ii) assessment of the didactic aspects of VR; (iii) assessment of the usability of VR by professors and students; (iv) level of perceived disadvantages of VR use in higher education; (v) perceived future use for VR in the universities of the region; and (vi) assessment of the didactic and formative effectiveness of VR use. All the explained variables were measured on Likert-type scales from 1 to 5, where the lowest rating corresponds to value 1 and the highest to value 5.

For measuring these explained variables, a validated questionnaire [32] oriented to university professors about the perception of the use of VR technologies in higher education was used (Appendix A). The questionnaire consists of 22 questions, each of which requests a rating of an aspect related to the didactic use of VR on a scale of 1 to 5, where 1 means a very low rating and 5 means a very high rating. The validation of the instrument refers to the construct, which consisted of an exploratory factor analysis that allowed the identification of six families of questions that explain the construct [32] (Table 1): (i) self-concept of participants' digital competence in using VR (questions 1 to 3); (ii) rating of technical aspects of VR, including realism, immersion, and three-dimensional design (questions 4 to 7); (iii) rating of usability aspects of VR, including user experience, employability of VR in lessons, and perceived possibility at the participant's university implementing VR technologies (questions 8 to 10); (iv) disadvantages of VR, including costs, space required, human and technical resources used, training required by technicians and professors, and technological obsolescence of equipment (questions 11 to 15); (v) assessment of the future projection of the use of VR in higher education, including both immersive and non-immersive VR (questions 16 and 17); and (vi) assessment of the didactic and formative aspects of VR, including student acceptance of VR, its impact on academic performance, induced student motivation, impact on the development of lessons, university capacity to implement VR technologies, and didactic employability (questions 18 to 22). This distribution of the questions into six families, which correspond to the explained variables of the present study, allows explaining 54.1% of the variance [32]. Likewise, the instrument was validated in terms of its internal consistency (notice that the Cronbach's alpha parameters of the different families mentioned vary between 0.70 and 0.84 [32]).

Table 1. Explained variables and questions of the instrument (Appendix A).

Variable	Questions
Digital competence	1 to 3
Technical aspects	4 to 7
Usability	8 to 10
Disadvantages	11 to 15
Future projection	16 to 17
Didactic aspects	18 to 22

3.3. Research Methodology

In this work, descriptive quantitative research was carried out on the assessments made by a sample of Latin American university professors of the didactic use of VR technologies. The core of the research consists of the statistical analysis of the comparison of the mean ratings of professors from CABEI countries with respect to professors from non-CABEI countries, and of private universities with respect to public universities. The research process was as follows (Figure 1): The authors provided a training session on the didactic use of VR as part of the data collection phase. After the session, the participants answered a questionnaire, which was used as a research instrument. After validation of the responses obtained (in the sense of checking for completeness), the data collection phase was concluded. These data were subjected to statistical analysis, which were finally discussed and conclusions were drawn.

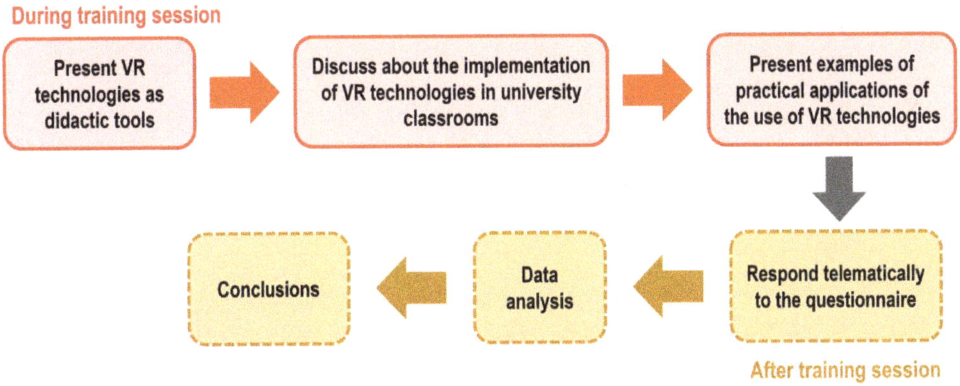

Figure 1. Research phases.

3.4. Data Analysis

This work is of a descriptive quantitative nature and is based on the statistical analysis of the responses obtained to the questionnaire used as a research instrument. For this purpose, it was confirmed, by means of a confirmatory factor analysis and the computation of internal reliability statistics, that the theoretical model of six families of questions that was presented explains the responses obtained. Descriptive statistics were then obtained for the responses, grouped by families of questions according to the model derived from the factor analysis. To answer the research questions, we obtained the statistics of the bilateral *t*-test, comparing the mean responses between CABEI countries and non-CABEI countries, with Welch's correction, without assuming equality of variances. Likewise, to contrast whether the gaps by university tenure in the responses are similar or different in CABEI countries and non-CABEI countries, the multifactor analysis of variance (MANOVA) test was used, again with Welch's correction, without assuming equality of variances.

4. Results

4.1. Distribution of Participants

A total of 1246 professors participated in the study, of which 746 come from nine CABEI countries (59.87% of the total) and 500 come from nine countries in the Latin American and Caribbean region that do not belong to CABEI (40.13% of the total). Of the participants from CABEI countries, 37.50% teach in private universities and 62.50% teach in public universities, so there is a slight majority of professors from public universities. Among participants from non-CABEI countries, 46.00% work in private universities and 54.00% work in public universities, so the majority are again in public universities, although the difference is smaller than in the case of CABEI countries. The distribution of participants by country of origin is shown in Table 2.

Table 2. Distribution of the participants by their country of origin.

CABEI Countries	Proportion (%)	Non-CABEI Countries	Proportion (%)
Argentina	16.6	Bolivia	10.4
Colombia	29.5	Brazil	4.0
Costa Rica	1.1	Chile	4.8
El Salvador	1.9	Ecuador	22.4
Guatemala	3.2	Paraguay	3.2
Honduras	1.1	Peru	44.4
Mexico	37.8	Puerto Rico	1.6
Panama	1.6	Uruguay	2.4
Dominican Republic	2.9	Venezuela	6.8
TOTAL	100	TOTAL	100

4.2. Validation of the Instrument

The Cronbach's alpha and composite reliability (CR) parameters computed on the responses obtained (Table 3), all greater than 0.70, show that the instrument enjoys good internal consistency.

Table 3. Cronbach's alpha and composite reliability (CR) parameters.

Family of Responses	Cronbach's Alpha	CR
Digital competence	0.7551	0.7421
Technical aspects	0.8491	0.8406
Usability	0.7814	0.7696
Disadvantages	0.8017	0.7933
Future projection	0.7941	0.7861
Didactic aspects	0.7640	0.7551

4.3. Responses

Participating professors express an intermediate average level of digital competence for VR use (between 3 and 4 out of 5) but higher ratings for technical and usability aspects (greater than or equal to 4 out of 5), according to the average responses shown in Table 4. On the other hand, the didactic aspects are rated lower than the technical and usability aspects (between 3 and 4 out of 5). Likewise, the level of disadvantage perceived by the professors is close to 4 out of 5. A bilateral t-test was performed to compare the mean ratings between teachers from CABEI countries and teachers from non-CABEI countries, the results of which are shown in Table 4 and Figure 2. Since the corresponding p-values are less than the significance level previously set (0.05) only for the usability and disadvantages variables, it can be concluded that there are significant differences between the mean ratings only for these variables. Specifically, professors from CABEI countries give better ratings of the usability of VR and identify a lower level of disadvantage in its use in lessons than professors from non-CABEI countries (Table 4).

The bilateral t-test performed for the comparison of means between private and public universities reveals significant differences (p-values lower than the 0.05 significance level) for the usability and didactic aspects variables. Therefore, professors from private universities give higher ratings to the usability and didactic aspects of VR than those from public universities (Table 5). However, no differences by university tenure were identified in the professors' self-concept of digital competence or in their ratings of the technical aspects of VR, its future projection or its disadvantages (Table 5 and Figure 3).

Table 4. Average responses distinguishing between CABEI countries and non-CABEI countries as well as statistics of the bilateral t-test for comparison of means, carried out with the Welch correction, without assuming equality of variances.

Family	Mean CABEI Countries (Out of 5)	Mean Non-CABEI Countries (Out of 5)	t-Statistic	p-Value
Digital competence	3.26	3.23	0.58	0.56
Technical aspects	3.97	3.91	0.91	0.36
Usability	4.29	4.15	2.81	<0.05 *
Disadvantages	3.80	3.92	−1.96	0.04 *
Future projection	4.00	3.90	1.62	0.10
Didactic aspects	3.08	3.14	−0.87	0.38

* $p < 0.05$.

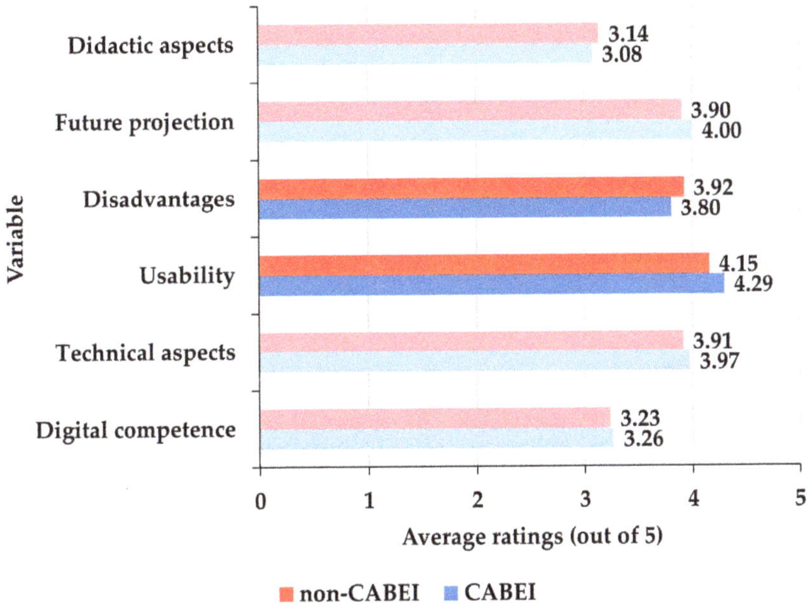

Figure 2. Average responses differentiated by geographic location (dark colors indicate significant differences between CABEI and non-CABEI countries).

Table 5. Average responses distinguishing between private and public universities as well as statistics of the bilateral t-test for comparison of means, carried out with the Welch correction, without assuming equality of variances.

Family	Mean Private	Mean Public	t-Statistic	p-Value
Digital competence	3.31	3.20	1.75	0.08
Technical aspects	3.98	3.92	1.06	0.29
Usability	4.36	4.15	4.27	0.00 *
Disadvantages	3.91	3.81	1.49	0.14
Future projection	3.97	3.95	0.38	0.70
Didactic aspects	3.27	2.98	4.40	0.00 *

* $p < 0.05$.

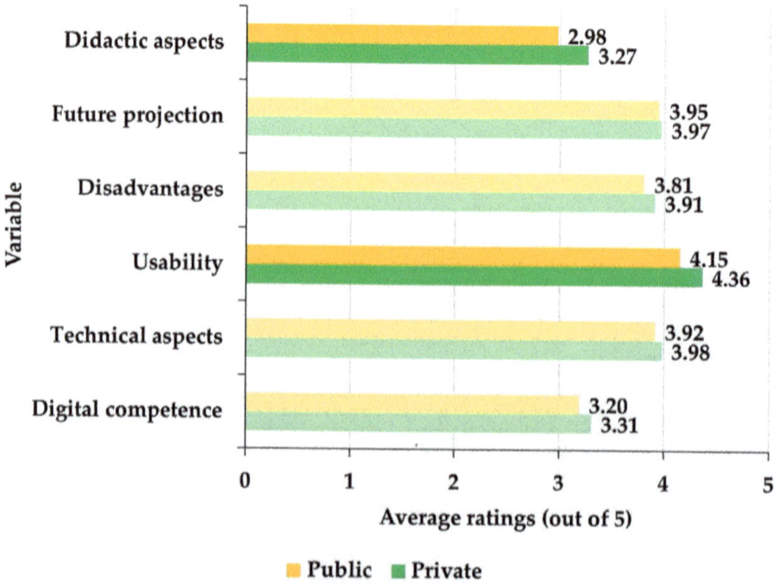

Figure 3. Average responses differentiated by university tenure (dark colors indicate significant differences between private and public universities).

The behavior of the gap between public and private universities depending on whether the professors are from CABEI or non-CABEI countries was studied using multifactor analysis of variance (MANOVA), the results of which are shown in Table 6 and Figure 4. Specifically, the behavior of the mean responses, distinguishing between private and public universities, is different for CABEI and non-CABEI countries in terms of self-concept of digital competence and assessment of the future projection of VR. Specifically, in the CABEI countries, professors in private universities report higher levels of digital competence and a better assessment of the future projection of VR than professors in public universities (Table 6). On the other hand, in countries outside CABEI, it is public university professors who show a slight superiority in their average self-concept of digital competence and also in their assessment of the future projection of VR compared to private university professors (Table 6).

Table 6. Average responses (out of 5) distinguished by university tenure within CABEI countries and non-CABEI countries as well as statistics from the multifactor analysis of variance (MANOVA) test with Welch's correction, without assuming equality of variances.

Family	CABEI Countries		Non-CABEI Countries		F-Statistic	p-Value
	Private	Public	Private	Public		
Digital competence	3.41	3.18	3.20	3.25	5.02	0.03 *
Technical aspects	3.99	3.95	3.97	3.86	0.47	0.49
Usability	4.45	4.20	4.25	4.06	0.28	0.60
Disadvantages	3.81	3.79	4.02	3.84	1.13	0.29
Future projection	4.08	3.95	3.84	3.96	4.36	0.04 *
Didactic aspects	3.26	2.97	3.29	3.01	0.02	0.89

* $p < 0.05$.

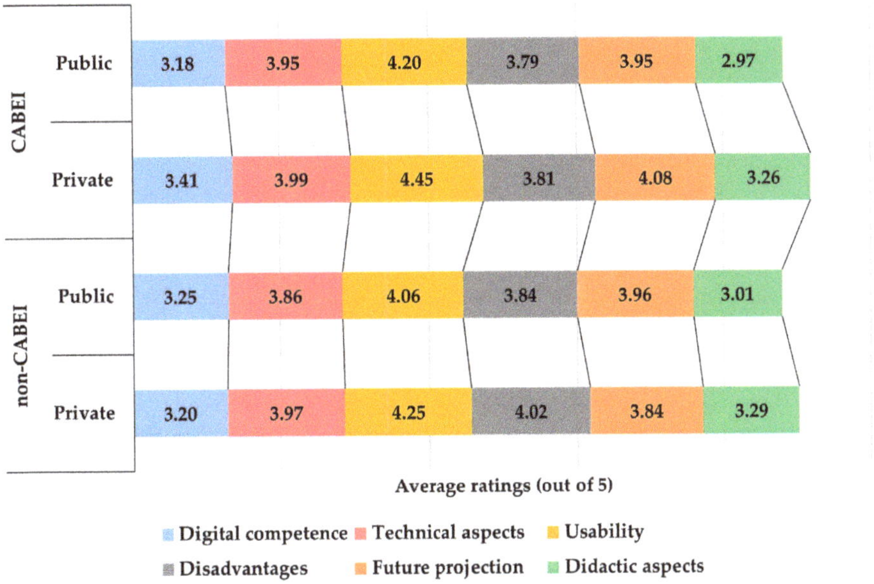

Figure 4. Average responses (out of 5) differentiated by geo-localization (CABEI and non-CABEI countries) and university tenure.

5. Discussion

The first novel contribution of the present research is to demonstrate that teachers from CABEI countries rate the usability and user experience dimensions of VR higher than teachers from non-CABEI countries (Table 4). In addition, the level of VR disadvantage perceived by CABEI members is lower than that of non-CABEI members (Table 4). This allows us to conclude, in response to RQ1, that belonging to the CABEI certainly influences professors' acceptance of VR, although not in all the dimensions analyzed. If there are no differences in the ratings of technical or didactic aspects, it is probably because these ratings are not so much conditioned by the digitization of the country or the experience of use, which seems to condition the rating of usability. This implies that professors in CABEI countries probably have greater knowledge and experience in the use of technologies such as VR.

In any case, the above results are in line with previous work that identifies the geographic variable as an influential factor in VR valuations [19,22,35]. Also, it is shown that CABEI policies regarding the egalitarian digital development of member states lead to higher acceptance of VR technologies by university professors. However, this higher acceptance, while significant, is still small (around 3.37% for usability aspects of VR and 3.16% for disadvantages; Table 4). In contrast, digital competence in CABEI countries is about 7% higher than in non-CBEI countries (Table 4). These two data together imply that membership in CABEI leads to an increase in the digital integration of its universities, but this increase has probably not yet sufficiently reached specific VR technologies.

University tenure has also been shown to be an explanatory variable for the evaluation of the didactic and usability aspects of VR (Table 5). Specifically, professors from private universities give higher ratings of these dimensions than professors from public universities. Again, these results are in line with previous work contextualized in specific areas of knowledge, such as Health Sciences [31] and Engineering [32]. Moreover, these results are extended here to a broader population of university faculty. This gap may be due to the greater experience and investment of private universities in the region in digital integration [32].

However, these university tenure gaps behave differently in CABEI and non-CABEI countries. Specifically, in CABEI countries, there is a larger gap in digital competence for VR use between private and public universities than in non-CABEI countries (Table 6). Indeed, the digital competence of professors at private universities is 7.23% higher than that of professors at public universities within CABEI countries. In contrast, the digital competence of professors at public universities is 1.6% higher than that of professors at private universities within countries outside the CABEI. This implies, in response to RQ2, that the gaps by university tenure are different depending on whether or not one belongs to the CABEI in terms of self-concept of digital competence, but not in the assessment of the different technical, didactic, or usability dimensions of VR. This probably means that CABEI countries are pursuing more determined university digitization policies than non-CABEI countries, but the impact of these policies is evident mostly in private universities. Again, the reality of the student body of these universities may explain this gap [32].

The implications of this study are as follows: (i) supranational alliances of an economic nature, such as CABEI, have a significant and positive impact on the digitization process in the region in which they are established; (ii) the previous digitization process carried out by CABEI countries has had very little impact on the use and acceptance of specific VR technologies in higher education; and (iii) the policies carried out by CABEI generate inequalities in terms of the digitization process between private and public universities, at least in terms of the digital training of faculty. Based on this second implication, it is suggested that CABEI member states take measures to ensure an increasing use of digital technologies in public universities, for example, by encouraging the design of protocols for their use in lessons.

Among the limitations of this study are the following: (i) the methodology employed is strongly quantitative, so that it is not possible to conduct an in-depth analysis of the reasons behind the gaps identified, which would be derived from a more qualitative or mixed approach; (ii) it is possible that there are extraneous variables influencing the perceptions analyzed, both sociological and academic, that have not been addressed in this research; and (iii) the geographic region analyzed, in the process of technological development, is specific and particular, so it is not possible to extend the results to other regions with higher levels of digitization. Thus, the following lines of future research are proposed: (i) to carry out a similar quantitative analysis, but with a sample of participants homogeneously distributed by country, so that the influence of the geographic variable can be studied in greater depth; (ii) to complete the study with a qualitative analysis that will make it possible to identify the exact reasons for the gaps identified; and (iii) to compare the results obtained with those of other geographic regions with different levels of digitization.

Central America faces significant challenges in its digital transformation, marked by a notable digital divide, limited technological infrastructure, and a lack of digital and innovation skills. These challenges, together with problems in cybersecurity and access to financing, hinder progress towards a digital economy. CABEI has responded to these challenges with significant initiatives, such as financing the expansion of educational infrastructure in Guatemala [23] and the development of an immersive virtual room at the National Museum of Art [25], in addition to supporting technological innovation projects in agriculture and education in other member countries [26]. In addition, CABEI has supported initiatives that promote technological innovation in various sectors, which could indirectly benefit education by improving the technological infrastructure available to educational institutions in the region. These efforts not only improve the access to and quality of education and culture but also foster greater integration with global value chains, paving the way for the incorporation of advanced technologies such as virtual reality. CABEI has thus played a fundamental role in the quest to mitigate these barriers through the financing of key projects.

CABEI's implementation of infrastructure and advanced technology offers a unique platform to explore the integration and perception of virtual reality in higher education in the region. The analysis of CABEI-supported projects, such as the creation of immersive facilities and support for research and development in countries such as Guatemala and Honduras, influence professors' perceptions of the didactic use of VR. In addition, these analyses make it possible to compare the differential situation between private and public universities, in order to understand the differences in the reception and application of Virtual Reality depending on the type of institution and the technological support provided by regional initiatives such as the National Artificial Intelligence Strategy in the Dominican Republic and educational innovation in Honduras, thus reflecting the impact of digitalization policies promoted by CABEI.

The results of the present study show that, despite funding for infrastructure improvements in universities and other educational institutions by CABEI in the Latin American and Caribbean region, the integration of technologies such as virtual reality in higher education in CABEI countries is still in its early stages. Integrating VR more deeply into academic curricula could improve the perception of its didactic benefits, thus aligning digital competence with positive evaluations of its practical applicability. While teachers in CABEI countries rate the usability aspects of VR positively and perceive fewer disadvantages in its use compared to their counterparts in non-CABEI countries, the increase in digital competence is not fully reflected in a high valuation of VR. This suggests that, while CABEI investments in technology infrastructure and training are critical, a more targeted and specific approach to VR training is needed for these technologies to be fully leveraged in educational contexts. These infrastructure projects would have the potential to incorporate advanced technological components such as computer labs and digital media, which can be critical in supporting VR technologies.

6. Conclusions

The participating professors give high ratings to the technical and usability aspects of VR but express an intermediate self-concept of their digital competence to use VR, an intermediate–high level of disadvantages, and an intermediate rating of its didactic benefits. Professors from CABEI countries express 3.37% higher ratings of the usability aspects of VR and 3.16% lower ratings of its disadvantages than those from non-CABEI countries. Also, within the CABEI countries, the digital competence expressed by private university professors is 7.23% higher than that of public university professors. However, within countries outside the CABEI, the digital competence expressed by public university professors is 1.6% higher than that of private university professors. Consequently, it can be affirmed that CABEI activity in its member states leads to a notable increase in the digital competence of professors in its universities, which is clearly concentrated in private universities. This is probably because private universities may have both a greater awareness of the digital integration process and a greater capacity to carry it out. Thus, this may have led them to a more optimal capacity to channel the investment received in the digitization of higher education than public universities. In addition, CABEI membership also significantly increases the valuations of VR technologies. However, this increase of just 3% is low (less than half of the increase in digital competence shown by CABEI countries). This means that the CABEI countries have not taken sufficient action in relation to specific VR technologies. From the results obtained, it is recommended that CABEI countries promote the design of protocols for the use of digital technologies, specifically VR, within their public universities, to reduce the existing gap with private universities, and that efforts to digitize higher education in non-CABEI countries be increased. In conclusion, the main original contribution of the article consists of a mathematical verification of the influence of CABEI's technological development policies in higher education on university professors' reception of digital teaching technologies, specifically VR.

Although it has been shown that there are significant differences in the acceptance of VR technologies depending on whether a country belongs to the CABEI, the methodology used cannot ensure that membership in the CABEI is the cause (at least the only cause) of these differences. This is a methodological limitation of this work. Thus, given that only a small part of the investment in higher education in CABEI countries can be assumed to be due to CABEI membership, it is possible that there are extraneous variables that cause the differences identified in this paper. Among these hidden causes could be, for example, the differences in socioeconomic levels that exist between CABEI and non-CABEI countries.

CABEI's commitment to improving digital infrastructure and training has facilitated a more receptive environment for VR in educational institutions in its member countries. This is inferred because the results obtained among participants from CABEI countries are better. However, despite CABEI funding for infrastructure improvements, the adoption of VR in higher education in CABEI countries is still in its nascent stages, because the superiority of the ratings to those of non-CABEI countries barely exceeds 3%. This implies that a more targeted approach to VR training is required to take full advantage of these technologies in educational contexts. Likewise, the results of the study indicate that, although there is a positive assessment of VR usability and recognition of its technical advantages, a concerted effort is still needed to build this improved infrastructure into an effective integration of VR into didactic processes, particularly in public universities, to close the gap with private institutions and maximize the educational potential of these advanced technologies. The difference in the reception of VR between private and public universities underscores the need for supportive policies that balance the distribution of technological resources and strengthen the capacity of all higher education institutions in the Latin American region.

Author Contributions: Conceptualization, P.F.-A. and D.V.; methodology, Á.A.-S., P.F.-A. and D.V.; validation, Á.A.-S., P.F.-A., E.A.A. and D.V.; formal analysis, Á.A.-S.; investigation, P.F.-A. and D.V.; data curation, Á.A.-S.; writing—original draft preparation, Á.A.-S., E.A.A. and D.V.; writing—review and editing, Á.A.-S., P.F.-A., E.A.A. and D.V.; supervision, Á.A.-S., P.F.-A., E.A.A. and D.V. All authors have read and agreed to the published version of the manuscript.

Funding: This research received no external funding.

Data Availability Statement: The data are not publicly available because they are part of a larger project involving more researchers. If you have any questions, please ask the contact author.

Conflicts of Interest: The authors declare no conflicts of interest.

Appendix A

The following are the questions of the survey used as the research instrument (all responses are measured on a Likert scale of 1 to 5, where 1 means a very low rating and 5 means a very high rating):

1. Self-concept of your digital skills to program or design new ICT-based educational tools.
2. Level of knowledge about virtual reality.
3. Do you feel that you have received sufficient training at your university on the possible applications of VR in education?
4. Level of importance of the following usability aspect of virtual reality when designing a virtual reality educational experience: 3D Design.
5. Level of importance of the following usability aspect of virtual reality when designing a virtual reality educational experience: Immersion.
6. Level of importance of the following usability aspect of virtual reality when designing a virtual reality educational experience: Realism.
7. Importance of interaction when designing an educational experience with virtual reality.
8. Importance of user experience when designing an educational experience with virtual reality.
9. Importance of employability when designing a virtual reality educational experience.
10. Possibility of your university implementing virtual reality in its teaching activities.
11. Level of inconvenience of the following aspects of virtual reality: Costs.
12. Level of inconvenience of the following aspects of virtual reality: Spatial limitations.

13. Level of inconvenience of the following aspects of virtual reality: Demand for technical and human resources.
14. Level of inconvenience of the following aspects of virtual reality: Requirement of specific knowledge on the part of teachers and technicians.
15. Level of inconvenience of the following aspects of virtual reality: Technological obsolescence of equipment.
16. Degree to which you think that the implementation of immersive virtual reality will increase in the future at your university.
17. Degree to which you think that the implementation of non-immersive virtual reality will increase in the future at your university.
18. Level of importance you give to the didactic usefulness of virtual reality when designing didactic actions.
19. Level of acceptance of virtual reality as a teaching resource that you think your students have (or would have).
20. Do you believe that the use of virtual reality in educational environments increases (or would increase) the academic performance of your students?
21. Do you believe that the use of virtual reality in educational environments increases (or would increase) your students' motivation to learn?
22. Do you consider that the application of virtual reality in educational environments helps (or would help) to improve the progress of lessons?

References

1. Onyesolu, M.O.; Eze, U.F. Understanding virtual reality technology: Advances and applications. In *Advances in Computer Science and Engineering*; Schmidt, M., Ed.; InTech: Houston, TX, USA, 2011; pp. 53–70. [CrossRef]
2. Newman, M.; Gatersleben, B.; Wyles, K.J.; Ratcliffe, E. The use of virtual reality in environment experiences and the importance of realism. *J. Environ. Psychol.* **2022**, *79*, 101733. [CrossRef]
3. Kyriakou, M.; Pan, X.; Chrysanthou, Y. Interaction with virtual crowd in immersive and semi-immersive virtual reality systems. *Comput. Animat. Virtual Worlds* **2017**, *28*, e1729. [CrossRef]
4. Zhou, Y.; Ji, S.; Xu, T.; Wang, Z. Promoting knowledge construction: A model for using virtual reality interaction to enhance learning. *Procedia Comput. Sci.* **2018**, *130*, 239–246. [CrossRef]
5. Milgram, P.; Kishino, F. A taxonomy of mixed reality visual displays. *IEICE Trans. Inf. Syst.* **1994**, *77*, 1321–1329. Available online: https://cs.gmu.edu/~zduric/cs499/Readings/r76JBo-Milgram_IEICE_1994.pdf (accessed on 18 June 2023).
6. Pavilionis, P.; Adhanom, I.B.; Moran, R.; Taylor, M.R.; Murray, N.G. Virtual reality application for vestibular/ocular motor screening: Current clinical protocol versus a novel prototype. *Sports Health* **2024**, *16*, 407–413. [CrossRef] [PubMed]
7. Cheng, D.; Duan, J.; Chen, H.; Wang, H.; Li, D.; Wang, Q.; Hou, Q.; Yang, T.; Hou, W.; Wang, D.; et al. Freeform OST-HMD system with large exit pupil diameter and vision correction capability. *Photonics Res.* **2022**, *10*, 21–32. [CrossRef]
8. Shi, Y.; Wan, C.; Dai, C.; Wang, Z.; Wan, S.; Zheng, G.; Zhang, S.; Li, Z. Augmented reality enabled by on-chip meta-holography multiplexing. *Laser Photonics Rev.* **2022**, *16*, 2100638. [CrossRef]
9. Liu, C.; Zheng, Y.; Yuan, R.-Y.; Jiang, Z.; Xu, J.-B.; Zhao, Y.-R.; Wang, X.; Li, X.-W.; Xing, Y.; Wang, Q.-H. Tunable liquid lenses: Emerging technologies and future perspectives. *Photonics Res.* **2023**, *17*, 2300274. [CrossRef]
10. Solmaz, S.; Kester, L.; Van Gerven, T. An immersive virtual reality learning environment with CFD simulations: Unveiling the Virtual Garage concept. *Educ. Inf. Technol.* **2024**, *29*, 1455–1488. [CrossRef]
11. Johnston, E.; Olivas, G.; Steele, P.; Smith, C.; Bailey, L. Exploring pedagogical foundations of existing virtual reality educational applications: A content analysis study. *J. Educ. Technol. Syst.* **2018**, *46*, 414–439. [CrossRef]
12. Duarte, M.L.; Santos, L.R.; Guimarães, J.B.; Peccin, M.S. Learning anatomy by virtual reality and augmented reality. A scope review. *Morphologie* **2020**, *104*, 254–266. [CrossRef] [PubMed]
13. Balamuralithara, B.; Woods, P.C. Virtual laboratories in engineering education: The simulation lab and remote lab. *Comput. Appl. Eng. Educ.* **2009**, *17*, 108–118. [CrossRef]
14. Potkonjak, V.; Gardner, M.; Callaghan, V.; Mattila, P.; Guetl, C.; Petrović, V.M.; Jovanović, K. Virtual laboratories for education in science, technology, and engineering: A review. *Comput. Educ.* **2016**, *95*, 309–327. [CrossRef]
15. Hutson, J.; Olsen, T. Virtual reality and art history: A case study of digital humanities and immersive learning environments. *Fac. Scholarsh.* **2022**, *417*, 50–65. [CrossRef]
16. Mäkinen, H.; Haavisto, E.; Havola, S.; Koivisto, J.-M. User experiences of virtual reality technologies for healthcare in learning: An integrative review. *Behav. Inf. Technol.* **2022**, *41*, 1–17. [CrossRef]

17. Natale, A.F.D.; Repetto, C.; Riva, G.; Villani, D. Immersive virtual reality in K-12 and higher education: A 10-year systematic review of empirical research. *Br. J. Educ. Technol.* **2020**, *51*, 2006–2033. [CrossRef]
18. Chang, C.-Y.; Sung, H.-Y.; Guo, J.-L.; Chang, B.-Y.; Kuo, F.-R. Effects of spherical video-based virtual reality on nursing students' learning performance in childbirth education training. *Interact. Learn. Environ.* **2022**, *30*, 400–416. [CrossRef]
19. Antón-Sancho, Á.; Vergara, D.; Fernández-Arias, P.; Ariza-Echeverri, E.A. Didactic use of virtual reality in Colombian universities: Professors' perspective. *Multimodal Technol. Interact.* **2022**, *6*, 38. [CrossRef]
20. Alnagrat, A.J.; Ismail, R.C.; Idrus, S.Z. The opportunities and challenges in virtual reality for virtual laboratories. *Innov. Teach. Learn. J.* **2023**, *6*, 73–89. [CrossRef]
21. Ebinger, F.; Buttke, L.; Kreimeier, J. Augmented and virtual reality technologies in education for sustainable development: An expert-based technology assessment. *TATuP-Z. Für Tech. Theor. Und Prax./J. Technol. Assess. Theory Pract.* **2022**, *31*, 28–34.
22. Liu, D.; Bhagat, K.K.; Yuan, G.; Chang, T.W.; Huang, R. The potentials and trends of Virtual Reality in education. In *Virtual, Augmented and Mixed Realities in Education*; Springer: Berlin/Heidelberg, Germany, 2017.
23. More than 107,000 Guatemalan Students Have Quality Educational Infrastructure with the Support of CABEI. 2023. Available online: https://www.CABEI.org/en/news-and-media/news/article/more-than-107000-guatemalan-students-have-quality-educational-infrastructure-with-the-support-of-cabei (accessed on 7 April 2024).
24. Programa de Mejoramiento Integral de la Infraestructura y Formación Educativa en Honduras (MIFE). Available online: https://adquisiciones.CABEI.org/planes-de-adquisiciones/plan/5886 (accessed on 13 April 2024).
25. CABEI Approves Donation of US$130 Thousand to Provide the National Museum of Art of Guatemala with an Immersive Virtual Room. 2023. Available online: https://www.CABEI.org/novedades/noticias/articulo/CABEI-aprueba-donacion-por-us130-mil-para-dotar-al-museo-nacional-de-arte-de-guatemala-de-una-sala-virtual-inmersiva (accessed on 7 April 2024).
26. Agtec—Innovación e Investigación. 2022. Available online: https://agtec.zamorano.edu/ (accessed on 9 April 2024).
27. Foro Organizado Por el CABEI Destaca Fortalecimiento de la Integración Regional a Partir de Sistemas de Ciencia y Tecnología, 2020. Forum: Science, Technology and Innovation for Development: The Necessary Normality. Available online: https://www.CABEI.org/novedades/noticias/articulo/foro-organizado-por-el-CABEI-destaca-fortalecimiento-de-la-integracion-regional-a-partir-de-sistemas-de-ciencia-y-tecnologia (accessed on 9 April 2024).
28. CABEI Apoya a República Dominicana en la Elaboración de Estrategia Nacional de Inteligencia Artificial. 2023. Available online: https://www.CABEI.org/novedades/noticias/articulo/CABEI-apoya-a-republica-dominicana-en-la-elaboracion-de-estrategia-nacional-de-inteligencia-artificial (accessed on 9 April 2024).
29. Cabero-Almenara, J.; Guillén-Gámez, F.D.; Ruiz-Palmero, J.; Palacios-Rodríguez, A. Digital competence of higher education professor according to DigCompEdu. Statistical research methods with ANOVA between fields of knowledge in different age ranges. *Educ. Inf. Technol.* **2021**, *26*, 4691–4708. [CrossRef]
30. Blayone, T.J.B.; Mykhailenko, O.; vanOostveen, R.; Grebeshkov, O.; Hrebeshkova, O.; Vostryakov, O. Surveying digital competencies of university students and professors in Ukraine for fully online collaborative learning. *Technol. Pedagog. Educ.* **2018**, *27*, 279–296. [CrossRef]
31. Cabero-Almenara, J.; Barroso-Osuna, J.; Gutiérrez-Castillo, J.-J.; Palacios-Rodríguez, A. The Teaching Digital Competence of Health Sciences Teachers. A Study at Andalusian Universities (Spain). *Int. J. Environ. Res. Public Health* **2021**, *18*, 2552. [CrossRef] [PubMed]
32. Vergara, D.; Antón-Sancho, Á.; Dávila, L.P.; Fernández-Arias, P. Virtual reality as a didactic resource from the perspective of engineering teachers. *Comput. Appl. Eng. Educ.* **2022**, *30*, 1086–1101. [CrossRef]
33. Saltos-Rivas, R.; Novoa-Hernández, P.; Rodríguez, R.S. Understanding university teachers' digital competencies: A systematic mapping study. *Educ. Inf. Technol.* **2023**, *28*, 16771–16822. [CrossRef] [PubMed]
34. Antón-Sancho, Á.; Fernández-Arias, P.; Vergara, D. Perception of the use of virtual reality didactic tools among faculty in Mexico. *Future Internet* **2023**, *15*, 72. [CrossRef]
35. Guillén-Gámez, F.D.; Cabero-Almenara, J.; Llorente-Cejudo, C.; Palacios-Rodríguez, A. Differential analysis of the years of experience of higher education teachers, their digital competence and use of digital resources: Comparative research methods. *Technol. Knowl. Learn.* **2022**, *27*, 1193–1213. [CrossRef]
36. Wells, T.; Miller, G. Teachers' opinions about virtual reality technology in school-based agricultural education. *J. Agric. Educ.* **2020**, *61*, 92–109. [CrossRef]
37. Rocha-Estrada, F.J.; Ruiz-Ramírez, J.A.; George-Reyes, C.E.; Glasserman-Morales, L.D. Evaluation of a virtual campus adapted to web-based virtual reality spaces: Assessments of teachers and students. *Front. Educ.* **2022**, *7*, 918125. [CrossRef]
38. Hamilton, D.; McKechnie, J.; Edgerton, E.; Wilson, C. Implementing immersive virtual reality in higher education: A qualitative study of instructor attitudes and perspectives. *Innov. Pract. High. Educ.* **2021**, *4*, 206–238. Available online: http://journals.staffs.ac.uk/index.php/ipihe/article/view/210 (accessed on 18 January 2024).
39. Alqahtani, E.S.; AlNajdi, S.M. Potential obstacles to adopting augmented reality (AR) technologies as pedagogical tools to support students learning in higher education. *Interact. Learn. Environ.* **2024**. *In press*. [CrossRef]
40. Krumsvik, R.J.; Jones, L.Ø.; Øfstegaard, M.; Eikeland, O.J. Upper secondary school teachers' digital competence: Analysed by demographic, personal and professional characteristics. *Nord. J. Digit. Lit.* **2016**, *11*, 143–164. [CrossRef]

41. Kuleto, V.; P., M.I.; Stanescu, M.; Ranković, M.; Šević, N.P.; Păun, D.; Teodorescu, S. Extended reality in higher education, a responsible innovation approach for generation Y and generation Z. *Sustainability* **2021**, *13*, 11814. [CrossRef]
42. Breiki, M.A.; Abri, A.A.; Moosawi, A.M.; Alburaiki, A. Investigating science teachers' intention to adopt virtual reality through the integration of diffusion of innovation theory and theory of planned behaviour: The moderating role of perceived skills readiness. *Educ. Inf. Technol.* **2023**, *28*, 6165–6187. [CrossRef] [PubMed]

future internet

MDPI

Article

Virtual Reality in the Classroom: Transforming the Teaching of Electrical Circuits in the Digital Age

Diego Alejandro Albarracin-Acero [1], Fidel Alfonso Romero-Toledo [2], Claudia Esperanza Saavedra-Bautista [3] and Edwan Anderson Ariza-Echeverri [4,*]

[1] Facultad de Ingeniería, Universidad Autónoma de Bucaramanga, Bogotá 680003, Colombia; dalbarracin848@unab.edu.co

[2] Grupo de Investigación GridsE, Ingeniería Electromecánica, Facultad Seccional Duitama, Universidad Pedagógica y Tecnológica de Colombia, Duitama 150461, Colombia; fidel.romero@uptc.edu.co

[3] Grupo de Investigación RESET, Licenciatura en Tecnología, Facultad Seccional Duitama, Universidad Pedagógica y Tecnológica de Colombia, Duitama 150461, Colombia; claudia.saavedra@uptc.edu.co

[4] Grupo de Investigación en Nuevos Materiales, Facultad de Ingeniería, Universidad del Magdalena, Santa Marta 470004, Colombia

* Correspondence: earizaec@unimagdalena.edu.co

Abstract: In response to the digital transformation in education, this study explores the efficacy of virtual reality (VR) video games in teaching direct current electrical circuits at a public university in Colombia. Using a mixed-method action research approach, this study aimed to design, implement, and evaluate a VR-based educational strategy to enhance undergraduate learning experiences. The methodology integrated VR into the curriculum, facilitating a comparison of this innovative approach with traditional teaching methods. The results indicate that the VR strategy significantly improved students' comprehension of electrical circuits and increased engagement, demonstrating the utility of immersive technologies in educational settings. Challenges such as the need for technological integration and curriculum adaptation were also identified. This study concludes that VR video games can effectively augment electrical engineering education, offering a model for incorporating advanced digital tools into higher education curricula. This approach aligns with ongoing trends in digital transformation, suggesting significant potential for broad applications across various educational contexts.

Keywords: electrical circuits; teaching; didactic strategy; virtual reality; emerging technologies; digital transformation; serious game

1. Introduction

The integration of digital technologies within educational paradigms is revolutionizing traditional teaching methodologies, fostering more interactive and engaging learning experiences [1]. Among these innovations, Virtual Reality (VR) stands out due to its capacity to create immersive and realistic environments that engage students more effectively than traditional methods [2]. This study explores the use of VR as a dynamic interface between humans and machines within educational settings, specifically targeting the instruction of direct current electrical circuits across various educational levels [3].

Emerging technologies such as virtual reality have become a significant topic of contemporary academic discussion due to their valuable contributions to teaching and learning processes [4,5]. These technologies are emerging as innovative approaches that break away from classic teaching methods and offer active and engaging learning environments for students and professionals in the field of electricity [6,7]. Thus, the emerging technology that was explored in this study is virtual reality, which, from a theoretical perspective, is defined as a human–machine interface that allows users to experience an immersive environment through 3-dimensional graphic simulations aimed at entering the metaverse [8]. This technology provides a realistic interaction with the content [9]. In this sense, this study aimed to develop a didactic strategy based on virtual reality video games for teaching the fundamentals of direct current electrical circuits in secondary, technical, and higher education. These tools are increasingly used to prevent electrical accidents, such as those occurring in substation control [10].

Virtual reality offers an interactive platform that significantly enhances the comprehension of complex scientific concepts through three-dimensional simulations. This immersive experience not only improves understanding but also increases student motivation and engagement, thereby making the learning process more appealing and effective. Despite initial barriers such as high costs and limited technological accessibility, recent advancements have rendered VR tools more accessible, spurring renewed interest and expanded research into their potential educational benefits [11,12].

The transformative impact of VR extends beyond mere visualization; it changes pedagogical approaches in science and technology education [13]. By enabling students to interact with virtual objects, VR facilitates a hands-on approach that is particularly advantageous in fields such as electrical engineering, where theoretical concepts can be abstract and difficult to grasp [14,15]. Research indicates that VR can significantly reduce cognitive load, providing a more intuitive understanding of complex theories [16,17].

Moreover, the inclusion of VR in educational settings enhances inclusivity and accessibility, catering to diverse learning needs and styles [18]. Studies have shown that VR's multisensory, immersive environments are particularly beneficial for students with learning disabilities, helping them engage with content in ways that are often unachievable through conventional methods [19,20].

Recent studies underscore VR's expanding role across various disciplines. For instance, Vergara et al. [21] demonstrated how VR platforms could simulate complex engineering tests like concrete compression, enhancing student familiarity with potentially hazardous equipment in a risk-free environment. Furthermore, Vergara-Rodríguez et al. [22] utilized VR for training in ultrasonic non-destructive testing, showing that VR not only reduces training costs but also prevents the risks associated with handling real equipment. These applications highlight VR's potential to transcend traditional educational boundaries, offering a versatile tool for both theoretical and practical instruction.

As VR technologies continue to evolve, their adaptability and scalability suggest that they could become foundational in educational systems globally, reshaping how educational content is delivered and experienced across various levels and disciplines. The empirical evaluation of this VR teaching strategy included both quantitative and qualitative assessments to determine its impact on learning effectiveness, usability, and student engagement. Findings suggest that VR significantly enhances educational experiences by providing interactive and engaging environments that support complex cognitive tasks such as understanding electrical circuits [23,24].

This research was conducted in collaboration with the Research and Development Group in Electromechanical Systems (GRIDSEs) and Research in Science, Education, and Technology (RESET) at the Pedagogical and Technological University of Colombia. It employs VR video games to teach the fundamentals of electrical circuits, integrating action research methodologies to ensure practical relevance and effectiveness. The initial phase involved a review of existing didactic strategies, followed by the development and implementation of a VR solution tailored to enhance learning outcomes in electrical circuit education. Thus, this study not only highlights the effectiveness of VR in enhancing electrical circuit education but also illustrates its potential as a transformative educational tool. The findings advocate for the integration of VR technologies in curriculum design, addressing the evolving demands of digital literacy in higher education [25,26].

2. Methodology

The methodological approach of this study was undertaken using a mixed method, supported by action research following Lewin's postulates, where the entire research proposal was structured into four stages: plan, act, observe, and reflect. Creswell [27] states that this type of research "is similar to mixed research methods as it utilizes a collection of quantitative, qualitative, or both types of data. However, it differs from these by focusing on solving a specific and practical problem" (p. 577). Notably, action research was first promulgated in 1944, envisioned as a research method with an experimental approach in social sciences, prioritizing action on social issues [28].

Currently, this method is widely utilized in the field of education, offering possibilities for intervention in communities with local problems that pave the way for transformation and reflection [29,30]. It also allows researchers to theorize about praxis and self-reflect on their teaching practices [31,32]. In action research, the researcher identifies a problem related to action, employing various instruments to define the topic of interest and diagnose significant weaknesses along with supporting theories, aiming to improve educational practices. This approach can be conducted individually or in teams [33].

During the planning phase, the need to incorporate an instructional design model was identified to plan the entire teaching strategy based on virtual reality effectively. To this end, the ADDIE model was employed, which involves structuring the sequence of content creation—didactic and interactive—based on five criteria: analysis, design, development, implementation, and evaluation. Muñoz and González [34] suggest that these steps can be followed sequentially or simultaneously to design teaching materials, as summarized in the diagram below (Figure 1).

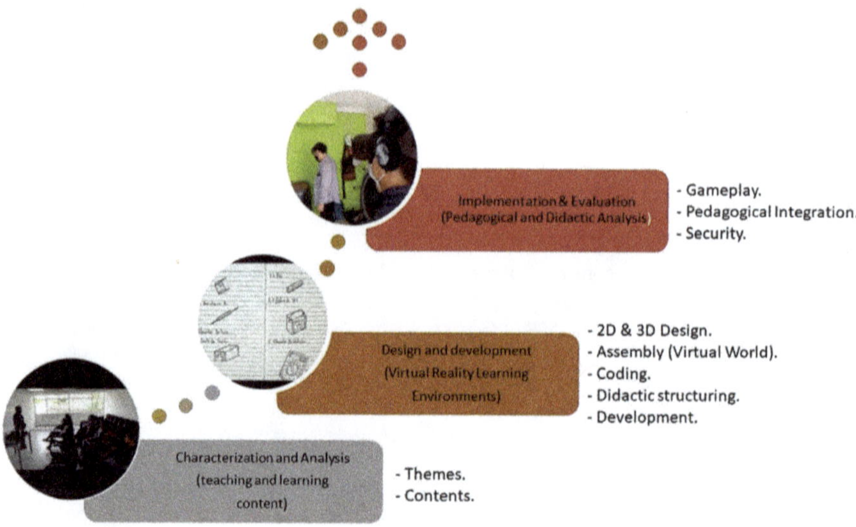

Figure 1. Methodological development diagram.

The virtual reality environment was developed using the Oculus Quest tool. This platform enables users to interact in real-time with a simulated three-dimensional environment via multiple sensory channels, emphasizing its main features such as visual and spatial representation, immersion, and 3D sound. These attributes are crucial for fostering the development of educational and interactive content.

The initial phases of this study involved a diagnostic analysis of the VR tool with students from the technology degree program enrolled in the "Fundamentals of Electrical Circuits" course. This cohort consisted of ten students, including two who were repeating the course, that were selected to explore their comprehension and challenges related to the topics of symbology, measurement, and circuit types in a controlled, virtual environment. To ensure a comprehensive evaluation, a supplementary assessment was conducted with an additional 17 students, bringing the total number of student evaluators to 27. This broader group allowed for a robust assessment of the VR system's usability, pedagogical integration, and safety in a wider educational context. Additionally, an evaluation panel comprising five experts in educational technology and electrical engineering was included to provide expert perspectives, ensuring the results reflect practical usability and pedagogical efficacy. The evaluation employed a Likert scale survey [35] to gather detailed and nuanced feedback, ensuring thorough vetting from both usability and educational perspectives. The survey used for this evaluation can be found in Supplementary Materials File S1.

To address potential risks associated with the use of virtual reality (VR) environments, such as falls, dizziness, and other symptoms [36], several precautionary measures were implemented. Prior to participation, all students were fully informed about the nature of this study and the potential risks involved. Informed consent forms were completed by each participant, ensuring that they were aware of the scope and responsibility entailed in the evaluation phase of the immersive VR resource developed.

To supplement our findings and mitigate the impact of having a smaller initial cohort, we established a second population comprising a panel of five experts with extensive experience in the electrical sector and educational gamification. This panel, detailed in Table 1, was meticulously selected based on rigorous inclusion criteria, primarily their professional experience exceeding ten years in relevant fields. The experts evaluated and analyzed the usability characteristics, pedagogical integration, safety measures, and the overall behavior of the virtual reality laboratory in teaching basic electrical circuits. Their insights were crucial for validating the effectiveness and educational value of the VR environment under conditions simulating real-life usage. This dual approach, combining both student interactions and expert evaluations, provided a comprehensive analysis of the VR application, ensuring robust testing and feedback that aligns with the high standards required for educational innovations in technical disciplines.

Table 1. Expert panel composition and qualifications.

Panel of Experts	Profession	Professional Experience	Virtual Reality Experience	Supervised Subjects
1	Electronic engineer, Master of Computer Science, and Ph.D. in engineering	18.3 years	No	Electrical circuits, electric drives, analog electronics, digital electronics, and power electronics
2	Industrial designer—with teaching experience in the area of 2D and 3D design	15.7 years	Yes, thesis supervision in gamification.	Basic and secondary education technology
3	Electromechanical engineer and Specialist of Industrial Automation and Master of Industrial Automation	28.4 years	No	Electrical circuits, electric drives, analog electronics, digital electronics, and power electronics
4	Electrical engineer, Master of Engineering with an emphasis in electrical engineering	20.2 years	No	DC electrical circuits
5	Graduate of Industrial Education, Master of E-learning, Ph.D. in creation	26 years	Yes, direction and chair of the postgraduate projects in gamification.	Educational digital ecosystems and educational innovation and information communication technology

The following description outlines the methodology used in this study, including details on the sample population, the various research methods applied at different stages, and the specific tools employed to evaluate the impact of virtual reality (VR) on students' learning experiences.

2.1. Methodological Process

2.1.1. Qualitative Methodology

Qualitative assessments were conducted at multiple stages to gather nuanced feedback on the VR environment. These included structured interviews and observational studies, which provided critical insights into the usability and educational value of the VR settings.

2.1.2. Quantitative Methodology

Quantitative data collection began with a baseline evaluation of students' understanding of key concepts in electrical circuits. This phase employed a structured questionnaire to identify initial knowledge gaps and measure learning outcomes post-intervention.

2.1.3. Measurement Tools

To rigorously assess the effectiveness of the VR application, a customized questionnaire was developed based on Olsen's frameworks for serious games' usability testing. The immersive quality of the VR experience was enhanced using Oculus Quest technology, which supports interactive learning through six degrees of freedom, ensuring a highly engaging and educational experience. Each session was carefully timed to last no more than thirty minutes to optimize focus and prevent cognitive overload.

3. Results

3.1. Initial Diagnosis

An assessment was conducted with ten students enrolled in the "Fundamentals of Electrical Circuits" course. The objective was to gauge their level of knowledge on key concepts. This assessment covered various topics, including symbols, electrical components and units, areas of measurement, series circuits, and mixed circuits (Table 2). Each question was categorized by theme and meticulously analyzed. This process enabled the identification of the students' strengths and weaknesses concerning their knowledge base.

Table 2. Knowledge level test responses.

Ask	Symbology (1a)	Units (1b)	Measurement Zones (2)	Series Circuit (3)	Mixed Circuit (4)
Correct answer	3	9	1	3	4
Wrong answer	7	1	9	7	6

The analysis of the preliminary data, as illustrated in the preceding table, reveals significant gaps in knowledge across most of the evaluated topics. This initial diagnostic exercise proved to be the most critical input for determining the specific subjects to be addressed within the teaching strategy, which was operationalized through the virtual reality laboratory. The analysis indicates that 90% of the students can identify and associate electrical components with their corresponding units. However, a majority struggles with other areas, including symbols, measurement domains, series circuits, and mixed circuits.

3.2. Design and Development of Virtual Reality Modules

For the design and development of the video game, two versions of the teaching strategy were developed, leveraging challenge-based learning to foster critical thinking, creativity, and curiosity among students. This approach facilitates a deeper understanding of the subject matter and enhances problem-solving skills, as supported by Romero-Yesa et al. [37] and Kaya and Ercag [38], who have documented the effectiveness of challenge-based learning in stimulating significant educational engagement and improvement in learning outcomes. A preliminary knowledge diagnosis was performed to identify the most challenging topics for students, which then informed the thematic content incorporated into the video game. The chosen topics were meticulously aligned with the course syllabus to ensure relevance and educational integrity.

Further detailing the video game's design, we incorporated instructional elements, interface designs, and safety measures tailored to the educational context. Notably, the gameplay was structured to include specific time allocations for each challenge, detailed in Table 3 below, ensuring that each session maintained optimal engagement without overwhelming the students. The sequence of scenes, evaluations, and feedback strategies were carefully orchestrated to provide both auditory and visual cues, enhancing the immersive experience while safeguarding the educational objectives. The sound environment and other design elements were chosen to minimize distractions and maximize learning efficacy, with the entire design process reflecting a meticulous approach to integrating educational technology effectively.

Table 3. Requirements for the design and development of the video game.

Requirements	Justification	Alternative
Characterization of the themes	To stop the design and development of the modules, the themes that represented the greatest difficulty in the contextualization of knowledge were taken into account.	The topics were selected based on the subject's curriculum and the application of the knowledge level test.
Virtual reality	Virtual reality was used due to its great benefits in terms of didactics and pedagogy, since significant learning has been demonstrated.	The total immersion of the user within the video game allows for a pedagogical and didactic connection.
Safety	Prevents the user (player) from suffering physical injuries. It is recommended to perform active pause practices every 15 min for a period of 30 min to use the virtual reality glasses again.	The Oculus Quest virtual reality device was used, due to its safety guardian system, which avoids collisions with the real world.
Gameplay	The video game was developed under a criterion of rules and conditions—Game Core, Game Engine, Game Interface—facilitating the response interaction between the user and machine.	Game Core: use of an interactive character that narrates and introduces the video game. The following system of rules was defined: The accumulation of points. This is an individual video game. Challenges only have one solution. There is a time limit for each challenge. If the player, at the end of each module, does not solve the challenge correctly, he must return to the beginning of it. If the player solves the challenge correctly in one module, he or she will automatically continue to the next. Game Engine: The 3D objects were designed under gravity parameters and high-quality rendering, obtaining a realistic appearance of the materials associated with each electrical element. Oculus Touch controls were used for the communication system. A VR display device, Oculus Quest, was used. Game Interface: Auditory feedback means (narrative audios, button sounds, and auditory timers) and visual feedback (images, colors, shapes, numbers, symbols, letters, and three-dimensional objects) were used.
Graphic section	The aim is for the content to be realistic and to have a high resolution, omitting distracting agents, and for the player to be the one who intuitively discovers the video game, within the user interface.	Naturalness in movements, quick interaction responses in real time, realistic renderings, and scales according to the real elements.
Music and sounds	During the experience, the user will need to be oriented and guided in each thematic module and have feedback on the practices.	Through narration and sound effects, the video game will be comfortable and intuitive to use.

Table 3. *Cont.*

Requirements	Justification	Alternative
Duration	Within each interaction, the user will have a time limit to be able to correctly solve the modules.	The video game will have a pop-up message in the last 10 s of each interaction.
Theme contextualization	The context of the video game and all the elements of the scenario are related to the topic of fundamentals of direct current electrical circuits.	The scenario was designed, simulating an electricity laboratory, ruling out any distraction within the practical experience.
Quantitative measurement of learning	As this is a video game focused on teaching, it is important to evaluate the results in each thematic module.	A scoring system was designed that allows for the measuring of the results by modules and additionally establishes a final sum of the victory of the video game.
Didactic environment	Electrical concepts, being ambiguous and intangible, become more difficult to understand and contextualize.	The scenario has the objects associated with a symbol and a type of electrical element.
Degrees of freedom	The controls and interface with the use of Oculus Quest offer six degrees of freedom, allowing free and natural movements in space.	At the time of immersion, the user has the option to move in all three axes and perform head rotations using the Oculus Quest devices.

3.3. Conceptual Modeling

In this phase, initial concepts for the video game were sketched by hand before being digitized. Figure 2 illustrates an initial layout of the game environment, detailing the quantities of electrical components utilized and establishing both the chronological sequence and the mechanics of the game, including the setting, immersion, interaction, and puzzles.

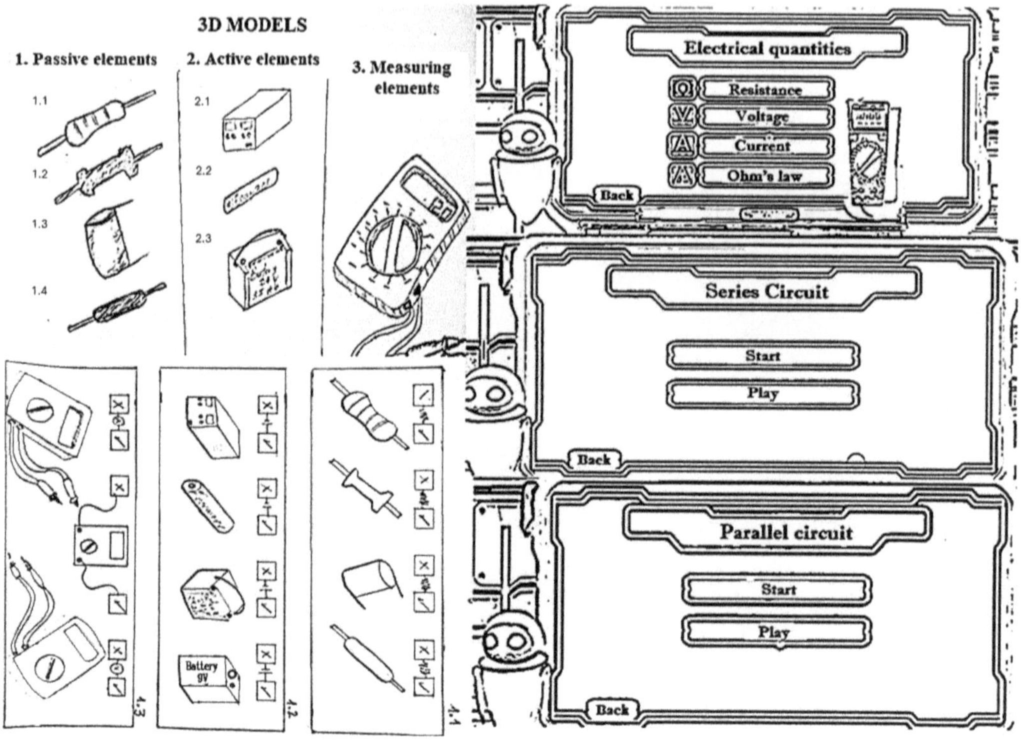

Figure 2. Spatial distribution of the module.

3.4. Production of Artistic Resources

During this stage, various artistic assets were created, including objects, textures, videos, illustrations, and audio narratives. The following tools were employed for their development: Blender was used for modeling three-dimensional objects in .blend format; Corel Draw was utilized for editing and creating vectors, specifically Sprites, in .png format; and Audacity was used for editing and creating narrative audio files in .mp3 format. For the rendering phase, a laptop equipped with an Intel Core I7 processor, 16 GB RAM (Intel Corporation, Santa Clara, CA, USA), and an NVIDIA GEFORCE RTX 2060 (NVIDIA Corporation, Santa Clara, CA, USA) graphics card was used.

3.5. 3D Modeling

The electrical objects were modeled in three dimensions with a high level of detail, coupled with the assignment of materials, which were rendered by the Cycles engine to achieve a realistic representation, as observed in Figure 3. The design of all objects within the learning environment utilized polygonal modeling techniques, favored for their ability to create complex shapes through the manipulation of vertices, edges, and faces. The primary tools employed in this process were Extrude and Subdivision, which are staple features of modeling software, particularly Blender in this instance. These tools enable the addition of intricate details to the mesh by starting with a basic geometric shape in edit mode and then selecting specific faces to extrude. The figure below displays examples of the modeled objects. The development of virtual reality equipment has led to significant advancements, particularly in the evolution from virtual reality helmets to virtual reality glasses. These glasses have enhanced scenario resolution, portability, and software development, including platforms like Unreal Engine™ and Unity™ © [39].

Figure 3. Element modeling.

3.5.1. Vectorized—Graphical User Interface

For the creation of buttons and electrical symbols, initial sketches were refined and subsequently vectorized using the Corel Draw program, specifically its free version. This approach facilitated the production of high-resolution vectors in .png format, ensuring that the graphical elements retained clarity and detail suitable for the educational content (Figure 4). The graph below displays the vectors and Sprites that were pre-designed and edited in .CDR format, sourced under a free license from the OpenGameArt repository, showcasing the variety and quality of these graphical components. Similarly, 2D elements play a crucial role in student tasks, as traditional methods utilize graphics and symbols that help connect concepts with student understanding [40].

Figure 4. Vectorized graphic elements.

As illustrated in the previous graph, symbols served as reference images to signify the type of electrical element each represented. Moreover, vectors were utilized to graphically underscore the concepts covered in each module, and a logo was crafted to encapsulate the essence of the game, serving as a key part of the virtual reality learning environment's identity.

The process for vectorizing images began with the initial sketching of buttons and symbols, followed by their vectorization in Corel Draw (X9). Subsequently, the hierarchy of the vectors was organized in terms of frames, titles, subtitles, and buttons. These vectors were then exported in .png format to the Unity3D engine. The final steps involved converting the .png vectors into 2D sprites and arranging the spatial distribution of buttons within the input menus.

3.5.2. Construction of the Scenario

For the construction of the setting, a 3D digitization was arranged, creating a futuristic electricity laboratory. This environment comprises three-dimensional elements including an instruction and menu screen, a workbench, and various 3D objects. The design draws inspiration from a futuristic laboratory theme, sourced from Unity's Asset Store. As depicted in Figure 5, the aim is to foster a gaming and immersive experience for the user. This immersion is further enhanced through visualization with virtual reality devices, such as Oculus Quest, thereby stimulating motivation during the execution of learning activities.

For the final arrangement of the scenario, the 3D objects were exported in .blend, .obj, and .fbx formats to the Unity video game engine. This step facilitated their integration within the scenario and its associated themes. Following this integration into Unity®, with the 3D elements designed by the authors, the appropriate lighting for the 3D environment was established. This meticulous process culminated in the creation of the environment depicted in Figure 6 as the result.

To ensure students' effective engagement and understanding, initial instructions are provided through 2D mediations such as texts and images. These instructions are presented on a monitor within the VR environment, explaining, in detail, the steps and tasks students need to perform. This preparatory phase helps students comprehend their roles and the activities involved in the immersive learning environment. Following this, students interact with the 3D resources and activities designed to achieve learning outcomes related to electrical circuits. The preliminary instructions are delivered via a computer, a familiar resource in the computer laboratories of the educational institution, facilitating a smooth transition to the immersive 3D experience. This method leverages both 2D and 3D elements, creating a comprehensive learning pathway that enhances educational outcomes. Figure 7a,b illustrate the interaction within the serious game. In the selection activities, students use controls to pick up 3D objects and place them in the correct category of circuit elements, as shown in Figure 7a. In the circuit-construction phase, students select elements such as sources, resistors, and conductors to assemble a series circuit on a giant breadboard within the 3D virtual environment, as depicted in Figure 7b. This structured integration of 2D and 3D instructions and activities ensures a progressive and engaging learning experience.

Figure 5. Scenario design in post-processing mode.

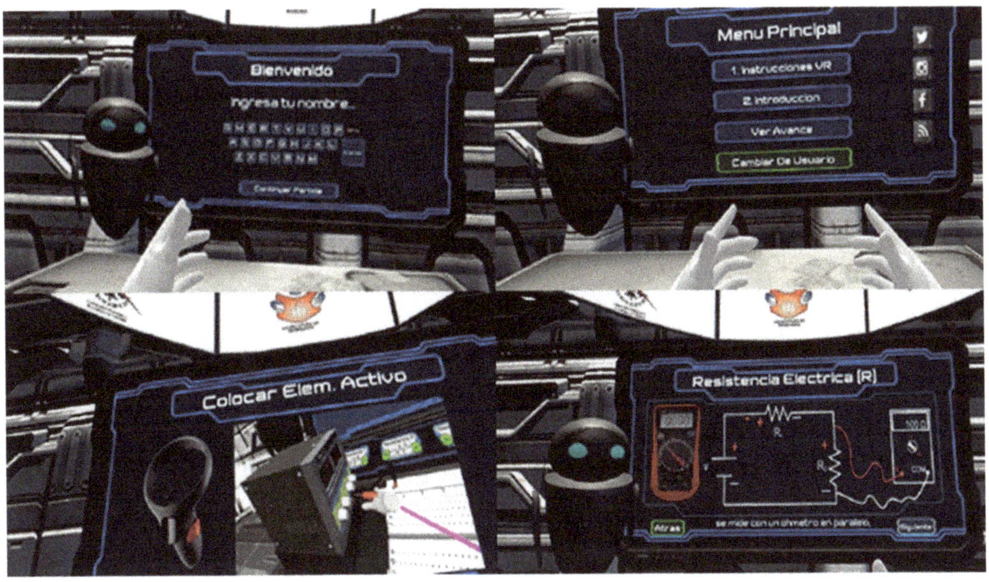

Figure 6. The Virtual Electrical Lab—the VE Lab.

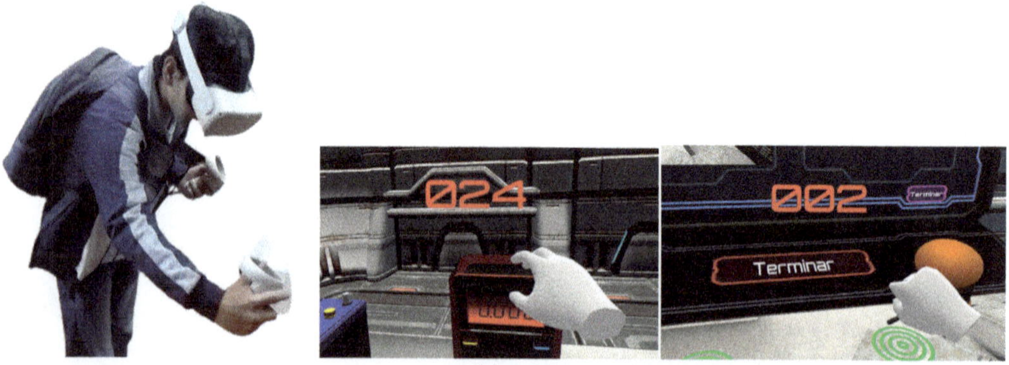

(**a**)

(**b**)

Figure 7. (**a**) Interaction with 3D objects for categorizing circuit elements. (**b**) Construction of a series circuit on a giant breadboard in the 3D virtual environment.

The graphical user interface (GUI) of the virtual laboratory features various menus that offer students the opportunity to temporarily register their names before proceeding with the different modules available in the learning environment. Additionally, an instruction menu provides guidance on using the controls to interact with 3D objects and integrate them into the construction of electrical circuits. Furthermore, the explanatory interface plays a crucial role in contextualizing the material through images, illustrations, and text, elucidating the electrical concepts and virtual reality principles necessary for engaging with the virtual world effectively.

In response to the innovative application of VR environments to simulate traditional educational tools like monitors displaying circuit diagrams, the well-documented educational benefits of serious games and digital game-based learning environments are harnessed. Studies by Protopsaltis et al. [41] and Anastasiadis et al. [42] illustrate how these digital platforms catalyze learning by enhancing student engagement through interactive and immersive experiences. Digital games, especially those designed for educational purposes, transform traditional learning landscapes into comprehensive and interactive environments where students actively participate and engage with content. This interactive modality, preferred by digital natives or modern learners who thrive in digital-rich settings, promotes a deeper understanding and retention of complex concepts such as those encountered in electrical circuits. The virtual display of a monitor in the VR laboratory serves more than a mere visual replication; it integrates with interactive elements that allow students to manipulate and experiment with circuits in ways traditional static displays cannot match. By incorporating serious games into education, the natural curiosity and engagement of learners are leveraged, transforming their interaction with content from passive reception to active involvement—a crucial shift in technical education where practical understanding and the application of knowledge are key. Moreover, the inclusion of game elements, such as points, levels, and feedback, not only makes the learning process more engaging but also aligns with pedagogical strategies that enhance motivation and improve learning outcomes. Embedding traditional educational content within a VR platform adheres to modern educational theories and provides a pedagogically enriched environment that is adaptive, interactive, and reflective of how students best learn today, aligning with the advantages of serious games in education which include improved cognitive gains, higher motivation and engagement levels, and enhanced problem-solving skills.

3.6. Logical Structuring of the GUI

Figures S1 and S2 (in the Supplementary Materials) showcase the class diagram (logical structure) of the GUI, detailing the various methods, variables, and plugins that facilitate user interaction. This diagram serves as the foundation for all user navigations within the GUI, enabling seamless interactions with menus, activities, and conceptual frameworks. In other research, interaction is crucial for familiarizing users with levels and tutorials to help them achieve each objective [43].

Figure S1 presents a concept map illustrating the relationship between the user interface and game controls within the virtual reality environment. The GUI is divided into two key elements: the "VR Instructions Menu" and the "Main Menu". This map highlights how the user interacts with the controls and various menus, showcasing the different activities involved in the application's use for teaching circuits. Figure S2 illustrates the interaction and components within the virtual world designed to teach concepts of electrical symbology, such as electrical resistance, voltage, and electrical current. The controls and gameplay modules are configured to allow for the selection and manipulation of various circuit elements, enabling users to identify passive, active, and measurement components. Additionally, users can engage in several questionnaire challenges where they must select the correct answers. Upon completing the questionnaire, users can build a circuit on a protoboard using different virtualized elements, enhancing their ability to manipulate and construct circuits.

The educational structure of the video game is divided into two main sections: the first part delivers theoretical content, introducing concepts through narratives and texts. The second part engages students with interactive puzzles, allowing them to apply the concepts they have learned. This dynamic approach is enhanced by the inclusion of a scoring system, timers, sounds, and pop-up messages, which provide feedback and signal achievement to the students.

3.7. Graphical User Interface Coding and Programming

The programming behind the graphical user interface (GUI) was executed in the C# (C Sharp) programming language, utilizing the Visual Studio 2019 Integrated Development Environment (IDE) and integrating it into the Unity video game engine. The development process involved coding various scripts related to entry, GUI navigation, instructions, question-and-answer interactions, final results, and circuit creation. These scripts underpin the interactions within each module of the virtual learning environment, facilitating a seamless and interactive educational experience.

3.7.1. Control Programming

Control programming was specifically designed to enable interaction with the input and grip buttons, allowing for the selection and manipulation of objects within the virtual space. Figure 8 illustrates the control mechanisms.

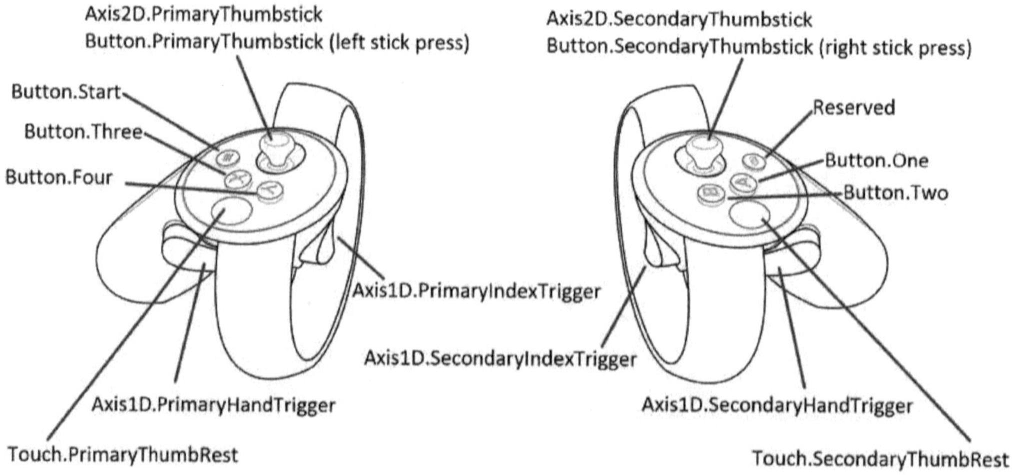

Figure 8. Oculus Touch input system in Unity. Source: Unity Manual [44].

The controller controls utilized were Oculus Touch, and the final coding was implemented within the Unity3D video game engine, version 2019. It was essential to identify the input buttons of the Oculus Touch controller within the Unity3D engine and utilize its native Oculus package, named Oculus Integration. This package comprises basic Oculus VR features, components, scripts, and plugins in Unity, facilitating certain user actions.

3.7.2. Generation and Installation of the Apk on the Oculus Quest Device

The final compilation of the virtual reality environment and the generation of the APK were conducted using Unity. Subsequently, the Oculus Quest device was connected, and the application was installed via the command prompt using the respective commands.

3.8. Implementation and Evaluation of the VR Teaching Strategy

A panel of five experts was selected to use and analyze the teaching strategy, named the Virtual Electrical Lab. This process allowed for the compilation of observations through a questionnaire to establish criteria for improvements. The observations, recommendations, and identified limitations aimed to enhance the video game in terms of usability, pedagogical integration, and safety.

At the start of the session, with each expert in the virtual reality laboratory, instructions for using the Oculus Quest virtual reality display device were provided, along with an introduction to the virtual learning environment. The progress within this environment was observable from outside the VR device via a screen.

In refining the assessment tools for the serious game, the necessity to adapt the evaluation strategy to better suit the developmental stage of the project was recognized. Initially guided by general frameworks from the literature [45], a comprehensive questionnaire was specifically designed to address usability, pedagogical integration, and safety aspects, drawing from established methodologies in usability testing for serious games. This approach ensures that the game not only meets technical standards but also aligns with educational goals, providing a safe and effective learning environment. The results from this structured evaluation are instrumental in directing ongoing adjustments and enhancements, confirming the game's readiness for eventual academic applications and highlighting its potential for broader educational impacts.

Usability and interaction (expert panel): The survey results from the results on usability (Table 4) indicate a highly positive reception of the VR tool's instructional quality and design features. Preliminary instructions provided by the developer or course instructor were rated as either "Excellent" (60%) or "Very Good" (40%), with no responses falling into lower categories. Similarly, the quality of in-game instructions for controls, object handling, and circuit building received the same high ratings, indicating clear and effective guidance for users. Satisfaction with the 3D environment design, including colors, textures, audio, voices, 3D objects, lighting, and scales, also scored highly, with 60% rating it as "Excellent" and 40% as "Very Good". This reflects the immersive and visually appealing nature of the VR environment. The 2D interface design (main panel) and the sense of immersion were similarly praised, with a majority of the ratings being in the "Excellent" and "Very Good" categories. Notably, questions related to interaction (Questions 6 to 11) showed that evaluators found the objects and buttons intuitive and easy to use, with 60% to 100% of the responses indicating "Almost always" or "Always". These results suggest that the VR tool is user-friendly and effectively engages users through its design and interactive elements.

Table 4. Evaluation results of expert panel: usability characteristics.

Question	Excellent [%]	Very Good [%]	Satisfactory [%]	Regular [%]	Deficient [%]
1	60	40	0	0	0
2	60	40	0	0	0
3	60	40	0	0	0
4	40	60	0	0	0
5	80	20	0	0	0
	Never [%]	**Almost Never [%]**	**Sometimes [%]**	**Almost Always [%]**	**Always [%]**
6	0	0	0	60	40
7	0	0	0	40	60
8	0	0	0	40	60
9	40	60	0	0	0
10	0	0	20	20	60
11	0	0	20	40	40

Pedagogical integration (expert panel): The survey results for pedagogical integration (Table 5) highlight the strong alignment of the VR system with educational content and its effectiveness in meeting learning needs. All evaluators (100%) agreed that the electrical concepts presented were appropriate for teaching basic DC electrical circuits and that the images and videos related to the concepts were clear. The degree of interaction with the 3D objects within the game was rated highly, with 60% of the responses indicating "5" (the highest rating) and 40% indicating "4". This suggests that the VR tool effectively engages students in interactive learning. Additionally, the circuit-building module was deemed to meet real electrical circuit practice needs to a great extent or completely by 60% of the evaluators. The implementation of the game as an innovative educational tool was also rated highly, with 60% of the evaluators believing it contributes to learning the fundamentals of DC electrical circuits completely. These findings affirm the effectiveness of the VR tool in enhancing pedagogical integration and providing an engaging and interactive learning experience, and the electrical concepts presented, in images, videos, 3D objects and symbols, were clear, relevant, and consistent for contextualization in the teaching of basic direct current electrical circuits.

Table 5. Evaluation results of expert panel: pedagogical integration characteristics.

Question	All [%]		Some [%]	None [%]	
12	100		0	0	
13	100		0	0	
Question	**Excellent [%]**	**Very Good [%]**	**Satisfactory [%]**	**Regular [%]**	**Deficient [%]**
14	60	40	0	0	0
Question	**5**	**4**	**3**	**2**	**1**
15	60	40	0	0	0
Question	**Completely [%]**		**Very Good [%]**	**Satisfactory [%]**	**Regular [%]**
16	20		40	40	0
17	60		20	20	0

Safety (expert panel): The safety results from the survey of the evaluators (Table 6) show a strong consensus on the safety of the VR tool and a lack of adverse effects. No evaluators reported detecting any errors during gameplay (100% "no"). Additionally, a majority of the evaluators (80%) indicated that they "never" experienced physical effects such as dizziness, nausea, or headaches while manipulating objects in the game, with the remaining 20% reporting "almost never" experiencing such effects. No evaluators reported that the guide induced them to make mistakes during immersion, nor did they encounter any obstacles or conflicts that hindered the completion of activities (100% "no"). Regarding the virtual reality learning environment, no errors in coding or effects related to vertigo or visual fatigue in the user were detected. These results suggest that the VR tool is not only safe but also well-designed to prevent common issues associated with VR usage, such as physical discomfort and navigation errors.

Table 6. Evaluation results of expert panel: safety characteristics.

Question	Yes			No	
18	0			100	
20	0			100	
21	0			100	
Question	**Always [%]**	**Almost Always [%]**	**Sometimes [%]**	**Almost Never [%]**	**Never**
19	0	0	0	20	80

The evaluation of the VR application involved a comprehensive assessment of its usability, pedagogical integration, and safety, utilizing a survey instrument detailed in Supplementary Materials File S1. This study initially included ten students from the "Fundamentals of Electrical Circuits" course and was later expanded to include an additional 17 students, resulting in a total of 27 student participants.

Usability and interaction (students): The usability results (Table 7) indicate a high level of satisfaction among the students regarding the VR system. For the preliminary instructions, 94% of the students rated them as either excellent or very good, suggesting that the guidance provided was clear and effective. Similarly, in-game instructions were highly rated, with 71% of the students giving them excellent or very good ratings, indicating that the controls and object handling were well-explained. Satisfaction with the 3D environment design was also high, with 89% of the students rating it as excellent or very good, reflecting the immersive and visually appealing nature of the game. The 2D interface design was positively received by 94% of the students, suggesting that the main panel's design elements were user-friendly. Lastly, the sense of immersion was rated highly by 94% of the students, highlighting the effectiveness of the VR environment in engaging students. The interaction section showed that while most students found the interaction with objects and buttons intuitive, a small percentage faced occasional challenges, potentially due to varying levels of familiarity with VR technology. The terminology and symbols used were clear to the majority, but a few students might benefit from additional context or explanation. Navigation through the main screen was smooth for most, though some adjustments could enhance the experience further. Although most students did not encounter difficulties during gameplay, ensuring consistent ease of use for all users remains important. The time allocated for each module and the feedback provided were generally sufficient, but minor tweaks could improve the overall learning experience.

Table 7. Evaluation results of student participants: usability and interaction characteristics.

Question	Excellent [%]	Very Good [%]	Satisfactory [%]	Regular [%]	Deficient [%]
1	65	29	0	6	0
2	53	18	0	0	0
3	71	18	12	0	0
4	59	35	6	0	0
5	53	41	6	0	0
	Never [%]	**Almost Never [%]**	**Sometimes [%]**	**Almost Always [%]**	**Always [%]**
6	59	29	6	6	0
7	82	12	6	0	0
8	59	29	12	0	0
9	6	6	18	41	29
10	12	53	18	18	0
11	41	18	24	12	6

Pedagogical integration (students): The results for pedagogical integration (Table 8) indicate a strong alignment between the VR system's educational content and the students' learning needs. A significant majority (94%) of the students found the electrical concepts appropriate for teaching basic DC electrical circuits, suggesting that the content was well-chosen and relevant. The clarity of images and videos was affirmed by 82% of the students, indicating that visual aids were effective in enhancing understanding. The 3D objects used to conceptualize elements and symbols were highly rated by 71% of the students as excellent or very good, reflecting the success of the visual representation in aiding comprehension. The degree of interaction with the 3D objects was rated highly, with 82% of the students giving the highest scores, suggesting that the interactive elements were engaging and functional. Most students felt that the circuit-building module met the needs of real electrical circuit practice, with 82% affirming this to a great extent or completely, highlighting the practical applicability of the VR tool. Additionally, 100% of the students believed the game contributed significantly to learning the fundamentals of DC electrical circuits, emphasizing the educational value of the VR environment. These results suggest that the VR tool effectively bridges theoretical knowledge and practical application, possibly due to its immersive and interactive nature, which enhances engagement and retention.

Safety (students): The safety results (Table 9) suggest that the VR system is generally safe and stable, with a few areas requiring attention. A slight majority (53%) of the students did not detect any errors during gameplay, indicating overall stability, though nearly half of them did report some issues, suggesting occasional glitches that need addressing. Most students (53%) never experienced physical effects such as dizziness or nausea, but 47% reported almost never or sometimes experiencing such effects, indicating that while the VR environment is mostly comfortable, some students may have sensitivity to VR experiences. Importantly, all students reported that the guide did not induce any mistakes during immersion, reflecting clear and effective instructions. Additionally, 82% of the students did not encounter any obstacles or conflicts that hindered the completion of activities, demonstrating a well-designed and smoothly functioning VR environment. These findings suggest that while the VR system is largely safe and user-friendly, ongoing monitoring and refinement are essential to ensure a consistently positive experience for all users. The occasional physical effects reported may be due to individual differences in susceptibility to VR-induced discomfort, highlighting the importance of offering guidelines for optimal use and ensuring that VR sessions are appropriately timed to minimize any adverse effects.

Table 8. Evaluation results of student participants: pedagogical integration.

Question	All [%]	Some [%]	None [%]
12	94	6	0
13	82	18	0

Question	Excellent [%]	Very Good [%]	Satisfactory [%]	Regular [%]	Deficient [%]
14	53	18	29	0	0

Question	5	4	3	2	1
15	41	41	18	0	0

Question	Completely [%]	Very Good [%]	Satisfactory [%]	Regular [%]
16	29	18	29	0
17	76	41	18	0

Table 9. Evaluation results of student participants: safety.

Question	Yes	No
18	47	53
20	0	100
21	82	18

Question	Always [%]	Almost Always [%]	Sometimes [%]	Almost never [%]	Never
19	0	12	6	29	53

4. Discussion

The development of this research underscores the transformative role of virtual reality (VR) in educational settings, emerging as a robust tool in the teaching and learning processes. Consistent with the observations by Escartín [46], VR is recognized not merely as a technological advancement but as a fundamental shift in the educational paradigm, supporting a more interactive and engaging learning process. Programs in developed countries have already begun integrating VR across various educational levels, reflecting a global trend towards immersive learning environments.

This study extends the current understanding of VR by demonstrating that a VR-based learning environment significantly enhances immersion and interaction with three-dimensional objects. This enhancement, as described by Miguélez-Juan et al. [47], promotes a realistic simulation of complex virtual worlds where users engage in real-time through tailored electronic devices, thereby boosting motivation and providing a lifelike experience during theoretical–practical activities. Furthermore, this approach mitigates traditional risks associated with electrical circuit training, such as electrical hazards and equipment damage, by providing a safe simulated environment for experimentation and learning.

The feedback from this study's VR laboratory experience aligns with findings by Botella et al. [48] and Paszkiewicz et al. [49], which reported a high approval rating for VR's application in primary education due to its capacity to safely replicate inaccessible or hazardous real-world environments. This correlation not only validates VR's utility in diverse educational settings but also highlights its potential in specialized fields such as electrical engineering education. Feedback from this study's VR laboratory experience aligns with findings by Singh [50] and Tanaka et al. [51], which reported a high approval rating for VR's application in electrical substation training due to its capacity to safely replicate inaccessible or hazardous real-world environments. This correlation not only validates VR's utility in diverse educational settings but also highlights its potential in specialized fields such as electrical engineering education.

Despite these advancements, challenges remain, particularly concerning the infrastructure required for implementing VR. The need for high-performance computers to process and display intricate simulations remains a significant barrier [46,51]. This infrastructure challenge is crucial for future research directions, as addressing these barriers could expand VR's accessibility and applicability.

Moreover, while this study focused on the benefits of VR in enhancing the understanding of direct current electrical circuits, its application in the social sciences and other fields suggests a broader potential. Future studies could explore interdisciplinary applications of VR, examining its impact on various educational outcomes and its integration into different curricular areas. Therefore, the findings from this research not only reinforce the efficacy of VR in enhancing educational experiences but also advocate for its broader adoption in curriculum design. As digital literacy becomes increasingly vital in higher education, VR's role in this domain is likely to expand, necessitating ongoing research into its integration, scalability, and long-term educational impacts.

Looking ahead, further research should focus on overcoming technological and infrastructural barriers to make VR more accessible across educational sectors. Additionally, studies could explore the long-term impacts of VR on learning retention and student engagement across diverse demographic groups. Another promising area for future investigation is the development of customizable VR content that educators can tailor to specific learning objectives and student needs, potentially transforming VR into a standard teaching tool across educational levels.

The constant advent of emerging technologies is creating disparities in access and usage within educational settings, exacerbating issues of digital illiteracy and constraining the pedagogical potential these advancements might offer. Often, traditional classroom strategies prioritize the transmission of theories and concepts in ways that isolate students from engaging and participatory learning processes. Such methods, which emphasize rote memory, repetition, and obedience, often position the teacher as the sole arbiter of educational success, thereby diminishing student motivation and hindering the development of knowledge, skills, and values. Conversely, the integration of emerging technologies, underpinned by educational theories such as constructivism and linked with innovative pedagogical methods, offers alternative teaching and learning modalities. Technologies like virtual reality introduce dynamic and disruptive learning environments that can significantly enhance student motivation, acknowledging and building upon students' prior knowledge and fostering the development of skills through problem-solving in real-world contexts [52]. Soler [53] highlights that while virtual reality holds substantial educational promise, it requires further research to optimize its content and extend its application broadly.

The survey results underscore the high usability, effective pedagogical integration, and robust safety of the VR system. A significant majority of the students rated the preliminary and in-game instructions, as well as the 3D environment and 2D interface design, as excellent or very good, indicating clear guidance and a user-friendly design. The sense of immersion was highly rated, with only minor interaction challenges noted. The pedagogical integration was strong, with most students finding the electrical concepts appropriate and the interactive 3D objects effective in enhancing understanding. The circuit-building module was well-received, meeting practical needs and contributing significantly to learning the fundamentals of DC electrical circuits. Security-wise, the system was stable and comfortable for most users, though a few reported minor physical effects. These findings validate the VR tool's effectiveness in enhancing educational experiences and highlight areas for continuous improvement, aligning with this study's objectives of exploring VR's potential in transforming teaching and learning dynamics in electrical engineering education.

The comparison of survey results between the expert panel and the students revealed several key insights into the usability, pedagogical integration, and security of the VR tool. Both groups rated the preliminary and in-game instructions highly, with the expert panel giving 60% "Excellent" ratings and students rating them at 94% for preliminary instructions and 71% for in-game instructions as excellent or very good. This suggests effective guidance for users, though the students showed slightly higher satisfaction. Satisfaction with the 3D environment and 2D interface design was also high for both groups, indicating that the VR tool's visual and interactive elements were well-received. The experts and students alike found the interaction intuitive, with a majority indicating "Almost always" or "Always", though a few students faced occasional challenges, possibly due to varying levels of familiarity with VR technology. In terms of pedagogical integration, both groups recognized the VR tool's effectiveness in presenting electrical concepts, with 100% of the experts and 94% of the students affirming its appropriateness. The experts rated the degree of interaction with 3D objects highly, and 71% of the students rated it as excellent or very good, reflecting successful engagement. Most notably, 60% of the experts and 82% of the students believed the circuit-building module met real practice needs to a great extent or completely. Regarding security, both groups reported minimal issues, with the experts indicating no errors or physical effects and most students reporting similar comfort levels, though a few noted occasional dizziness or nausea. These findings suggest that the VR tool is well-designed, user-friendly, and effective in enhancing learning, though ongoing refinement and attention to individual user experiences could further optimize its impact. The slight differences in ratings between the two groups may be attributed to the experts' familiarity with VR technology and educational tools, compared to students' varying levels of prior exposure and experience.

Consequently, this study explores the potential of VR to transform educational environments, focusing on how immersive technologies can enhance teaching and learning dynamics. By simulating realistic environments, VR significantly improves upon traditional educational methods. It provides students with immersive and interactive experiences that are crucial for understanding and retaining complex concepts, such as electrical circuits. This research contributes to the evolving understanding of how VR can be effectively integrated into educational methodologies to facilitate deeper learning.

Theoretically, this research aligns with constructivist learning theories which emphasize active learning through experience and interaction, rather than a passive absorption of information. VR allows students to 'learn by doing' in a risk-free environment, which is particularly beneficial in technical disciplines where practical experience is crucial but often constrained by access to resources or safety concerns.

Practically, the findings from this study demonstrate VR's potential to increase engagement and motivation among students, which are critical factors in educational success. By incorporating VR into the curriculum, educators can offer students a more engaging learning experience that not only improves comprehension but also encourages continuous learning and curiosity.

Based on the results of this study, the following are recommended for the application of VR in educational settings: 1. the integration of VR into existing curricula to provide students with hands-on experience in a virtual environment, thereby enhancing their understanding of theoretical concepts; 2. the development of customizable VR content that educators can tailor to specific educational needs and learning outcomes, making VR a versatile tool across various subjects; and 3. a continuous evaluation and adaptation of VR applications in education to ensure they meet the evolving technological standards and educational requirements. These recommendations aim to assist educators and policymakers in leveraging VR technology to transform educational environments and meet the diverse needs of students. By doing so, VR can play a pivotal role in bridging the gap between traditional education methods and the digital future, making learning more accessible, engaging, and effective for everyone.

5. Conclusions

Virtual reality (VR) has emerged as a significant advancement in educational technology by enhancing simulation, immersion, and interaction with three-dimensional objects. These elements are essential for achieving educational objectives, particularly in technical disciplines such as electrical engineering. This study demonstrates VR's transformative impact, facilitating hands-on, interactive learning experiences that significantly enhance comprehension and engagement, especially in the study of electrical circuits.

During the testing of the VR game "The Virtual Lab", no programming errors were identified that compromised user safety, nor were instances of vertigo or visual fatigue reported. This confirms the game's safety and comfort for educational use. It is recommended that the use of this virtual environment be moderated, with sessions ideally kept under thirty minutes, particularly for inexperienced users or those with visual and cognitive disabilities.

The immersive VR game surpasses traditional educational methods such as video games and educational software, particularly in boosting motivation, concentration, and the incorporation of gamification elements. In the context of electrical circuits, VR supports the acquisition of complex scientific knowledge more effectively and significantly enhances learner motivation and attention.

The integration of VR into classrooms has proven to promote equity by providing students from diverse backgrounds access to innovative learning tools. This inclusivity is crucial for creating an equitable educational environment where all students can benefit from advanced technological tools and engage more effectively with challenging subjects like electrical circuits.

A major challenge in expanding VR in education is the need for adequate infrastructure, such as high-performance computers and specialized software, necessary to support the sophisticated simulations required for teaching complex topics like electrical circuits. This infrastructure challenge underscores the importance of technological readiness in realizing the full benefits of VR in education.

Future research should focus on overcoming these technological barriers to make VR more accessible and feasible for widespread educational use. Further studies should explore the long-term impacts of VR on learning outcomes, including retention rates and the development of practical skills in electrical engineering, to provide deeper insights into VR's comprehensive benefits and challenges within the educational sector.

The practical implications of this study are extensive, particularly in the field of electrical engineering, where VR enables a hands-on learning experience that traditional methods cannot replicate. By integrating VR technologies into the curriculum, educators can enhance educational effectiveness and better align learning experiences with educational objectives. A continuous evaluation and adaptation of VR applications are recommended to ensure their ongoing relevance and efficacy, making learning more accessible, engaging, and effective for students of all backgrounds.

Supplementary Materials: The following supporting information can be downloaded at: https://www.mdpi.com/article/10.3390/fi16080279/s1, Supplementary Materials File S1: Survey Instrument for Evaluating Usability, Pedagogical Integration, and Safety of the VR Application; Figure S1: GUI coding structure; Figure S2: GUI coding structure continued.

Author Contributions: Conceptualization, D.A.A.-A., F.A.R.-T., and C.E.S.-B.; methodology, D.A.A.-A., F.A.R.-T., and C.E.S.-B.; validation, D.A.A.-A., F.A.R.-T., C.E.S.-B., and E.A.A.-E.; formal analysis, D.A.A.-A., F.A.R.-T., C.E.S.-B., and E.A.A.-E.; investigation, D.A.A.-A., F.A.R.-T., and C.E.S.-B.; resources, D.A.A.-A., F.A.R.-T., and C.E.S.-B.; data curation, D.A.A.-A., F.A.R.-T., C.E.S.-B., and E.A.A.-E.; writing—original draft preparation, D.A.A.-A. and F.A.R.-T.; writing—review and editing, D.A.A.-A., F.A.R.-T., C.E.S.-B., and E.A.A.-E.; visualization, D.A.A.-A., F.A.R.-T., C.E.S.-B., and E.A.A.-E.; supervision, F.A.R.-T. and C.E.S.-B.; project administration, F.A.R.-T. and C.E.S.-B.; funding acquisition, F.A.R.-T. and C.E.S.-B. All authors have read and agreed to the published version of the manuscript.

Funding: This research was part of the SGI—3080 project, conducted from June 2019 to June 2020, funded by the Pedagogical and Technological University of Colombia through the Call for Management, Strengthening, and Research Productivity. La Universidad del Magdalena provided financial support to pay for the publication.

Data Availability Statement: The original contributions presented in the study are included in the article/supplementary material, further inquiries can be directed to the corresponding author.

Acknowledgments: The authors are grateful to the GRIDSE and RESET research groups of the Duitama Sectional Faculty at the Pedagogical and Technological University of Colombia for providing the necessary scenarios and support for this project. Additional thanks go to the Research Directorate—DIN—for funding initiatives that explore emerging technological trends in education. To the Universidad del Magdalena for financial support for publication.

Conflicts of Interest: The authors declare no conflicts of interest.

References

1. Al-Ansi, A.M.; Jaboob, M.; Garad, A.; Al-Ansi, A. Analyzing augmented reality (AR) and virtual reality (VR) recent development in education. *Soc. Sci. Humanit. Open* **2023**, *8*, 100532. [CrossRef]
2. Schott, C.; Milligan, A.; Marshall, S. Immersive VR for K-12 experiential education—Proposing a pedagogies, practicalities, and perspectives informed framework. *Comput. Educ.* **2024**, *4*, 100068. [CrossRef]
3. Wen, J.; Gheisari, M. VR-Electricians: Immersive storytelling for attracting students to the electrical construction industry. *Adv. Eng. Inform.* **2021**, *50*, 101411. [CrossRef]
4. Moral-Sánchez, S.N.; Sánchez-Compaña, M.T.; Romero-Albaladejo, I. Uso de realidad virtual en Geometría para el desarrollo de habilidades espaciales. *Enseñanza Ciencias. Rev. Investig. Exp. Didácticas* **2023**, *41*, 125–147. [CrossRef]
5. Anacona Ortiz, J.D.; Millán Rojas, E.E.; Gómez Cano, C.A. Aplicación de los metaversos y la realidad virtual en la enseñanza. *Entre Cienc. Ing.* **2019**, *13*, 59–67. [CrossRef]
6. García-Delgado, M.Á.; Rodríguez-Cano, S.; Delgado-Benito, V.; Lozano-Álvarez, M. Emerging Technologies and Their Link to Digital Competence in Teaching. *Future Internet* **2023**, *15*, 140. [CrossRef]
7. AlGerafi, M.A.M.; Zhou, Y.; Oubibi, M.; Wijaya, T.T. Unlocking the Potential: A Comprehensive Evaluation of Augmented Reality and Virtual Reality in Education. *Electronics* **2023**, *12*, 3953. [CrossRef]
8. Sabatucci, L.; Augello, A.; Caggianese, G.; Gallo, L. Envisioning Digital Practices in the Metaverse: A Methodological Perspective. *Future Internet* **2023**, *15*, 394. [CrossRef]
9. Antón-Sancho, Á.; Fernández-Arias, P.; Vergara, D. Perception of the Use of Virtual Reality Didactic Tools among Faculty in Mexico. *Future Internet* **2023**, *15*, 72. [CrossRef]
10. Cyrino, G.F.; Barreto, C.L.; Mattioli, L.R.; Cardoso, A.; Lamounier, E.A.; Lima GF, M.; Ramos, D.S. An Intuitive VR-based Environment for Monitoring and Control of Electrical Power Substations. *Procedia Comput. Sci.* **2022**, *201*, 551–558. [CrossRef]
11. Allcoat, D.; von Mühlenen, A. Learning in virtual reality: Effects on performance, emotion and engagement. *Res. Learn. Technol.* **2018**, *26*, 2140. [CrossRef]
12. Bailenson, J. *Experience on Demand: What Virtual Reality Is, How It Works, and What It Can Do*; W.W. Norton & Company: New York, NY, USA, 2018.
13. Sural, I. Augmented reality experience: Initial perceptions of higher education students. *Int. J. Instr.* **2018**, *11*, 565–576. [CrossRef]
14. Freina, L.; Ott, M. A literature review on immersive virtual reality in education: State of the art and perspectives. *Int. Sci. Conf. Elearning Softw. Educ.* **2015**, *1*, 133–141. [CrossRef]
15. Huang, H.M.; Rauch, U.; Liaw, S.S. Investigating learners' attitudes toward virtual reality learning environments: Based on a constructivist approach. *Comput. Educ.* **2010**, *55*, 1171–1182. [CrossRef]

16. Jensen, L.; Konradsen, F. A review of the use of virtual reality head-mounted displays in education and training. *Educ. Inf. Technol.* **2018**, *23*, 1515–1529. [CrossRef]
17. Lee, E.A.L.; Wong, K.W.; Fung, C.C. How does desktop virtual reality enhance learning outcomes? A structural equation modeling approach. *Comput. Educ.* **2010**, *55*, 1424–1442. [CrossRef]
18. Segura Ruiz, M.Y.; Osorio Diaz, R. Usability in Accessible and Inclusive Immersive Virtual Reality applications Multi-scenario: Practical case. *Res. Innov. Eng.* **2021**, *9*, 82–92. [CrossRef]
19. Makransky, G.; Terkildsen, T.S.; Mayer, R.E. Adding immersive virtual reality to a science lab simulation causes more presence but less learning. *Learn. Instr.* **2019**, *60*, 225–236. [CrossRef]
20. Merchant, Z.; Goetz, E.T.; Cifuentes, L.; Keeney-Kennicutt, W.; Davis, T.J. Effectiveness of virtual reality-based instruction on students' learning outcomes in K-12 and higher education: A meta-analysis. *Comput. Educ.* **2014**, *70*, 29–40. [CrossRef]
21. Vergara, D.; Rubio, M.P.; Lorenzo, M. Interactive Virtual Platform for Simulating a Concrete Compression Test. *Key Eng. Mater.* **2013**, *572*, 582–585. [CrossRef]
22. Vergara-Rodriguez, D.; Rodriguez-Martin, M.; Rubio-Cavero, M.; Ferrer-Marin, J.; Nuñez-Garcia, F.; Moralejo-Cobo, L. Technical Staff Training in Ultrasonic Non-Destructive Testing Using Virtual Reality. *Dyna* **2018**, *93*, 150–154. [CrossRef]
23. Mikropoulos, T.A.; Natsis, A. Educational virtual environments: A ten-year review of empirical research (1999–2009). *Comput. Educ.* **2011**, *56*, 769–780. [CrossRef]
24. Parong, J.; Mayer, R.E. Learning science in immersive virtual reality. *J. Educ. Psychol.* **2018**, *110*, 785–797. [CrossRef]
25. Radianti, J.; Majchrzak, T.A.; Fromm, J.; Wohlgenannt, I. A systematic review of immersive virtual reality applications for higher education: Design elements, lessons learned, and research agenda. *Comput. Educ.* **2020**, *147*, 103778. [CrossRef]
26. Slater, M.; Antley, A.; Davison, A.; Swapp, D.; Guger, C.; Barker, C.; Pistrang, N.; Sanchez-Vives, M.V. A virtual reprise of the Stanley Milgram obedience experiments. *PLoS ONE* **2009**, *4*, e1005. [CrossRef]
27. Creswell, J.W. *Educational Research: Planning, Conducting, and Evaluating Quantitative and Qualitative Research*, 4th ed.; Pearson: Boston, MA, USA, 2012.
28. Brydon-Miller, M.; Coghlan, D. *The SAGE Encyclopedia of Action Research*; SAGE Publications Ltd.: Thousand Oaks, CA, USA, 2014; 904p.
29. Lake, D.; Wendland, J. Practical, epistemological, and ethical challenges of participatory action research: A cross-disciplinary review of the literature. *J. High. Educ. Outreach Engagem.* **2018**, *22*, 11–42.
30. Doria, R.; Castro, M. La investigación-acción en la transformación de las prácticas de enseñanza de los maestros de lenguaje [Action research in the transformation of teaching practices of language teachers]. *Lenguaje* **2012**, *40*, 447–468. [CrossRef]
31. Herr, K.; Anderson, G. *The Action Research Dissertation—A Guide for Students and Faculty*, 2nd ed.; SAGE: Thousand Oaks, CA, USA, 2015; ISBN 978-1-4833-3310-6.
32. Latorre, A. *La Investigación-Acción, Conocer y Cambiar la Práctica Educativa [Action Research, Knowing and Changing Educational Practice]*; Editorial Graó: Barcelona, CA, USA, 2005; ISBN 9788478272921.
33. Rosenbaum, E.; Klopfer, E.; Perry, J. On Location Learning: Authentic Applied Science with Networked Augmented Realities. *J. Sci. Educ. Technol.* **2007**, *16*, 31–45. [CrossRef]
34. Muñoz, P.C.; González, M. *The Design of Multimedia Learning Materials and the New Teacher Competencies in Teletraining Contexts [El Diseño de Materiales de Aprendizaje Multimedia y las Nuevas Competencias del Docente en Contextos Teleformativos]*; Bubok Publishing: Madrid, Spain, 2009.
35. Joshi, A.; Kale, S.; Chandel, S.; Pal, D. Likert Scale: Explored and Explained. *Br. J. Appl. Sci. Technol.* **2015**, *7*, 396–403. [CrossRef]
36. Cobb, S.V.G.; Nichols, S.; Ramsey, A.; Wilson, J.R. Virtual Reality-Induced Symptoms and Effects. *Presence Teleoperators Virtual Environ.* **1999**, *8*, 169–186. [CrossRef]
37. Romero-Yesa, S.; Fonseca, D.; Aláez, M.; Amo-Filva, D. Qualitative assessment of a challenge-based learning and teamwork applied in electronics program. *Heliyon* **2023**, *9*, E22739. [CrossRef]
38. Kaya, O.S.; Ercag, E. The impact of applying challenge-based gamification program on students' learning outcomes: Academic achievement, motivation and flow. *Educ. Inf. Technol.* **2023**, *28*, 10053–10078. [CrossRef] [PubMed]
39. Checa, D.; Bustillo, A. A review of immersive virtual reality serious games to enhance learning and training. *Multimed. Tools Appl.* **2020**, *79*, 5501–5527. [CrossRef]
40. Pellas, N.; Mystakidis, S.; Kazanidis, I. Immersive Virtual Reality in K-12 and Higher Education: A systematic review of the last decade scientific literature. *Virtual Real.* **2021**, *25*, 835–861. [CrossRef]
41. Proopsaltis, A.; Pannese, L.; Pappa, D.; Hetzner, S. Serious Games and Formal and Informal Learning. *E-Learn. Pap.* **2011**, *25*, 1542.
42. Anastasiadis, T.; Lampropoulos, G.; Siakas, K. Digital Game-based Learning and Serious Games in Education. *Int. J. Adv. Sci. Res. Eng.* **2018**, *4*, 139–144. [CrossRef]
43. Tan, Q.P.; Huang, L.; Xu, D.; Cen, Y.; Cao, Q. Serious Game for VR Road Crossing in Special Needs Education. *Electronics* **2022**, *11*, 2568. [CrossRef]
44. UnityManual. Unity-Manual: Input for Oculus. 2020. Available online: https://docs.unity3d.com/560/Documentation/Manual/index.html (accessed on 21 February 2021).

45. Olsen, T.; Procci, K.; Bowers, C. Serious Games Usability Testing: How to Ensure Proper Usability, Playability, and Effectiveness. In *Design, User Experience, and Usability. Theory, Methods, Tools and Practice*; Marcus, A., Ed.; DUXU 2011. Lecture Notes in Computer Science; Springer: Berlin/Heidelberg, Germany, 2011; Volume 6770. [CrossRef]
46. Escartín, E.R. Virtual reality, an educational technology within our reach [La realidad virtual, una tecnología educativa a nuestro alcance]. Pixel-Bit. *Rev. Medios Educ.* **2000**, *15*, 5–21.
47. Miguélez-Juan, B.; Nuñez Gómez, P.N.; Mañas-Viniegra, L. Immersive Virtual Reality as an educational tool for social transformation: An exploratory study on the perception of students in Post-Compulsory Secondary Education [La Realidad Virtual Inmersiva como herramienta educativa para la transformación social: Un estudio exploratorio sobre la percepción de los estudiantes en Educación Secundaria Postobligatoria]. *Aula Abierta* **2019**, *48*, 157–165. [CrossRef]
48. Botella, A.M.; Hurtado-Soler, A.; Ramos, S. Educational Innovation through Virtual Reality and Soundscape [Innovación Educativa a Través de la Realidad Virtual y el Paisaje Sonoro]. In *Creativity and Educational Innovation Review*; Universitat de Valencia: Valencia, Spain, 2018. [CrossRef]
49. Paszkiewicz, A.; Salach, M.; Strzałka, D.; Budzik, G.; Nikodem, A.; Wójcik, H.; Witek, M. VR Education Support System—A Case Study of Digital Circuits Design. *Energies* **2022**, *15*, 277. [CrossRef]
50. Singh, G.; Mantri, A.; Sharma, O.; Kaur, R. Virtual reality learning environment for enhancing electronics engineering laboratory experience. *Comput. Appl. Eng. Educ.* **2021**, *29*, 229–243. [CrossRef]
51. Tanaka, E.H.; Paludo, J.A.; Cordeiro, C.S.; Domingues, L.R.; Gadbem, E.V.; Euflausino, A. Using immersive virtual reality for electrical substation training. In Proceedings of the International Association for Development of the Information Society (IADIS) International Conference on E-Learning, Las Palmas de Gran Canaria, Spain, 21–24 July 2015; pp. 136–140. [CrossRef]
52. Losada, N.; Jorge, F.; Teixeira, M.S.; Sousa, N.; Melo, M.; Bessa, M. Place Attachment Through Virtual Reality: A Comparative Study in Douro Region (Northern Portugal) with Video and 'Real' Visit. In *Marketing and Smart Technologies: Proceedings of ICMarkTech 2021*; Springer: Singapore, 2021; Volume 279, pp. 585–594.
53. Soler-Domínguez, J.L. Influencia del diseño de interacción sobre la experiencia de usuario en entornos de aprendizaje en realidad virtual: Un estudio centrado en las metáforas de navegación. Doctoral Dissertation, Universitat Politécnica de Valencia, Valencia, Spain, 2020. [CrossRef]

future internet

Article

Assessing User Perceptions and Preferences on Applying Obfuscation Techniques for Privacy Protection in Augmented Reality

Ana Cassia Cruz , Rogério Luís de C. Costa *, Leonel Santos , Carlos Rabadão , Anabela Marto and Alexandrino Gonçalves

Computer Science and Communication Research Center (CIIC), Escola Superior de Tecnologia e Gestão (ESTG), Polytechnic University of Leiria, 2411-901 Leiria, Portugal; ana.v.cruz@ipleiria.pt (A.C.); leonel.santos@ipleiria.pt (L.S.); carlos.rabadao@ipleiria.pt (C.R.); anabela.marto@ipleiria.pt (A.M.); alex@ipleiria.pt (A.G.)

* Correspondence: rogerio.l.costa@ipleiria.pt

Abstract: As augmented reality (AR) technologies become increasingly integrated into everyday life, privacy-maintenance concerns about their capacity to capture and process sensitive visual data also increase. Visual data sanitization and obfuscation may effectively increase the privacy protection level. This study examines user perceptions of privacy protection strategies within AR environments. We developed and disseminated a questionnaire to assess users' preferences, experiences, and concerns related to visual obfuscation techniques, namely masking, pixelation, and blurring. We collected and analyzed the responses using both qualitative and quantitative methodologies. The results indicate that user perceptions varied based on the AR context and individual preferences. Participants identified blurring as a versatile option that provides the best aesthetic appeal. Users recognized masking as the most secure method but less visually appealing. This study also revealed that demographic factors, such as age, education, and occupation, influenced privacy concerns and the acceptance of obfuscation methods. These findings enhance the understanding of user preferences and the effectiveness of obfuscation techniques in AR. These insights can guide the development of privacy-preserving AR applications tailored to accommodate diverse user needs.

Keywords: augmented reality; blurring; masking; obfuscation techniques; pixelation; privacy; security

1. Introduction

In the modern era of pervasive digital technology within an increasingly interconnected society, safeguarding privacy and security has emerged as a critical concern. The extensive volume of visual data generated and disseminated daily—via security cameras, social media platforms, and mobile devices—poses substantial privacy risks [1]. Visual media, such as images and videos, frequently encapsulate sensitive information, including personal details, geolocations, and identities, underscoring the necessity for robust privacy protection mechanisms [2].

The evolution of privacy threats has paralleled technological advancement, creating a complex landscape where traditional privacy protection methods often prove insufficient [3]. As technologies become more immersive and pervasive, the lines separating private and public spheres are becoming increasingly blurred due to rising immersion and pervasiveness. This shift highlights the pressing need for novel approaches or advancements in privacy protection [4].

A notable immersive technology in recent years is augmented reality (AR), which superimposes digital data onto the real environment [5]. Through the integration of virtual content with the physical world, AR offers an interactive experience [6]. Its uses are found in several domains, such as industry, gaming, healthcare, and education [7–10].

However, integrating AR into our daily lives also introduces a new wave of privacy and security concerns [11]. As AR devices continuously scan our surroundings, they inadvertently collect sensitive information, raising concerns about bystander privacy [12]. Furthermore, real-time data processing and storage, coupled with location tracking and behavioral pattern recognition, pose significant risks to the exposure of personal information [13]. The advent of shared AR spaces further complicates the privacy landscape as individuals with diverse privacy preferences engage in a common digital environment [14].

To address these privacy challenges, some techniques can be used to anonymize or obscure visual data captured by AR devices to ensure that the identities and sensitive information of individuals are protected [15]. Common methods include blurring, blocking, and pixelating sensitive information while preserving the overall visual context. However, the effectiveness and suitability of these techniques can vary depending on the specific application, context, and the required level of privacy [13]. Thus, we developed SafeAR (https://safear.ipleiria.pt/ accessed on 13 December 2024), a funded project to enhance privacy in AR environments. SafeAR focuses on developing services [16] and libraries [17] to apply privacy-preserving techniques to sensitive visual data captured by AR devices. Using machine learning to identify sensitive data and obfuscation methods such as blurring, blocking, and pixelation, SafeAR seeks to protect the identities of individuals and personal information without compromising the functionality of AR applications.

In this paper, we explore user preferences and perceptions of these privacy-enhancing techniques, examining which method is considered more secure or effective in different scenarios. We address the following research questions:

- **RQ1:** what is the relationship between demographics (age, education, and occupation) and the perceived security of different obfuscation methods?
- **RQ2:** how do different obfuscation techniques (masking, pixelation, and blurring) affect user experience in AR applications?
- **RQ3:** what is the relationship between the level of familiarity with AR and the acceptance of different obfuscation methods?

To answer these questions, we developed and disseminated a questionnaire to a diverse group of participants. The questionnaire was designed to capture information on user demographics, their familiarity with AR, and their perceptions of pixelation, masking, and blurring obfuscation techniques. The collected data were analyzed using statistical methods to validate the results.

The remainder of this paper is organized as follows. Section 2 provides essential background information on AR technology and existing privacy protection techniques and reviews relevant research in AR privacy protection and user studies. To systematically explore the research question, Section 3 details the research methodology and study design. Subsequently, Section 4 presents the findings of our study and we analyze the effects of these findings, offering insight into the considerations of AR privacy. Finally, Section 5 summarizes the conclusions and recommendations for future research directions and potential solutions to address the privacy challenges posed by AR technology.

2. Background and Related Work

The integration of digital information into the physical world has reached new levels of sophistication with advancements in AR technology. AR systems seamlessly incorporate computer-generated content, including images, sounds, and 3D models, into users' real-time view of their environment. This augmentation is typically experienced through smart glasses or mobile devices equipped with cameras and sensors that analyze the surroundings to accurately position and display digital content [18].

As AR applications become more prevalent, particularly on mobile platforms, they present new challenges related to the exposure of sensitive information in both personal and professional contexts. The technology's capacity to overlay digital content onto the real world, while innovative, raises significant privacy concerns that require careful consideration and management [19].

2.1. *Privacy Challenges in AR Environments*

Privacy challenges in AR environments are inherently multifaceted and complex. AR systems continuously scan and process their surroundings, often capturing sensitive information that may inadvertently appear in the background of a user's view. This continuous environmental scanning creates a persistent stream of data that must be carefully managed to protect user privacy [20]. The complexity increases in multi-user scenarios, where different users may have varying privacy requirements and familiarity levels with shared AR experiences [21]. Furthermore, the context-dependent nature of AR applications makes it particularly challenging to implement universal privacy protection measures that work effectively across all situations [22]. The potential for AR systems to store or process captured information also raises important questions about data retention and security [23].

2.2. *Visual Privacy Protection Techniques*

To address these privacy concerns, several visual privacy protection techniques have been developed and implemented in AR systems. These techniques offer different approaches to evalute privacy protection with user experience and functionality.

Each of these privacy protection techniques offer distinct advantages and limitations, making them suitable for different use cases and privacy requirements. The choice between these methods often depends on factors such as the sensitivity of the information being protected, the required level of privacy, and the desired user experience. The effectiveness of these techniques in AR environments is particularly important as the technology continues to evolve and become more integrated into our daily life.

To illustrate the impact of different obfuscation techniques, Figure 1 compares the effects of masking (Figure 1b), pixelation (Figure 1c), and blurring (Figure 1d) when applied to an AR system. These techniques are used to conceal sensitive information displayed on the screen, demonstrating various methods of privacy protection in AR environments.

Masking: Figure 1b illustrates how this technique involves completely covering sensitive information with solid shapes or patterns, effectively creating a visual barrier between the protected content and any observers. While masking provides possibly better privacy protection and is computationally efficient to implement, it can significantly impact the user experience by removing all visual context from the protected area [24,25].

Pixelization: In Figure 1c, the pixelization technique, also known as the mosaic effect, offers a different approach to privacy protection. This technique reduces image resolution in specific areas by averaging pixel values within defined blocks. The result maintains the visual structure of the protected content while making specific details unclear [26].

Blurring: Figure 1d illustrates how this technique applies a smoothing effect that preserves general shapes and colors while obscuring specific details that might be sensitive or private. Blurring can be implemented with varying intensity levels, offering adaptable privacy protection based on specific needs [27].

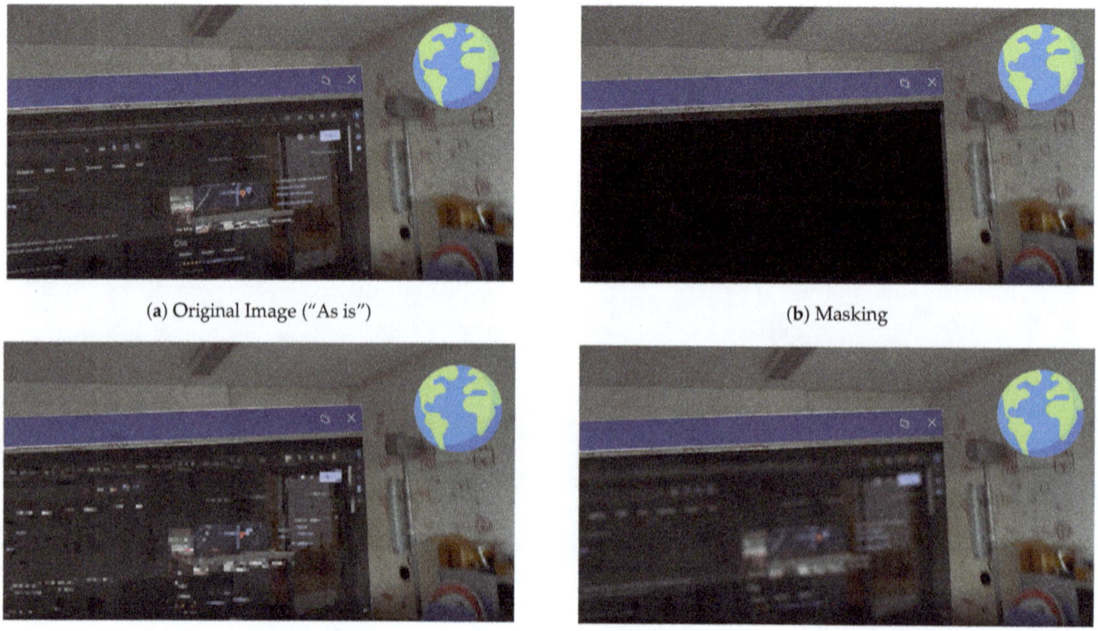

(a) Original Image ("As is") (b) Masking (c) Pixelation (d) Blurring

Figure 1. Visualizations of privacy protection techniques in AR. The "As is" image shows the original image, while masking, pixelation, and blurring can be used to obscure sensitive information on screens within AR environments.

2.3. Related Work

Important research addresses privacy and security challenges associated with the protection of personal information, alongside obfuscation techniques that are applied to visual data.

In Roesner et al. [28], the authors examine security and privacy challenges in AR systems, focusing on how sensitive information can inadvertently be displayed or recorded by AR devices. The study discusses how AR-specific contexts, such as shared visual data and continuous environmental scanning, create privacy risks. The authors propose mechanisms like access controls for data streams, the obfuscation of sensitive elements, and user-consent mechanisms that address privacy without interrupting the AR experience. The study is relevant as it focuses on developing privacy techniques that are uniquely adapted to the immersive and interactive characteristics of AR environments.

Li et al. [29] explore the effectiveness of blurring and pixelation obfuscation techniques in protecting the privacy of individuals depicted in images. The study examines how well these techniques prevent the recognition of sensitive content while balancing the need for interpretability in different contexts. The study indicates that while both blurring and pixelation can obscure facial features, their effectiveness varies depending on the context and the observer's familiarity with the target subjects.

In Oh et al. [30], the authors explore techniques for person recognition while omitting facial features, such as relying on body shape, clothing, and pose. The authors address how these methods can still allow for recognition in social media contexts, raising privacy concerns even when facial details are obscured. Their findings suggest that solely obscuring faces may be inadequate for ensuring comprehensive privacy protection.

Demiris et al. [31] assess the privacy concerns associated with vision-based monitoring systems, which capture video or images for safety monitoring. The study finds that while monitoring enhances safety, privacy concerns arise from the continuous capture of personal spaces. They propose obfuscation techniques that extend beyond face concealment, incorporating methods such as low-resolution imagery and the selective masking of sensitive areas.

While a few studies have explored the integration of obfuscation techniques within AR systems, to the best of our knowledge, none have conducted surveys with volunteers to empirically measure the effectiveness of these techniques in AR-specific contexts.

3. Methodology

This section provides an overview of the research methodology adopted in this study. It describes the systematic approach taken, detailing the planning, data collection, and analysis. By outlining each stage, the methodology illustrates how the research was structured to achieve the study's objectives in five distinct phases:

- **Phase 1—Preparation:** This initial step involved defining the core research objectives, reviewing related studies, and structuring the questionnaire. The goal was to outline the research questions and ensure that the questionnaire was thoughtfully designed to collect the necessary data.
- **Phase 2—Questionnaire:** In this phase, the questionnaire was created, using Google Forms [32] to design and distribute the digital survey. Each question was crafted to try to align it with the research objectives.
- **Phase 3—Dissemination:** This phase involved disseminating the survey link through social media messages and in-person requests for participation. The survey was also shared in class with students to further extend its reach.
- **Phase 4—Data Analysis:** Once the survey responses were collected, we began the data analysis. Using statistical methods, we examined the data to identify patterns and insights that addressed the research questions.
- **Phase 5—Reporting and Documentation:** Finally, we compiled the results of our data analysis, drew conclusions, and interpreted the significance of the findings.

This study examined user perceptions of privacy protection strategies in AR using a primarily quantitative research approach, supplemented with qualitative analysis. The aim was to explore user preferences, experiences, and concerns regarding visual obfuscation techniques in AR contexts.

The research methodology was structured to address three primary research questions. We sought to identify how different obfuscation techniques (masking, pixelation, and blurring) affect user experience in AR applications. Additionally, we aimed to explore the relationship between demographics (age, education, and occupation) and the perceived security of different obfuscation methods. Finally, we explored the relationship between the level of familiarity with AR and the acceptance of different obfuscation methods.

The survey was implemented using Google Forms and was thoughtfully structured with four distinct sections: demographic user information, privacy and obfuscation awareness, obfuscation technique preference in an AR context, and the adoption and application of obfuscation techniques. These built upon each other to provide a comprehensive understanding of user preferences and perceptions.

Demographic information. The first section of the SafeAR questionnaire gathered demographic information from participants, including gender identity, age, education level, and current occupation. The questions are visualized in the Appendix in Table A1; these demographic data were essential for analyzing how different population segments perceive and accept various privacy protection methods. Also, questions related to smartphone usage at work and prior AR experience were included to assess participants' familiarity with technology, which could influence their acceptance of and engagement with AR solutions.

Privacy and obfuscation awareness. The second section of the questionnaire, detailed in the Appendix in Table A2, focused on participants' habits, concerns, and knowledge related to privacy and obfuscation techniques. This section was designed to capture both behavioral data and awareness levels, providing insight into how participants handle privacy when sharing visual content online and their familiarity with methods used to protect that privacy. Participants were inquired about their prior knowledge of different obfuscation methods and their awareness of potential security vulnerabilities in these techniques.

Obfuscation technique preference in an AR context. The third section focused on privacy and obfuscation awareness, introducing participants to fundamental concepts of privacy and obfuscation in digital contexts. As shown in the Appendix in Table A3, we examined the participants' perceptions of different obfuscation techniques (masking, pixelating, and blurring) across a variety of AR contexts, as can be seen in Figure 2. This section aimed to evaluate the suitability of each technique for different scenarios, such as outdoor environments (bike or people) and indoor environments (document or screen). They were asked to rate how appropriate each obfuscation technique is for these contexts on a scale ranging from "Not at all" to "Extremely", offering insights into their preferences for privacy protection based on situational needs.

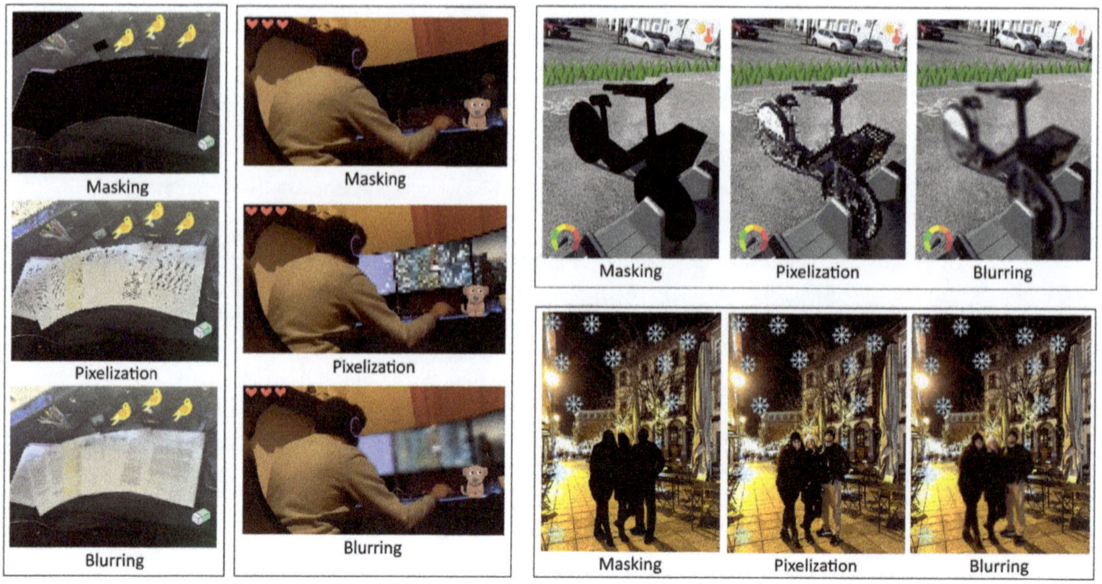

(**a**) AR in an indoor context (**b**) AR in an outdoor context

Figure 2. Examples of obfuscated images in different AR contexts (indoor and outdoor), demonstrating techniques such as masking, pixelation, and blurring.

In addition to contextual suitability, the questionnaire also explored participants' perceptions of using each obfuscation method across all AR contexts. Specifically, it addressed aesthetic appeal, information preservation, satisfaction, security, and trust, allowing us to assess how these factors influence users' approaches toward each technique.

The adoption and application of obfuscation techniques. The final section, detailed in the Appendix in Table A4, offered an overview of users' experiences and approaches toward incorporating obfuscation techniques into their daily lives. Participants were asked to evaluate the suitability of obfuscation techniques, such as masking, pixelating, and blurring, in different AR contexts. In addition to this, the interest in having control over the degree of obfuscation applied provided insights into how much autonomy users expect when managing privacy settings. It also assessed their familiarity with obfuscation applications by asking if they had ever used apps to obfuscate data.

Over the course of a week, the full data collection process was conducted. An introductory note outlining the goal of this study and its relationship to the project was included at the start of the questionnaire. In order to balance collecting thorough data with preserving participant involvement, the survey was developed so that it could take less than 10 min to complete. No personal identifiable information was taken during the procedure, and all replies were gathered anonymously to protect participant privacy.

After collecting the data from the questionnaire, the results were analyzed using the Pandas library [33], which facilitated efficient data manipulation and analysis. Necessary libraries for data analysis and visualization include Pandas, NumPy, Seaborn, Matplotlib, SciPy, and Scikit-learn [34].

The analysis focused on understanding the relationship between the level of familiarity with AR and the acceptance of different obfuscation methods (masking, pixelation, and blurring). Various statistical methods and visualizations were employed to analyze the data. Descriptive statistics were calculated, including the mean, median, standard deviation, minimum, and maximum values for satisfaction ratings across different AR familiarity levels. Boxplots were used to visualize the distribution of satisfaction ratings for each obfuscation method across different AR familiarity levels. The Kruskal–Wallis (H) test [35] was conducted to determine if there were statistically significant differences between the satisfaction ratings of different obfuscation methods.

4. Results and Discussion

In this section, we present and discuss the results of our study, where we analyze the responses collected using various data analysis techniques.

4.1. Participant Demographic

Our study included 54 participants (33 were male, 19 were female, and 2 preferred not to answer) with ages ranging from 15 to 77 years. The mean age ($\bar{x}$) was 30.6 years, with a standard deviation (s) of 13.1 years. Participants primarily consisted of students and professionals in education and information technology fields; most of them were familiar with AR technology.

4.2. Open-Ended User Responses Analysis

Responses about familiarity with obfuscation techniques revealed that over 85% of participants had limited knowledge of these methods. Nonetheless, some participants mentioned specific techniques like inpainting [36]—a common approach in visual data obfuscation—indicating recognition of its applications. One participant noted image swirling as an obfuscation method, while privacy-preserving photo sharing (P3) [37] and techniques like halftone and image quantization were also mentioned, reflecting some awareness of privacy-focused approaches among participants.

The analysis of open-ended responses about barriers to the adoption of visual data obfuscation techniques revealed various perceived obstacles. Respondents noted technical and implementation challenges, usability concerns, and security issues. For example, some highlighted the "technical complexity" required to obfuscate visual data accurately without losing precision or causing high computational costs, which could impact device performance.

Usability was another concern. Participants expressed reluctance toward functionalities that add complexity to image-sharing processes, suggesting "convenience" as an essential factor. Some suggested integrating optional obfuscation features within social media and photo-sharing platforms to reduce friction and improve user experience.

Finally, concerns about the effectiveness and security of obfuscation methods were raised, with some participants worried about the potential for reversed obfuscation techniques. This emphasizes that trust in the security of these methods is crucial for widespread adoption.

4.3. Addressing Research Questions

(RQ1): The first research question examined the relationship between demographics and the perceived security of different obfuscation techniques. Figure 3 shows privacy concerns by age group, highlighting a trend of increasing concern with age. Younger participants (ages 15–25 and 26–35) generally showed fewer privacy concerns, with many expressing little or no concern. Conversely, those aged 55+ expressed the most privacy concerns, with a significant proportion showing extreme concern. The age groups 36–45 and 46–55 exhibited moderate concerns. This suggests that younger generations may be more accustomed to sharing personal information online, while older generations, more aware of privacy risks, demonstrate greater caution.

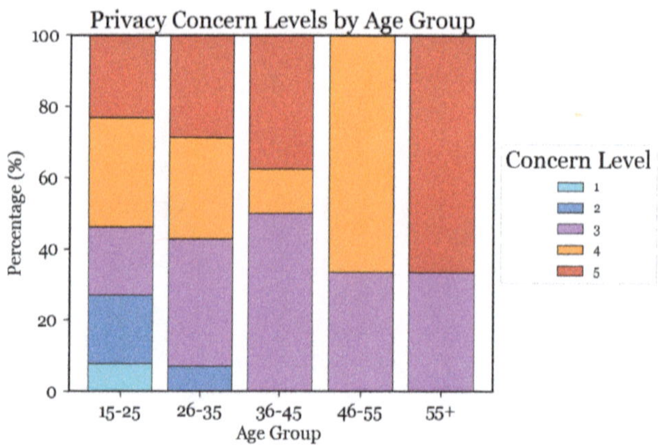

Figure 3. The distribution of privacy concern levels across five age groups (18–25, 26–35, 36–45, 46–55, 55+). The different colored segments within each bar correspond to the percentage of individuals who selected a particular level of privacy concern on a Likert scale (1 = Not at all; 5 = Extremely).

Figure 4 presents an analysis of privacy concern levels by educational level. Elementary school graduates tended to have fewer privacy concerns, possibly due to less exposure to online activities or a lack of awareness about privacy issues. High school graduates showed a more varied distribution of privacy concerns, with a noticeable increase in moderate to high levels when compared to elementary school graduates. Participants with a higher technical qualification exhibited a higher percentage of moderate to high privacy concerns, likely due to their technical background and awareness of privacy issues.

Bachelor's degree holders had a significant proportion of high levels of privacy concerns, indicating more awareness and concern about privacy issues. Master's degree holders showed a high level of privacy concerns, similarly to bachelor's degree holders, suggesting that higher education levels correlate with increased privacy awareness and concern. Finally, due to their extensive education and potential involvement in research and data processing, PhD holders exhibited the highest levels of privacy concerns.

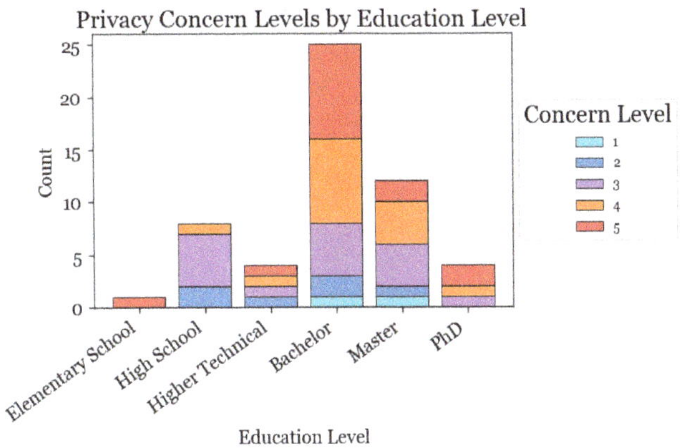

Figure 4. Privacy concern levels vary across different education levels. The chart shows the distribution of privacy concern levels (1 = Not at all; 5 = Extremely) for individuals at six different education levels.

Figure 5 shows the distribution of privacy concerns across occupations. Students revealed the most variation and generally fewer concerns. Participants with backgrounds in technology and educational fields displayed more concern, suggesting a greater awareness of privacy risks in these fields. Health professionals, in particular, had concentrated concerns at level 4, likely due to their sensitivity to patient privacy. Retirees exhibited moderate concern, and unemployed participants showed lower levels, with responses centered around levels 2 and 3.

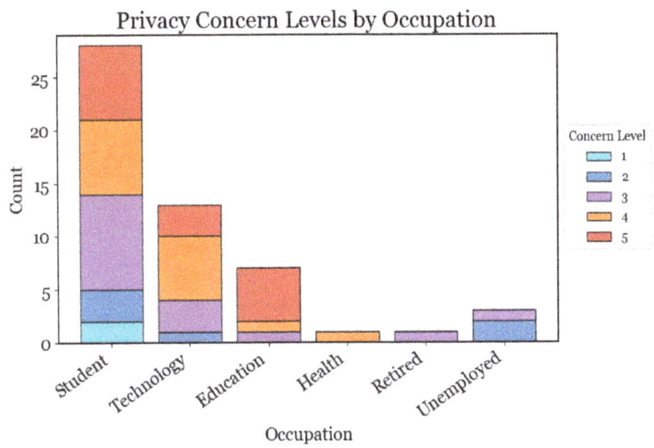

Figure 5. The distribution of privacy concern levels across six different occupations (student, technology, education, health, retired, unemployed). The different colored segments within each bar correspond to the percentage of individuals who selected a particular level of privacy concern on a Likert scale (1 = Not at all; 5 = Extremely).

The analysis indicates that privacy concerns tend to vary across different occupations. Careers in technology, education, and health are more likely to have high levels of privacy concerns. This trend suggests that professional background plays a significant role in raising awareness about privacy issues and the importance of protecting personal information online.

(RQ2): The second research question examined how different obfuscation techniques affect user experience in AR applications. Figure 6 exhibits the adequacy ratings for three obfuscation techniques (masking, pixelation, and blurring) in four distinct AR contexts: the outdoor bike, outdoor people, the indoor document, and the indoor screen. We used the Kruskal–Wallis test (H) to analyze how the different obfuscation techniques affect user experience across the four different AR contexts. The test aimed to determine if there were statistically significant differences in the perceived adequacy of obfuscation methods between these various AR contexts.

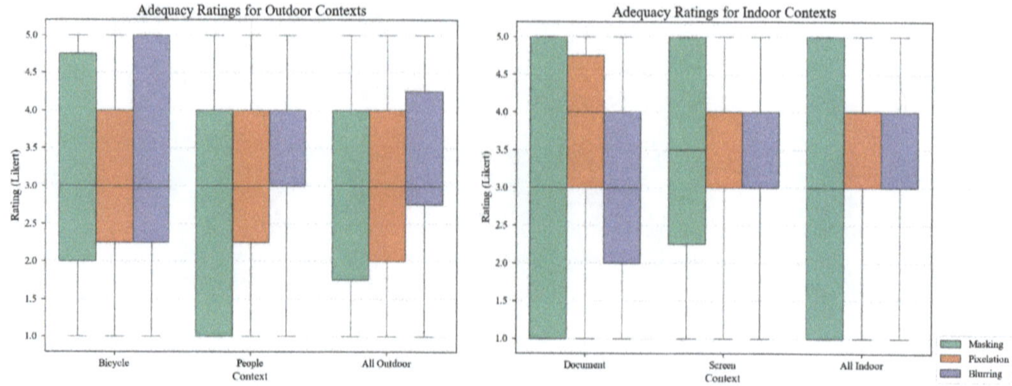

Figure 6. Mean adequacy ratings for masking, pixelation, and blurring techniques in four different AR contexts: outdoor bike, outdoor people, indoor document, and indoor screen.

Our results revealed that the best privacy protection method depended on the specific situation, while no single obfuscation technique was superior. For the outdoor AR contexts, we obtained the following results:

- **Bicyle:** People did not strongly prefer any particular technique (H = 3.58; p = 0.1670), and they had a slight preference for blurring (M = 3.46; σ = 1.35), followed by pixelation (M = 3.15; σ = 1.03) and masking (M = 2.91; σ = 1.55).
- **People:** Significant differences were observed (H = 6.00; p = 0.0499). Blurring (M = 3.46; σ = 1.11) was the most preferred, significantly more so than masking (M = 2.80; σ = 1.44), with pixelation (M = 3.26; σ = 1.04) in the middle.

For the indoor AR contexts, we obtained the following results:

- **Document:** Significant differences emerged between the methods (H = 7.91; p = 0.0191). Pixelation (M = 3.70; σ = 1.19) was the most favored, significantly outperforming masking (M = 2.87; σ = 1.63), and blurring (M = 3.11; σ = 1.27) fell in the middle.
- **Screen:** People did not state strong preferences, rating all three techniques—blurring (M = 3.46; σ = 1.03), masking (M = 3.41; σ = 1.47), and pixelation (M = 3.37, σ = 1.16)—similarly (H = 0.18; p = 0.9120).

These findings suggest that the suitability of obfuscation techniques can vary depending on the specific AR context and the type of visual content involved.

Figure 7 presents the average rating of the three different methods of obfuscation, masking, pixelation, and blurring, providing comprehensive insight into this question, comparing these techniques across the following five metrics: aesthetic, information, satisfaction, security, and trust.

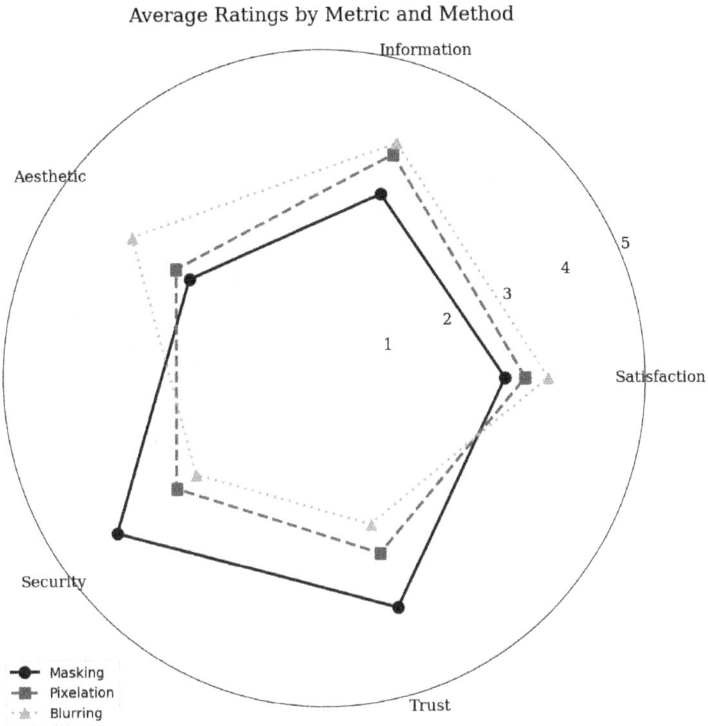

Figure 7. A comparative analysis of three obfuscation techniques (masking, pixelation, and blurring) based on five key metrics: aesthetic, information, satisfaction, trust, and security. The radial axis represents the rating scale using the Likert scale (1 = totally disagree; 5 = totally agree), with higher values indicating better performance.

Masking was suggested as the most trusted and secure method, but it compromised aesthetic appeal and user satisfaction. Pixelation offered a balanced approach, preserving information while maintaining moderate levels of trust and security, albeit at the cost of aesthetic appeal. Blurring prioritized aesthetic appeal and information retention, but it significantly underperformed in terms of security and trustworthiness. This can indicate that the optimal choice depends on the specific requirements of the application. If prioritizing trust and security is paramount, masking could be the ideal choice. For applications where information preservation and aesthetic appeal are crucial, blurring might be considered. However, pixelation offers a middle ground, balancing information preservation with reasonable levels of trust and security, even though it sacrifices aesthetic appeal.

(RQ3): Our third research question studied how users' familiarity with AR technology influenced their acceptance of different obfuscation methods. Table 1 presents the mean satisfaction ratings for the blurring, masking, and pixelation methods across different AR familiarity levels (1 = Not at all; 5 = Extremely).

The data demonstrate that blurring received consistent preference across both ends of the AR familiarity spectrum, with its highest satisfaction score at AR level 4 (3.75) and its lowest at AR level 1 (2.33). It still stood out with the highest mean score overall (3.45), suggesting that it may be the most generally acceptable technique for users across different familiarity levels. This could indicate that blurring is more universally suited for various AR environments, making it the most versatile option.

Table 1. Mean satisfaction – Comparison of blurring, masking, and pixelation across different AR familiarity levels.

AR Level	Blurring	Masking	Pixelation
1	2.33	3.67	3.33
2	3.67	3.33	2.00
3	3.29	2.94	3.00
4	3.75	2.75	3.44
5	3.60	2.47	3.13
Mean	3.48	2.81	3.13
Std. Dev.	1.37	1.33	1.10

Masking had a lower mean satisfaction score (2.81) and showed moderate variability in the satisfaction scores, with a standard deviation of 1.33. The highest satisfaction score for masking was at AR level 1 (3.67), and the lowest was at AR level 5 (2.47). This suggests that while masking may not be the most preferred method overall, it still has specific contexts (like AR level 1) where it performs relatively well. The moderate variability indicates that user experiences with masking can differ, which might imply that it is more context-dependent and may not provide a uniformly reliable experience across all AR familiarity levels.

Pixelation had a mean satisfaction score of 3.13 and showed higher variability, especially with a score of 2.00 at AR level 2. This indicates that while some participants found pixelation acceptable, it may not be as effective across the full range of AR familiarity levels. The variability in user responses suggests that pixelation may be less suitable for diverse AR contexts.

4.4. Discussion

The results of our study provide some insights into user perceptions and preferences regarding obfuscation techniques for privacy protection in AR applications. Firstly, demographic factors such as age, education level, and occupation significantly influence privacy concerns. Older participants and those with higher education levels or technical backgrounds tended to exhibit more privacy concerns, highlighting the importance of tailoring privacy solutions to different user groups.

Secondly, the user acceptance of obfuscation techniques varied depending on the AR context and the type of visual content. Blurring emerged as the most preferred technique for outdoor contexts involving people, while pixelation was favored for indoor document contexts. This suggests that a standard approach may not be suitable, and context-specific solutions are necessary to balance privacy protection and user experience.

Thirdly, user familiarity with AR technology played a crucial role in the acceptance of obfuscation methods. Blurring was consistently preferred across different familiarity levels, indicating its versatility. However, masking and pixelation showed more variability in user satisfaction, suggesting that these techniques may be more context-dependent.

Overall, our findings emphasize the need for a nuanced approach to implementing obfuscation techniques in AR applications. Privacy protection solutions should take into account demographic factors, contextual requirements, and the varying levels of user familiarity with AR technology.

5. Conclusions and Future Work

As AR evolves and is applied in fields such as education, healthcare, and entertainment, addressing privacy concerns becomes more critical for its sustainable adoption. This work is on the interplay between AR and user privacy, aiming to identify user preferences and perceptions regarding obfuscation techniques. By understanding user preferences for obfuscation techniques, one can design AR applications that align with user expectations while mitigating privacy risks. In this work, we conducted a comprehensive survey.

An analysis of the obtained results led to valuable insights on how users perceived various obfuscation methods in an AR context. Users generally expressed concerns about privacy in AR environments but had varying preferences for obfuscation techniques. Blurring emerged as a popular choice for its ability to maintain visual appeal and preserve information, making it suitable for scenarios in which one prioritizes aesthetics. Masking was regarded as the most secure and trusted method, though its intrusive nature often detracted from the overall user experience. However, pixelation was perceived as a median method across all evaluated criteria. It did not emerge as the best or worst in terms of visual appeal, preserving information, user satisfaction, trust, and security, positioning it centrally within the spectrum of user preferences. This indicates that while pixelation may not excel in any specific category, it offers a balanced approach that could be suitable for general use cases where a moderate level of obfuscation is acceptable.

Also, results demonstrated that user familiarity with AR technology influenced the acceptance of obfuscation methods. Although all three methods (blurring, masking, and pixelation) were generally well received, blurring emerged as the most universally accepted technique, particularly among users with higher AR familiarity levels. Pixelation had a medium preference overall and demonstrated consistent user satisfaction across different familiarity levels. Masking showed more variability in user acceptance, indicating that it may not be the optimal choice for all AR contexts, especially for high AR familiarity levels.

Demographic factors significantly influenced perceptions of privacy and the acceptance of obfuscation methods. Younger individuals and those with a high-school education tended to have fewer privacy concerns, while older individuals and those with higher education levels exhibited greater awareness and caution. Similarly, professional background emerged as a significant factor, with individuals in the technology, education, and health sectors demonstrating heightened privacy awareness and concern.

The methods explored in this study have the potential to be applied in safeguarding sensitive information in shared AR spaces, such as obscuring bystander identities or protecting proprietary data in industrial settings.

In future work, we intend to incorporate these results into the automatic selection of obfuscation methods in AR environments, in order to combine the protection of sensitive data with the quality of user experience.

To address the limitations highlighted by the small sample size and demographic diversity, future research will focus on expanding the participant pool to enhance the reliability and generalizability of our findings. We will aim to recruit a larger and more diverse sample, allowing for more robust conclusions across different user demographics.

Also, some findings can be generalized to other populations and contexts, considering limitations and specific variables. Excessive generalization may lead to premature conclusions, warranting further research. Obfuscation methods can protect data privacy and security but require consideration of ethical and legal implications. Transparent and auditable methods that preserve data integrity must be developed.

Exploring different cultural and social contexts can provide more valuable insights into obfuscation methods. Quantitative approaches have limitations, particularly regarding "unknown unknowns". Qualitative methods, such as interviews or content analysis, can provide a deeper understanding of phenomena, enabling the identification of patterns and relationships not captured by quantitative approaches.

Author Contributions: Conceptualization, A.C., R.C., A.M., A.G. and L.S.; data curation, A.C.; formal analysis, A.C.; funding acquisition, C.R. and R.C.; investigation, A.C., C.R., R.C., A.M., A.G. and L.S.; project administration, C.R. and R.L.; supervision: A.G. and A.M.; visualization, A.C.; writing—original draft, A.C., A.G., A.M., C.R., R.L. and L.S.; writing—review and editing, A.C., A.G., A.M., C.R., R.L. and L.S. All authors have read and agreed to the published version of the manuscript.

Funding: This work is partially funded by national funds through FCT—Fundação para a Ciência e a Tecnologia, I.P., in the context of projects SafeAR—2022.09235.PTDC and UIDB/04524/2020 and under the Scientific Employment Stimulus—CEECINS/00051/2018.

Data Availability Statement: The source code used to analyze the responses to the questionnaire is available at https://github.com/ipleiria-ciic/safe-ar-questionnaire (accessed on 13 December 2024).

Conflicts of Interest: The authors declare no conflicts of interest.

Appendix A

This appendix presents the questionnaires used in our study to evaluate the AR System. The SafeAR questionnaire was structured into four distinct sections to collect detailed data on user profiles (Table A1), privacy awareness (Table A2), preferences for obfuscation techniques (Table A3), and overall perceptions (Table A4).

In some questions in the questionnaire, we evaluated user perceptions of three obfuscation techniques: masking, pixelating, and blurring. For clarity, each technique is represented by a number throughout the tables:

1. Masking
2. Pixelating
3. Blurring

Similarly, when evaluating user perceptions of these techniques across different criteria, we used a similar approach:

1. Aesthetic: the visual appeal of the technique.
2. Information: the clarity and usability of information after obfuscation.
3. Satisfaction: overall satisfaction with the technique.
4. Security: the perceived security enhancement provided by the technique.
5. Trust: the trustworthiness and reliability of the technique.

Each question was rated individually in a multiple-choice grid format, as indicated by the symbol #.

Table A1. SafeAR Questionnaire 1° section: user profile questionnaire.

Question	Options
Gender	☐ Female ☐ Male ☐ Prefer not to answer
Age	______
Education level	☐ Primary ☐ Secondary ☐ Technical ☐ Bachelor's ☐ Master's ☐ Doctorate

Table A1. *Cont.*

Question	Options
Professional field	☐ Student ☐ Healthcare ☐ Education ☐ IT ☐ Legal ☐ Finance ☐ Services ☐ Unemployed
Previous AR experience	☐ Glasses/Headset ☐ Smartphone/Tablet ☐ Spatial projection
Familiarity level with AR	☐ 1—Not at all ☐ 2—Slightly ☐ 3—Moderately ☐ 4—Very ☐ 5—Extremely

Table A2. SafeAR Questionnaire 2° section: privacy and obfuscation.

Question	Options
Sharing photos or video online	☐ Never ☐ Rarely ☐ Sometimes ☐ Often ☐ Very often
Concerned about privacy	☐ 1—Not at all ☐ 2—Slightly ☐ 3—Moderately ☐ 4—Very ☐ 5—Extremely
Heard about obfuscation technique # 1-Pixelating 2-Blurring 3-Masking	☐ Yes, I use it regularly ☐ Yes, I have used it ☐ Yes, but I don't use it ☐ Yes, but I don't know what they are ☐ I've never heard of it
Knowledge of reversal of obfuscation methods	☐ Yes ☐ No ☐ Maybe
Knowledge about others obfuscation methods	______

Table A3. SafeAR Questionnaire 3° section: masking vs. pixelating vs. blurring.

Question	Options
Suitable of obfuscation for the current context # (Bike outdoor) 1-Masking 2-Pixelating 3-Blurring	☐ 1—Not at all ☐ 2—Slightly ☐ 3—Moderately ☐ 4—Very ☐ 5—Extremely

Table A3. *Cont.*

Question	Options
Suitable of obfuscation for the current context # (Document indoor) 1-Masking 2-Pixelating 3-Blurring	☐ 1—Not at all ☐ 2—Slightly ☐ 3—Moderately ☐ 4—Very ☐ 5—Extremely
Suitable of obfuscation for the current context # (Screen indoor) 1-Masking 2-Pixelating 3-Blurring	☐ 1—Not at all ☐ 2—Slightly ☐ 3—Moderately ☐ 4—Very ☐ 5—Extremely
Suitable of obfuscation for the current context # (People outdoor) 1-Masking 2-Pixelating 3-Blurring	☐ 1—Not at all ☐ 2—Slightly ☐ 3—Moderately ☐ 4—Very ☐ 5—Extremely
User perception using Masking to all contexts AR # 1-Aesthetic 2-Information 3-Satisfaction 4-Security 5-Trust	☐ 1—Disagree totally ☐ 2—Disagree somewhat ☐ 3—Neither agree nor disagree ☐ 4—Agree somewhat ☐ 5—Agree totally
User perception using Pixelating to all contexts AR # 1-Aesthetic 2-Information 3-Satisfaction 4-Security 5-Trust	☐ 1—Disagree totally ☐ 2—Disagree somewhat ☐ 3—Neither agree nor disagree ☐ 4—Agree somewhat ☐ 5—Agree totally
User perception using Blurring to all contexts AR # 1-Aesthetic 2-Information 3-Satisfaction 4-Security 5-Trust	☐ 1—Disagree totally ☐ 2—Disagree somewhat ☐ 3—Neither agree nor disagree ☐ 4—Agree somewhat ☐ 5—Agree totally

Table A4. SafeAR Questionnaire 4° section: overview of using obfuscation techniques.

Question	Options
Importance of control over the level of obfuscation # 1-Masking 2-Pixelating 3-Blurring	☐ 1—Not at all ☐ 2—Slightly ☐ 3—Moderately ☐ 4—Very ☐ 5—Extremely
Have ever used an app to obfuscate data	☐ Yes, frequently ☐ Yes, sometimes ☐ No

Table A4. *Cont.*

Question	Options
Interested in including obfuscation techniques in daily life	☐ 1—Not at all ☐ 2—Slightly ☐ 3—Moderately ☐ 4—Very ☐ 5—Extremely
Obfuscation techniques should be applied automatically	☐ Yes ☐ No ☐ Maybe
Obstacles in the process of adopting obfuscation on a daily basis	______

References

1. Orekondy, T.; Schiele, B.; Fritz, M. Towards a Visual Privacy Advisor: Understanding and Predicting Privacy Risks in Images. In Proceedings of the 2017 IEEE International Conference on Computer Vision (ICCV), Venice, Italy, 22–29 October 2017; pp. 3706–3715. [CrossRef]
2. Zhao, Y.; Wei, S.; Guo, T. Privacy-preserving Reflection Rendering for Augmented Reality. In Proceedings of the 30th ACM International Conference on Multimedia, Lisboa, Portugal, 10–14 October 2022; ACM: Lisboa, Portugal, 2022; pp. 2909–2918. [CrossRef]
3. Moon, J.; Bukhari, M.; Kim, C.; Nam, Y.; Maqsood, M.; Rho, S. Object detection under the lens of privacy: A critical survey of methods, challenges, and future directions. *ICT Express* **2024**, *10*, 1124–1144. [CrossRef]
4. Fuchs, C. Social media and the public sphere. In *Culture and Economy in the Age of Social Media*; Routledge: London, UK, 2015; pp. 315–372.
5. Minaee, S.; Liang, X.; Yan, S. Modern Augmented Reality: Applications, Trends, and Future Directions. *arXiv* **2022**, arXiv:2202.09450.
6. Azuma, R.T. A Survey of Augmented Reality. *Presence Telepper. Virtual Environ.* **1997**, *6*, 355–385. [CrossRef]
7. Francisco, D.; Cruz, A.; Rodrigues, N.; Gonçalves, A.; Ribeiro, R. Augmented Reality and Digital Twin for Mineral Industry. In Proceedings of the 2023 International Conference on Graphics and Interaction (ICGI), Tomar, Portugal, 2–3 November 2023; pp. 1–8. [CrossRef]
8. Leitão, B.; Costa, C.; Gonçalves, A.; Marto, A. Defend Your Castle–A Mobile Augmented Reality Multiplayer Game. In Proceedings of the 2023 International Conference on Graphics and Interaction (ICGI), Tomar, Portugal, 2–3 November 2023; pp. 1–7. [CrossRef]
9. Marto, A.; Almeida, H.A.; Gonçalves, A. Using Augmented Reality in Patients with Autism: A Systematic Review. In *VipIMAGE 2019*; Tavares, J.M.R.S., Natal Jorge, R.M., Eds.; Series Title: Lecture Notes in Computational Vision and Biomechanics; Springer International Publishing: Porto, Portugal 2019; Volume 34, pp. 454–463. [CrossRef]
10. Kesim, M.; Ozarslan, Y. Augmented Reality in Education: Current Technologies and the Potential for Education. *Procedia—Soc. Behav. Sci.* **2012**, *47*, 297–302. [CrossRef]
11. King, A.; Kaleem, F.; Rabieh, K. A Survey on Privacy Issues of Augmented Reality Applications. In Proceedings of the 2020 IEEE Conference on Application, Information and Network Security (AINS), Kota Kinabalu, Sabah, Malaysia, 17–19 November 2020; pp. 32–40. [CrossRef]
12. Xue, J.; Hu, R.; Zhang, W.; Zhao, Y.; Zhang, B.; Liu, N.; Li, S.C.; Logan, J. Virtual Reality or Augmented Reality as a Tool for Studying Bystander Behaviors in Interpersonal Violence: Scoping Review. *J. Med. Internet Res.* **2021**, *23*, e25322. [CrossRef] [PubMed]
13. Heller, B. Reimagining Reality: Human Rights and Immersive Technology. Harvard Carr Center Discussion Paper Series. 2020. Available online: https://scholar.google.com/citations?view_op=view_citation&hl=en&user=DJmbBPIAAAAJ&citation_for_view=DJmbBPIAAAAJ:IjCSPb-OGe4C (accessed on 5 November 2024). [CrossRef]
14. Ruth, K.; Kohno, T.; Roesner, F. Secure Multi-User Content Sharing for Augmented Reality Applications. In Proceedings of the 28th USENIX Security Symposium (USENIX Security 19), Santa Clara, CA, USA, 14–16 August 2019; pp. 141–158.
15. Guzman, J.A.d.; Thilakarathna, K.; Seneviratne, A. Security and Privacy Approaches in Mixed Reality: A Literature Survey. *ACM Comput. Surv.* **2020**, *52*, 1–37. [CrossRef]

16. Alves, M.; Ribeiro, T.; Santos, L.; Marto, A.; Gonçalves, A.; Rabadão, C.; de C. Costa, R.L. Evaluating Service-based Privacy-Protection for Augmented Reality Applications. In Proceedings of the 16th International Conference on Management of Digital Ecosystems (MEDES 2024), Naples, Italy, 18–20 November 2024.
17. Ribeiro, T.; Marto, A.; Gonçalves, A.; Santos, L.; Rabadão, C.; de C. Costa, R.L. SafeARUnity: Real-time image processing to enhance privacy protection in LBARGs. In Proceedings of the 14th International Conference on Videogame Sciences and Arts (VideoJogos'24), Leiria, Portugal, 5–6 December 2024.
18. Van Krevelen, D.; Poelman, R. A Survey of Augmented Reality Technologies, Applications and Limitations. *Int. J. Virtual Real.* **2010**, *9*, 1–20. [CrossRef]
19. Grubert, J.; Langlotz, T.; Zollmann, S.; Regenbrecht, H. Towards Pervasive Augmented Reality: Context-Awareness in Augmented Reality. *IEEE Trans. Vis. Comput. Graph.* **2017**, *23*, 1706–1724. [CrossRef] [PubMed]
20. Jana, S.; Narayanan, A.; Shmatikov, V. A Scanner Darkly: Protecting User Privacy from Perceptual Applications. In Proceedings of the 2013 IEEE Symposium on Security and Privacy, Berkeley, CA, USA, 19–22 May 2013; pp. 349–363. [CrossRef]
21. Lebeck, K.; Ruth, K.; Kohno, T.; Roesner, F. Towards Security and Privacy for Multi-user Augmented Reality: Foundations with End Users. In Proceedings of the 2018 IEEE Symposium on Security and Privacy (SP), San Francisco, CA, USA, 20–24 May 2018; pp. 392–408. [CrossRef]
22. Ramajayam, G.; Sun, T.; Tan, C.C.; Luo, L.; Ling, H. Saliency-Aware Privacy Protection in Augmented Reality Systems. In Proceedings of the First Workshop on Metaverse Systems and Applications, Helsinki, Finland, 18–22 June 2023; ACM: New York, NY, USA, 2023; pp. 1–6. [CrossRef]
23. Diyora, V.; Khalil, B. Impact of Augmented Reality on Cloud Data Security. In Proceedings of the 2024 15th International Conference on Computing Communication and Networking Technologies (ICCCNT), Mandi, Himachal Pradesh, India, 24–28 June 2024; pp. 1–4. [CrossRef]
24. Enireddy, V.; Somasundaram, K.; Mahesh, M.P.C.S.; Ramkumar Prabhu, M.; Babu, D.V.; Karthikeyan, C. Data Obfuscation Technique in Cloud Security. In Proceedings of the 2021 2nd International Conference on Smart Electronics and Communication (ICOSEC), Trichy, India, 7–9 October 2021; pp. 358–362. [CrossRef]
25. Martínez, S.; Sánchez, D.; Valls, A.; Batet, M. Privacy protection of textual attributes through a semantic-based masking method. *Inf. Fusion* **2012**, *13*, 304–314. [CrossRef]
26. Fan, L. Image Pixelization with Differential Privacy. In Proceedings of the Data and Applications Security and Privacy XXXII, Bergamo, Italy, 16–18 July 2018; Kerschbaum, F., Paraboschi, S., Eds.; Springer International Publishing: Berlin/Heidelberg, Germany, 2018; pp. 148–162.
27. Neustaedter, C.; Greenberg, S.; Boyle, M. Blur filtration fails to preserve privacy for home-based video conferencing. *ACM Trans. -Comput.-Hum. Interact.* **2006**, *13*, 1–36. [CrossRef]
28. Roesner, F.; Kohno, T.; Molnar, D. Security and privacy for augmented reality systems. *Commun. ACM* **2014**, *57*, 88–96. [CrossRef]
29. Li, Y.; Vishwamitra, N.; Knijnenburg, B.P.; Hu, H.; Caine, K. Blur vs. Block: Investigating the Effectiveness of Privacy-Enhancing Obfuscation for Images. In Proceedings of the 2017 IEEE Conference on Computer Vision and Pattern Recognition Workshops (CVPRW), Honolulu, HI, USA, 21–26 July 2017; pp. 1343–1351. [CrossRef]
30. Oh, S.J.; Benenson, R.; Fritz, M.; Schiele, B. Faceless Person Recognition; Privacy Implications in Social Media. In Proceedings of the Computer Vision–ECCV 2016: 14th European Conference, Amsterdam, The Netherlands, 11–14 October 2016; pp. 19–35.
31. Demiris, G.; Oliver, D.P.; Giger, J.; Skubic, M.; Rantz, M. Older adults' privacy considerations for vision based recognition methods of eldercare applications. *Technol. Health Care* **2009**, *17*, 41–48. [CrossRef] [PubMed]
32. Vasantha, R.N.; Harinarayana, N. Online survey tools: A case study of Google Forms. In Proceedings of the National Conference on Scientific, Computational & Information Research Trends in Engineering, Chennai, India, 20–21 October 2016.
33. W3Schools. Pandas Tutorial—Introduction. Available online: https://www.w3schools.com/python/pandas/pandas_intro.asp (accessed on 9 December 2024).
34. Ranjan, M.; Barot, K.; Khairnar, V.; Rawal, V.; Pimpalgaonkar, A.; Saxena, S.; Sattar, A.M. Python: Empowering Data Science Applications and Research. *J. Oper. Syst. Dev. Trends* **2023**, *10*, 27–33. [CrossRef]
35. Vargha, A.; Delaney, H.D. The Kruskal-Wallis test and stochastic homogeneity. *J. Educ. Behav. Stat.* **1998**, *23*, 170–192. [CrossRef]
36. Li, Y.; Vishwamitra, N.; Knijnenburg, B.P.; Hu, H.; Caine, K. Effectiveness and Users' Experience of Obfuscation as a Privacy-Enhancing Technology for Sharing Photos. *Proc. ACM -Hum.-Comput. Interact.* **2017**, *1*, 1–24. [CrossRef]
37. Ra, M.R.; Govindan, R.; Ortega, A. P3: Toward Privacy-Preserving Photo Sharing. In Proceedings of the 10th USENIX Symposium on Networked Systems Design and Implementation (NSDI 13), Lombard, IL, USA, 2–5 April 2013; pp. 515–528.

future internet

Article

CityBuildAR: Enhancing Community Engagement in Placemaking Through Mobile Augmented Reality

Daneesha Ranasinghe [1], Nayomi Kankanamge [2], Chathura De Silva [1], Nuwani Kangana [1], Rifat Mahamood [1] and Tan Yigitcanlar [3,*]

1 Department of Town & Country Planning, University of Moratuwa, Katubedda 10400, Sri Lanka; madumadhirad.23@uom.lk (D.R.); chathurads@uom.lk (C.D.S.); kanganakmnd.23@uom.lk (N.K.); mahamoodmr.23@uom.lk (R.M.)
2 School of Law and Society, University of the Sunshine Coast, Moreton Bay, QLD 4502, Australia; nkankanamge@usc.edu.au
3 QUT Urban AI Hub, School of Architecture and Built Environment, Queensland University of Technology, 2 George Street, Brisbane, QLD 4000, Australia
* Correspondence: tan.yigitcanlar@qut.edu.au; Tel.: +61-7-3138-2418

Abstract: Mostly, public places are planned and designed by professionals rather engaging the community in the design process. Even if the community engaged, the engagement process was limited to hand drawings, manual mappings, or public discussions, which limited the general public to visualize and well-communicate their aspirations with the professionals. Against this backdrop, this study intends to develop a mobile application called "CityBuildAR", which uses Augmented Reality technology that allows the end user to visualize their public spaces in a way they want. CityBuildAR was developed by the authors using the Unity Real-Time Development Platform, and the app was developed for an Android Operating System. The app was used to assess community interests in designing open spaces by categorizing participants into three groups: those with limited, average, and professional knowledge of space design. The open cafeteria of the University of Moratuwa, Sri Lanka served as the testbed for this study. The study findings revealed that: (a) Mobile Augmented Reality is an effective way to engage people with limited knowledge in space design to express their design thinking, (b) Compared to professionals, the general public wanted to have more green elements in the public space; (c) Compared to the professionals, the general public who were not conversant with the designing skills found the app more useful to express their ideas. The study guides urban authorities in their placemaking efforts by introducing a novel approach to effectively capture community ideas for creating inclusive public spaces.

Keywords: mobile augmented reality; placemaking; public spaces; participatory planning; community engagement; smart city; urban technology; artificial intelligence (AI); generative AI

1. Introduction

Placemaking is a multifaceted concept that has emerged since the late 20th century [1]. Originally grounded in urban planning and design, it concentrated mostly on developing functional places that addressed certain requirements. Over time, the concept has evolved to encompass community engagement, social connection, and environmental sustainability, illustrating a more comprehensive understanding of how spaces transform into meaningful places through the active participation of their residents [1]. This shift highlights the growing importance of community involvement in designing public places [2].

The primary focus on community in placemaking has transitioned from a marginal aspect to a fundamental component of the process, highlighting the growing importance of participatory development [3–7]. For instance, the transformation of the Comuna 13 neighborhood—Medellin in Colombia [8], the development of an extensive public transportation system—Curitiba in Brazil [9], communities are regarded as active contributors in defining their environments, promoting ownership and collaboration in urban planning processes [10]. This shift recognizes the importance of social capital, highlighting that strong community connections are vital for successful and sustainable placemaking. As an example, "The High Line" in New York City exemplifies successful placemaking through community-driven action, where local residents, artists, and activists collectively advocated for the project, secured funding, and shaped its design, strengthening the sense of ownership that ensures its long-term sustainability [11,12].

However, despite these improvements, community engagement has not always led to positive outcomes. Superficial participation is common, where communities are invited to be involved but often only in a limited or symbolic way, leading to feelings of distrust [13]. Additionally, the flexibility of placemaking is sometimes exploited, leading to projects that mainly benefit specific groups, exacerbating social inequalities and undermining community cohesion [14,15]. These challenges highlight the ongoing struggle to effectively address community needs and ensure that participatory approaches are both sustainable and equitable.

Participatory tools such as hand-drawn sketches, cultural mapping, community meetings, participatory mapping, community surveys, public exhibitions, social media platforms, etc. play a vital role in the placemaking process by enabling citizens to actively contribute to shaping their environments [16–18]. However, these tools face several challenges that can limit their effectiveness in truly engaging all members of the community. For example, community surveys have been used in various urban planning projects to gather input on public space usage, but these often fail to capture the complexities of urban dynamics [19]. For instance, the redevelopment of Pruitt-Igoe in St. Louis, Missouri —an infamous public housing project that was demolished in the 1970s despite initial positive feedback from residents in surveys. However, these surveys failed to capture the social and economic realities of the residents, their deep-rooted community ties, and the negative impacts of isolation and displacement that the demolition would cause [20,21].

Similarly, hand-drawn sketches have been used in participatory design workshops to visualize community ideas, yet their lack of precision limits their integration into formal planning processes [22]. Cultural mapping, which integrates artistic approaches to explore the cultural significance of spaces, has been effective in some cases but struggles with a lack of standardized methodology, hindering its widespread adoption [23]. For example, in the Grecanic Area of Southern Italy, a culturally rich region known for its historical traditions and natural landscapes, cultural mapping was used to capture both material and immaterial heritage through community surveys and visual data representation. This approach successfully enhanced local identity and supported sustainable tourism development beyond seasonal seaside activities [24]. Community meetings, such as those held in local councils, aim to gather input from residents but can often perpetuate existing power imbalances, leading to unequal participation and marginalization of more vulnerable groups [19]. Participatory mapping has been successfully used in neighborhood planning to allow community members to mark areas of significance, yet its effectiveness can be limited by varying levels of spatial literacy [25,26].

Public exhibitions are commonly used to display public space design proposals and collect feedback, promoting transparency, though they are often constrained by the scale of participation and the type of feedback they gather [17]. Finally, social media platforms, like Facebook or X, have been used to engage a broader audience in the planning process, yet they require careful management to prevent the digital exclusion of less connected groups [27,28]. These tools, while invaluable, face significant challenges that hinder their ability to produce inclusive and equitable outcomes. A common issue is inequality in participation, where marginalized groups are often excluded from meaningful engagement, resulting in skewed representation in the decision-making process [19].

Additionally, technological limitations, such as the lack of access to social media platforms for certain populations, reduce the inclusivity of digital tools [27]. Another significant challenge is the lack of consistency in methods, as tools like cultural mapping and hand-drawn sketches often lack standardized methodologies, limiting their ability to be integrated into broader planning practices effectively [23]. Moreover, generative artificial intelligence-based design tools, such as MidJourney, etc., are not freely accessible to the public and may pose usability challenges for general users. Despite these challenges, the potential for these participatory tools to enhance community engagement remains significant. Overcoming these issues, particularly related to representation and methodology, is crucial for their success in placemaking initiatives.

In response to the challenges discussed above, such as limited access to advanced technology in certain communities, lack of consistency and standardized methodologies, and the need for more inclusive digital tools, this study explores the use of Mobile Augmented Reality (M-AR) technology as a tool to bridge the gap between professionals and the community in designing places. By integrating real-time visualizations and interactive features, M-AR provides an opportunity for communities to actively participate in designing their public spaces in ways that were previously inaccessible. The research questions addressed by this study include: (a) How can M-AR applications enhance community engagement in placemaking? and (b) How does the City BuildAR app (version 1.0) bridge the gap between professionals and the general public in placemaking?

2. Literature Background

The growing interest in M-AR as a tool for participatory planning is driven by its potential to bridge the gap between digital technology and community engagement. This literature review examines current research on the application of M-AR in urban planning, highlighting its advantages and constraints in promoting meaningful community engagement, and establishing the rationale for the study of CityBuildAR 1.0 as a tool to improve urban planning outcomes.

2.1. *What Is M-AR and Why?*

Mobile-Augmented Reality (M-AR) is an interactive technology that overlays computer-generated visuals and, in some cases, audio onto the real-world environment using mobile devices such as smartphones and tablets. While M-AR predominantly relies on mobile devices due to their accessibility and cost-effectiveness, it can also be supported by AR headsets such as Meta Quest, providing an enhanced and immersive user experience by merging the physical and digital domains [29]. The origin of AR dates to the 1960s with Ivan Sutherland's invention of the first head-mounted display system. However, the term "augmented reality" was officially introduced by Tom Caudell in the early 1990s [30]. Initially, AR systems were confined to industrial and academic uses due to high costs and technological limitations. With advancements in mobile computing and smartphones, M-AR become popular and was become more accessible to the general population.

Today, M-AR finds applications across diverse sectors including education, healthcare, urban planning, and entertainment, enabling users to experience an interactive and immersive overlay of digital content in their real environments [31,32]. In education, AR enhances learning by offering immersive, interactive experiences, for instance the "HoloHuman" AR app (version 1.0.2) designed for anatomy visualizations for medical students, which have become integral to contemporary medical school curricula [33]. The "Google Expeditions" which is an educational platform that uses AR to take students on virtual field trips to various locations around the world [34]. Retailers use AR for virtual product trials, like IKEA's furniture placement app, improving customer satisfaction [35]. Tourism also benefits from AR through apps that enhance visitor experiences, such as interactive historical site tours [36]. Military and defense applications use AR for real-time situational awareness, with systems like the US military's IVAS helmets [37]. AR's influence in entertainment, particularly gaming, is evident in games like Pokémon GO, which merges virtual and real environments for player engagement [38]. In automotive industries, AR improves navigation and car design through systems like BMW's augmented HUDs [39]. Although AR is less frequently utilized in disciplines like philosophy, literary studies, and traditional sociology, there is growing potential for its use in areas like philosophical simulations, interactive literary experiences [40].

In M-AR interfaces, three-dimensional virtual images and objects are integrated into real-world scenes through mobile phone cameras, allowing users to interact with both simultaneously [41]. For example, M-AR enables architects and planners to visualize urban designs in realistic settings and support better communication of ideas easily through their handheld device at any time [42]. This capability not only enhances comprehension and decision-making but also democratizes participation by making complex design concepts understandable to non-experts.

M-AR technology can be classified into different types, each providing unique functionality and applications across diverse industries. They are: (a) Marker-Based AR, (b) Projection-Based AR, and (c) Superimposition-Based Augmented Reality. Marker-Based Augmented Reality utilizes visual markers, such QR codes, to overlay digital content onto the physical environment. It is extensively employed in education to develop engaging and problem-solving-oriented learning experiences [43,44]. For instance, the "HoloHuman" AR application enables medical students to visualize and interact with 3D models of the human body by scanning markers on anatomical charts, allowing them to rotate, zoom, and dissect virtual models for a deeper understanding of complex structures [45]. Similarly, "Quiver Vision" enhances language learning by bringing children's colored artwork to life with 3D animations and sounds, creating an interactive way to learn vocabulary, grammar, and cultural concepts [46]. Markerless augmented reality, in contrast, does not necessitate predefined markers; it utilizes GPS, accelerometers, and digital compasses to provide adaptable and immersive experiences, rendering it especially efficacious for gaming, navigation, and urban planning applications [47–49]. For example, Pokemon Go (version 0.91.1—Android/version 1.61.1 IOS), which is primarily a gaming application, demonstrated the potential of devisor's sensors to encourage exploration and increase foot traffic in urban areas [50].

Projection-based AR superimposes virtual pictures onto tangible surfaces, enabling users to engage with digital material directly within real-world environments. This is particularly advantageous in design and architecture for visualizing concepts in realistic contexts [51,52]. Superimposition-Based Augmented Reality augments or substitutes aspects of the physical environment with digital overlays, frequently utilized in medical training and maintenance activities to deliver real-time, contextually relevant information [53]. These classifications demonstrate AR's varied capabilities and its transformational potential across numerous fields.

2.2. M-AR as a Participatory Tool

M-AR is widely recognized as an effective participatory tool, enhancing interaction, engagement, and understanding across multiple fields by integrating digital components onto physical situations [54]. This technology improves the capacity of individuals and groups to visualize and engage with complex information, particularly beneficial in collaborative and decision-making contexts through mobile devices such as mobile phones, tablets, etc. M-AR is revolutionizing individual and community engagement in projects, conversations, and solutions across sectors such as education, healthcare, design, and public participation [55]. With the extensive use of mobile phones, M-AR transforms conventional decision-making tools into contemporary digital solutions, integrating AR, Virtual Reality (VR), and Geographic Information Systems (GIS) to create interactive, portable platforms for collaborative engagement [42]. Despite its potential, M-AR remains less popular due to technical challenges such as limited device compatibility, high computational demands, and the need for robust internet connectivity [56]. Additionally, its adoption is hindered by a lack of user familiarity, high development costs, and the absence of standardized frameworks, which collectively restrict its widespread implementation and scalability.

M-AR has emerged as a powerful participatory planning tool, enabling a more inclusive, interactive, and accessible approach to urban and spatial planning. By overlaying digital elements onto the physical environment, AR enhances visualization, interaction, and comprehension for planning professionals, stakeholders, and community participants [55]. Traditional participatory methods, reliant on static tools like paper maps, drawings, and physical models, often fall short in conveying the complexity and spatial dynamics of urban projects. For instance, MIT's CityScope project integrates AR with 3D physical models to allow stakeholders to collaboratively explore urban scenarios, such as transportation network changes or housing developments, in an understandable format [57]. However, this approach often requires expert assistance for setup and operation, as it involves technical devices like projectors or tablets. This complexity makes it less community-friendly compared to more accessible tools like M-AR platforms, which are easier to use and require minimal technical expertise.

AR has been widely used as a participatory tool to engage communities in the urban planning process, providing an interactive platform for understanding and contributing to urban planning initiatives. In Amsterdam, numerous grassroots projects have utilized digital tools, including websites and interactive applications, to enhance citizen engagement in urban development. These technologies empower communities to address urban challenges, cooperate on solutions, and see project outcomes, thereby improving their capacity to provide informed feedback [58]. In Oslo, Norway, AR was used to support community-driven planning for urban green initiatives, including the proposal of planting 100,000 trees. This initiative incorporated participatory activities such as visual presentations, drawings, and AR-enhanced simulations, allowing community members to see and interact with proposed changes in real time [59], and highlighted that AR facilitated community understanding and participation, encouraging meaningful contributions to urban planning processes. Similarly in Bandung City, Indonesia, community members actively participated in data collection and research to identify and address urban planning issues in their local environment [60].

Out of the 33 AR applications found in literature (Table 1), five are relevant to urban planning and community engagement. These applications aim to improve urban design, facilitate community participation, and enhance planning processes through interactive and immersive technologies. A detailed review of these applications is as follows. In-Citu AR allows users to visualize urban proposals in real time, improving communication between planners and residents, though it relies on accurate mapping data and faces accessibility challenges. The CitySense App provides real-time data visualization on urban metrics such as air quality and traffic, fostering greater awareness but risking information overload and limited user comprehension [61]. The ARPP engages the public in the planning process by enabling interactive participation in urban design, enhancing transparency, but is resource-intensive and may face challenges related to digital literacy and device access [62]. Urban Sketcher encourages community creativity in urban design, promoting collaboration, though it may lack the professional tools necessary for detailed planning [63]. Wikitude overlays data on real-world environments, enriching public understanding of urban spaces, yet its reliance on accurate data and potential privacy concerns may limit its effectiveness [64].

Table 1. Overview of 33 AR applications.

No	AR Application	Type	Focus	Developer	Reference
1	ways2gether	Mobile	Traffic Planning	Jauschneg & Stoik—Vienna	[65]
2	Augmented Reality UJI (ARUJI)	Mobile	AR guiding app for the students and visitors around the University of Jaume I and available for Android devices as an unsigned application	Francisco Ramos, Sergio Trilles, Joaquín Torres-Sospedra, and Francisco J. Perales—Malaysia	[66]
3	Green Living Augmented + virtual ReAlity (GLARA)	Mobile	Microclimatic effects	Fluxguide—Slovenia	[67]
4	Smart [AR] Mini-Application	Mobile	Digital placemaking app	Samaneh Sanaeipoor; Khashayar Hojjati Emami—Romania	[68]
5	City 3D-AR	Web/ Mobile	Provide 3D object placement in real space for enhanced visualization	Arnis Cirulisa, Kristaps Brigis Brigmanisb—Latvia.	[42]
6	Junaio	Web/ Mobile	Create, explore and share information in a completely new way using augmented reality	Metaio—web browser used in many countries, Latvia, Spain, etc.	[42,69]
7	Change Explorer	Watch/mobile/web	A smartphone app that notifies the public when they are close to an area that has plans for redevelopment	Alexander Wilson—UK	[70]
8	In-Citu AR	Mobile	City Governments. Make urban development accessible and visible using AR, city-wide	Dana Chermesh-Reshef—US	[71]
9	CitySense App	Mobile	Co-creation of buildings, spaces	H2020 European Projects—Italy	[72]
10	Augmented Reality Participatory Platform (ARPP)	Mobile	Platform uses mobile augmented reality (M-AR) to engage residents, particularly in under-resourced communities, in identifying the design improvements necessary to enhance neighborhood walkability	Saeed Ahmadi Oloonabadi, Perver Baran—US, UK, Netherlands, Germany	[62]
11	Tinmith-Metro	Mobile	Visualisation of designed buildings	Thomas, Piekarski, and Gunther	[63]
12	StudierStubeES Software (StbES)	Mobile	Tracking and visualisation framework	Schmalstieg and Wagner	[63]

Table 1. *Cont.*

No	AR Application	Type	Focus	Developer	Reference
13	City View AR	Mobile	Disaster Visualization—Earthquake	Mark Billinghurst, Gun Lee, Jason Mill, Rob Lindeman, Adrian Clark, Thammathip Piumsomboon, Rory Clifford, Shunsuke Fukuden—Austrailia	[73]
14	Architeque—3D and AR	Mobile	Platform for Product Presentations in 3D and Augmented Reality	Architeque LLC—Germany	[74]
15	Vidente	Mobile	Demonstrating underground infrastructure virtualization in the field	Schall & Mendez	[63]
16	Urban Sketcher	Computer Based	Users can directly alter the real scene by sketching 2D images which are then applied to the 3D surfaces of the augmented scene	Sareika & Schmalstieg	[63]
17	Wikitude	Mobile	M-AR application which captures images from the surrounding environment (e.g., sights, restaurants, streets, and shops) and displays relevant information, on the screen of the mobile device	Wikitude GmbH—Athens Greece	[42,75]
18	Nokia city lens	Mobile	Uses your device's camera to display nearby restaurants, stores, and other notable locations in augmented reality style	Andrew Webster	[42]
19	ARQuake game	Computer Based	ARQuake is an Augmented Reality (AR)version of the popular Quake game. Augmented Reality is the overlaying of computer-generated information onto the real world	Thomas & Piekarski—Austrailia	[76]
20	Archeoguide	Mobile	Augmented Reality based Cultural Heritage On-site GUIDE	Vlahakis, Ioannidis, Karigiannis, Tsotros, Gounaris, Stricker, Gleue, Daehne & Almeida—Italy	[65]
21	Mentira	Mobile	Example of location-based M-AR for Albuquerque city. The purpose of the game is learning Spanish as a foreign language and addresses visitors among others	Prof. Chris Holden, Prof. Julie Sykes—Albuquerque	[77]
22	LocatAR	Mobile	Personal tour guide using location data to identify points of interest in AR	Chowdhury & Iqbal—Bangladesh & Pakistan	[78]
23	Frequency 1550	Mobile	City mobile game enabling students to learn about the history of Amsterdam	Montessori Scholengemeenschap Amsterdam, IVLOS, Uva -ILO, OSB Open Schoolgemeenschap, Bijlmer—Amsterdam	[75]

Table 1. *Cont.*

No	AR Application	Type	Focus	Developer	Reference
24	Dow Day	Mobile	Uses a journalistic narration genre and player takes the role of a news reporter and investigate the different perceptions of virtual characters who participated in protests against Dow Chemical Corporation for making napalm for the war in 1967	Aris Games—Vietnam	[75]
25	Road of Rhodes game		A game application which introduces the user in the cultural history of the island, and it was created using the ARIS authoring tool	Aris Games—Greece	[75]
26	CityScope	Mobile	Community engagement platform	MIT Media Lab's Changing Places Group (CPG)	[79]
27	Urban CoBuilder	Mobile	Outdoor urban simulation tool based on AR	Hyekyung Imottesjo, Jaan-Henrik Kai—Germany	[80]
28	EduPARK	Mobile	Use image-based AR, with marker-based tracking, to display mainly botanical content	Lúcia Pombo, Margarida Morais Marques—Portugal	[81]
29	ARGarden	Mobile	Enabling AR handheld device with multi-user interaction to create 3D outdoor designs	F E Fadzli, M A Mohd Yusof, A W Ismail, M S Hj Salam and N Aismail—Malaysia	[82]
30	Vítica	Mobile	Reactivation of Cisneros Market Square's cultural heritage and its surroundings using GPS and augmented reality	Mauricio Hincapi, Christian Díaz, Maria-Isabel Zapata-Cardenas, Henry de Jesus Toro Rios, Dalia Valencia, David Güemes-Castorena	[83]
31	Magical Park	Mobile	Encourages children to explore the park and run around, by engaging them in games played inside a blended virtual environment	GEO AR Games	[84]
32	Minecraft Earth	Mobile	This game brings the blocky construction set into the physical world. Minecraft Earth users do not pursue any specific goal; they can merely create, build, and explore in freedom while playing alone or cooperatively in a real territory or in an environment created by the players	Mojang Studios in 2009	[84]
33	Geocaching	Web Based/	This high-tech treasure hunting game, users hide a cache (typically a small waterproof container) in some location and post its coordinates along with some clues on the Internet	Stuart Aldrich, Erika Zhou, Thomas M., Thomas Manoka, Ruhais Li	[84]

Despite advancements, AR applications face critical limitations. High production costs restrict accessibility and scalability for community-driven initiatives [85]. Technical challenges such as battery drain, GPS inaccuracies, and network failures compromise AR reliability in dynamic outdoor environments, for an example in EduPARK App [81].

Marker-based tracking is often less effective in natural settings, where moving elements and sunlight interference hinder performance [86]. Moreover, AR tools frequently focus on visualization overactive co-creation of public spaces, limiting their utility in placemaking. Inclusivity remains another major concern, with barriers such as digital literacy, device accessibility, and technological complexity marginalizing underrepresented voices in participatory processes, for an example the Urban Co Builder AR tool [80]. Privacy concerns and dependency on high-quality data further complicate AR implementation [64].

To fully harness AR's potential, several key challenges must be addressed. Enhancing accessibility through affordable, intuitive solutions compatible with common devices and resolving connectivity issues is essential for real-time collaboration. Developing standardized frameworks for AR tools that integrate features for continuous community feedback can bridge the gap between visualization and active participation. Furthermore, addressing technical performance issues, such as GPS reliability and marker tracking, will improve AR's applicability in diverse urban contexts.

2.3. *Placemaking and AR*

AR has the potential to enhance user engagement in placemaking by overlaying digital elements onto physical environments that enrich their interaction and understanding of the space [15]. In addition, AR fosters place-based storytelling and community engagement by integrating digital artworks with public spaces, facilitating community-driven placemaking and creating meaningful connections to the space [27].

As placemaking is a multifaceted process that transforms public spaces into meaningful places, the concept is built around three primary attributes: sociability, physical setting, and image [13,87]. Sociability refers to the degree to which a place promotes interpersonal relationships and social interactions. The environment's layout and design determine the physical setting, which makes sure the area is safe, usable, and accessible. A space character and emotional appeal are derived from its identity, history, and aesthetic attributes. Together, these attributes contribute to a place's overall sense of belonging, functionality, and emotional significance, playing a crucial role in creating spaces that serve the needs of the community.

2.3.1. Sociability and M-AR

The sociability aspect of placemaking emphasizes the promotion of social interactions in public settings. Placemaking seeks to establish situations that facilitate engagement, communication, and relationship-building among individuals. AR technology amplifies social interaction by enabling users to engage with their environment in a more dynamic and immersive manner [88]. By using AR applications, the users have the ability to co-design the space with diverse activities that might be missing in the existing situation and create more social interactions in co-designing one space (play area, seating, visual appeal). Further, it fosters social cohesion by providing immersive, interactive experiences that enhance individuals' understanding and connection with their environment and one another in a more engaging way [17,25]. The connectedness and inclusiveness of placemaking enabled by collaborative designs, AR allows communities to express their interests and unique identities for combating social isolation [88].

2.3.2. Physical Setting and M-AR

The physical setting attribute in placemaking involves the design of the space to ensure it is functional, accessible, and welcoming [13]. A well-designed physical space promotes comfort, safety, and usability, which are essential for encouraging people to engage with it. M-AR technology enhances the physical setting by allowing users to visualize proposed changes in real time and interact with 3D models of the space in a more flexible way. This helps community members and planners understand how new designs will look and feel in the real world, leading more informed decision-making. With AR, public spaces can be tested and adjusted before implementation, ensuring they meet the community's needs and enhance usability [25].

2.3.3. Image and M-AR

The image of a place is deeply tied to its identity, which emerges from cultural and social engagement, as well as emotional connections [89] It encompasses the visual attributes of the environment, as well as the memories and associations it evokes in the people who use it. AR plays a significant role in enhancing the image of public spaces by integrating cultural, historical, and artistic elements through digital overlays [90,91]. By providing an interactive platform for displaying local history, art, and cultural narratives, AR helps strengthen the emotional connection between the community and the space. It also enables residents to visualize how proposed changes will impact the image of the area, ensuring that new designs align with the cultural and symbolic significance of the place [17]. Through AR, communities can actively participate in shaping the image of their environment, contributing to a more meaningful and inclusive placemaking process.

3. Research Design

This research utilizes a systematic approach consisting of four key phases. As shown in Figure 1, initially, a background analysis provides a fundamental comprehension of planning methods and formulates the research hypothesis. Secondly, an examination of applications based on literature highlights technological and scientific deficiencies to anchor the study in relevant results. The development and testing of application encompass iterative design, production, and evaluation with various stakeholder groups, ensuring the practical validation of AR tools for placemaking.

3.1. Background Analysis

This phase entails performing a brief literature analysis to examine existing planning and design methods, encompassing conventional as well as contemporary tools. To guarantee thorough coverage, pertinent keywords such as public participation, urban planning, and participatory tools were employed to search academic databases, including Google Scholar, ScienceDirect, and Scopus. The hypothesis, "AR applications are effective in placemaking", was derived from a brief literature review that identified gaps in community engagement tools and approaches in the current placemaking process. It also considered the increasing use of M-AR across various sectors to enhance community participation. This study aims to test the hypothesis to determine whether AR can improve community engagement in placemaking.

3.2. Literature-Based Application Review

The literature review concentrated on discovering AR applications pertinent to participatory urban planning by the utilization of certain keywords, including 'Participation', 'Augmented Reality', 'Planning', and 'Public Spaces'. The criteria for selecting research papers were restricted to peer-reviewed articles, journal publications, and conference proceedings authored in English. Grey literature, book chapters, and non-English language publications were excluded. Skim reading was initially conducted, followed by a full reading of the main body, and papers lacking AR and placemaking content were subsequently excluded.

Academic databases like Google Scholar, Scopus, and ScienceDirect were employed to guarantee thorough coverage in the search. Furthermore, the snowballing technique was employed to broaden the review's scope. This involved scrutinizing reference lists (backward snowballing) and evaluating citations (forward snowballing) to uncover supplementary articles of interest.

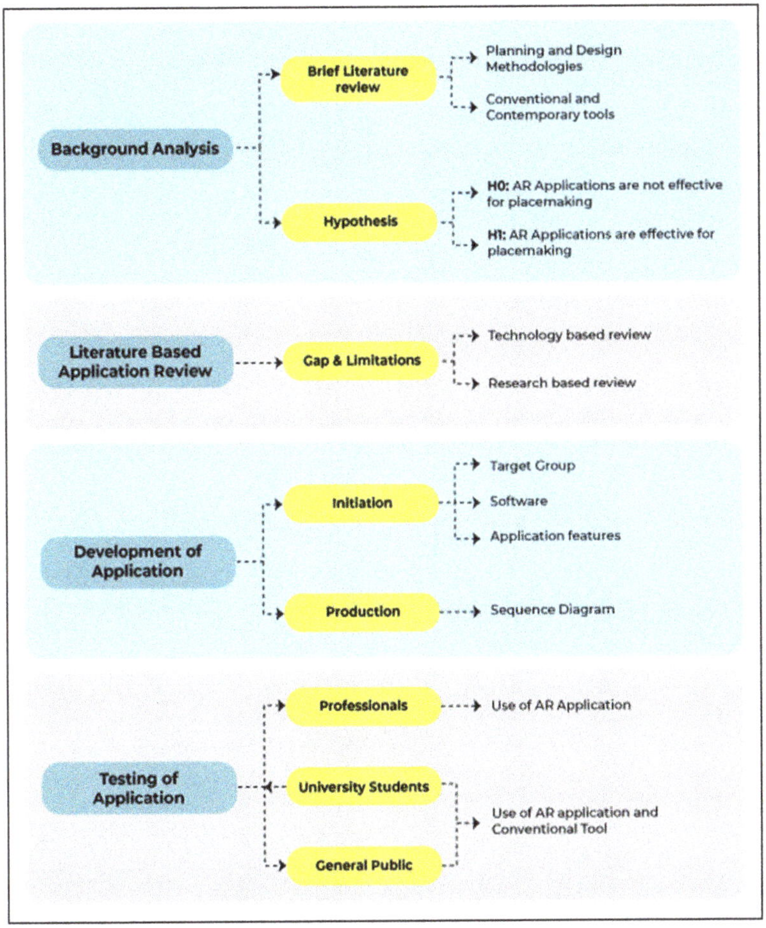

Figure 1. Methodology flowchart.

A total of 33 AR applications were discovered, of which only 13 expressly focused on participatory urban planning components, including traffic planning, disaster visualization, infrastructure planning, and digital placemaking. However, the remaining 20 AR applications show the potential of using AR for community engagement, enhanced user interaction through real-time visualization, and user experience in various other sectors. Therefore, all the applications identified using the keywords were included in the study.

Table 1 provides an overview of 33 AR applications, categorizing them by type (Mobile/Web), focus areas, and developers. The majority of these applications are mobile-based, while a few are web-based. Developers range from individual creators to research institutions, reflecting a wide array of AR innovations across various sectors, including urban planning, tourism, education, and business. The results underscore considerable deficiencies and constraints in the existing realm of AR tools for urban planning, establishing the foundation for the development of the CityBuildAR—application. Current AR applications designed for placemaking encountered technological issues, including location retrieval failures, the absence of a personalized user platform, and restricted functionalities in certain applications, such as displaying information on screen and enabling comments instead of facilitating substantial contributions to placemaking.

3.3. Development of Application

The development of the application consisted of two phases: initiation and production, as mentioned in the Figure 1. In the initiation phase, identifying the target group, selecting software and developing the core-features of the app was completed. The production phase involved with creating the sequence diagram outlining the entire concept of the application, including both front-end and back-end operations.

3.3.1. Target Group

The primary target demographic for this application is the general public. The program seeks to be user-friendly and accessible, enabling non-technical users to interact with its features and meaningfully participate to urban planning processes. To ensure user-friendliness, the app features an intuitive interface with simple navigation similar to any other basic crowdsourcing app, and clear instructions through the process to reduce the learning curve for first-time users in the future. In addition, accessibility is enhanced by optimizing the app for common mobile devices, such as smartphones and tablets, without requiring high-end hardware or specialized equipment. The spatial literacy is addressed through the incorporation of simple, interactive visual aids that simplify complex spatial data, making it easier for users to comprehend. Furthermore, the app enhances users' understanding of existing spatial context by providing accurate scale representations, and high-definition virtual objects, enabling a more realistic design experience.

3.3.2. Software

The application is made using Unity 3D, selected for its intuitive interface, which is suitable for novice developers. Unity's capability to export projects across several platforms, such as iOS, Android, and the web, renders it appropriate for engaging a wide audience. The program encompasses essential tools for developing AR-based apps, including the AR Foundation package, which offers comprehensive support for AR functions. Moreover, 3D models necessary for the application were procured from the Unity Asset Store, facilitating rapid prototyping and development.

The user engagement is enhanced through the design choices available in Unity 3D and AR foundation such as integrating real-time AR visualization, intuitive user interfaces, and especially object placement in the real world. Additionally, user-friendly navigation and the ability to customize options are available to ensure equal accessibility and understanding for both experienced and novice users.

3.3.3. Application Features

The application includes various features to facilitate participatory urban planning and placemaking. The study identified crucial placemaking elements, including trees, benches, tables, lamp posts, dustbins, and bushes, as determined by the literature review. Therefore, a similar set of elements were incorporated in the CityBuildAR app as shown in the Figure 2. These components enable users to construct and see urban environments interactively in AR. The application allows users to record photographs of their designs, facilitating documentation and sharing of their ideas. This feature improves user involvement and facilitates collaborative planning by offering a visual documentation of suggested ideas.

Figure 2. Used placemaking elements in the application.

3.3.4. Production

The production phase entails developing the application prototype, built specifically for the Android operating system. The application was created utilizing Unity Engine version 2021.3.15f1, capitalizing on its strong features for AR development. Multiple Unity packages were included to facilitate AR functionality: AR Foundation version 4.2.9, ARCore XR Plugin version 4.2.9, ARKit XR Plugin version 4.2.9 and XR Interaction Toolkit version 2.0.4.

These tools permitted the incorporation of sophisticated AR features and guaranteed interoperability among AR-capable devices. Sequence diagrams were employed in the development process to delineate user interactions and application operations, hence facilitating a seamless and intuitive user experience. Figure 3 illustrates the Unity 3D interface, which enabled the integration of AR features in the app development process.

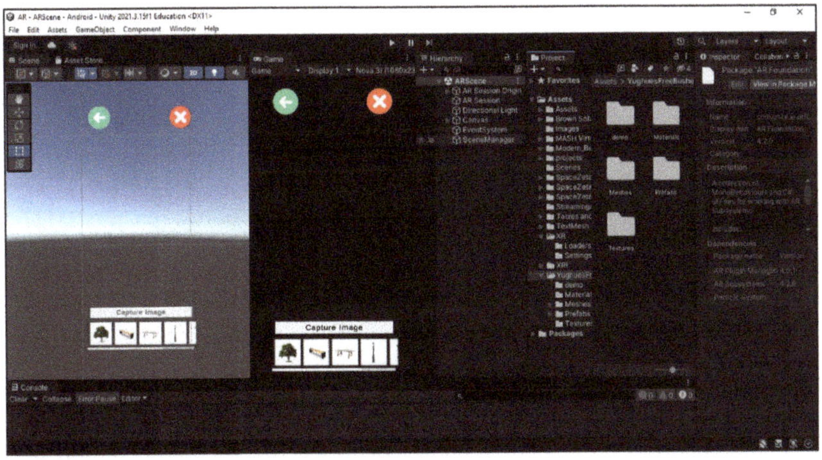

Figure 3. Unity 3D interface.

The app sequence diagram was initially created, followed by the development of the app prototype based on it.

The author initially created the sequence diagram on top of the deficiencies and constraints identified from the reviewed 33 AR application. The 'CityBuildAR' application was built to address these concerns, functioning as a crowdsourcing platform that allows users to create personal accounts, join up or log in, and participate in placemaking by constructing locations according to their preferences. "CityBuildAR" integrates placemaking elements such as trees, benches, lamp posts, etc. directly into the AR environment, enabling users to create interactive designs and save them to a cloud-based system to review further by professional urban planners. Therefore, this app enables community-driven placemaking by leveraging smartphones as the only required device.

Figure 4 illustrates that the application was designed in three primary phases: user registration/login, placemaking utilizing provided elements, and saving the design for reference by other users or professionals.

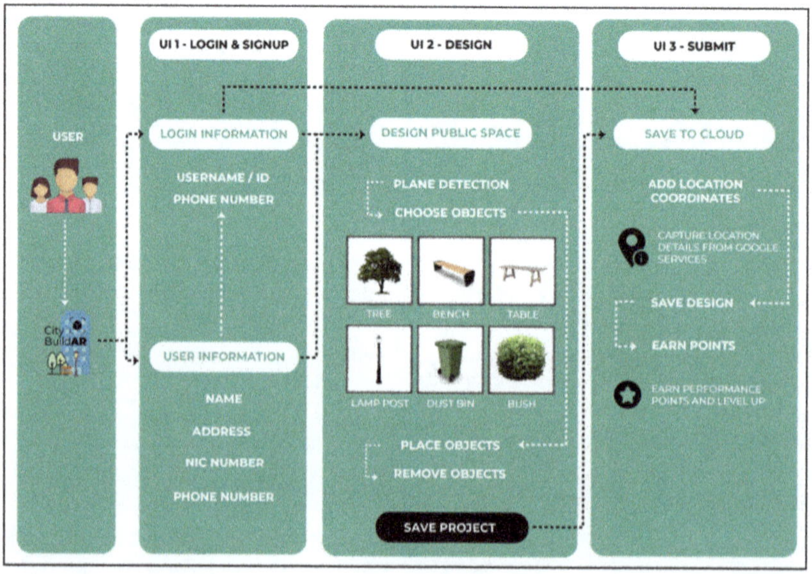

Figure 4. Sequence diagram.

The prototype development has been finalized as shown in the Figure 5, and all user interfaces have been built to improve the app's user-friendliness. The colors selected for the user interfaces and the intended placemaking components aim to increase interaction with the application.

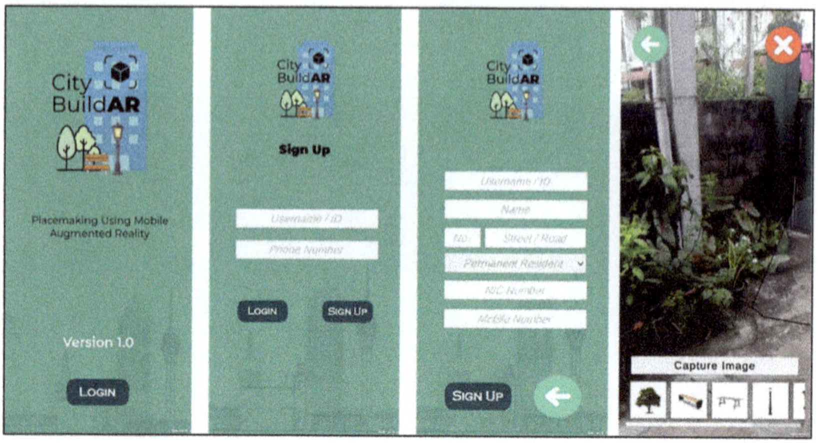

Figure 5. Prototype development.

In the subsequent phase, a preliminary demonstration was executed to evaluate the application's functions, its compatibility with the Sri Lankan setting, and the efficacy of employing a M-AR application as a placemaking instrument.

3.4. Testing the Application

The application underwent testing with three separate user groups: professionals, university students, and the general public. The rationale for selecting these three groups is based on the varying levels of knowledge and experience related to placemaking. Professionals were selected for the test because they practice placemaking in both academic settings and real-world contexts. Meanwhile, university students represent a transitional group where they learn about theories under academic modules and await to apply them gradually. Comparatively, the general public lacks formal knowledge or practice regarding placemaking concepts, with their ideas influenced by day-to-day experiences. Including a diverse participant profile enables a comprehensive outcome regarding placemaking enabling a wide range of perspectives.

To attract a broader audience, all individuals interested in placemaking using M-AR were encouraged to join through a Facebook event (Figure 6), and further information was disseminated via WhatsApp groups. The open café area of the University of Moratuwa (Figure 7) was chosen as the location of the study, offering a familiar and approachable setting for participants. Participants' consent to participate in the demonstration was obtained from everyone before engaging in the activities. All the participants were well-informed that the data collected would be used solely for research purposes and assured that none of their personal information would be shared.

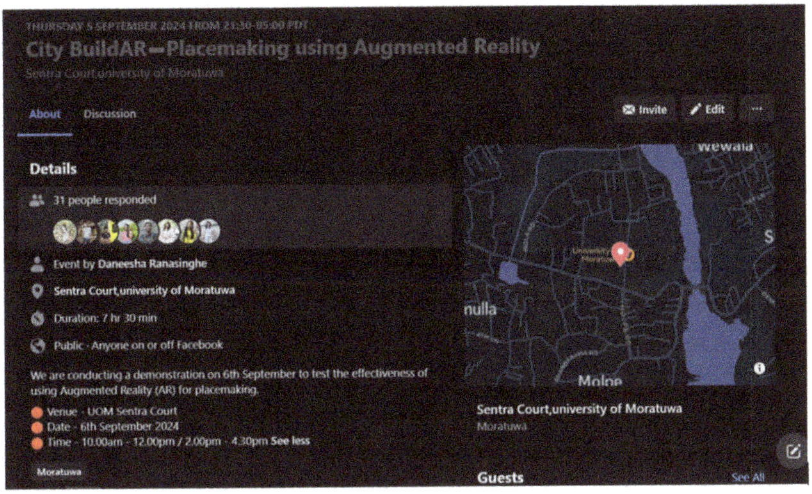

Figure 6. Invitation through Facebook.

The study was performed in two sessions. Session A was for the university students and the general public. Session B was for the professionals. During session A, a registration form was given to the participants, which collected the details of participant's age, gender, present role/status at the university, and subject of study/profession. The form collected data regarding their expertise and experience in placemaking and AR, their acquaintance with the study location, their readiness to utilize AR for placemaking purposes, and their preference in sketching —hand sketch, use of 3D SketchUp software, or other. Then, as demonstrated in Figure 8a,b, they were asked to design the open café area of the university using the preferred sketching method.

Figure 7. Case study area.

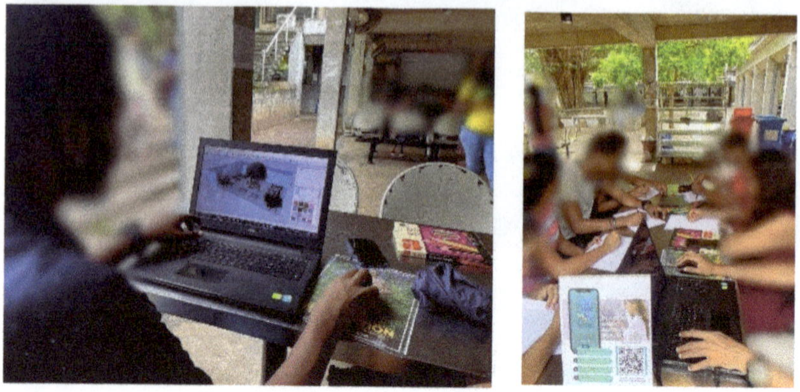

(a) (b)

Figure 8. Designing using: (a) Sketchup Modelling and (b) Hand-sketching.

Secondly, they were asked to use the City BuildAR application to redesign the same area. Finally, feedback was collected. An overview of the feedback form is given in Table 2.

Unlike session A, session B did not go with an initial sketching exercise as all the professionals are experienced architects or urban planners with sketching skills. Therefore, the CityBuildAR app was directly introduced to them, and they were asked to design the open café areas. Similarly, the feedback form was given to professionals at the end the session.

Figure 9 shows some examples of user engagement in designing the UOM cafeteria during the user demonstration of the CityBuildAR app. As shown in Figure 9, some participants gathered as groups to discuss the requirements and interests while designing, and some of them individually designed the space.

Table 2. Overview of the feedback form.

No	Question Type	Question	Metric
Q1	Closed-ended	How comfortable were you using hand sketching (2D drawing) techniques for placemaking?	5-Point Likert Scale
Q2	Mixed	What are the positives you experienced while using hand sketching (2D drawing) for placemaking?	Multiple checkboxes and text
Q3	Mixed	What challenges did you face while using hand sketching (2D drawing) for placemaking?	Multiple checkboxes and text
Q4	Closed-ended	How comfortable were you using SketchUp software (3D modelling) techniques for placemaking?	5-Point Likert Scale
Q5	Mixed	What are the positives you experienced while SketchUp software (3D modelling) for placemaking?	Multiple checkboxes and text
Q6	Mixed	What challenges did you face while using hand sketching (2D drawing)/SketchUp software (3D modelling) for placemaking?	Multiple checkboxes and text
Q7	Closed-ended	To what extent do you think AR is effective in visualizing and understanding placemaking concepts?	5-Point Likert Scale
Q8	Closed-ended	How easy was it to navigate and use the AR application for placemaking?	5-Point Likert Scale
Q9	Mixed	What challenges did you face, and positives did you experience while using the AR app for placemaking?	Multiple checkboxes and text
Q10	Closed-ended	Compared to hand sketching/3D modelling software, do you find AR to be a better tool for placemaking?	5-Point Likert Scale
Q11	Closed-ended	Do you believe that AR can enhance your involvement in urban planning and placemaking?	5-Point Likert Scale
Q12	Closed-ended	Rate your interaction and experience with "Activities—Diversity, People's activities, Cafes, etc." during placemaking activity using these tools.	3-Point Likert Scale
Q13	Closed-ended	Rate your interaction and experience with "Physical Setting—Human and Building scale, walkability, accessibility, etc." during placemaking activity using these tools.	3-Point Likert Scale
Q14	Closed-ended	Rate your interaction and experience with "Imageability—attractiveness, physical comfort, attachment, etc." during placemaking activity using these tools.	3-Point Likert Scale
Q15	Closed-ended	Rate app features according to your experience	3-Point Likert Scale
Q16	Open-ended	Are there any features you believe should be added or modified in the AR app?	Text
Q17	Closed-ended	How willing are you to use AR applications for placemaking activities in the future?	5-Point Likert Scale

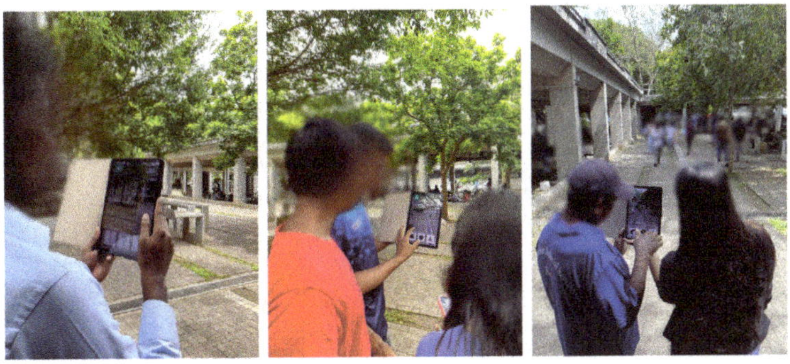

Figure 9. Users engaging in placemaking using the CityBuildAR app.

4. Analysis and Results

This section provides an overview of the results of the user demonstration conducted under study, followed by a comprehensive image analysis and an opinion analysis to highlight the effectiveness of using CityBuildAR for placemaking.

4.1. Overview

Figure 10 indicates the participant breakdown including the three participant groups—university students, professionals, and the general public—considered in the study. 23 undergraduates between the 18–34 age group participated in the session A. As shown in Figure 10 below, the participants were from different educational backgrounds, including urban planning (26%), architecture (6%), business studies (8%), engineering (4%), and quantity surveying (2%). The majority of the participants were somewhat familiar (54.5%), and the rest of the participants were very familiar (21.3%) with the placemaking concept as most of them heard about it through different methods such as academic modules or studies (80%), from professionals or authorities (32%), and also from social media (40%), which indicates that some of them were exposed to the concept via multiple methods. In comparison, 24.2% of the participants were unfamiliar with the concept.

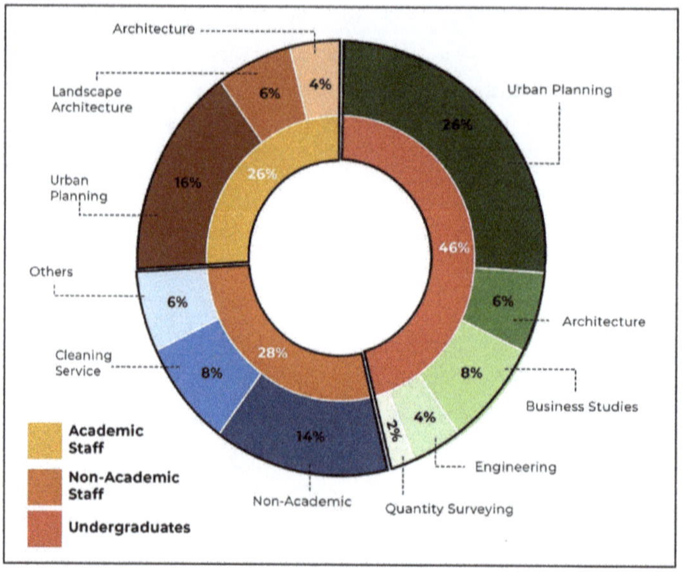

Figure 10. Participants' Profile.

The non-academic staff members, including technical assistants, drivers, and the cleaning staff, attended session A to represent the general public's perspective on using AR for placemaking. As indicated in Figure 10, a total of 14 individuals, including seven non-academic members (14%), four cleaning service members (8%), and three others (6%) aged 35–54 participated in the demonstration. Among them, only three participants heard about placemaking, and only one participant engaged in placemaking activity by coordinating a placemaking workshop.

Academic staff from urban planning, architecture, landscape architecture, and engineering fields were taken as professionals to evaluate the CityBuildAR application for designing the university cafeteria at the University of Moratuwa in session B. A total of 13 academic staff members participated in the demonstration, with the majority representing the fields of urban planning (eight participants—16%), landscape architecture (three participants—6%), and architecture (two participants—4%), respectively. According to their feedback, a majority of them familiar with placemaking (84.6%) through academic modules (68.1%), from professionals and authorities in the field (81.3%), through stakeholder meetings and workshops (56.3%), and some of them through media (18.8%).

The professionals' role in the previous placemaking activities was described as actively contributing to the design and planning of green and recreational spaces by integrating community input, providing technical guidance for infrastructure improvements, and collaborating with stakeholders through workshops and urban planning projects, refined through academic modules and practical experiences. Commonly used placemaking methodologies were participatory mapping, stakeholder meetings, and discussions, while the tools used to design through hand sketching, AutoCAD 2024, SketchUp 2024 modeling, physical models, and GIS (10.8.2) tools.

The participants' familiarity with the selected location (university cafeteria) for the study was evaluated. The majority of the university students (78.8%—18), general public (92.86%—13), and professionals—(84.6%—11) who participated were familiar with the location, while the rest of the participants also responded as somewhat familiar with it. The university students and professionals responded to the use of cafeteria space for dining, gathering, using ATM, and other recreational activities, while the general public responded to dining and cleaning the space. Additionally, the willingness to engage in placemaking through AR has been considered, and the majority (55.9%) of university students were very interested in it, while the professionals (52.6%) and general public (51.5%) responded as somewhat interested in it.

4.2. Comparing Hand Sketching, Software with CityBuildAR

Figures 11 and 12, shows the responses for Q1–Q3, which examined the university students' opinions in using hand sketches in visualizing and designing the open café areas during session A.

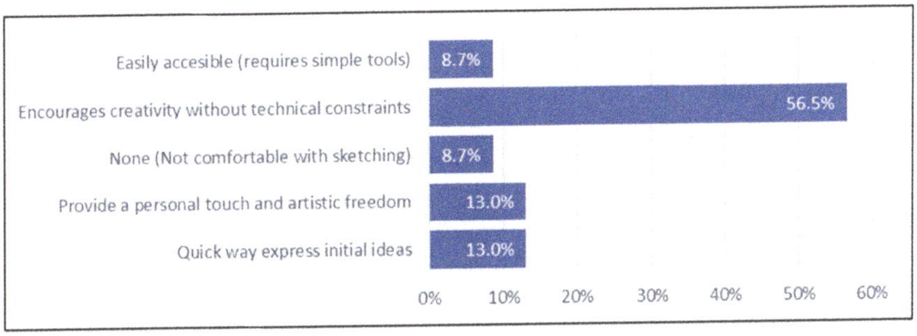

Figure 11. Positive aspects of using hand sketching for placemaking—university students.

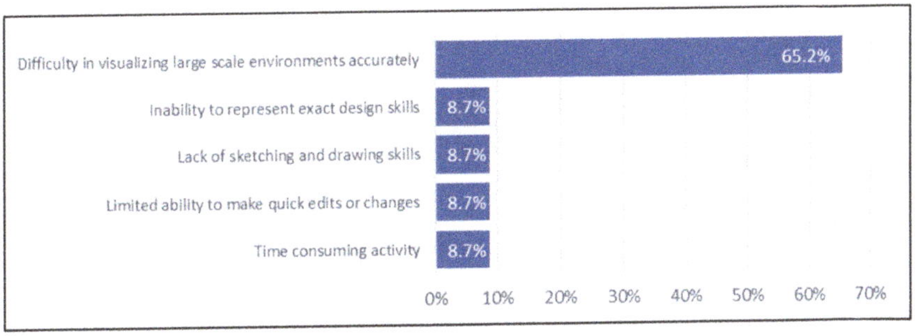

Figure 12. Challenges of using hand sketching for placemaking—university students.

Accordingly, most university students selected the hand sketching option and most felt comfortable (43.5%), while some were uncomfortable (17.4%) with sketching. However, 60.9% of them identified sketching as an accessible method that provides artistic freedom and encourages creativity without any technical constraints (56.5%), as shown in Figure 11. Nevertheless, as shown in Figure 12, participants highlighted challenges such as difficulty in visualization (65.2%), limitations with making edits to the design (60.9%), time-consuming (47.8%), and lack of drawing skills (69.6%).

Q4–Q6 examined university students' feedback for 3D modelling using the SketchUp software during the study. As shown in Figure 13, even though university students identified the positive aspects of 3D modelling compared to hand sketching such as the ability to visualize design from different perspectives (60.9%), facilitate quick adjustments and changes (73.9%), and support detailed elements (texture, lighting, etc.) (60.9%), they mentioned the challenges they faced while using Sketch Up 3D modelling at the demo as shown in Figure 14.

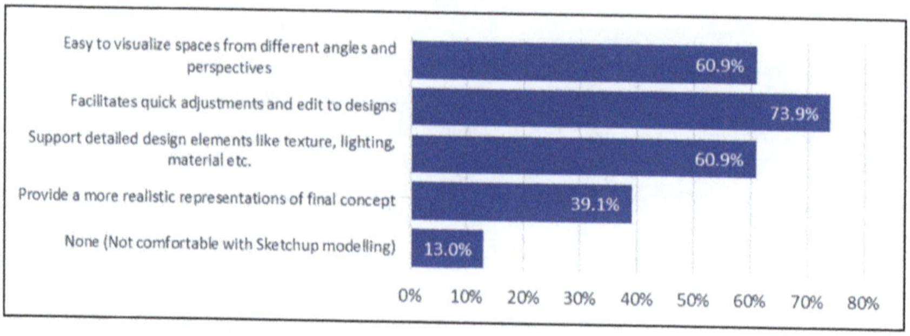

Figure 13. Positive aspects of using 3D modelling—university students.

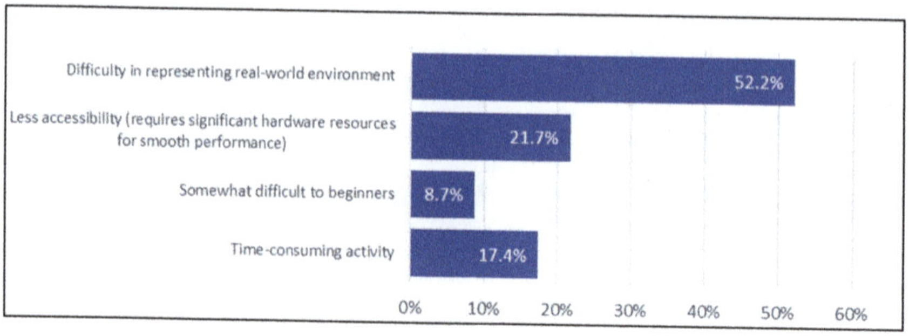

Figure 14. Challenges of using 3D modelling—university students.

However, none of the participants from the general public category were comfortable with two alternatives provided at session A— hand sketching and SketchUp 3D modeling. As indicated in Figure 15, most of them responded about lack of personal drawing skills and identified it as a time-consuming activity. Further, they have never participated in placemaking activities using these tools, which was a challenge for them.

Although the study initially excluded Session A for professionals with placemaking experience, assuming their proficiency in sketching, the participants highlighted challenges stemming from their limited drawing skills to effectively illustrate and customize designs—Figure 16. Additionally, 15.4% of professionals emphasized the need for specialized software for designing, noting that existing tools pose challenges when used for placemaking.

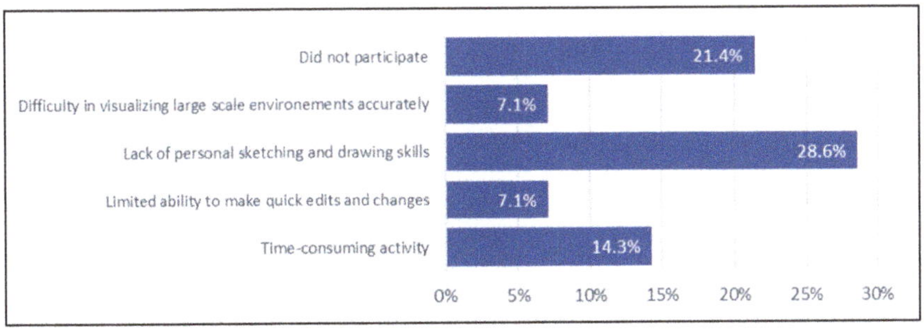

Figure 15. Challenges of using hand sketching for placemaking—general public.

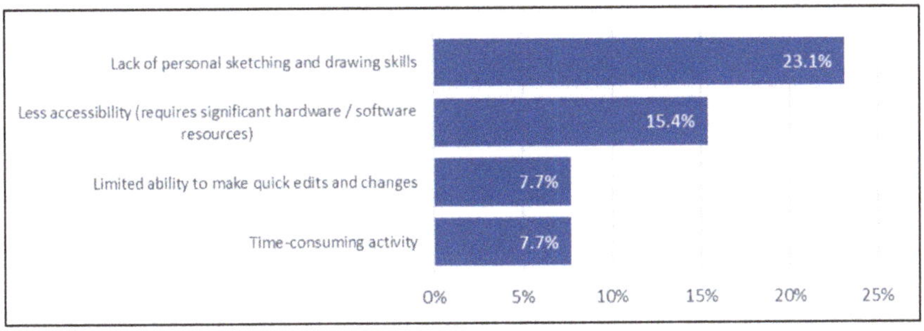

Figure 16. Challenges of using existing tools for placemaking—professionals.

4.3. Placemaking with CityBuildAR

In the feedback form shared after session A, Q7-Q13 discussed the participants' experience regarding placemaking using CityBuildAR.

The university students' feedback indicated that the majority considered the AR application easy (43.5%) or very easy (17.4%) to navigate and use for placemaking, while the rest of them answered neutrally (39.1%). As shown in Figure 17, the ability to visualize designs in real time, the immersive experience in the real context, and ability to design multiple scenarios within a limited time were identified as positives. Yet, according to Figure 18, University students identified technical issues with the app, including app instability, loading, and performance issues, as well as difficulties in aligning virtual objects with the real-world environment while using the AR app for placemaking.

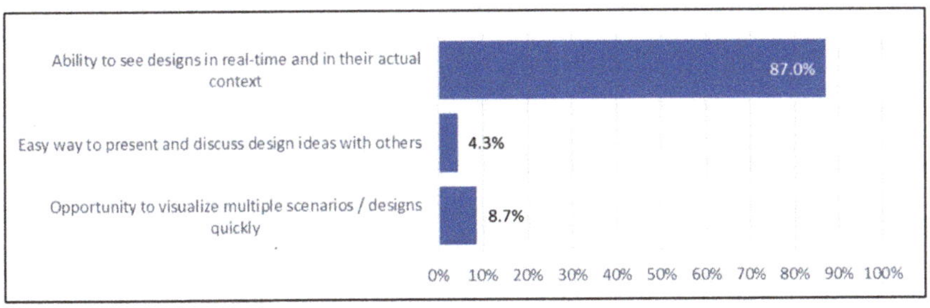

Figure 17. Positive aspects of using AR—university students.

Out of 14 individuals which represented the general public group, seven have used AR apps previously for gaming (Pokemon Go—developed by Niantic, Inc. software company in San Francisco, California, USA), advertisements (Dilmah Tea—Sri Lankan Beverage

Company in Peliyagoda, Western Province, SL), (Coca-Cola—AR billboard for Christmas in Finland), and other (University Vesak Lantern App—A product of Department of Computer Science Engineering, University of Moratuwa, Sri Lanka). All 14 participants agreed that the ease of use and accessibility of AR apps serves as a strong motivation to utilize AR in placemaking.

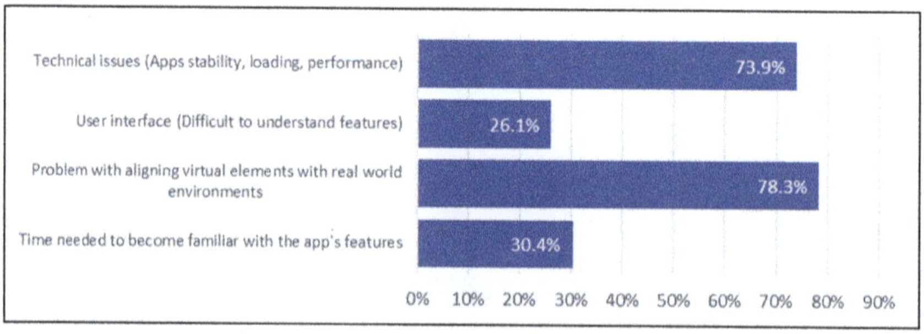

Figure 18. Challenges of using AR—university students.

As shown in Figure 19, the general public has identified using AR as an opportunity to see designs in real time, and it is easy to handle with minimal expertise and knowledge about the field. However, after using the CityBuildAR app, all of them have identified challenges as negatives, including the difficulty in understanding the app elements, and functionality (rotate, delete), and they need time to get familiar with the app before designing.

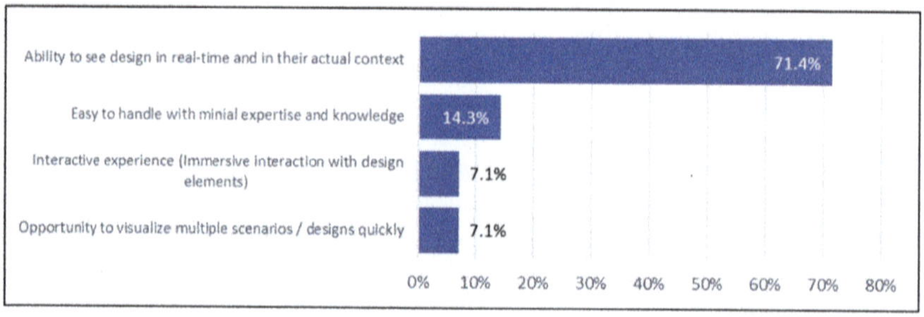

Figure 19. Positive aspects of using AR—general public.

Among the professionals who participated, a total of 10 has used AR apps previously for gaming, advertising, infrastructure project simulations, and storytelling (DEVAR app). Therefore, the motivating factors for professionals to use AR for placemaking has been identified as the ability to visualize the designs real-time, ability to design a space with limited skills, ease of use and accessibility and collaborative features of the app as indicated in Figure 20.

Nevertheless, after using the AR app the professionals responded with the challenges they faced, such as technical issues (app stability, loading, performance) and difficulty aligning virtual objects with the real ground situation, and most of them highlighted that they needed more time to be familiar with the app before starting the design. Overall, professionals evaluated the app's features, including user interface (colors, graphics), functionalities (rotate, remove), and design components (tables, chairs, trees, benches, garbage bins, etc.) as good (64.23%), poor (15.38%), and neutral (15.38%).

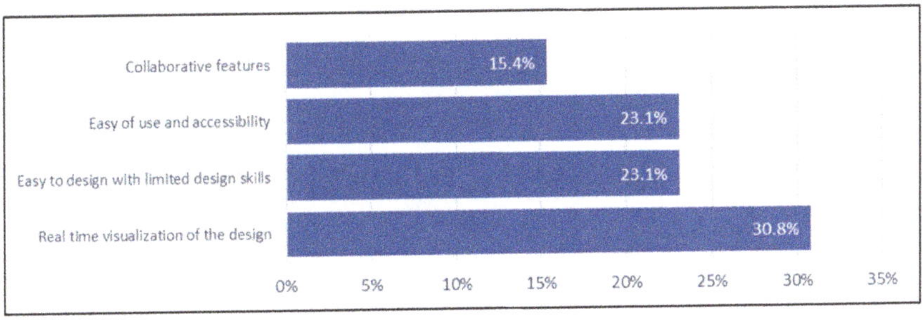

Figure 20. Motivations for using AR—professionals.

Based on the app demonstration conducted with three groups—professionals, university students, and the general public—it was observed that professionals mostly preferred existing tools such as 3D software over the AR application due to its limited features, which restrict the ability to create unique designs. However, university students identified AR as a more convenient tool for placemaking as it is easily accessible and does not require technical expertise or drawing skills. Also, it highlighted its ability to collaborate and visualize the design in real time. The general public indicated that using the AR app for placemaking is inclusive and accessible for everyone rather than the existing methodologies, but sometimes it can be limited due to the unavailability of a compatible smartphone to run the AR app. All three groups have responded that they need more time to get familiar with the app before starting designing and the app needs modifications, including more design elements and functionality (scaling, moving, etc.).

4.4. Image Analysis

Image analysis aims to identify similarities and differences in design methodologies among different groups and evaluate the impact of M-AR technology on design outputs. Figures 21–23 indicate the visualizations of university cafeteria designs created by the three groups during the app demonstration. Three designs from each participant group are included here to represent how the groups individually applied design elements, considered the existing context, and incorporated placemaking attributes.

As of Table 3 the designs were classified into three categories and evaluated according to certain criteria: use of element, functionality, user interaction, and incorporation of AR features. Table 3 presents a detailed breakdown of the element counts for each design criterion, providing insights into the specific elements utilized in every individual design.

Table 3 indicated that professionals used limited components in the designs such as one garbage can in all designs and only a few (15) lampposts, benches (37), and tables (10) as well. Comparatively, University students included more elements in the design such as trees (45), bushes (104), tables (26), benches (87), lampposts (35), and garbage bins (15). The general public added elements comparatively higher than professionals and lower than university students.

Greenery was added in seven (53.8%) designs of professions without changing the existing setting of the cafeteria. However, the university students' designs highlight their requirements such as more seating (100%) and lighting (82.6%) in the space. Use of shady trees is emphasized commonly in all designs, while the bushes have been placed for visual appeal. Comparatively, the general public's designs indicate familiar layouts, such as having seating under shades with garbage bins near to them that are replicating existing patterns. University students prioritized their requirements to gather in visually appealing and comfortable surroundings.

(a) (b) (c)

Figure 21. Exemplary visualizations completed using CityBuildAR by Professionals (**a**) Design 1; (**b**) Design 2; and (**c**) Design 3.

(a) (b) (c)

Figure 22. Exemplary visualizations completed using CityBuildAR by Undergraduate (**a**) Design 1; (**b**) Design 2; and (**c**) Design 3.

As shown in Table 3, the functionality, including seating, walking paths, lighting, and greenery, has been considered by the university students when designing, but when it comes to the general public, the functionality was comparatively not considered, because the existing paths were covered and used for the design and no shades were provided for the seating area. However, the university students prioritized visual appeal and comfort except for the existing real ground context, but the professionals highly considered the existing layout by not adding many elements in the design. The general public considered functionality by having usual requirements such as seating in this space.

(a) (b) (c)

Figure 23. Exemplary visualizations completed using CityBuildAR by General Public (**a**) Design 1; (**b**) Design 2; and (**c**) Design 3.

Table 3. Image analysis.

Criteria		Professional	University Student	General Public
Use of element	Tree	23 (1.77) [1]	43 (1.87)	33 (2.36)
	Bushes	55 (4.23)	104 (4.52)	30 (2.14)
	Table	10 (0.77)	26 (1.13)	13 (0.93)
	Benches	37 (2.85)	87 (3.78)	28 (2.00)
	Lamp posts	15 (1.15)	35 (1.52)	11 (0.79)
	Garbage bins	1 (0.08)	15 (0.65)	7 (0.50)
Functionality	Seating	Y—11, N—2	Y—23, N—0	Y—11, N—3
	Walking	Y—13, N—0	Y—17, N—6	Y—8, N—6
	Lighting	Y—7, N—6	Y—19, N—4	Y—8, N—6
	Greenery	Y—7, N—6	Y—20, N—3	Y—11, N—3
User Interaction	Physical Setting	Y—13, N—0, M—0	Y—23, N—0, M—0	Y—6, N—0, M—8
	Sociability	Y—10, N—0, M—3	Y—18, N—0, M—5	Y—2, N—4, M—8
	Imageability	Y—7, N—0, M—6	Y—21, N—0, M—2	Y—5, N—8, M—1
Incorporating AR features	Designing	Y—9, N—0, M—4	Y—23, N—0, M—0	Y—5, N—0, M—8
	Visualizing	Y—0, N—0, M—13	Y—23, N—0, M—0	Y—5, N—0, M—8

[1] Count (Mean), Y = Yes/ N = No/M = Moderate.

User interaction with the placemaking, and community engagement aspects while designing the space, were evaluated under the attributes of physical setting, sociability, and imageability. According to the analysis, professionals considered the existing setting more than attractiveness and physical and social comfort. However, university students have considered the physical setting, including aspects such as accessibility, walkability, climate comfort, and spatial characteristics. Additionally, visual appeal, attractiveness, and comfort, which represent imageability, were also highlighted in the designs. However, the general public group neglected the accessibility and walkability of space. University students considered the sociability aspect by incorporating density, diversity of space, and furniture availability, but the professionals did not add many inputs towards enhancing diversity or density to the place. The general public moderately considered sociability by incorporating density and functionality into the design but did not consider the imageability aspect in the designs.

All three groups—professionals, university students, and the general public—incorporated AR elements and features in designing and visualizing the space. University students used AR to create transformative and experimental designs while professionals focused on enhancing the existing layout with minimal alterations. However, compared to university students and professionals, the general public used fewer design elements and focused on familiar layouts resulting in simple visualizations.

This image analysis revealed diverse design methodologies influenced by participants' backgrounds and the role of AR as a placemaking tool to aid in visualizing the design ideas.

4.5. Opinion Analysis

The participants' feedback included insights replated to their placemaking exercise using the CityBuildAR app. Out of all the participants, 81% have expressed their insights. The study considered all the open-ended responses and classified them into three themes based on the response nature. Out of them, 43% have expressed positive sentiments about the app.

4.5.1. Ability to Visualize and Design with Limited Skills

Some participants identified the CityBuildAR app as an effective tool for visualizing, and it enabled users to design spaces with limited drawing skills, technical expertise, and less hardware/software requirements.

- Opinion 1—"I have limited drawing skills, so I usually engaged in collaborating with ideas as a group member while another member will visualize. But using this AR app I can do my own design by myself. But the list of elements and features should expand to make a unique design".
- Opinion 2—"I really liked the interface and elements of the app. It creates a nice design of myself with limited skills. Wish I had more time to get familiar with this app".
- Opinion 3—"Simple and effective for non-designers".

4.5.2. Impact on Creativity of Users

Majority of the participants indicated that the restricted elements and options available have constrained the individual design and unique qualities of one another. Additionally, the app crashes have interrupted the design process often.

- Opinion 4—"Great concept for enhancing placemaking through real-time visualization. However, the limited design options and occasional bugs limit its potential in professional landscape projects. Expanding its feature set would make it more versatile".
- Opinion 5—"App doesn't allow us to create & visualize unique designs. It generalizes the designs and with the given elements, it's limited to create my own design. Realtime visualization is interesting somehow".

- Opinion 6—"Expanding the range of features and addressing performance concerns would make it a highly effective tool for professional urban planning and participatory processes".

As indicated in the above opinions, the AR app has limited the creativity of participants and it requires modifications in the app elements, features and scaling to enhance the uniqueness of designs.

4.5.3. Technical Constraints

Apart from the limited features and elements mentioned above, a majority of them shared their opinion about the lack of time given to familiarize themselves with the app before designing. According to their responses, the app familiarity is significant to develop a proper design.

- Opinion 7—"App elements are difficult to understand in the beginning, needed assistance to understand. I had the ability to do a design for cafeteria using this app, which I wouldn't be able to do with sketching or other software".
- Opinion 8—"Expanding the range of features and addressing performance concerns would make it a highly effective tool for professional urban planning and participatory processes".
- Opinion 9—"Using app for designing is good for me because I have poor drawing skills. However, it is difficult to understand and design within this limited time given".

Participants' feedback highlighted the app potential as a placemaking tool specifically for enhanced engagement of communities in different levels of knowledge and expertise. However, as indicated in Figure 24, technical issues such as limited elements and difficulty in understanding at first need to be addressed to get more creative and unique designs.

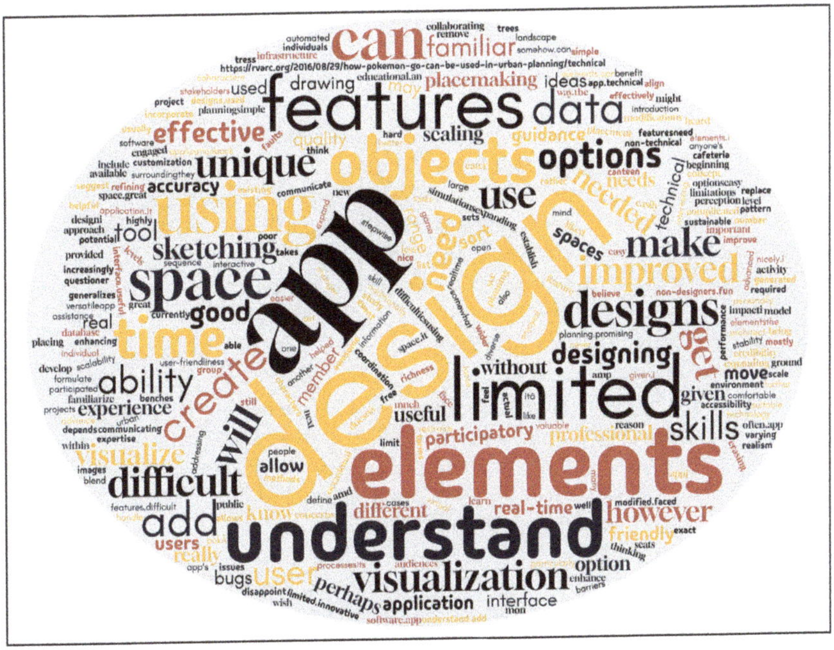

Figure 24. Word Cloud representing participant opinions.

5. Findings and Discussion

5.1. To What Extent Does the CityBuildAR App Bridge the Gap Between Professionals and the General Public in Placemaking?

The CityBuildAR app allows the general public to design and visualize public spaces using their mobile phones similar to a professional, which significantly enhances their ability to participate in placemaking. The conflict between community preferences and the preferred engagement techniques of the public has caused a lack of public participation in urban planning with existing conventional methods [92,93].

Furthermore, real-time visualization encourages users to redefine spatial designs with limited time and expertise because realistic visualizations are more effective than abstract presentations, especially when it comes to engaging a non-specialist audience like the general public [93]. AR models can influence people to participate in the planning process and to provide immediate feedback using AR [94,95]. Especially, CityBuildAR app enables users to engage in placemaking using high-tech software with limited technical expertise and experience, which enhances public participation in the process. Therefore, utilizing AR for placemaking has the potential to bridge the gap between planning practitioners and the general public when it comes to design and visualization. The use of technologically advanced applications (AR, VR) can support professionals in creating an inclusive and accessible participatory planning methodology for all citizens, including students [26,96].

Accordingly, the CityBuildAR app has the potential to support participatory planning and enhance stakeholder engagement, thereby facilitating the planning process of authorities. The app could be integrated into community-driven urban planning and regeneration projects, allowing the community to design and visualize their interests in real time and provide immediate feedback to the authorities. As an example, in Vienna, Austria, AR has been used for two urban planning projects to assess its effectiveness in participatory planning, and the results indicate that AR facilitated better communication between stakeholders and planners [55].

However, despite its advantages, the application reveals an important gap in the design process, which is the rationale for designs. During the app demonstration, the professionals considered the existing layout of the university cafeteria. They added features to the existing layout without replacing it or ignoring the existing setting because as professionals they prioritized the functionality and feasibility based on their knowledge and experience resulting in more grounded designs. In contrast, university students were innovative and transformative, and they ignored the existing setting in imposing their design. It shows that as undergraduates, they are often encouraged to think creatively, and according to their feedback, university students were more familiar with the AR tools and willing to experiment without any constraints. Comparatively, the general public used the app to visualize existing patterns and spatial layouts with minimum requirements, which reflects that using CityBuildAR for designing has been a complete experimental activity for them. It indicates that knowledge and expertise have a direct impact on the design when using CityBuildAR. Further, it highlights the app's flexibility to adapt and address the needs of different layers in the society in expressing their design thinking.

Overall, the CityBuildAR app allows professionals and the general public to equally engage in placemaking activities using the application and bridge the gap in terms of visualization and conceptualization. However, the app allows users to visualize their requirements and interests through design. Therefore, the designs are biased to each individual's personal preferences and in some cases, the design might not meet the significant placemaking attributes such as physical setting, imageability, and sociability. On some occasions, important aspects such as walkability, accessibility, comfort, and density of activities might not be considered as discussed under image analysis (Figures 20–22). The university students' designs and visualizations consist of a total transformative layout that requires the replacement of the existing elements (concrete pavements).

The general public only focused on their basic requirements such as seating and shading while the professional designs were more focused on keeping the same layout by adding a few elements. Therefore, the necessity of incorporating the knowledge of placemaking to the app using other alternatives such as incorporating gamified can be emphasized.

5.2. Can Mobile-AR Tools Like CityBuildAR Replace Traditional Participatory Planning Methods?

The CityBuildAR app facilitates the use of M-AR in placemaking by engaging with the three primary attributes: sociability, physical setting, and imageability. This app fosters sociability by offering an immersive, real-time, interactive experience for modifying public spaces and promoting collaborative decision-making. Unlike traditional methods that rely on drawings, 3D renderings that require expertise or public hearings with limited interaction with the actual space, the CityBuildAR app enables users to visualize designs, and place and adjust virtual objects in the real-world context, offering a tangible connection between designs and the physical setting. Additionally, it enhances spatial perception by enabling users to integrate visual and cultural elements into public spaces and explore the impact of design elements on the overall character and identity of space, which strengthens the imageability of space.

The strengths of this app, such as real-time visualization, interactive platform, and accessibility, eliminate the barriers associated with traditional methods like discussions, public hearings, and stakeholder meetings, enabling the ability for it to be used as a contemporary tool for placemaking.

In comparison with the 34 apps reviewed in the literature review, CityBuildAR avoids location-based errors and GPS inaccuracy [81,97] as this app does not require location fetching to do the design. The CityBuildAR app relies on markerless AR technology using real-time place detection and surface tracking through the device's camera, and the virtual objects are placed relative to the detected plane. This method allows users to quickly place objects. Still, this limits the ability to edit/reproduce the same design with high precision, as it is saved as an image to the cloud. However, the location coordinates and design configurations are saved to the cloud for later access. Therefore, the CityBuildAR app enables any individual from any part of the world to create a design and then save the image to the cloud database, which is handled by the relevant authorities in that area. Other constraints, like technical complexity and high costs of other AR apps [85,97], were eliminated by this app, as it requires a smartphone to install the app and then do the design and save to the cloud. However, the CityBuildAR app also has some inherited limitations, such as it requires access to a compatible smartphone to run the AR app, basic technical knowledge to install and operate the app, and an internet connection to connect the app to the cloud to save the designs. In addition to that, the AR apps identified in the review do not support citizen engagement in the planning context directly. Even though 13 apps are related to the urban planning context, only the Smart AR mini application [68] and ChangeExplorer app [70] enable the real-time engagement of citizens in the real-world context. Other apps such as City View AR, Wikitude, etc. support only visualization. Meanwhile, the rest of the 21 apps discussed in the literature are not directly relevant to the urban planning context, yet they enable community engagement in other fields such as construction.

Yet, the CityBuildAR app does not provide the capability to replace traditional participatory methods completely. As discussed above, this app allows each individual to do their own unique design and enhance their level of engagement and understanding in placemaking. But according to the image analysis (Table 3), the consideration of significant aspects such as physical setting, sociability, and imageability in placemaking was not highlighted in the designs when using the app. However, the limited time allocated, and the limited space used to design, the characteristics of the space (cement pavements, existing table, bench layout) have influenced the professionals' designs. Therefore, the feedback highlights that collaboration between planning practitioners and the community using AR is essential for effective placemaking.

According to [98], decisions can be made by incorporating the public's knowledge into the decision's calculus. As an example, the local community knows about crimes or traffic problems in a particular area, and that knowledge can be taken into consideration by the planners through participatory planning [99]. The collaboration of traditional aspects and AR apps is effective in communicating the placemaking knowledge with participants easily. Based on the app demonstration, the CityBuildAR app is somewhat difficult for people to understand and navigate, and also, this app only enables individual experience of users, which causes the lack of dialogue and collaborative design of spaces.

Accordingly, mobile AR applications like CityBuildAR can be considered as complementary tools rather than a replacement for traditional tools. This AR app excels in visualization and enhancing accessibility to the design process, but it should be leveraged with the professionals' interpretation before the actual implementation process. The study highlights that CityBuildAR has the potential to enhance community engagement. However, when considering placemaking, the necessity of incorporating professional insights into the general public's designs is necessary. It can avoid neglect of important aspects like inclusivity to place, density and diversity of activities, and so on.

5.3. Limitations

CityBuildAR app has technical limitations such as limited elements provided, the inability to design without being familiar with the app, and the lack of knowledge shared through the app. The constant addition of new versions and tools to the applications, rewarding participants by recognizing each input, and continuous responsiveness are required to enhance user motivation in using these tools and applications for urban planning [100]. Also, the app does not provide any guidance to the users before the design process, which needs to be addressed before officially launching the app.

The AR application is presently in the development phase and contains several technological bugs and constraints that affect its performance.

- Plane-detection problems: The program necessitates the completion of plane detection before object placement, as it is incapable of identifying additional planes after objects have been positioned.
- Restricted design elements: Participants were given a limited array of items for space design, perhaps hindering their creativity and design alternatives.
- Scaling limitations: Users cannot resize items, constraining design flexibility.
- Deletion errors: Specific elements experience faults during deletion, resulting in difficulties in altering the design.

Notwithstanding these constraints, the program functions as a prototype for participatory placemaking utilizing augmented reality. Insights garnered from the testing sessions will inform subsequent enhancements, rectifying these concerns and augmenting its usability and functionalities.

6. Conclusions

This research investigated the potential of M-AR technology through the CityBuildAR app, to bridge the gap between professionals and the general public in placemaking. By analyzing the experiences of university students, general public members, and professionals, the study revealed that AR can significantly enhance public participation and engagement in the design process. The study reveals that the general public and university students are more flexible in using novel technologies compared to the professionals who have been active in placemaking for years. Further, the study reveals that the general public and university students are concerned about green and seating arrangements, whereas the professionals have considered walking as a fact to think in designing the open space. However, university students have identified green as a key component in designing open spaces compared to both professionals and the general public.

As most of the results emphasized, the CityBuildAR app empowers individuals with limited design skills to visualize and create spatial designs, fostering a sense of ownership and agency in shaping their surroundings. By combining the strengths of traditional participatory methods with the innovative capabilities of AR, a more inclusive and effective approach to placemaking can be achieved. However, the technical errors of the app, including plane detection errors, limited design elements, and occasional app crashes, caused less detailed feedback and limited the ability to create participant's designs.

Future research should explore ways to establish an interactive login within the app for multiple users to work interactively in designing spaces. The CityBuildAR is to be developed to enhance collaborative placemaking by introducing ratings, adding comments to others' designs, and gamified elements such as scoring, leaderboard, etc. Furthermore, to prevent server crashes, a guest option is recommended, allowing users to log in and design once without saving their login information on the server, and only the designs with location coordinates are saved.

Improving app stability and expanding features such as gamified elements is necessary to avoid limited participant engagement and to optimize app performance [100–102]. In future iterations, it is essential to enhance the technology to maintain app stability and facilitate a more user-centric design by analyzing user-engagement levels and the effectiveness of CityBuildAR in real-world placemaking scenarios. Additionally, real-world integration through collaboration with authorities and stakeholders is crucial to address the current limitations and evaluate the long-term impact of the app. Furthermore, the opinion analysis highlighted that technical constraints limit the ability to create unique design proposals of each individual, and professionals with experience were somewhat technology-resistant due to this issue. Therefore, in future studies, the need to address how to get unique and specific designs and ideas from individuals using technical tools is significant.

By harnessing the transformative potential of M-AR, cities can foster more inclusive, dynamic, and resilient communities. This technology empowers individuals from diverse backgrounds to actively participate in shaping urban spaces, ensuring that development reflects the needs, aspirations, and identities of all residents. By integrating M-AR into urban planning and design, cities can promote more collaborative, transparent, and innovative decision-making processes, ultimately leading to more equitable and people-centered environments.

Author Contributions: Conceptualization, D.R., N.K. (Nayomi Kankanamge) and C.D.S.; Methodology, D.R., N.K. (Nayomi Kankanamge) and R.M.; Software, R.M.; Validation, D.R., R.M. and N.K. (Nuwani Kangana); Formal analysis, D.R., N.K. (Nuwani Kangana) and N.K. (Nayomi Kankanamge); Investigation, D.R. and R.M.; Writing—original draft preparation, D.R.; Writing—review and editing, D.R., N.K. (Nuwani Kangana), N.K. (Nayomi Kankanamge) and T.Y.; Visualization, D.R., R.M. and N.K. (Nuwani Kangana); Supervision, N.K. (Nayomi Kankanamge) and C.D.S.; Project administration, N.K. (Nayomi Kankanamge) and C.D.S.; Funding acquisition, N.K. (Nayomi Kankanamge) and C.D.S. All authors have read and agreed to the published version of the manuscript.

Funding: This research received no external funding.

Informed Consent Statement: The participants in this study were recruited voluntarily through an open Google Form. Before participation, they were provided with information outlining the purpose of the research and the use of the collected data. It was explicitly stated that the data gathered during the session, including any photographs taken, would be used solely for research purposes.

Data Availability Statement: Data is available upon request to the corresponding author.

Acknowledgments: Authors acknowledge the reviewers and journal editors.

Conflicts of Interest: The authors declare no conflicts of interest.

References

1. Akbar, P.N.G. Placemaking. In *Encyclopedia of Tourism Management and Marketing*; Edward Elgar Publishing: Cheltenham, UK, 2022; pp. 515–517. [CrossRef]
2. Amirzadeh, M.; Sharifi, A. The evolutionary path of place making: From late twentieth century to post-pandemic cities. *Land Use Policy* **2024**, *141*, 107124. [CrossRef]
3. Palmer, L. New inroads on community-centric placemaking. *Nat. Cities* **2024**, *1*, 2–4. [CrossRef]
4. Wichowsky, A.; Gaul-Stout, J.; McNew-Birren, J. Creative Placemaking and Empowered Participatory Governance. *Urban Aff. Rev.* **2023**, *59*, 1747–1774. [CrossRef]
5. Kankanamge, N.; Yigitcanlar, T.; Goonetilleke, A.; Kamruzzaman, M. How can gamification be incorporated into disaster emergency planning? A systematic review of the literature. *Int. J. Disaster Resil. Built Environ.* **2020**, *11*, 481–506. [CrossRef]
6. Baum, S.; Yigitcanlar, T.; Horton, S.; Velibeyoglu, K.; Gleeson, B. *The Role of Community and Lifestyle in the Making of a Knowledge City*; Griffith University: Brisbane Australia, 2007.
7. Pancholi, S.; Yigitcanlar, T.; Guaralda, M. Place making for innovation and knowledge-intensive activities: The Australian experience. *Technol. Forecast. Soc. Chang.* **2019**, *146*, 616–625. [CrossRef]
8. Naef, P. Touring the 'comuna': Memory and transformation in Medellin, Colombia. *J. Tour. Cult. Chang.* **2018**, *16*, 173–190. [CrossRef]
9. Prestes, O.M.; Ultramari, C.; Caetano, F.D. Public transport innovation and transfer of BRT ideas: Curitiba, Brazil as a reference model. *Case Stud. Transp. Policy* **2022**, *10*, 700–709. [CrossRef]
10. Hamdi, N. *The Placemaker's Guide to Building Community*; Routledge: London, UK, 2010. [CrossRef]
11. Song, Y.; Yang, R.; Lu, H.; Fernandez, J.; Wang, T. Why do we love the high line? A case study of understanding long-term user experiences of urban greenways. *Comput. Urban Sci.* **2023**, *3*, 18. [CrossRef]
12. Loughran, K. Imbricated Spaces: The High Line, Urban Parks, and the Cultural Meaning of City and Nature. *Sociol. Theory* **2016**, *34*, 311–334. [CrossRef]
13. Ellery, P.J.; Ellery, J. Strengthening Community Sense of Place through Placemaking. *Urban Plan.* **2019**, *4*, 237–248. [CrossRef]
14. Hale, V. Good Places Through Community-Led Design. In *Sustainable Development and Planning IX*; WIT Press: Southampton, UK, 2018; pp. 155–164. [CrossRef]
15. Fingerhut, Z.; Alfasi, N. Operationalizing Community Placemaking: A Critical Relationship-Based Typology. *Sustainability* **2023**, *15*, 6371. [CrossRef]
16. Abesinghe, S.; Kankanamge, N.; Yigitcanlar, T.; Pancholi, S. Image of a City through Big Data Analytics: Colombo from the Lens of Geo-Coded Social Media Data. *Future Internet* **2023**, *15*, 32. [CrossRef]
17. Kangana, N.; Kankanamge, N.; De Silva, C.; Goonetilleke, A.; Mahamood, R.; Ranasinghe, D. Bridging Community Engagement and Technological Innovation for Creating Smart and Resilient Cities: A Systematic Literature Review. *Smart Cities* **2024**, *7*, 3823–3852. [CrossRef]
18. Yigitcanlar, T.; Kankanamge, N.; Regona, M.; Ruiz Maldonado, A.; Rowan, B.; Ryu, A.; Li, R.Y.M. Artificial intelligence technologies and related urban planning and development concepts: How are they perceived and utilized in Australia? *J. Open Innov. Technol. Mark. Complex.* **2020**, *6*, 187. [CrossRef]
19. Sokolaj, U. Understanding Inclusive Placemaking Processes through the Case of Klostergata56 in Norway. *J. Public Space* **2022**, *7*, 193–204. [CrossRef]
20. Gąsowska-Kramarz, A. Pruitt Igoe vs. City of the Future. *Archit. Civ. Eng. Environ.* **2020**, *12*, 15–21. [CrossRef]
21. Pınar, E. Entangled Histories of Architecture and Dispossession in The Pruitt-Igoe Myth (2011). *GRID—Archit. Plan. Des. J.* **2025**, *8*. [CrossRef]
22. Beckus, A.; Atia, G.K. Sketch-based community detection in evolving networks. *Phys. Rev. E* **2022**, *106*, 044306. [CrossRef]
23. Abeynayake, T.; Meetiyagoda, L.; Kankanamge, N.; Mahanama, P.K.S. Imageability and legibility: Cognitive analysis and visibility assessment in Galle heritage city. *J. Archit. Urban.* **2022**, *46*, 126–136. [CrossRef]

24. Assumma, V.; Ventura, C. Role of Cultural Mapping within Local Development Processes: A Tool for the Integrated Enhancement of Rural Heritage. *Adv. Eng. Forum* **2014**, *11*, 495–502. [CrossRef]
25. García-Esparza, J.A.; Nikšič, M. Revealing the Community's Interpretation of Place: Integrated Digital Support to Embed Photovoice into Placemaking Processes. *Urban Plan.* **2024**, *9*. [CrossRef]
26. Hunter, M.; Soro, A.; Brown, R.; Harman, J.; Yigitcanlar, T. Augmenting community engagement in city 4.0: Considerations for digital agency in urban public space. *Sustainability* **2022**, *14*, 9803. [CrossRef]
27. Yigitcanlar, T.; Kankanamge, N. *Urban Analytics with Social Media Data: Foundations, Applications and Platforms*; Chapman and Hall/CRC: London, UK, 2022.
28. Rotta, M.; Sell, D.; Pacheco, R.; Yigitcanlar, T. Digital commons and citizen coproduction in smart cities: Assessment of Brazilian municipal e-government platforms. *Energies* **2019**, *12*, 2813. [CrossRef]
29. Carmigniani, J.; Furht, B. Augmented Reality: An Overview. In *Handbook of Augmented Reality*; Springer: New York, NY, USA, 2011; pp. 3–46. [CrossRef]
30. Azuma, R.T. A Survey of Augmented Reality. *Presence Teleoperators Virtual Environ.* **1997**, *6*, 355–385. [CrossRef]
31. Kesim, M.; Ozarslan, Y. Augmented Reality in Education: Current Technologies and the Potential for Education. *Procedia-Soc. Behav. Sci.* **2012**, *47*, 297–302. [CrossRef]
32. Shalender, K.; Singla, B. Augmenting Reality (AR) and Its Use Cases: Exploring the Game Changing Potential of Technology. In *Augmented Reality and the Future of Education Technology*; Aggarwal, R., Gupta, P., Singh, S., Bala, R., Eds.; IGI Global Scientific Publishing: Hershey, PA, USA, 2024; pp. 1–10. [CrossRef]
33. Boyanovsky, B.B.; Belghasem, M.; White, B.A.; Kadavakollu, S. Incorporating Augmented Reality Into Anatomy Education in a Contemporary Medical School Curriculum. *Cureus* **2024**, *16*, e57443. [CrossRef]
34. Cardullo, V.; Wang, C. Pre-service Teachers Perspectives of Google Expedition. *Early Child. Educ. J.* **2022**, *50*, 173–183. [CrossRef]
35. Ozturkcan, S. Service Innovation: Using Augmented Reality in the IKEA Place App. *J. Inf. Technol. Teach. Cases* **2021**, *11*, 8–13. [CrossRef]
36. Kounavis, C.D.; Kasimati, A.E.; Zamani, E.D. Enhancing the Tourism Experience through Mobile Augmented Reality: Challenges and Prospects. *Int. J. Eng. Bus. Manag.* **2012**, *4*, 10. [CrossRef]
37. Tanwar, V.; Anand, V.; Aggarwal, P.; Kumar, M.; Kumar, G.R. Revolutionizing Military Training: A Comprehensive Review of Tactical and Technical Training through Augmented Reality, Virtual Reality, and Haptics. In Proceedings of the 9th IEEE International Conference for Convergence in Technology (I2CT), Pune, India, 7–9 April 2024; pp. 1–5. [CrossRef]
38. Qin, Y. Attractiveness of Game Elements, Presence, and Enjoyment of Mobile Augmented Reality Games: The Case of Pokémon Go. *Telemat. Inform.* **2021**, *62*, 101620. [CrossRef]
39. Boboc, R.G.; Gîrbacia, F.; Butilă, E.V. The Application of Augmented Reality in the Automotive Industry: A Systematic Literature Review. *Appl. Sci.* **2020**, *10*, 4259. [CrossRef]
40. David, R.S. Immersive Learning Experiences: Technology-Enhanced Instruction, Adaptive Learning, Augmented Reality, and M-Learning in Informal Learning Environments. *I-Manag. J. Educ. Technol.* **2019**, *15*, 17. [CrossRef]
41. Singh, S. Designing AR Interfaces for Enhanced User Experience. *J. Adv. Sch. Res. Allied Educ.* **2024**, *21*, 96–102. [CrossRef]
42. Cirulis, A.; Brigis, K.; Brigmanis, B. 3D Outdoor Augmented Reality for Architecture and Urban Planning. *Procedia Comput. Sci.* **2013**, *25*, 71–79. [CrossRef]
43. Shree, N.; Selvarani, G. Mobile Marker-Based AR Children App for Learning Map. In Proceedings of the 7th International Conference on Circuit Power and Computing Technologies (ICCPCT), Kollam, India, 8–9 August 2024; pp. 60–64. [CrossRef]
44. Blazhko, O.; Shtefan, N. Development of Marker-Based Web Augmented Reality Educational Board Games for Learning Process Support in Computer Science. In Proceedings of the 6th Experiment@ International Conference (exp.at'23), Évora, Portugal, 5–7 June 2023; pp. 146–151. [CrossRef]
45. Dhar, P.; Rocks, T.; Samarasinghe, R.M.; Stephenson, G.; Smith, C. Augmented reality in medical education: Students' experiences and learning outcomes. *Med. Educ. Online* **2021**, *26*, 1953953. [CrossRef]
46. Kisno, B.; Wibawa, K.; Khaerudin. Digital Storytelling for Early Childhood Creativity: Diffusion of Innovation '3-D Coloring Quiver Application Based on Augmented Reality Technology' in Children's Creativity Development. *Int. J. Online Biomed. Eng. IJOE* **2022**, *18*, 26–42. [CrossRef]
47. Antoro, M.F.A.P.; Anistyasari, Y. Implementasi Markerless Location-Based Dalam Aplikasi Peta Augmented Reality Fakultas Teknik Unesa Berbasis Android. *J. Inform. Comput. Sci. JINACS* **2022**, *4*, 117–130. [CrossRef]
48. Messi, L.; Spegni, F.; Vaccarini, M.; Corneli, A.; Binni, L. Infrastructure-Free Localization System for Augmented Reality Registration in Indoor Environments: A First Accuracy Assessment. In Proceedings of the IEEE International Workshop on Metrology for Living Environment (MetroLivEnv), Chania, Greece, 12–14 June 2024; pp. 110–115. [CrossRef]
49. Yigitcanlar, T.; Degirmenci, K.; Butler, L.; Desouza, K. What are the key factors affecting smart city transformation readiness? Evidence from Australian cities. *Cities* **2022**, *120*, 103434. [CrossRef]
50. Chong, Y.; Sethi, D.; Loh, C.Y.; Lateef, F. Going forward with Pokemon Go. *J. Emergencies Trauma Shock.* **2018**, *11*, 243. [CrossRef]

51. Prananta, A.W.; Biroli, A.; Afifudin, M. Augmented Reality for Science Learning in the 21st Century: Systematic Literature Review. *J. Penelit. Pendidik. IPA* **2024**, *10*, 38–44. [CrossRef]
52. Uhrík, M.; Kupko, A.; Krpalová, M.; Hajtmanek, R. Augmented reality and tangible user interfaces as an extension of computational design tools. *Archit. Pap. Fac. Archit. Des. STU* **2022**, *27*, 18–27. [CrossRef]
53. Aggarwal, R.; Singhal, A. Augmented Reality and its effect on our life. In Proceedings of the 9th International Conference on Cloud Computing, Data Science & Engineering (Confluence), Noida, India, 10–11 January 2019; pp. 510–515. [CrossRef]
54. Jindal, A. Augmented Reality Applications in Mechanical System Design and Prototyping. *Darpan Int. Res. Anal.* **2024**, *12*, 1–13. [CrossRef]
55. Reinwald, F.; Berger, M.; Stoik, C.; Platzer, M.; Damyanovic, D. Augmented Reality at the Service of Participatory Urban Planning and Community Informatics—A Case Study from Vienna. *J. Community Inform.* **2014**, *10*. [CrossRef]
56. Braud, T.; Bijarbooneh, F.H.; Chatzopoulos, D.; Hui, P. Future Networking Challenges: The Case of Mobile Augmented Reality. In Proceedings of the 37th IEEE International Conference on Distributed Computing Systems (ICDCS), Atlanta, GA, USA, 5–8 June 2017; pp. 1796–1807. [CrossRef]
57. Baeza, J.L.; Stephenson, G.; Samarasinghe, R.M.; Rocks, T.; Smith, C. CityScope Platform for Real-Time Analysis and Decision-Support in Urban Design Competitions. *Int. J. E-Plan. Res.* **2021**, *10*, 121–137. [CrossRef]
58. Niederer, S.; Priester, R. Smart Citizens: Exploring the Tools of the Urban Bottom-Up Movement. *Comput. Support. Coop. Work* **2016**, *25*, 137–152. [CrossRef]
59. Reaver, K. Augmented Reality as a Participation Tool for Youth in Urban Planning Processes: Case Study in Oslo, Norway. *Front. Virtual Real.* **2023**, *4*, 1055930. [CrossRef]
60. Argo, T.A.; Prabonno, S.; Singgi, P. Youth Participation in Urban Environmental Planning through Augmented Reality Learning: The Case of Bandung City, Indonesia. *Procedia-Soc. Behav. Sci.* **2016**, *227*, 808–814. [CrossRef]
61. Mao, Y.; Zhang, Z.; Sun, H.; Chen, Y. CitySense. In Proceedings of the 16th ACM Conference on Embedded Networked Sensor Systems, Shenzhen, China, 4–7 November 2018; ACM: New York, NY, USA, 2018; pp. 379–380. [CrossRef]
62. Ahmadi Oloonabadi, S.; Baran, P. Augmented Reality Participatory Platform: A Novel Digital Participatory Planning Tool to Engage Under-Resourced Communities in Improving Neighborhood Walkability. *Cities* **2023**, *141*, 104441. [CrossRef]
63. Allen, M.; Regenbrecht, H.; Abbott, M. Smart-Phone Augmented Reality for Public Participation in Urban Planning. In Proceedings of the 23rd Australian Computer-Human Interaction Conference, Canberra, Australia, 28 November–2 December 2011; ACM: New York, NY, USA, 2011; pp. 11–20. [CrossRef]
64. Amin, D.; Govilkar, S. Comparative Study of Augmented Reality SDKs. *Int. J. Comput. Sci. Appl.* **2015**, *5*, 11–26. [CrossRef]
65. Reinwald, F.; Schober, C.; Damyanovic, D. From Plan to Augmented Reality—Workflow for Successful Implementation of AR Solutions in Planning and Participation Processes. Available online: https://programm.corp.at/cdrom2013/papers2013/CORP2013_110.pdf (accessed on 29 December 2023).
66. Alam, F.; Reaz, M.B.I.; Ali, M.A.; Samad, S.A.; Hashim, F.H.; Hamid, M.H.A. New Trends in Using Augmented Reality Apps for Smart City Contexts. *ISPRS Int. J. Geo-Inf.* **2018**, *7*, 478. [CrossRef]
67. Höftberger, K.; Konrath, A.; Berger, A.; Allerstorfer, D.; Krebs, R. XR-Supported Communication in Green Urban Projects. Participating in Urban Change through Virtual and Augmented Reality. In Proceedings of the 28th International Conference on Urban Development, Regional Planning and Information Society, Ljubljana, Slovenia, 18–20 September 2023; pp. 1071–1080. Available online: https://www.corp.at/archive/CORP2023_116.pdf (accessed on 29 December 2023).
68. Sanaeipoor, S.; Emami, K.H. Smart [AR] Mini-Application: Engaging Citizens in Digital Placemaking Approach. In Proceedings of the 4th International Conference on Smart City, Internet of Things and Applications (SCIOT), Mashhad, Iran, 16–17 September 2020; pp. 84–90. [CrossRef]
69. Fonseca, D.; Martí, N.; Redondo, E.; Navarro, I.; Sánchez, A. Relationship between Student Profile, Tool Use, Participation, and Academic Performance with the Use of Augmented Reality Technology for Visualized Architecture Models. *Comput. Hum. Behav.* **2013**, *29*, 1048–1056. [CrossRef]
70. Wilson, A.; Tewdwr-Jones, M.; Comber, R. Urban Planning, Public Participation, and Digital Technology: App Development as a Method of Generating Citizen Involvement in Local Planning Processes. *Urban Plan.* **2017**, *2*, 28–39. [CrossRef]
71. inCitu. inCitu AR App: Empowering Urban Planning with Augmented Reality. Available online: https://www.incitu.us (accessed on 29 December 2023).
72. Piga, B.; Cacciamatta, S.; Boffi, M. *Smart Co-Design for Urban Planning: Augmented and Virtual Reality Apps in Collaborative Processes*; PoliMi Springer Brief: Milan, Italy, 2021; ISBN 978-3-030-67842-5. Available online: https://re.public.polimi.it/handle/11311/1175121 (accessed on 29 December 2023).
73. Lee, G.; Duenser, A.; Kim, S.; Billinghurst, M. CityViewAR: A Mobile Outdoor AR Application for City Visualization. In Proceedings of the IEEE International Symposium on Mixed and Augmented Reality—Adjunct (ISMAR-AMH 2012), Atlanta, GA, USA, 5–8 November 2012; pp. 57–64. [CrossRef]

74. Architeque. Architeque—3D and Augmented Reality Platform for Product Presentations. Available online: https://www.architeque.com (accessed on 29 December 2023).
75. Markouzis, D.; Fessakis, G. Enriching the City Environment with Mobile Augmented Reality Edutainment Applications for Residents and Tourists: The Case of "Roads of Rhodes" Game. In Proceedings of the 3rd International Biennial Conference, Hybrid City 2015: Data to the People, Athens, Greece, 17–19 September 2015; Theona, I., Charitos, D., Eds.; National and Kapodistrian University of Athens: Athens, Greece, 2015; pp. 290–297, ISBN 978-960-99791-2-2.
76. Piekarski, W.; Thomas, B.H. ARQuake: The Outdoor Augmented Reality Gaming System. *Commun. ACM* **2002**, *45*, 36–38. [CrossRef]
77. Holden, C.; Sykes, J. Leveraging Mobile Games for Place-Based Language Learning. *Int. J. Game-Based Learn.* **2011**, *1*, 1–18. [CrossRef]
78. Chowdhury, R.R.; Iqbal, A. LocatAR—An Augmented Reality Application for Local Points of Interest Identification. In Proceedings of the International Conferences on Computing Advancements, Dhaka, Bangladesh, 10–12 March 2022. [CrossRef]
79. Noyman, A.; Holtz, T.; Kröger, J.; Noennig, J.R.; Larson, K. Finding Places: HCI Platform for Public Participation in Refugees' Accommodation Process. *arXiv* **2018**, arXiv:1811.10123. Available online: https://arxiv.org/abs/1811.10123 (accessed on 13 November 2023). [CrossRef]
80. Imottesjo, H.; Kain, J.-H. The Urban CoBuilder—A Mobile Augmented Reality Tool for Crowd-Sourced Simulation of Emergent Urban Development Patterns: Requirements, Prototyping and Assessment. *Comput. Environ. Urban Syst.* **2018**, *71*, 120–130. [CrossRef]
81. Pombo, L.; Marques, M.M. Marker-Based Augmented Reality Application for Mobile Learning in an Urban Park: Steps to Make It Real under the EduPARK Project. In Proceedings of the 12th International Conference on Computer Supported Education (CSEDU 2020), Prague, Czech Republic, 2–4 May 2020; Volume 2, pp. 16–25. Available online: https://ieeexplore.ieee.org/document/8259669 (accessed on 29 December 2023).
82. Fadzli, F.E.; Mohd Yusof, M.A.; Ismail, A.W.; Hj Salam, M.S.; Ismail, N.A. ARGarden: 3D Outdoor Landscape Design Using Handheld Augmented Reality with Multi-User Interaction. *IOP Conf. Ser. Mater. Sci. Eng.* **2020**, *979*, 012001. [CrossRef]
83. Hincapié, M.; Díaz, C.; Zapata-Cárdenas, M.-I.; Toro Rios, H.d.J.; Valencia, D.; Güemes-Castorena, D. Augmented Reality Mobile Apps for Cultural Heritage Reactivation. *Comput. Electr. Eng.* **2021**, *93*, 107281. [CrossRef]
84. Nekoui, Y.; Roig, E. Children and the Mediated City: Place Attachment Development Using Augmented Reality in Urban Spaces. *Interact. Des. Archit. J. (IxD&A)* **2022**, *52*, 144–157.
85. Silva, C.; Zagalo, N.; Vairinhos, M. Towards Participatory Activities with Augmented Reality for Cultural Heritage: A Literature Review. *Comput. Educ. X Real.* **2023**, *3*, 100044. [CrossRef]
86. Goudarznia, T.; Pietsch, M.; Krug, R. Testing the Effectiveness of Augmented Reality in the Public Participation Process: A Case Study in the City of Bernburg. *J. Digit. Landsc. Archit.* **2017**, *2*, 244–251. [CrossRef]
87. Ali, A.S.; Baper, S.Y. Assessment of Livability in Commercial Streets via Placemaking. *Sustainability* **2023**, *15*, 6834. [CrossRef]
88. Cocchia, L.; Spegni, F.; Vaccarini, M.; Corneli, A.; Binni, L. The Impact of Social Environment and Interaction Focus on User Experience and Social Acceptability of an Augmented Reality Game. In Proceedings of the 16th International Conference on Quality of Multimedia Experience (QoMEX), Ghent, Belgium, 18–20 June 2024; pp. 160–166. [CrossRef]
89. Hammack, P.L. Narrative and the Cultural Psychology of Identity. *Personal. Soc. Psychol. Rev.* **2008**, *12*, 222–247. [CrossRef]
90. Zhang, M. Research on the Application of AR Technology in Reconstructing the Digital Presentation of Urban Identity. In Proceedings of the 15th International Conference on Digital Image Processing, Beijing, China, 6–8 May 2023; ACM: New York, NY, USA, 2023; pp. 1–7. [CrossRef]
91. Khor, C.Y.; Mubin, S.A. AR Mobile Application for Enhancing National Museum Heritage Visualization. *Int. J. Softw. Eng. Comput. Syst.* **2024**, *10*, 1–19. [CrossRef]
92. Caldeira, T.; Holston, J. Participatory urban planning in Brazil. *Urban Stud.* **2015**, *52*, 2001–2017. [CrossRef]
93. Al-Kodmany, K. Visualization Tools and Methods for Participatory Planning and Design. *J. Urban Technol.* **2001**, *8*, 1–37. [CrossRef]
94. Othengrafen, F.; Sievers, L.; Reinecke, E. Using augmented reality in urban planning processes: Sustainable urban transitions through innovative participation. *GAIA-Ecol. Perspect. Sci. Soc.* **2023**, *32*, 54–63. [CrossRef]
95. Yigitcanlar, T. *Rethinking Sustainable Development: Urban Management, Engineering, and Design*; IGI Global: Hersey, PA, USA, 2010.
96. Sabah, S.; Hossain, I.; Weiss, D.; Tillmann, A. Towards Increasing Active Citizen Involvement in Urban Planning through Mixed Reality Technologies. In Proceedings of the 34th Central European Conference on Information and Intelligent Systems (CECIIS), Dubrovnik, Croatia, 20–22 September 2023; pp. 435–439.
97. Santana, J.M.; Wendel, J.; Trujillo, A.; Suárez, J.P.; Simons, A.; Koch, A. Multimodal location-based services—Semantic 3D city data as virtual and augmented reality. In *Progress in Location-Based Services 2016*; Springer: Berlin/Heidelberg, Germany, 2017; pp. 329–353. [CrossRef]
98. Pissourios, I. Top-down and bottom-up urban and regional planning: Towards a framework for the use of planning standards. *Eur. Spat. Res. Policy* **2014**, *21*, 83–99. [CrossRef]

99. Gordon, E.; Baldwin-Philippi, J.; Balestra, M. Why we engage: How theories of human behavior contribute to our understanding of civic engagement in a digital era. *SSRN Electron. J.* **2013**, *21*, 12–15. [CrossRef]
100. Yigitcanlar, T. Australian local governments' practice and prospects with online planning. *URISA J.* **2006**, *18*, 7–17.
101. Gonsalves, K.; Foth, M.; Caldwell, G.A. Radical Placemaking: Utilizing Low-Tech AR/VR to Engage in Communal Placemaking during a Pandemic. *Interact. Des. Archit.* **2021**, *48*, 143–164. [CrossRef]
102. Kankanamge, N.; Yigitcanlar, T.; Goonetilleke, A. Gamifying Community Education for Enhanced Disaster Resilience: An Effectiveness Testing Study from Australia. *Future Internet* **2022**, *14*, 179. [CrossRef]

MDPI AG
Grosspeteranlage 5
4052 Basel
Switzerland
Tel.: +41 61 683 77 34

Future Internet Editorial Office
E-mail: futureinternet@mdpi.com
www.mdpi.com/journal/futureinternet

www.ingramcontent.com/pod-product-compliance
Lightning Source LLC
Chambersburg PA
CBHW040812250926
51850CB00007BA/1148
* 9 7 8 3 7 2 5 8 4 9 9 1 8 *